DICTATORS

IN THE MIRROR

OF MEDICINE

Other publications by Anton Neumayr

Music & Medicine, Volume 1
Haydn, Mozart, Beethoven, Schubert
Notes on Their Lives, Works, and Medical Histories

Music & Medicine, Volume 2
Hummel, Weber, Mendelssohn, Schumann, Brahms, Bruckner
Notes on Their Lives, Works, and Medical Histories

Music & Medicine, Volume 3
Chopin, Smetana, Tchaikowsky, Mahler
Notes on Their Lives, Works, and Medical Histories
(English edition available Summer of 1996)

ANTON NEUMAYR

DICTATORS
IN THE MIRROR
OF MEDICINE

NAPOLEON • HITLER • STALIN

Translated by David J. Parent

M
Medi-Ed Press

Copyright © 1995 by MEDI-ED PRESS
Printed in the United States of America. All Rights Reserved.
ISBN 0-936741-09-0

The original edition of this work, Diktatoren im Spiegel der Medizin, by Anton
Neumayr, has been published by J&V Edition Wien Dachs-Verlag Ges.m.b.H.

Library of Congress Cataloging-in-Publication Data:
Neumayr, Anton.
  [Diktatoren im Spiegel der Medizin. English]
  Dictators in the mirror of medicine : Napoleon, Hitler, Stalin /
Anton Neumayr. ; translated by David J. Parent.
    p. cm.
  Includes bibliographical references and index.
  ISBN 0-963741-09-0
  1. Napoleon I, Emperor of the French, 1769-1821--Health.
2. Napoleon I, Emperor of the French, 1769-1821--Mental health.
3. Hitler, Adolf, 1889-1945--Health. 4. Hitler, Adolf, 1889-1945-
-Mental health. 5. Stalin, Joseph, 1879-1953--Health. 6. Stalin, Joseph, 1879-
1953--Mental health. 7. Europe--History. 8. Diseases and history. I. Title.
D108.N48413 1995
909.8'092'2--dc20
[B]
               95-23605
               CIP

MEDI-ED PRESS
Constitution Place, Suite A
716 East Empire Street
Bloomington, Illinois 61701
1-800-500-8205

Contents

STALIN

PREFACE

Three powerful political figures, Napoleon, Hitler, and Stalin, had an extraordinary influence on the course of European history over the past two centuries; the traces of their exploits are still visible today around the world. In the following pages, the spectacular rise and catastrophic fall of each of these despots will be subjected to a medical analysis.

World history has recorded similar historical figures who flashed across the world stage like comets and, by their extraordinary energy—similar to forces of nature—and their almost demonic eloquence, succeeded in mobilizing tremendous masses of their countrymen for personal, egoistic goals. Napoleon was the first to introduce this sort of obsession with power into modern history, but the activities of all three men showed a disdain for human life on a scale that far outshadowed anything seen previously. Without hesitation, they were ready to sacrifice hecatombs of people on the altar of their greed for power and fame, their sadistic vindictiveness, or their pathological delusions, while shamelessly pretending to be moved by honorable national and ideological motivations.

The gruesome events on the European battlefields, in the Soviet GULAGs, and in the German concentration camps, as well as the unimaginable violations of human rights, even outright genocide, have been described in countless reliable biographies and historical treatises in greater or lesser detail and analyzed according to the attitudes of the various authors. Until now, only a few publications have tried to trace the factors that contributed to the development of such eerie historical figures and to examine what specific psychological traits must predominate for such brutal and relentless actions to be possible and at the same time achieve almost unlimited power over millions of people. For it is almost inexplicable today, especially for the younger generation, how people could fall prey to the utopian and unreal delusions of a single individual, to such an extent as to be willing to gladly give up even their own lives to achieve the predetermined goals of their respective idol, almost in a kind of mass hysteria.

The present medical analysis, therefore, will not concern itself merely with clarifying their somatic diseases, which is possible with great certainty based on the biographical sources. In Napoleon's case, especially, the retrospective diagnosis will require the correction of several medical errors. Of greater interest, certainly, is the elaboration of a psychograph, as well as a psychiatric, psycho-historical, and above all, a criminal-psychological analysis of Hitler and Stalin, because these fields of study can bring some of their deeds and crimes closer to our understanding. No doubt, a few chauvinistic or ideologically blinded readers will be disappointed by the effort to maintain relentless objectivity, but that is a self-evident precondition for any medical analysis. On the contrary, it can be expected that knowledge of the true character of an idol, magnified into a hero by concerted propaganda, will lead to the discarding of some traditional and uncritically accepted ideas.

Some readers also will realize how irresponsible it is to submit to the seductive spell of demagogic eloquence and to place oneself uncritically in the service of the unreal delusionary fantasies of egoistic tribunes obsessed with the intoxication of power. For such a formation of consciousness, it is necessary to lay to rest the many existing legends and idealizations and to communicate a realistic image of those three historical figures of recent European history as it emerges from a medical viewpoint.

In that sense, this book is intended not only for readers interested in medicine or history, but for every human being who is politically aware and has an intact social conscience.

NAPOLEON BONAPARTE

What Napoleon did will in the long-run
amount to what he did justly;
what Nature with her laws will sanction.
To what of reality was in him; to that and nothing more.
The rest was all smoke and waste.

Thomas Carlyle,
On Heroes, Hero-Worship and the Heroic in History, 1841

According to legend, Napoleon's goal was the liberation of the nations, and only his enemies, under Great Britain's leadership, prevented him from realizing his goal; the legend was fabricated by Napoleon himself during the years in exile on St. Helena. Expanded and elaborated romantically by Napoleon III, this legend still continues to circulate in some circles and literary writings. Only in recent decades has a more realistic and differentiated image of Napoleon developed, in which his actions become recognizable as both a destructive and a constructive power, and his role as one of the essential shapers of modern European history has been put in the proper light. As a herald of the nineteenth century, he brilliantly combined the ideas of the Enlightenment and the French Revolution with an absolutist will to dominate. In his boundless urge for power, he triggered the destruction of the *ancien régime* far beyond the Bourbon domains of Louis XIV into the far reaches of Europe, thereby releasing tremendous political and economic energies. In France, his organizing and progressive spirit is still felt to this day in the judiciary system and in many areas of administration and forms of society. Even in Italy and Germany, Napoleon promoted the modern idea of government and sense of nationhood which replaced the system of feudal privileges and fragmentation into tiny states, and he set in motion the process of development to constitutional and national government.

It is not surprising that the literary image of Napoleon in the nineteenth and, in part, still in the twentieth century shows two faces, depending on who sketched it; one is the face of a brutal tyrant, a megalomaniac obsessed with power and a charlatan, and the other is the face of the celebrated perfecter of the Revolution, the conqueror of nations and a superman. As a military leader, Napoleon was unanimously admired and idolized by his troops and often imitated by his opponents. His fabulous rise from a Corsican rebel to the Emperor of the French and ruler of the European continent lets him appear in the eyes of the world as a unique world-historical personality, who basically escapes any attempt at rational comprehension. The sobriquet, "the Great," would certainly be accurate after his name, for, as Jacob Burckhardt once paraphrased it so accurately:

> History at times loves to concentrate itself in one man whom the world then obeys. The great individuals are the coincidence of the universal and the particular, of being and becoming, concentrated in one single personality. They epitomize states, religions, cultures and crises.

Although Napoleon did not have the talent to draw the masses under his spell by political speeches or to win them to himself and to his wide-ranging ideas by the power of his voice, he was well aware of the importance of directly swaying the masses; and he had an instinctive feeling for the best way he could win them over and enthuse them for his breathtaking plans for the future. Looking back at outstanding world-historical personalities, he came to this conviction:

> The men who have changed the world never did it by winning the leaders to their cause, but always only by motivating the masses. The first method falls in the area of intrigue and leads only to second-rate results, the second is the path of genius, and it changes the face of the world.

Napoleon's character—in which demonic passions were combined with a cool, calculating, extremely sharp intellect—his burning ambition, his absolutely unwavering self-confidence, his unhesitatingly accurate instinct, his unbending will, and his almost unlimited energy have been just as clearly elaborated in his great biographies as the historical background before which the trajectory of his cometlike rise and fall occurred. But whereas almost all previous historians who tried to describe Napoleon's character agreed on the striking duality of his personality, they hardly tried to give more serious thought to the causes of this dichotomy. In order to better understand his character, it will be necessary to subject his childhood biography to an objective medical study. An extensive biographical survey will also enable us to explain various military and personal crises in his life which have puzzled historians because of medical particulars or events which, until now, have received little or no attention. For "it is not Wellington who defeated Napoleon at Waterloo."

Napoleon's medical biography offers many surprising aspects during his time as military commander, statesman, and Emperor of the French; but above all, at St. Helena it gives us a truly shattering image of an exile condemned to life in a long-lasting death agony. The humiliations endured on that remote rock of an island probably contributed in no small measure to his painful death, which, incidentally, is still being interpreted wrongly in recently published medical articles. A summary of Napoleon's life and death from a medical point of view should be suited to rounding out the life of this historically significant personality and making it humanly more understandable.

BIOGRAPHICAL SURVEY

CHILDHOOD AND SCHOOL YEARS

Since Napoleon was born on the island of Corsica, he is generally called a Corsican. But although his ancestors had been living in Corsica for more than two centuries and in the course of time felt like genuine Corsican patriots, genealogical research surprisingly points to the probability that the original ancestors of the Bonapartes were of Germanic origin. Whether they were of Frankish or Lombard origin remains uncertain. The first ancestor who took the name Bonaparte was Count William of the Cadolingian family. The Cadolingians were spread out from Lombardy to Tuscany; they took part in various Crusades and, as Ghibellines, sided with the Imperial party in the thirteenth century. Until 1529, the Bonapartes remained in the region of Genoa and at that time first settled on the island of Corsica, where in Ajaccio they soon counted as one of the most respected and wealthiest families.

Carlo Maria Bonaparte was born on March 27, 1746, and lived only to the age of thirty-eight, but he attained immortality as Napoleon's father and thus was responsible for his family going down in history with elemental force. He himself was a man of many talents, with a lively temperament and cultural interests, but he was also an extremely ambitious man, whose lifelong yearning for wealth, honor, and fame never gave him any rest. A thousand bold plans and fantastic ideas chased through the brain of this Count Bonaparte, as he liked to call himself with pride in the venerable length of his lineage.

The father, Carlo Maria Bonaparte, with his son, Napoleon I, and his wife, Maria Letizia Ramolino (contemporary etching)

Napoleon's mother, Maria Letizia Ramolino, was born in Ajaccio on August 24th, 1750, and belonged to a family of Italian origin which absolutely matched the Bonapartes in antiquity and reputation. The marriage of the two young people stood from its first day under the sign of the Corsican War of Liberation, which was waged under the leadership of Pasquale Paoli to liberate the island from the Genoese yoke, under which the freedom-loving mountain people of Corsica had bowed for more than two centuries. By 1764, the Corsicans had rid the entire island of the Genoese troops; the Republic of Genoa, sufficiently tired of the continual struggle with the rebellious mountain people, finally had ceded the island to the French for suitable financial compensation.

Now Louis XV tried to change Corsica's inhabitants into obedient subjects. But Paoli did not give up and began waging a desperate guerrilla war against the invading French forces. Carlo Bonaparte sided enthusiastically with this independence movement. But neither Paoli's obstinate resistance nor Bonaparte's fiery zeal could save Corsican independence, since in the long run the small Corsican militia was no match for the vastly superior French military forces. After an overwhelming defeat, Paoli had to leave the island.

During the guerrilla war, Letizia had accompanied her husband everywhere, taking care of the wounded and carrying ammunition to the soldiers fighting in the front lines; she was already pregnant with her second child, who was literally conceived amid the thundering of cannons. She gave birth to him in Ajaccio on August 15, 1769, a few months after the heroic resistance had collapsed. The child was baptized Napoleone Buonaparte. The bell that rang for his baptism was, so-to-speak, still vibrating from the remote storm signals and the infant breathed the sultry air of the mutual hatred between the Corsicans and the French.

Napoleon later described the circumstances of his birth in the following words:

> The cries of pain of the dying, the complaints of the oppressed, tears and despair surrounded my cradle. My birth came suddenly and unexpectedly....My mother, who had shared the deprivations and hardships of the War of Liberation, now was at the end of her pregnancy. It happened to be the Feast of the Assumption of Mary. She still felt strong enough to go to Mass, but she overestimated her strength. Hardly had she arrived at the church when her first contractions began. Quickly she returned home and hardly reached the parlor, where she gave birth to me on an old blanket. I was given the name Napoleon, which the second-born sons of our family always had.

The story, still repeated even in the most recent biographies, that Napoleon was born in the lobby of the house on a rug depicting the heroes from Homer's *Iliad*, is, according to a statement by Napoleon himself on the island of St. Helena, nothing more than a pious legend. Similar legends embellish his youth, attributing a striking temperament to the lad. But Napoleon's own confessions and descriptions by the Countess of Abrantès, a friend of the Bonaparte family, inform us that, at most, only faint nuances of little Napoleon's temperament suggested that someday he would be an extraordinary man. In his memoirs, however, he wrote a few revealing remarks:

Room in which Napoleon was born in Ajaccio

I was a headstrong child. Nothing impressed me, nothing disconcerted me. I was quarrelsome and pugnacious and afraid of nobody. I hit one person, scratched another, and everyone was afraid of me....But although I grew up wild and unruly, I did respect my mother's authority. To my mother and her excellent principles, I owe my whole happiness and anything good I have done....Indeed, I do not hesitate to assert that a child's future depends on its mother. From earliest childhood I loved to play soldiers, and when I saw real soldiers marching by, I ran out to watch them. My preference for the exact sciences was impressed upon me at an early age, and my mother often told me that while my brothers and sisters spent their time at childish games, I was drawing mathematical figures on the wall.

From Napoleon's nursemaid, the Countess of Abrantès learned of various events of the future Emperor's childhood. She related:

> Napoleon almost never cried when he was punished. If he was spanked, the pain sometimes brought tears to his eyes but that did not last long, and if he was innocent then he absolutely refused to apologize.

His mother was the parent who tried to keep this unruly and stubborn offspring under control, to some extent with blows. His father, on the contrary, was so proud of him that he let him get away with mostly anything. Even later, Napoleon had genuine respect for his mother, who came to be called "Madame Mère." In his opinion, she had the head of a man on the body of a weak woman, and even later she was able to withstand losses and deprivations of the most varied kind with admirable magnanimity.

His nurse Saveria later told the following details about his external appearance:

> Napoleon was not a pretty child like his brother Joseph; his head was much too large in proportion to the rest of his body, a beauty blemish, incidentally, which often occurred in the Bonaparte family. What was especially pleasing about young Napoleon was his glance and especially the expression of mildness mirrored in it during moments of benevolence....Of all Madame Letizia's children [four other brothers and three sisters survived] the later Emperor was the one who showed the least signs of future greatness.

Yet a strange and independent nature manifested itself in the cheerful child and set him off distinctly from his average playmates. Besides his mother's memories, his uncle Michele Durazzo's less well-known sketches also document the boy's strangeness, when he says:

> Since we had no children, I paid more attention to those of my relatives, especially little "Nabulio," who always displayed such a mysterious nature but often also could be adventurous, unruly, and extremely irascible. At times he also became very odd, crude, and brutal. Despite his father's strictness he always managed to get his way, and so he was considered a spoiled brat and incorrigible scalawag....Little Nabulio was very

vain. He openly displayed this vanity, for it was the
energetic expression of his innermost nature....The
little Abbé, who was his first teacher, had a good deal
of trouble with the unruly boy....During the lessons
he was at times distracted, inattentive, enthusiastic, passionate, or indifferent. He offended his teacher's
religious feelings and ignored his criticism. Once he
was supposed to be spanked; he defended himself de-
fiantly against this punishment and bit the Abbé on
the hand....As a child he very easily got angry. Often
he had such tantrums that he became sick and
screamed, beside himself with rage. Out of a simple
spirit of contradiction and obstinacy, he refused to stand
in the corner, shook as if from fever, and refused to
eat....One night I was awakened by screams—the
scrub-bushes on the foothills were ablaze and Nabulio
was not in the house! The thought that the madcap lad
could have lit the fire and now be dying in the flames
made me tremble. Suddenly a shepherd called: "There
is someone in the tower." That will be the boy, I
thought. Yes, it was really Nabulio. He had wanted to
enjoy a magnificent spectacle. So he had set fire to
the heath and then climbed up into the tower.

Since Napoleon showed a great preference for everything military
at so early an age, his father decided to have him pursue a military
career. At nine years of age, Napoleon was sent to the college in Autun
in Burgundy, in order to learn quickly the rudiments of the French language, for until now, he had spoken only the dialect of his native island.
A few months later, his father succeeded in arranging for his son to be
admitted to the Royal Military Academy in Brienne, exclusively intended for training sons of the nobility for the military profession. On
the list of Brienne pupils, one finds this entry: "Today, on April 23,
1779, Napoleon Buonaparte, nine years, eight months, and five days of
age, entered the Royal Military Academy at Brienne-le-Chateau."

Since the poor son of a dubiously noble Corsican, with his spindly
little appearance, was not taken very seriously by his comrades, he
soon felt sorely offended by their arrogance. He had enough, he wrote
home, "of being the target of a few aristocratic dolts, who, proud of
amusing themselves at my expense, criticize and mock me for the
deprivations I impose on myself." But since he could not leave the

military academy, he tried very early to distance himself and to put a barrier between himself and his comrades, and this barrier never completely disappeared. Bourrienne, later Napoleon's secretary and state councilor, reports in his memoirs about his former fellow pupil:

> His need for solitude was caused by impressions which the misfortunes of Corsica and of his own family had stamped upon him during his early childhood....There was always an element of bitterness in his words, his nature had nothing lovable about it; probably the reason was partly the bad circumstances afflicting his family at the time of his birth, and partly the impressions that the subjugation of his fatherland had made on the child.

Actually, he hated the very thought of Corsica's subjugation by France, which made him—the only Corsican at the military academy in Brienne—appear like the conquered among the conquerors. His national sensitivity went so far that he even criticized his father for his courtesy toward the French. Once, when during a meal his professors spoke disparagingly of Paoli, Napoleon exclaimed with annoyance:

> Paoli was a great man who loved his fatherland as the Romans did, and I will never forgive my father, who was his adjutant, for contributing to linking Corsica with France; he should have followed the star of his general's fortune and fallen with him.

In his withdrawal, he found refuge in studying the heroic world of Plutarch, and he was often found reading and daydreaming in the part of the garden assigned to him, which he especially enjoyed tending in his spare time. So he remained a pupil in the military academy in Brienne for five years; every humiliation and discrimination nurtured a revolutionary, rebellious feeling in him, and the inner sense of his own value grew apace with his contempt for men. His rejection by his comrades led him more and more clearly to resolve to pay them back someday and to avenge himself on France for the humiliations he was suffering. Above all, he felt a vague premonition that he would someday liberate his home island from the French yoke.

A well-grounded general education could not be expected from this military academy. As his graduation certificate states, he "always excelled in Mathematics by his talent and industriousness. History and Geography, quite good; Fine Arts exercises and Latin, less

*Napoleon at the military academy in Brienne reading classical authors
(drawing by Karl Girardet)*

satisfactory….Deserves to be accepted at the military academy in Paris."
When he arrived there in October 1784, he faced even greater alienation and hostility than before. At this Parisian school for cadets, after
only one year, he had earned the rank of Second Lieutenant in the Artillery Regiment La Fère in Valence after passing an examination with
a mediocre grade. The certificate reads:

> Reserved and studious, he prefers studies of all sorts
> to conversation and takes a lively interest in good
> writers….He is silent, loves solitude, is moody, proud,
> and very egoistic. Without talking much, he is defi-
> nite in his answers, quick-witted and judicious in
> debates. Much self-love and an ambition that strives
> for everything.

In the boring garrison town of Valence he would probably have reached
the point of despair, had he not withdrawn into a literary world. Later
he reported:

> When I had the honor of being a simple lieutenant in
> the artillery, I was stationed in Valence for three years.
> I was no friend of parties and lived extremely with-
> drawn. But by a fortunate coincidence, I lived near a
> very knowledgeable and
> pleasant book-dealer.
> During those three years
> in garrison I read his en-
> tire library again and
> again, nor did I omit
> works not dealing with
> my profession. More-
> over, nature had endowed
> me with a very good
> memory for numbers.

How serious he was about expanding his general knowledge by
zealous autodidactic studies is
proven by the excerpts he made
in an almost illegible handwriting
in a series of notebooks, whose
printed version takes up four hundred pages by itself! At the same

*Napoleon Bonaparte as artillery
lieutenant, ca. 1790*

time Napoleon also began doing his own original writing. He drafted short stories and began to write a novel about Corsica—all filled with hatred of France—but he finished nothing.

By preoccupying himself more and more in his imagination with Corsica's hopeless state, he felt the anomalies that he encountered in his real social environment all the more clearly, which resulted in a kind of weariness with life, a mood of melancholy (*Weltschmerz*), and real spells of depression. When barely sixteen years of age, he wrote: "What place is there for me in the world? Since I must die someday anyway, couldn't I just kill myself right now?" Although this probably did not involve any genuine suicidal intentions, such a depressive mood is still quite striking for a precocious boy.

In such a mental state, in September 1786 he went on leave to his homeland, where he all too soon was caught between the two fronts. For his Frankophile friends he acted too Corsican, while the national-minded Corsicans saw him only as wearing the uniform of the French king. His diary states:

> Always alone, even among people, I come home to devote myself to my lonely dreams and the waves of my melancholy. To where is this mood inclined today? Toward death. And yet I am standing on the threshold of life and can hope to continue breathing for a long time....Since I am always unhappy and nothing gives me joy, why should I endure a life in which I succeed at nothing!...What a spectacle here at home!...Such a look at my fatherland, yet complete impotence to help: reason enough to flee a world in which I must praise those whom I hate....Life is just a burden for me; I have no enjoyment, everything becomes painful.

After a dull year spent in Corsica amid the money difficulties and family problems, he had to return to a garrison in France, still in this hopeless, depressive mood. He arrived in the spring of 1788 at Auxonne where his regiment was located; there he enjoyed increasing respect from his general, and his mood soon changed. He wrote to his uncle that he was instructed by his highest superior officer "to construct at the firing range various works that required difficult calculations," and he was given writings on modern warfare and tactical operations for precise study, with which he speedily acquired the foundations for his ensuing greatly admired strategies. Moreover, he was introduced to political writings and was especially impressed by Rousseau and Voltaire. Significantly, his diary contains, among other things, a "Draft for a Monograph on the Royal Power," in which he tried to portray the details of the usurped power of the kings in the then-existing twelve monarchies of Europe and came to the conclusion that "there are only a few among them that would not deserve to be deposed." As can be gathered from his "Letters from Corsica," Louis XVI seemed to him in many ways ripe to be deposed from his throne: first, as the King of France ruling absolutely; and second, as Corsica's usurper and colonial master.

CORSICAN ADVENTURE

When Napoleon's mother had visited him in 1782 at the military academy in Brienne, she was appalled at her son's extremely haggard appearance, which made him almost unrecognizable; but at the garrison in Auxonne his general condition became even worse. Compelled by the extremely scanty salary of a young artillery lieutenant to live in a particularly modest style, he followed almost exclusively an "animal and vegetable principle," as he himself expressed it, in which his meals consisted of bread and milk and occasionally corn. Proudly he reported to his mother that he habitually made do with only one meal per day, and since he constantly overexerted himself in his zeal as an officer, it is no wonder that he gradually became extremely thin.

On top of it all, in the summer of 1788 he fell sick with a fever, from which many of his comrades in the garrison also suffered and which apparently lasted for quite a long time. In a letter to his clergyman uncle, Cardinal Joseph Fesch, dated August 22, 1788, he said on this topic: "I am somewhat ill. The great projects I had to complete lately are the cause of that....I am worried mostly about my health, which seems somewhat run-down." It is typical of his boundless ambition that, despite his frail, bean-pole thin appearance and his generally weakened state, he did not shy away from any tasks, however difficult, required by the hard camp life.

Soon the revolutionary events in Paris, starting on July 14, 1789, with the conquest of the Bastille, which was regarded as a bastion of absolutism, were reverberating throughout the country, all the way to the little garrison town of Auxonne. When the Declaration of Human Rights, "Liberty, Equality, Fraternity," was proclaimed on August 27, 1789, young Lieutenant Napoleon was full of hope and expected a

Corsican declaration of independence to follow. Therefore, in September 1789, he hastily took leave from the army in order to seize the favorable moment in Corsica. Meanwhile, in Ajaccio his older brother Joseph was elected chairman of the district council by a Corsican assembly that had been convoked. And Pasquale Paoli, under whose leadership Napoleon hoped to win Corsican independence with the National Guard, had already returned from exile in England. This goal, however, failed to be achieved due to the disunity and discord among the Corsican political and social groups, and so in February 1791, Napoleon returned disappointedly to his unit in Auxonne, where he soon was promoted to First Lieutenant.

A very informative document from that period gives a look into Napoleon's thinking at the time and into his later actions, namely, the essay in reply to the highly endowed prize question of the Academy of Lyons: *"Which truths and which feelings should be most impressed upon people for their happiness?"* For the first time, this essay shows very clearly the two souls in his breast—the coldly calculating reason on the one hand, and the unrestrained, passionate emotions on the other—two sides of his character that would be displayed repeatedly in his future deeds and misdeeds. In response to the dominant ideas of the time, in this essay he advocated a balanced mixture of feeling and reason and warned against coupling "feeling with unrestrained fantasy"; otherwise, misfortune is the inevitable result. People with unrestrained fantasy should therefore "not be allowed to volunteer to maintain order, since they violate its supreme laws." As proof for the correctness of his demand, he cited a historical example:

> Ambition, this unruly desire to satisfy pride or immoderation, though these can never reach their limit, led Alexander of Thebes to Persia, from Granicus on the Issus to Arbella and from there to India. Ambition led him to conquer and devastate the world, yet without satisfying him.

He did not apply his wise insight to his own life at the time he wrote these lines, and later he increasingly lost sight of it. On leave once more, he showed up again in Corsica to take the fate of his country into his own hands. Aflame with uncontrolled ambition and driven by a mania for fame and honor, he now began to do exactly what he had so strongly condemned in his essay. With Machiavellian methods he tried, through election manipulation, bribery and slander, indeed, even by threatening violence against an election commissioner, to obtain a command in the Corsican militia and an elected office. On April 1, 1792, chosen by these wrongful methods to be a lieutenant major of a volunteer battalion, he tried unscrupulously, with the support of radicals, to make himself the military and political master of Ajaccio. In doing so, he deceived even his former idol, Pasquale Paoli, the supreme commander of the Corsican national guard with a purposeful lie, so that soon Napoleon had turned almost all Corsicans against him, and he had to withdraw from Corsica in the greatest haste. By the end of May, 1792, he was back in Paris applying for reinstatement in the army. In France, he was regarded as a lieutenant who had more or less deserted. In Corsica, he was seen as a deposed lieutenant major, exposed to a most embarrassing trial. Totally finished and ruined in both places and facing hunger tomorrow, he saw that his only hope lay in supporting the radicals. So he joined Robespierre, since the only way for him to advance in his career was if the royal dynasty fell.

Reinstated in the army on July 8, 1792, Napoleon was promoted to captain after only two days. However, seeing the disgusting behavior of the revolutionary masses and the Jacobins, who were "acting like madmen, without common sense," as he wrote to his brother Joseph, he was not motivated to fight at the front in the war which France had declared against its arch-enemy Austria in April, 1792. It seemed much more rewarding to him to become engaged again for the Corsican cause, so in September he left Paris, where the Committee of Public Safety soon dominated the entire "public safety." The Revolutionary Tribunal was getting ready to condemn as class enemies all citizens who opposed it, including the King, and send them to the guillotine. In Corsica, he hoped that a military victory would finally give him personal glory and a position of political power. However, his rather dishonorable behavior toward his commander, to whom he was subject as a battalion leader, soon lost him Paoli's good will; when Luciano, Napoleon's brother and fellow combatant, denounced Paoli (the patriot and popular hero) as a separatist and counterrevolutionary, the signal was definitively given for the Bonaparte family to be hunted down. The Bonapartes' family residence was demolished and the mother was forced to flee with her children. Napoleon himself left the island on June 11, 1793.

Three times he had wanted to conquer it as a liberator. Now he was being hunted down as a Frenchman in utter disgrace together with his family, and cooperation with the Jacobins was his only hope of satisfying his ambitions. Since, by his actions in Corsica, he had already disregarded many of the principles advocated in his essay for the Academy of Lyons, he no longer had any qualms about openly professing in a political tract that he was a Jacobin. In this work of political agitation he showed his lightning-fast adaptability to given facts—insofar as they worked to his advantage—and he also demonstrated for the first time his extraordinary talent for propaganda and for effective psychological control of the masses, which he later would manipulate so skillfully in order to realize his ambitious plans. As a result of his adaptation to Jacobinism, he soon was given the nickname of a "Robespierre on horseback," though it was not realized that ideological principles left him completely cold and that all he was seeking with the support of the Jacobins was to win money, power, and fame, as quickly as possible.

FROM BRIGADIER GENERAL TO FIRST CONSUL

Employed by the National Convention, he soon got the chance to demonstrate his military knowledge for the cause of the Jacobins, namely, by putting down the revolt of the citizens of Toulon. Since the artillery commander was incapacitated by a wound, young Captain Napoleon was put in charge of the siege of the city. His plan of operations was approved by the commanding general, Dugommier; and, after little more than three months, Toulon, weakened by constant bombardment until ready for storming, was captured on December 17, 1793. Napoleon's revolutionary attitude and his successful military campaign were rewarded by the Commissars of the National Convention by his promotion to brigadier general, supported among the Jacobins mainly by Augustin Robespierre, brother of the leader of the "reign of terror" in Paris. This could soon have led to his doom after the elder Robespierre himself ended on the guillotine on July 28, 1794. As "Robespierre's brother's man," Napoleon was sent to prison, but was released after a short time.

The execution of eleven hundred people after the capture of Toulon did not seem to make much impression on him. A wound in his thigh by a bayonet stab also did not worry him. But he felt considerably bothered by a very itchy skin ailment, allegedly a case of scabies, which he had caught during the siege.

Reportedly trying in vain to find a satisfactory assignment as a brigadier general, in May 1795, he was seriously thinking of applying for a position as a military adviser in Turkey. But the Directory's takeover of political control in France opened a promising new possibility for his military career, since he was recommended for membership on the Commission for Army Command and Operational Plans, in case of military conflicts. The news then came all the more surprisingly for him that on September 15, 1795, for various political and personal reasons, he was, nonetheless, crossed off the list of French generals. Then suddenly he was reinstated due to the fact that, meanwhile, in Paris

Napoleon, before his promotion to brigadier general, 1793

an opposition movement was being formed, consisting of monarchists and liberals who were trying to topple the new regime with the help of the civilian National Guard. To clear up this dangerous situation, the new commander of the Military Forces of the Interior, rather incompetent militarily, saw himself compelled to call back Brigadier General Napoleon, who had just been dismissed, to immediately recommend a strategic plan to repress the uprising. When on October 5, 1795, the government palace at the Tuileries was attacked by the National Guard, Napoleon dealt the rebels a devastating blow simply by placing cannons in optimal locations and brutally blasting them with grapeshot, which won him the sobriquet of "Grapeshot Shooter" [*mitrailleur*]. Later, he apparently was ashamed of this ruthless behavior against his own countrymen, for he swore that his opponents, not himself, were to blame for this "crime against the French people." In fact, however, Bonaparte probably ordered the first shot, for just shortly before the massacre he had told Barras, the most powerful of the five Directors at that time:

Nominate me, then I am responsible and must have a free hand. Do you perhaps expect the people to give us permission to shoot at the people?

And he wrote to his brother on the very night after his quick victory in the Battle of Paris:

Finally, it is all over....We lined up our troops, the enemy attacked us at the Tuileries, we killed swarms of them, it cost us 30 dead and 60 wounded....All is quiet. As always, I was not wounded at all....Luck is on my side.

As reward, the young brigadier general was promoted to division general and supreme commander of the Army of the Interior. The Tribunes of the National Convention gave him resounding applause; the people of Paris, however, were learning to hate him, for hundreds of unarmed citizens, curious bystanders, and women had been killed in that evening hour. But his mind was not at all set on being loved. As an adventurer of the Revolution, rapidly promoted to a high position, he was beginning to enjoy the joys and privileges of the new class of society, and since he suddenly also had money, he used his high position and his influence—as often done by newly arrived politicians before and after him—to raise his family members and closest friends to influential offices. Although he seemed quite provincial to the Parisians and, with his crude manners and unkempt appearance, with dark, oily hair that hung down to his shoulders, he did not "exactly give the impression of a man of intellect"; still everyone, including the ladies, agreed that General Bonaparte was an extraordinary man, despite his short stature and somewhat oversized head, limbs too short compared with his upper-torso, his thin almost sickly-seeming figure, and the yellowed complexion of his face, with noticeable nervous twitchings.

General Bonaparte in 1795 after his dismissal from the army

Like all men of the new class, Napoleon soon was introduced into the salons of those beautiful ladies who were jokingly referred to among the people as "government property" and to whom Josephine, the widowed Marquise Beauharnais, also belonged. She was a favorite mistress of the mighty Barras, who intended her for his new favorite, Bonaparte. With his impetuous Corsican temperament, which he had until now been able to keep very well under control, he immediately fell so head over heels in love with that flirtatious Creole lady from the Antilles island of Martinique that on March 9, 1796, just a few months after first meeting her, he married her in a civil wedding. To appear approximately of the same age, the aristocratic lady and the Corsican upstart agreed to change their baptismal certificates to make her four years younger and him a year and a half older.

Two days after the wedding, Napoleon left Paris hastily for the front—he had meanwhile been promoted to Commanding General of the Army in Italy. Whereas his love and affection for Josephine became stronger each day, he vanished from her heart and mind on the very day of his departure. For the French revolutionaries, Italy was a preferred target of attack because they hoped thereby to eliminate the quintessence of the conservative reaction, namely, the Habsburg Empire, and in this way to lend a hand to the progressive-minded people in Italy in dispossessing both the clergy and the noble ruling houses. If Napoleon at first was looked upon with suspicious eyes as an appointee of the civilian government, he soon inspired confidence in both officers and enlisted men. Propaganda leaflets were distributed among the soldiers glorifying him as a genius of a military commander, and soon all would have gone through fire for him, spurred by slogans such as: "He flies like lightning and strikes like thunder. He is everywhere and sees everything." Success would prove him right. Using new tactics of war and

Joséphine Beauharnais (1763-1814). (miniature by Jean Baptiste Isabey)

Napoleon as supreme commander of the French troops in Italy, 1796

a superior strategy in a kind of modern blitzkrieg, he defeated Austria's old-fashioned armies. As he later said of himself, since the victory near Lodi on May 10, 1796, he had become convinced that he was chosen by fate for special deeds. Aware of the boundless possibilities of his forces, he revealed for the first time to his friend Marmont: "I feel that deeds are in store for me of which the current generation has no idea." And when he wrote to Paris: "I have received your peace treaty with Sardinia. The Army has approved it," fear ran through the Directory's bones. When had a general ever dared to speak to his government in such a tone!

Napoleon made an eerie impression not only on the Directors in Paris, but also on the citizens of Milan, whose city he entered like a Roman *triumphator*. No one was particularly enthusiastic; indeed, everyone was somewhat astonished. Yet there seemed to be no element of pride in this victor; rather, he was all determination and unbending iron will, to which one was compelled to bow without resistance. The commander rested in the archbishop's palace and took ever longer and hotter baths—the only recreation of his nerves and the only luxury he indulged in, more and more capriciously, until the time of his death.

With the fall of Mantua Fortress, Austria had lost its predominance in Italy. By forming the "Cisalpine Republic," with Milan as its capital, and the Ligurian Republic, with Genoa as its capital, which were vassal states of France from then on, Bonaparte performed a creative act he would repeat in ever wider circles, in order to draw closer to his goal of a united Europe. He proclaimed to the previously oppressed masses the advantages intended by the French Revolution for the welfare of the people, but at the same time, during a period of greatest financial distress, he was pouring money and natural resources back to France and filling the Louvre with more valuable works of art than a king, in all his glory, ever could. The magnificence of his court at Montebello Palace, near Milan, emulated that of a prince in the *ancien régime*, always with the personal aim of being respected and feared. His parvenu-like behavior and his increasingly arrogant deportment were clear manifestations of a deep-seated insecurity. A Roman contemporary wrote:

> You cannot imagine the conceitedness and pride with which he received me, you have no idea. He swore high and mighty that he wanted to invade the capital and as he did so, he tore with his teeth at a document he was holding.

Whether this was really the spontaneous behavior of an unbridled temperament or whether he intentionally wanted to impress and frighten his interlocutor is an unanswerable question. This arrogant and tumultuous behavior was also displayed to French diplomats, for instance, when he exclaimed: "What I have accomplished till now is nothing. I am just at the beginning of my career." On his own authority, he actually marched toward Vienna as far as the Semmering and then signed the truce of Leoben with the Habsburgs on April 18, 1797. The peace treaty signed in Campo Formio on October 1797 was also done completely on his own authority and contrary to the Directory's intention. He made it clear to the lawyers who were convoked in the Directory that he no longer intended to follow their instructions. "I have felt the pleasure of ruling and can no longer do without it." His avidity for glory and power, one of Bonaparte's main driving mechanisms in his future actions, had been aroused and he could by no means settle merely for what had been achieved up to this point. But before leaving Italy, he told Bourrienne that he already felt some satisfaction: "A few more such campaigns and we will have assured ourselves of a tolerable place in posterity."

Madame de Staël, a famous and extremely intelligent lady, saw through Bonaparte more clearly than most men in France at that time when she met him in person, after his triumphal entry into Paris:

> I have seen enough important men, including wildly temperamental ones, but the fear I feel of this one is strange. This man is neither good nor ugly, neither gentle nor cruel....He is more and at the same time less than human. Character, mind, language, everything

has a strange stamp, and that is an additional advantage for winning the hearts of the French....He hates no more than he loves; for him, only he himself exists, all others are numbers. A great chess-player, whose opponent is mankind, and he intends to checkmate it....He despises the nation whose applause he seeks; not a spark of enthusiasm mingles with his need to astonish all mankind....I was never able to breathe in his presence.

Perhaps wishful thinking more than a realistic assessment, some contemporaries at the time believed the small-chested man, with sunken cheeks and scraggly appearance, must be suffering from consumption, and, during the Italian campaign, many a French emigrant drank to his likely impending death. Actually, during the whole Italian campaign, he was suffering from constant coughing and repeated feverish states, as can be gathered from his letters to his wife. Indeed, in 1797 he even asked the Directory in Paris to release him from military service for that reason: "I can hardly remain on horseback any more. I need two years of rest," he confided to Talleyrand, although these lines may have referred more to his hemorrhoid ailment, from which he was already suffering, than to his generally diminished state of health.

In Paris his behavior was rather modest. At the festive reception in the Palais Luxembourg, just a few days after his return from Italy, it was noticed that he entered in a field uniform—could one be more modest?—and stepped up to the platform with a serious and reserved air to give his speech. With clever calculation, he acted more like a citizen than a general, but it soon became clear that his reputation would turn paler and paler if he kept that up. "In Paris they have a short memory. If I remain inactive for long, I am finished." Again we see his burning ambition to attach new glory to his military pennants. The most obvious idea, which would fall on willing ears in the Directory, too, was to defeat England; for whoever defeated England would be the unrestricted master of Europe. But since he could not, at that point in time, become involved in the hopeless adventure of invading that island, the only operation that seemed sensible was a military expedition to Egypt, since that would block England's land route to India, its richest colonial possession. At the same time, this would be a first step toward fulfilling his childhood dream of marching to India in the footsteps of Alexander the Great. The Directory agreed to this proposal of

Napoleon's almost with relief, because it enabled them to remove a dangerous man to a distance, presumably for a rather long time and, if such an enterprise failed, perhaps even forever.

In the battle near the pyramids on July 21, 1798, the French at first won an easy victory over the Mamelukes' far inferior force. Nonetheless, the morale of the troops soon reached its nadir because of the endless hardships they had endured. Then the alarming news was received that, in the sea battle of Abukir on August 1, 1798, the French fleet had been destroyed by the English under Admiral Horatio Nelson. This not only cut off reinforcements from France, but also the Army's return path. Cheated of his long-desired glory of returning to Paris as a victorious hero and hard-pressed by an uprising of the Egyptians, which was strongly supported by Turkish troops, Napoleon began behaving like a barbaric Oriental despot such as Alexander the Great. In Cairo, according to his own data, he ordered at least two thousand Moslems beheaded, and when he faced the Turks on the way to Syria and successfully took Jaffa by storm, he had all the inhabitants, even if they had surrendered, massacred without pity. It reminds one of the war crimes of the twentieth century when one reads that several thousand prisoners of war were led to the beach and pitilessly chased into the sea or slain. Napoleon's later attempt to justify himself with the argument that he had no means to guard them or feed them sounds almost cynical and shows this man's cold inconsideration and contempt for other human beings. As Madame de Staël said, for him only he himself existed and all others were worthless numbers. A letter to Josephine, written by Napoleon only a few days before the fateful day of Abukir, casts a significant light on this person, where it says, among other things:

Humanity nauseates me....My feelings are confused....
My only recourse is to be a complete egoist.

Napoleon's visions of the future were still alive. Instead of going to India, he now wanted to advance on Damascus and Aleppo, and finally to take Constantinople: "I will defeat Turkey and establish a new great empire. Thus I will assure myself of a name for posterity." Again and again his thoughts circled only around his later fame, for which his soldiers had to endure unspeakable toils, sufferings, or death, without contradiction and, with the help of propagandistic slogans, even joyfully. Only after the abortive siege of Acre did general discouragement set in. A retreat to Cairo was begun, without roads, without water, and with the plague as rearguard. The sick and wounded were left behind.

In Jaffa, Napoleon visited the field hospital full of plague victims. Although Desgenettes, the main doctor there, appealing to his Hippocratic oath, refused to obey the order, Napoleon ordered the administration of opium to about thirty men with the plague so as to give them a gentle death. In later justification he said, "Under such circumstances I would have had my own son poisoned," and he insisted that he would himself have taken this assistance to die if he had caught the plague. "Napoleon's Visit to the Plague Field Hospital of Jaffa," an idealized painting by his court painter Gros, was made at his request. Similarly, after returning to Cairo with the remaining five thousand men, "he reported of his deeds like an Arabian teller of tales."

As far as his own person was concerned, the influence of Egypt's warm climate was advantageous to his state of health. The coughing that had never left him since the Italian campaign disappeared completely, and he felt physically fit again, as he had before the start of the war with Italy. However, during the Egyptian enterprise, an itchy skin rash appeared again, such as he had observed during the siege of Toulon and associated with an alleged scabies. The doctors spoke only in general terms of an eczema, without going into more specific details.

He now realized that his goal of creating a basis for his further rise in France by glorious military operations in the Orient was not being met. Since nothing more could be achieved with the French Orient Army for his highly ambitious plans—in his own words "its career was finished"—and he did not have enough ships to take home the pitiful remnant of his army, he decided simply to put what was left of the Army under General Kléber's command; and he, himself, would return to France by ship. The Directory, which had suffered a bankruptcy of its domestic policies and, meanwhile, was involved in the second Coalition War against England, Austria and Russia, had changed its mind about Bonaparte and was now waiting impatiently for his return. Even the opposition press wrote: "His campaign in Egypt has failed, but what harm does it do?...And yet everything he has dared, seems to give us hope again." With his return, however, Napoleon was thinking less of France, which was already hard pressed by its war against the Coalition, than of the welcome chance to be received, not as a defeated commander, but rather as one bringing hope to his fatherland, despite the failure of his Egyptian campaign. Even before his

*General Bonaparte visits patients suffering from the plague in Jaffa on March 11,
1799 (detail from a painting by Antoine Gros)*

departure for Egypt, he had hoped that the impending conflict of France with the European great powers might erupt during his absence, so that he could return as savior of the Republic and occupy the position for which he believed himself to be predestined. These ideas can clearly be read in a letter to his brother written before his journey to Egypt: "If the war breaks out and is waged unsuccessfully, then I will come back and be more certain of public opinion than now." What his soldiers, whom he was leaving behind in Egypt, would say to the news that their General boarded ship for home in absolute secrecy on August 23, 1799, is another page in the book of Napoleon's ambitious plans.

To achieve his plans, he set to work very cautiously and cleverly. He received leaders of the Jacobins, as well as agents of the Bourbons, gave suitable advice to each, told no one what he was really thinking, acted like a prominent gentleman who had been traveling for a long time, and listened with feigned nonchalance to the reports of their quarrels. Napoleon later recalled:

> It was the time of my life in which I acted most skill-fully. I visited Sieyès [a new and especially influential member of the Directory] and promised to implement his lengthy draft of a constitution; I received leaders of the Jacobins and agents of the Bourbons, denying no one my advice, but I gave it only in the interest of my own plans. Each one fell into my net.

The result of the plot Napoleon forged, together with the Abbé Sieyès, was a *coup d'état* that began on November 9, 1799, and was supposed to replace the five Directors with two or three Consuls who would remain in office for ten years. However, in the Council of the Five Hundred, he suffered a political defeat; not only was he reviled, he was even thrown out the door. The General, not used to such parliamentary customs, suffered a severe attack of fainting. He felt deeply humiliated and swore to himself that he would soon put an end to this parliamentary "chattering room." Only by the intrusion of grenadiers into the plenary hall was the Council of Elders forced to confirm the planned provisional government consisting of three Consuls. Again Napoleon used concerted and carefully targeted propaganda on the people, announcing:

A hundred murderers are attacking me and aiming for the heart....The shout of "Outlaw!" is directed against the defender of the law....Frenchmen! You will, without a doubt, recognize in my behavior the zeal of a soldier of freedom, of a citizen devoted to the Republic.

In truth, even at this time he was already toying with the idea of being placed at the head of France with the help of the Army. But first it seemed urgent to him to elaborate a form of constitution useful for his own ambitious plans, namely, "a formal democratic constitutional paper [as cover] for a Caesaristic constitutional reality." He worked for such a constitution by a series of adroitly and persistently conducted negotiations with the technical commissions. In this way, by December 24, 1799, a consular constitution was adopted, conveying on him the title of First Consul. Following a formula well proven in more recent history, he decided to disguise his possibilities for autocratic rule achieved *de facto* by this nomination under the appearance of democracy. He also decided to secure and consolidate his power position once and for all over the heads of parliament by calling for a referendum of the entire nation. Although by irregularities in the counting and a very high number of abstentions—less than one-third of the eligible voters voted "Yes"—the First Consul was satisfied with the outcome, and he set the constitution in force.

One of the most urgent tasks of the newly elected First Consul was to put an end to the Second Coalition War. He tried to achieve peace by diplomatic means, not so much out of personal conviction, but because of his people's longing for peace. But since, as could be expected, England and Austria rejected his offers for peace, he could present himself to the French as a "disappointed lover of peace." Then, appealing to his soldiers to move against the enemy states, he won public opinion to support his decision to force the enemy to accept peace by military means.

In the spring of 1800, Napoleon's army crossed the great St. Bernard's Pass in order to strike the surprised Austrians in Upper Italy, in the style of Hannibal crossing the Alps in 218 B.C. Napoleon's victory near Marengo on June 14, 1800, was, however, not as flawless as he later tried to describe it. If General Desaix had not joined him in time with a fresh division, Napoleon would surely have lost the battle.

To admit this was unthinkable for the vain, glory-seeking commander, and fate helped him to cast this rather dubious victory in a favorable light. Since General Desaix was mortally wounded during his relief operation, Napoleon was able to claim the glory for himself alone and to exploit the victory for his own purposes. After the peace treaties of Lunéville (1801/02) and later of Amiens, he was able to present himself credibly to his people as a peace-maker and to get Europe to make friends with such a peace-loving Napoleon. His subsequent proclamation involuntarily calls to mind memories of similar words heard in the twentieth century in the Third Reich:

> Frenchmen! Now you have it at last, this peace you have deserved by such long and heroic efforts. The government, faithful to your wishes and its promises, has not let itself be carried away by either ambition for conquests or by the allures of bold and extraordinary enterprises. It was its duty to give peace and quiet back to mankind and to unite the great European family, whose task it is to determine the fate of the world, with firm and enduring bonds.

With these and similar words, Napoleon succeeded in impressing even foreign negotiators, such as the new English prime minister, Charles James Fox, who, after a visit to Paris, returned home with enthusiastic praise for the famous Anglophobe.

After successfully signing the peace treaties, Napoleon had to pay more attention to problems of domestic policy. First, he hastened to reconcile his state with the Church after ten years of enmity, not however because he was a believer, but merely because on rational grounds one must get along with this oldest of all powers if one wants to use it for one's own purposes.

> Catholicism won the Pope for my side and, with my influence and my power in Italy, I did not give up hope of being able to steer him according to my will sooner or later. And then what influence! What a means toward Europe!

But he also passed a new education law for the whole country, and he increased internal security by strengthening the security forces. While he turned aside the Bourbons' attempts at *rapprochement* with courteous smoothness, he tended to be more favorable toward the Royalists from the Vendée. What seemed most reliable to him, however, was to know that the great democratic center was on his side because they felt secure under him. Like a real "father of his country," he did everything he could to diminish social hardship.

Conspiracies against the First Consul came from the Jacobins who tried to stab him on October 10, 1800, in an opera box. But the Royalists, too, tried to murder him by throwing a bomb at his carriage during his trip to the opera on December 24th. The ambition of the coachman, who wanted to leave on time, saved his life, while nine unfortunate pedestrians were killed. Napoleon appeared quite calmly at his theater-box for the premiere of Haydn's *Creation*; but the next day he had 130 Jacobins deported without a trial to the Seychelles Islands in the Indian Ocean and did not retract this measure even when it turned out that the Royalists were responsible for the assassination attempt. He had two Royalist assassins guillotined in the red shirt of patricides, because they had tried to kill the "father of the fatherland," as he said. Napoleon also took stern measures against writers who seemed dangerous to him, as, for instance, against Madame de Staël-Holstein, whom he banished from Paris in 1802 for her sharp words directed against Napoleon's enlightened absolutism. Later, from abroad, she gave important support to the European resistance against him.

Like other dictators, he considered himself the representative and, if necessary, the violent implementer of the will of the people. The methods required for this were broadly similar to those employed by dictatorial states of the twentieth century. In addition to skillful manipulation of the popular will by propaganda, an important tool was the creation of a state police whose job was to watch the citizens as constantly as possible. The man whom he selected as most suitable to be Minister of Police was Joseph Fouché, a former Jacobin and later turncoat, who went down in the history of the Revolution as the "Butcher of Lyons" and whose network of agents was so finely meshed that he could secretly spy even on the First Consul. But, as a precaution, Napoleon kept the dissemination of propaganda, so important for his plans for power, in his own hands. Its task was constantly to remind the French people of the unique greatness of his glorious deeds and to convince the citizens with passionate, nationalistic pathos that only he, and no other, was the outstanding leader, with the abilities, willpower, and razor-sharp intellect to successfully guide France's destiny.

Even at this early date Napoleon was convinced that he could create a "new France as the model for a French Europe." To achieve this, he needed, in his opinion, not only superior understanding and superhuman will, but, above all, untiring endurance and energy. Actually, he worked incessantly, whether at home, on journeys, or in the field, both day and night, and his coworkers were quite exhausted by such restless activity. Such a work-style was possible for him only because he needed very little sleep and he got it when and where it happened to suit him.

This hectic way of working, however, also had some negative effects in the sense of psychosomatic ailments that now showed up for the first time. His stomach proved to be especially susceptible. Even during his schooling at Brienne, under mental stress or excitement he repeatedly had suffered stomach ailments of an indefinite sort, but they had abated quickly. But now this organ first began to act up with painful attacks that were reportedly almost unbearable. A report by his secretary Fauvlet de Bourrienne from the year 1802 tells how Napoleon, during an intensive phase of work, groaned the words: "How I'm suffering!" In the midst of his work, he leaned hard against the edge of the desk, tore open his vest, and pressed his right upper abdominal regions with both hands.

The stabilization of the currency, the creation of a balanced budget for the government, and other successes in the economic and social field improved his reputation and his credibility among the people. He also knew how to exploit human vanity by granting medals and honors in order to recruit reliable coworkers in the various fields. "With children's toys one attracts men," he said. Finally, a special concern of his was to create civil equality by means of the "*Civil Code of the French,*" published on March 21, 1804, and later called the "*Code Napoléon.*" One result of this codification of laws was, among other things, that he could count on the bourgeoisie's support in the civilian area. This Napoleonic Code later influenced the civil law of many European countries and became the basis for future human rights legislation. All children were equally entitled to inherit; all parents had the duty to support their children. Jews had equal rights, and civil marriage was introduced for everyone, together with the possibility of divorce. All these beneficial actions understandably led the people to want to retain their benefactor for life.

NAPOLEON I, EMPEROR OF THE FRENCH

Should Napoleon Bonaparte be Consul for life?" Impatiently pressing for an affirmative answer, he quickly arranged for a plebiscite to decide this question, and that is exactly how the text submitted to the people read. In that referendum 3,600,000 citizens voted "YES," compared with only 80,370 negative votes. Now he could finally tell himself with his chest swelling with pride: "From now on I stand on the same level as other monarchs." This satisfying outcome soon gave rise to the ambitious idea of making his position as absolute head of state hereditary, in order to secure the position in the future for his descendants or his family. With unnoticed but rapid strides, he was advancing toward a real monarchy, for, as he assured private circles, with the help of his devoted supporters, he could achieve whatever he wanted.

His plan was favored by a neomonarchistic wave that was becoming ever stronger in France. Nor could this development remain hidden from the Senate and even from the Tribunate, which was still occupied by a few Jacobins. Since the Jacobins considered the restoration of Bourbon rule unthinkable, the Tribunate preferred to promote the idea of a monarchy under Bonaparte, and, therefore, it proposed a bill to "declare Napoleon Bonaparte, now First Consul, to be the Emperor of the French and to make the imperial dignity hereditary in his family."

On May 18, 1804, the new constitution was adopted by the Senate. It reads, in part, as follows: "The government of the Republic is transferred to an Emperor, who bears the title 'Emperor of the French.'" Submitted to the people in a third referendum, the new constitution was approved by more than 3,500,000 votes on November 6, 1804, an overwhelming approval by the French citizens. Therefore, with open pride Bonaparte said:

> Never has a prince sat on his throne with more legitimate rights to the throne than Napoleon. Hugh Capet received the throne from the hands of a few bishops and a few great men of the realm. The imperial throne was given to Napoleon by the will of all citizens.

But Bonaparte had even more in mind. In order to be able to present himself to European sovereigns and to his believing citizens as a monarch in the old style, he considered the confirmation of his imperial dignity by a papal anointing to be absolutely necessary. However, he insisted that the Pope come to him in Paris, where the coronation ceremonies were to take place in the cathedral of Notre Dame. Pope Pius VII consented under pressure, but under condition that the previous civil marriage between Bonaparte and Josephine first be confirmed by a church wedding; only when he received news that this had been done did the Holy Father reply with satisfaction: "Now we will no longer resist the coronation of the illustrious Emperor."

The grandiose spectacle took place on December 2. About one hour after the Pope's arrival at the cathedral, the Emperor and the Empress arrived, saluted by thundering cannons. The Emperor did not permit the Pope to touch the crown, but placed it on his own head; then he took the crown intended for the Empress and placed it on her head, as she knelt before him. Then he had himself anointed by the Pope. Even at that solemn moment, he was not self-conscious. Accompanying Josephine to the festive table, he said only: "Thank God that is over! I would have preferred a day on the battlefield."

Despite all triumphal grandeur of that day, a shadow did fall on his insatiable longing for glory and power, as a skeptical, pathetic remark to his trusted Decrès shows:

> I was born too late, there is nothing great left to do....I admit I have had a beautiful career, but what a difference from antiquity! Just take Alexander! After having conquered Asia, he declared himself to be Jupiter's son, and the entire Orient believed him—except his mother, Aristotle, and a few Athenian pedants. But if I were to declare myself today to be the son of the Almighty Father and were to go to Notre Dame to thank him for it, every fishwife would ridicule me. The nations of today are too intelligent, one cannot do anything great anymore.

These words spoken a few hours after the imperial coronation show once again that nothing could satisfy his unrestrained striving for greater heights. Since he saw how easy it is to assure oneself of the obedience and loyalty of men by outstanding deeds and skillful leadership, he felt that the demands of the Enlightenment no longer applied to him, the strongest person on earth. How could he wish for democracy, government by the people, now that he had seen so precisely the weakness of their instincts. To become ever greater, to carry his name farther and

Napoleon Bonaparte in coronation regalia (painting by François Gérard)

farther and to write pages in the book of history with golden letters was the only thing that seemed to him the goal and reward of his life. When, in those days, the design for an Imperial seal containing the sketch of a sitting lion was shown to him, he crossed out the drawing right away and wrote in his own handwriting next to it: "An eagle in flight."

The hour of the Imperial coronation meant the final end of the Republic, and in all Europe, the vanguard of intellectual freedom, disappointed by their idol as herald of freedom and equal human rights, now began to fall away from him: two examples are Lord Byron, who had praised him, and Beethoven, who immediately retracted the dedication to him of his "Heroic Symphony" *(Eroica)*.

Moreover, Napoleon was not satisfied with one crown. On March 17, 1805, the unification of the Kingdom of Italy with France was offered to him by the Cisalpine Republic, and on May 26 in the Cathedral of Milan, whose cornerstone had been laid by Galeas Visconti, he received the iron crown of the old Lombard kings, which Charlemagne had worn and which he now set upon his head with the words: "God has given it to me, woe to him who touches it!"

As Emperor of the French, he wanted to make Paris the center of Europe. To do this, he had to present himself in monarchic style and to shape his courtly life accordingly. As under the Bourbons, there were in the palace courtly positions for the most varied duties; and, even for these imperial positions, he adopted the practices of the *ancien régime*. While the old feudal nobility had disappeared, he created a new, popular nobility of merit, within which the introduction of the Legion of Honor was a first step. The naming of fourteen general field marshals was intended to reward those meritorious generals who had performed especially valuable services for him during his military campaigns. Soon, however, he also began to provide members of his family with princely titles and to assign profitable posts to them. So, after just a few years, all the old titles of nobility had been reintroduced; they had become necessary in order to lead and supervise the new society, consisting mostly of *parvenus*. But these titles brought neither feudal property nor tax privileges nor hereditariness to those who received them.

While the Empress Josephine acquired a wardrobe of dresses and jewelry that far outdid that of all previous queens, Napoleon was satisfied with the soldier's uniform, replacing it only on festive occasions with the blue jacket of a guard of the grenadiers. He gave great

significance to the celebration of Sunday, which was intended to impress both citizens and foreign diplomats. That this ploy succeeded
can be seen from the description by one of his marshals: "It is Sunday;
he is awaited in the Grand Gallery. As soon as the cry 'The Emperor!'
is heard, we turn pale; I know a few bold fellows who tremble in their
entire body." Most "instructive for friend and foe" was how Napoleon
rated the great parade he mustered from horseback, which, with its
drums and fanfares, its magnificent flags and standards, used to stir up
genuine enthusiasm—a phenomenon only too well known to some dictators in our century, with their repertory of effective methods for
influencing the masses.

Like many tyrants and dictators, Napoleon, too, preferred to talk
about himself. His personality was marked by an often brusque change
from relaxed merriment to brooding melancholy, and he never could
hide his momentary mood and spontaneous thoughts. His handwriting,
hard to read even in his youth, became more and more distorted with
the years because of his myopia. Like Hitler, he was gifted with an

Napoleon's handwriting

incredibly quick comprehension and an astonishing memory, which he
never lost. His daily schedule was marked by restless and untiring
activity, which on some days left very few hours for sleep. He usually
got up at 7 a.m. and quickly scanned the most important files and reports, then he also scanned the newspapers for possible deviations from
the official policy, after which he went to his bathtub. From his valet
Constant Wairy, we learn that the water could never be hot enough for
him, because he was extraordinarily sensitive to the cold; and, since he
took a notion to bathe at any hour day or night, warm bathwater had to
be kept ready at all times.

During his bath he received reports on the content of various dispatches, or even private tales, and the servant had to add hot water
constantly during this time—the bath often took longer than an hour.
The bathroom also had to be well heated, even in the summer, so that

his servant finally had to let the sauna-like air out by opening all the doors and windows. His head too, incidentally, was very sensitive to the cold, so that Constant had to have all his hats padded for him. After the bath he slipped into a morning coat of white flannel, put his night-cap on again, drank one or two cups of tea, and began to shave himself. He then washed his hands with almond paste and with a soap perfumed with rose essence, cleaned his face with a fine sponge, sprinkled his toothbrush with a fine powdered coral and rinsed his mouth with diluted brandy. Finally he had Constant massage him with cologne, and he finished the whole procedure of his morning toilette with a dose of snuff. Then he immediately dressed to go to his office, where his secretary was already awaiting the Emperor with pen in hand.

Toward ten o'clock, breakfast was served. Lunch was eaten quickly and seldom lasted longer than twelve minutes. This habit of eating so fast often had a bad influence on the Emperor's health, as an incident reported by Constant proves:

> One day I was called to the Emperor, with whom the noon meal had disagreed very much. I found him lying stretched out on the carpet, the Empress was kneeling next to him with his head in her lap; he was groaning and swearing. He found it harder to bear this kind of suffering (which he tried to alleviate by stretching out full length on the floor) than any discomfort, any dangers in the field....Napoleon drank three cups of tea and felt some relief. The Empress stroked his brow and rubbed his stomach....I often witnessed such touching scenes.

This and similar portrayals by Constant led the Italian psychiatrist Cesare Lombroso to diagnose epilepsy for Napoleon, but there is absolutely no evidence to support this assumption. The legend that Napoleon suffered from epilepsy comes from Talleyrand, who reports in his memoirs that in September 1805, during a stay in Strasbourg, the Emperor suffered an attack in his presence, falling to the floor and twisting with cramps for fifteen minutes. Since in this context there was no mention of him biting his tongue, nor foaming at the mouth, nor even of falling unconscious, it probably could not have been an epileptic seizure. Besides, Napoleon's immediate circle expressly report that they had never observed any epileptic attacks in Napoleon. Probably the incident described by Talleyrand was triggered by a violent, cramplike stomachache, such as his servant Constant often witnessed. That

Napoleon often acted theatrically during these attacks was due to the extremely tense state of his nerves, manifested on other occasions by secondary muscular reactions, quite familiar to the people around him. For instance, after long hours of work, his right shoulder sometimes would begin to quiver, a nervous tic that signaled a heightened nervous tension. Similarly his closer associates always noticed a visible quivering of the calf muscles under his silk stocking when a more violent emotional outbreak was imminent.

His meals consisted of a soup, three meat entrees, among which a chicken fricassee—*poulet à la marengo*—was one of his favorite dishes, two kinds of vegetables, coffee and chambertin wine. The menu was, however, reduced considerably as the years went by. Napoleon, to whom "eating meant merely the intake of fuel for the working machine," often hardly noticed what food was set before him, since his thoughts were already preoccupied with continuing his interrupted work. This almost pathological dedication to work was also the reason why he frequently took his meals very irregularly, and therefore the foods often were served reheated, which incidentally did not bother him. He set as little store on table manners as on the makeup of the menu and liked to serve himself with his fingers instead of with a fork, which often left traces of the hastily swallowed foods on the table and also on his clothing.

His behavior with regard to eating seems also to have applied to love-making. For Napoleon, a woman was, in the judgment of one historian, "nothing more than a means of recreation from work." To court a woman seemed to him a waste of time, so that he came directly to the point without any digressions. He considered social equality for women practically deviant: "Women are our property....They belong to us just like a fruit-bearing tree belongs to the gardener." He saw the positive role of woman as a chaste, faithful wife and a mother with many children. Since he was, moreover, of the view that since the *ancien régime* "the French had in this regard become much stricter and no longer would forgive their ruler public love affairs and mistresses," the keeping of mistresses was absolutely frowned upon in his court.

In other ways, too, life at the court was stiff and, because of the unpredictable changes of mood of the master of the house, boring and muted, so that Franz Herre said "it was the most unpleasant and boring court France ever had." The conversational partners he liked to spend time with were his court painters, such as Jacques Louis David and François Gérard, to whom he gave instructions about how his deeds and his image were to be depicted most effectively. He also expected his architects to lend to his Empire the impression of ancient grandeur with suitable classical buildings. Despite his physical appearance, which had become somewhat corpulent, he soon was compared with famous figures of antiquity, although his physical build had little in common with a Greek statue. Although Napoleon was a boundless dreamer both militarily and politically, he obviously had inhibitions about having superdimensional monumental structures built in the manner of a Roman Emperor and, in this restraint, he differs from Hitler's pathological construction megalomania. He rejected plans of that sort with the remark: "Too much ambition leaves unfinished palaces."

A year before his coronation, the war with England had erupted again. It was more a state of war than a military campaign, and it was not to end until Napoleon himself was finished. Just as he had done before going to Egypt, he now examined all conceivable possibilities of a landing, but the alien element of the sea misled him to considerations designed more by an amateur than a technician. An incident also occurred that was a warning symptom of his stormy and tyrannical nature: he had ordered a review of the fleet, despite a mounting storm, and the commanding general refused to carry out the orders for the fleet movements; Napoleon sent him away with a threatening gesture of his riding whip and insisted stubbornly that his order be carried out. Twenty boats tipped over, and the next day about two hundred dead sailors were washed ashore as victims of this cruel example of a power-mad tyrant—a high price for the unconditional satisfaction of the arrogant and irresponsible mood of a dictator.

This war with England, which had found Austria and Russia as mighty allies for this third coalition war, would soon prove to be the beginning of the end for Napoleon. But first, there came one conquest after another. A masterful commander, Napoleon introduced a new military science that, according to Marshal Ferdinand Foch, would set the direction for the nineteenth and twentieth centuries and totally change "the nature and dimensions of war." So he succeeded in encircling the entire Austrian army before they were even lined up for battle.

> I have achieved my purpose of destroying the Austrian army by simple marches. Now I will turn against the Russians. They are lost!

He pictured the destruction of the Russian military power as being so simple. But then as his armies were marching forward, he received the bad news that his fleet had been almost completely annihilated near Trafalgar by Admiral Nelson, who lost his life in that naval battle. Nonetheless, Napoleon did not let this detain him from continuing on the path prescribed for him by his overpowering ambition and his belief in his mission to found a European empire. He hoped to attain this objective by satisfying both the French quest for supremacy and his own unlimited urge to extend his Imperial sphere of influence. The realization of his plans of operation sometimes brought him to the limits of the bearable by incessant and, in part, hectic expenditure of all his energies, as is evidenced by an incident reported by Talleyrand:

> I pulled off his necktie, for he seemed to be choking.
> He did not vomit, but he was groaning, and spittle was
> pouring out of his mouth.

Finally on December 2, 1805, in the famous battle on the plains of Austerlitz, a battle in which three emperors were present, he defeated the Austrians and the Russians and made the desolate place famous for all time. He wrote to Josephine:

> I am somewhat tired. I've bivouacked outdoors for a
> week on rather cool nights. Today I am lying in bed in
> the beautiful castle of Prince Kaunitz…and intend to
> sleep for two or three hours.

This unexampled victory at the same time marked the demise, in 1806, of the Holy Roman Empire of the German Nation, and from the ruins of the old Reich, Napoleon created "a French fortress, to which he gave the veneer of a German citadel," to quote Franz Herre. The introduction of the *Code Napoléon* in the confederation of German states now created the basis for a bourgeois society by abolishing the privileges of the nobility, freeing the peasants of the feudal impositions, emancipating the Jews, and tolerating all religious denominations. The Holy Roman Empire of the German Nation was replaced by a "Roman Empire of the French Nation" in the spirit of enlightened absolutism, in which, however, there was to be one sole ruler, namely, Napoleon. To remove all misunderstandings from the start, in 1809 he abruptly annexed the Papal States and took Pope Pius VII prisoner. "Now I am the Emperor of Rome," Napoleon said after the victory at Austerlitz, and he began to plan for a modern empire modeled on the Roman one. He installed his son as King of Rome and his brother Joseph as King of Naples. As he wrote at the time:

> I want to incorporate the Kingdom of Naples in my
> family, so that it will belong to my federative states, or
> in truth to the French Empire, just as do Italy, Switzer-
> land, Holland, and the three German Kingdoms,
> Bavaria, Würtemburg, and Saxony.

This idea, confided to his brother, fit perfectly into his firmly decided plan for a European empire under the leadership of the Emperor of the French.

Under these circumstances, it depressed him that he could expect no heirs from Josephine. So he began looking for a second wife and found one in the person of Marie-Louise, the daughter of the Austrian Emperor. While some of his old comrades-at-arms were displeased that Napoleon sought to establish marriage ties with an old, established dynasty, he himself regarded it "as a great success, equal to the victory at Austerlitz."

The Prussians had given him an ultimatum to withdraw from southern Germany and to give the Prussian King Friedrich Wilhelm III freedom of action there. After dealing them a crushing defeat in the battle near Jena and Auerstadt on October 14, 1806, he now also had northern Germany, including Silesia, all the way to the Weichsel, in his hands, and victory began visibly to go to his head. Intoxicated with power, he now believed that he could force England to its knees by a total trade war via the so-called Continental Blockade. Almost simultaneously with the decree issued on November 21, 1806, Czar Alexander and his army started marching toward the West.

If Napoleon believed that he could defeat the Russians quickly, he was in error. Winter, cold, and snow, but especially the Russian tactic of scorched earth threatened to cause Napoleon's strategy to fail and the important battle on February 8, 1807, near Eylau ended indecisively, which did considerable damage to his reputation in Paris as an undefeatable military commander. So it seemed wisest to Napoleon to come to an agreement with Russia, and this was assured by a Franco-Russian treaty signed on July 9, 1807. In the Peace of Tilsit, half of the Prussian national territory was ceded to France, and Napoleon carved it out into the Duchy of Warsaw and the Kingdom of Westphalia, which he intended for his brother Jerome.

The Prussian Countess von Voss described Napoleon as "corpulent, short, and totally without a figure....The expression of his features is hard; he looks like the incarnation of success." But his constitution was apparently not as ironclad as he tried to demonstrate by his majestic deportment. During the campaign against the Russians, he often suffered violent stomach cramps, which began to worry him. "I bear the germ of an early death in me. I will die of the same ailment as my father." With these words he alluded to cancer, the family ailment which took the lives of his grandfather, his father, his uncle, a brother, and a sister. But his external deportment was marked by decisiveness and, if necessary, cruel hardness. While his brother, King Jerome, tried to explain the intentions of the French Emperor, that he "always was victorious only for the nations, and every peace-treaty he signed was one more step toward the goal his genius had set of giving entire nations a political existence and government by wise laws, and of building a fatherland for each of them," Napoleon forcefully warned the French military governor:

> If the defeated people show the least movement of any
> kind, set a terrible example. The first village that rebels
> is to be plundered and burned down.

That is the reality behind the "noble simplicity and silent grandeur" that Goethe saw in this man whom he felt to be the great organizer of Europe.

Goethe's idea of Napoleon as a "demigod," who acted outside morality, "ultimately like physical causes, like fire and water," calls to mind the original estimation of Hitler by Thomas Mann or Martin Heidegger. Napoleon, too, in his "noble simplicity and silent grandeur" knew how to impress the people around him by wearing the simple green infantry jacket, as a conscious understatement, to put his role as the "controller of the masses and overcomer of chaos" all the more convincingly in the right light.

Napoleon was more and more frequently plagued by stomach cramps and was able to alleviate the increasing irritability of his nerves only by hot baths lasting for hours. His behavior toward the people around him became colder and colder, and he forbade even his brothers to address him. Sometimes he got up in the middle of the night to dictate until morning, and sometimes melancholy darkened his mood, a melancholy such as he had experienced previously only in his youthful years. Now that his fantastic dream was gradually beginning to be fulfilled, all that he had achieved seemed to be too little. When a minister wanted to congratulate him after signing the Treaty of Tilsit, he replied gruffly: "You are just like the crowds. I will be master only when I have signed the Treaty of Constantinople." The dream of world power, of ruling Asia, still hovered before his mind.

THE TURNING POINT APPROACHES

But the turning point in Napoleon's destiny was beginning to show its contours. The Continental Blockade was unable to break England's position of power; Austria was preparing for a new war; and Talleyrand, with a premonition of what was coming, took the precaution of stepping down as foreign minister. At the meeting of princes at Erfurt in October 1808, Talleyrand, by secret intrigues, convinced the Czar of the Emperor's blind mania for conquest, and so Alexander I began to distance himself from Napoleon. Then came the uprising of the Spaniards against the French, so that in July 1808 Joseph Bonaparte, who had been installed as King, had to flee out of his capital together with the French army, retreating beyond the Ebro.

Napoleon was now denounced by the oppressed nations as the violator of the Spanish people, and gradually the view glimmered in the mind of the French people too, that Napoleon was not sincere with his often proclaimed noble intention of wanting to bring freedom to the nations, along with the rights they had coming to them. Instead, the genuine driving force behind his far-flung imperial endeavors was his ambition and his mania for conquest, in order to create a single European empire under his sole authority. In complete ignorance of the passionate Spanish nationalism, he tried to prevent disaster by sending in elite troops under his own command. The Spanish had nothing with which to oppose such massive military superiority and so on December 4, 1808, they had to surrender their capital, Madrid, to the Imperator. But now a guerrilla war flared up, waged with unimaginable hardness and cruelty, bringing Napoleon's strategy down in defeat. "The Spanish war destroyed my reputation in Europe," he later admitted and, since he had started this war only to win a new crown for his dynasty and to increase his own glory, he also lost a lot of his reputation in France, too. Above all, this successful defensive war against the conqueror by the Spanish was a rallying signal for other repressed nations. This was true especially of Freiherr von Stein, whose opinion was confirmed that, on the model of Spain, together with the Generals Gneisenau and Scharnhorst, he could break the oppressor's yoke in Germany, too. Austria, as well, was mobilizing for a fifth war after it had allied itself anew with England and, this time, also with Turkey. But precisely in the role of an aggressor, Austria did Napoleon the favor of placing in his hands the role of defender of France, thus raising his damaged prestige in the homeland and the fighting spirit of his troops.

On May 12, 1809, the French troops moved into Vienna for the second time, although the Austrian army had not yet been defeated. And now it turned out that Napoleon's usually victorious strategy had reached the limit of its possibilities, since the enemy had already learned too much about the skillful commander's tactical maneuvers. On the battlefield of Aspern, Napoleon suffered his first defeat; the only reason he was able to make up for this loss with a victory in the battle on July 6 near Wagram—having received reinforcements from his armed forces in Italy—was that Archduke Karl did not know how to exploit his own success.

After the battle near Wagram, which marked an especially distressing and stressful situation in his life, Napoleon's skin disease flared up again. His doctors were so worried that they sought the advice of Johann Peter Franck, the court physician of the Austrian Imperial family and first director of the General Hospital in Vienna. This doctor apparently assumed the existence of a boil, caused by the rubbing of his coat collar on the skin of the neck, and proposed a long-lasting treatment because of the possible danger of a "brain congestion." Since Napoleon absolutely rejected such methods of treatment, he had his personal physician, Professor Jean Nicolas Corvisart summoned from Paris, and he apparently was able to heal this boil quickly by means of a blistering plaster.

After signing the peace treaty of Schönbrunn on October 14, 1809, which he imposed on the Austrians, an embarrassing incident occurred during the victory parade: an attempt was made by Friedrich Staps, the son of a Protestant clergyman, to stab the Emperor Napoleon to death. After his arrest, he claimed to have formerly been an ardent admirer of the Imperator and to have recognized Napoleon's true character only because of his policy of violence and conquest. The change of attitude of this young man, who just before his execution cried out, "Long live freedom, death to the tyrant!" is said to have put Napoleon into a very pensive mood. Elsewhere in Germany, the intellectual resistance was also stirring and various pamphlets were already striking a dubious and threatening tone. Johann Philipp Palm, from Braunau on the Inn, was the publisher of such a pamphlet directed against Napoleon. When he was arrested by the French occupation forces, Napoleon wanted to set an example with him, so Palm was executed in Braunau on the Inn on August 26, 1809.

But Napoleon had a domestic enemy of quite a different stature: Reichs-Baron von Stein, who tried to pry reforms out of the Prussian King Friedrich Wilhelm III in a tenacious struggle, and who eagerly longed for a popular uprising in northern Germany, such as had taken place in Spain. In a letter intercepted and forwarded to Paris, he wrote:

> The Spanish example shows how far cunning and ambition to dominate can go, and on the other hand what a nation can do if it has strength and courage. Bitterness is increasing in Germany day by day, and it is advisable to foster it and spread it among the people.

After he was outlawed by the Emperor of the French, Baron von Stein fled to Austria and later to Russia, and he became a martyr in the eyes of the people. Together with Madame de Staël, he organized and led the national opposition to Napoleon's ever more blatant imperialism.

Even in the mother country, the increasingly dictatorial nature of Napoleonic rule was causing dissatisfaction to spread. The number of yearly conscriptions kept climbing—for wars that served not to defend France, but merely to expand the domains ruled by Napoleon—while the number of soldiers who had fallen in battle had long since passed one million. Typical of Napoleon's view of the role of young men in achieving his ambitious goals is that he called France his mistress, "who would gladly pay the price for the good fortune of devoting herself to me." For, as he boasted literally: "If I need 500,000 men, she gives them to me." In the memoirs of Fouché, his unpopular yet indispensable police minister, he is quoted as saying:

> I need 800,000 men, and I have them; I will drag all Europe behind me, Europe is nothing but an old woman with whom I can do whatever I want with my 800,000 men....Didn't you tell me that you recognize genius because it knows no impossibilities?...Can I help it if excessive power drives me to become dictator of the world? I have not yet fulfilled my destiny, I want to finish what I have merely begun....I want to make one people out of all the nations.

Again we have his vision of a United States of Europe.

The more intensely Napoleon's world plans pressed for further recruitments, the more troops he had to assign to maintain internal peace. And the consequent sharpening of the dictatorship caused the mood of the citizens to become all the more dismal. Since thousands of young

Napoleon's personal physician Jean-Nicolas Corvisart (1755-1821) (after an anonymous etching)

men had already avoided conscription by fleeing, he had to coerce families and communities to provide young men for service in the army by threats and the use of "flying columns." The network of agents of the government surveillance service reached down to the smallest corner of the country and the least sign of criticism was persecuted without mercy. More than three thousand "state criminals" were already sitting without a trial in protective custody, as it was already called then, foreshadowing the practice of dictators of our century, "because he hates the Emperor" or "because of statements against the government in private letters." When a Dutch newspaper expressed the opinion that the Pope could excommunicate a king, not only was the newspaper banned, but the author, too, was arrested. Formerly Napoleon had consulted public opinion on every step he took, but now under the spell of developing his power and with an eye only on the goal of his life, he utterly disregarded the moral impression that his actions made on the citizens of his country: "What do I care about the opinion of the salons and the gossipers!"

Outside the mother country, the bitterness about Bonaparte's policies increased even more. The confiscation and burning by the French military of commodities that illegally got through the Continental Blockade, reaching German cities, acted like smoke signals for the oppressed peoples. But every attempt at resistance or sedition was snuffed out.

When a famine revolt occurred in Normandy in 1812, he ordered troops to march in and set a deterrent example by eight executions. The French people were subjected more and more to the will of a single dictator, an "autocrat who appealed to the will of the people but ruled arbitrarily like a monarch by God's grace. A throne-robber founded a dynasty and collected crowns." Equality and liberty had long since been trodden underfoot. In a self-glorifying intoxication with power, his instructions and resolutions now served only his own interests and the increase of his fame; and the more the people's dissatisfaction grew, the more the repressions were strengthened. All writings that could diminish the Emperor's reputation were confiscated or corrected by the censors, and books like those of Madame de Staël or Chateaubriand were put on the Index. Like Hitler, Napoleon, too, regarded intellectuals as ideologists who merely stood in the way of his policies and were deeply repugnant to him. In 1807 he abolished the parliamentary tribunal, which he considered to be "a chattering room for ideologues and a playground for oppositionists," thus reducing the state council to a merely formal rubber-stamping agency for his solitary decisions. "I am a Roman Emperor, one of the best kind of Caesars," he boasted.

From then on, the laws were merely edicts issued by Napoleon, who also saw to it that they were obeyed to the letter, and with the introduction of a probationary period for judges, he was also well on the way to appropriating the judiciary power, too. Again, similarly to the Third Reich, there were among the French ecclesiastical dignitaries some who, despite the abolition and annexation of the Papal States in 1809, believed they owed their Emperor "love, respect, obedience, and loyalty," since they were of the view that God had "made him their sovereign, an implement of his power, his likeness on earth." A formulation which Napoleon commented on with modest, self-satisfied words: "I absolve you from comparing me with God."

By the Emergency Law of 1808, he tried to proceed against the Jews, who had been emancipated by the Revolution, apparently because by this action he hoped to win supporters and to improve his declining popularity with the broad masses. But he became more and more unpopular with the masses, and his overbearing arrogance made him appear less respectable, indeed ridiculous, even among his circles of sympathizers. In his self-glorification and self-adulation, he gradually lost all sound self-critique, for instance, when he stated "that he had more knowledge in his little finger than his subjects in all their heads."

The Empress Marie-Louise (1791-1847), Napoleon's second wife (contemporary etching)

When the young, eighteen-year-old daughter of the Austrian Emperor, Marie-Louise, moved into the Tuileries on April 2, 1810, after the church wedding, Napoleon expected no particular demonstrations of sympathy from the French. After their experiences with Marie-Antoinette, they had even worse memories of the Habsburgers than of the Bourbons. The marriage to Marie-Louise had certainly not been made out of political considerations, but was based exclusively on his wish to assure a male successor for his dynasty, since his illegitimate son Alexander, whom the Polish Countess Walewska had borne him, did not qualify to fulfill this wish. On March 20, 1811, after a difficult forceps delivery, his throne-heir was born and given the title of King of Rome.

Meanwhile, the conflicts of interest between France and Russia were becoming threateningly more acute. Although Napoleon, in his "Proclamation to the Nation" on June 16, 1811, gave the consoling assurance that peace on the continent would not be jeopardized, at the

The Countess Maria Walewska (1789-1817), Napoleon's most faithful mistress (after a painting by R. Lefèvre)

same time the mobilization plans against Russia were already in progress, and on June 24, 1812, one year after this treacherous message, the war began. With 600,000 men—the largest army in history—and with the belief that he would receive strong support from his satellite states, he thought he could defeat Russia in a blitzkrieg within a few months and, by conquering Asia, become the ruler of the world. However, despite all warnings that the French would expose themselves to famine and cold in the endless spaces of Russia and would suffer drastic attrition, he crossed the boundary river, Memel, on June 24, with his victory-bound appeal to his army: "Russia is heading for its doom! Its fate is sealed."

The Emperor was seeking a battle; the Russians avoided it. So the swift advance of the French army literally struck into the void. With the call for a "holy war" against the French usurper, the Czar fanned the patriotic flame among his troops, and it was expressed symbolically in the Russian defense system of the "scorched earth." Soon the French army ran short of food. Their horses ate straw from the roofs and some fell over dead, so that for stretches of the way even the Emperor himself had to march on foot. Ahead of him the smoke of destroyed villages, behind him the smell of decay of countless corpses, dysentery as his constant companion, he lost over 100,000 men just in the first four weeks without even once having come into military contact with the enemy. On September 7, 1812, the Russian Army finally stood its ground for battle near Borodino and was beaten back by the French, but could not be destroyed. For the first time, Napoleon did not leave his position during that entire day. Suffering from a severe cold, with fever, coughing, difficulty in breathing, and swollen legs, he sat on his horse and did not allow his troops to pursue the fleeing enemy.

Yet the battle near Borodino opened the gateway to Moscow for the French. However, fire already flamed up in all parts of Moscow, abruptly shattering the exhausted soldiers' dreams of at last finding quarters for some much-needed sleep. Allegedly, the fires had been set on the order of the Russian military governor, but could it not also have been caused partly by plundering soldiers? Looking back, Napoleon described his situation at the time:

> If Moscow had not been set on fire, I would have entered winter quarters there and offered the world the rare spectacle of an army peacefully wintering in the middle of an enemy country.

The truth looked quite different, for his enterprise had already failed before Moscow began to burn. His mental and physical strength were no longer the same as Goethe had so admired in him near Erfurt, because of the exertions he had endured, with "little sleep, little food and at the same time always the highest mental strain." In addition, there were stomach cramps, painful bladder blockages when he tried to urinate and intestinal pains stemming from hemorrhoid problems. All this made it impossible for him to decide whether he should sound the retreat or continue with his "Alexander-like campaign to India," whereby he hoped to deprive England of its most important source of supply for its tremendous accumulation of wealth. On September 20th, he had offered the Czar a peace settlement and was still awaiting the Czar's answer, but increasingly the Czar was being pressed by Napoleon's opponents into the role of the liberator of Europe. In the forefront of all of them was Baron von Stein, who, expelled from Prussia, was now living in Russian exile and who urged the European powers "all to unite and pounce upon the filthy animal that is disturbing the peace of Europe."

Meanwhile, the Russian winter was drawing near, although less severe than usual and beginning relatively late. By long hesitation, nonetheless, the retreat ordered by Napoleon on October 19, 1812, soon became a hopeless flight. Hampered by sick and wounded men, the Grand Army dragged itself along; and, as much as it had sought battle in its eastward march, now it feared it during the retreat. Similarly as in the guerrilla war in Spain, Napoleon now saw himself beset by snipers and guerrillas of the Russian Army; on one occasion, only the Emperor's presence of mind prevented his own capture by a band of Cossacks. This incident caused him to have his doctor give him a poison, which he henceforth carried around his neck in a black silk bag, for use in case of capture. Under no circumstances would Czar Alexander be able to harness him before his triumphal chariot!

In the second half of November, the Russian cold set in and began to snatch away men by the thousands. Arriving at the Beresina, the engineers constructed two pontoon bridges amid the drifting ice-floes with feverish haste, and all the men at once tried to get across them from November 26 to 28.

After this icy inferno, Napoleon's Grand Army numbered only about twenty-five thousand men; the accounting he believed he had to make for himself after this ghastly spectacle was summed up in the following words:

> In such a state of things it is important that I regard my presence in Paris as necessary for France, for the Empire and even for the Army.

He said it, and on the night of December 5, 1812, just as in Egypt many years before, he left his frantically retreating troops after placing them under General Joachim Murat's command.

After these unspeakable losses—the war with Russia swallowed almost four hundred thousand men—Napoleon acted like an adventurer upon his arrival in Warsaw. He pretended to the Poles that he still had an army, although it had long since perished under gruesome conditions; he reported of battles that had never been fought, and he ascribed his retreat to the cold, though, in reality, the cold weather decimated only pitiful remnants of his defeated army. Expecting the Poles to transmit his reports to France, he boasted:

> The army is magnificent! I still have 120,000 men! I defeated the Russians everywhere. They did not dare to stand up and fight. We will take quarters in Vilna. I want to fetch 300,000 men from Paris. In six months I will be back at the Memel.

Even before his arrival in Paris, he heard of a failed *coup d'état,* and he was fully aware of how much damage his military reputation had suffered. Once back home again, he made every effort to present himself as undefeatable as ever. He put all the blame on the pitiless winter and did not hesitate to restore his damaged reputation as a brilliant commander by lies and slanders. He announced that his Army, which he had left in Russia, had perished only after it was under General Murat's command In spite of everything, with methods of calumny

Napoleon's retreat from Russia (aquarell by Johann Adam Klein)

and false pretenses that defied the facts, he managed to dupe the people so that they once more recognized him as their lord and master despite his disaster in Russia. By April 1813, by a general conscription of even the youngest boys, he again managed to have at his disposal an army of over half a million men, just as he had predicted to the Prussian ambassador: "The French people will follow me unconditionally, and if necessary I will arm even the women." Even the German princes, including the Habsburgs, obeyed and once again collected money and troops, "happy to give the Emperor the chance for new glory," as one of his vassals added.

DOWN TO TOTAL DEFEAT

Meanwhile the Allies were busily mobilizing, since a war was to come after all. Napoleon now had just about everybody against him: the ruling dynasties, who had never forgiven him for implementing most of the revolutionary ideas, as well as the nations to whom he had brought those ideas, which now revolted against his reactionary side. Napoleon saw clearly that the Allied forces were numerically superior to his own and that his advantage lay only in his superior mastery of military science. With his slogan: "I will wage this war as General

Bonaparte," he plunged into the first battle near Lützen, from which he emerged victorious, so that on May 10, 1813, he could march into Dresden. Completely surprised by Napoleon's lightning-swift operations, a few days later the Russians and Prussians were forced to retreat. But he was no longer the "man of granite," as Goethe had seen him, who could exploit all circumstances to bring about quick victories.

The change in Napoleon was noticed by his top field surgeon, Baron Dominique Larrey, during the Russian campaign. This excellent doctor, who assisted the wounded at the front lines with his famous "flying ambulance" organization and whom Napoleon had often observed amputating limbs on the battlefield, described the change of the Emperor as follows:

> The same man who cheerfully endured long marches through the desert in the glaring heat and who in Spain surprised even the Spaniards by his endurance, now complained about the cold, liked to remain sitting in his wagon, and lay undressed for hours on his couch.

Not only his entourage noticed the increasing contrast between the lean and formerly tremendously energetic General Bonaparte and this Emperor who had meanwhile become fat and clumsy. By Austerlitz (at the latest) he too had become aware of the limits of his strength, as he resignedly remarked: "One can wage war only for a certain time. I will be useful for it only six more years, then I will have to stop." In the battle near Borodino during the Russian campaign he had managed only through the most extreme effort of will to remain in the saddle all day long, despite fever, coughing, and painful bladder blockages. At that time he confided openly to Mestivier, a doctor living in Moscow who had been recommended to him by Professor Corvisart:

> I feel old, my legs are swollen, I cannot urinate. No doubt the dampness of the bivouac is to blame, for I am always soaked to the bone.

Particularly noticeable to him and his entourage was his changed sleeping behavior. In his youth, he had looked upon sleep as an unavoidable waste of time and considered three or four hours of sleep sufficient to maintain health; now, he was frequently overcome with sudden sleepiness. A remarkable episode illustrating this change occurred in August 1813 during the battle near Dresden, where his initial success was changed into a defeat by his sluggishness and indecision,

*Dominique Larrey amputating a
hand in the battle of Hanau*

just as the exhaustion of his energies and the frequent hesitation in giving commands probably had contributed to the unhappy outcome of the Russian campaign. Contemporaries' accounts of the battle of Dresden narrate that in the midst of headlong pursuit of the already defeated enemy, he suddenly stopped short and after a brief indecision turned back—a situation which he later tried to explain with the words: "I suddenly had terrible stomach pains, which were so violent that I could no longer continue."

This must not have been the sole reason for his strategic error, however, for we know that he spent the four weeks in Dresden mostly sleeping, so that dispatches and important news sometimes lay unanswered on his desk for several days.

Insufficiently informed about the actual difficulties of the enemy troops, he accepted a limited truce on June 4, 1813, which he later called the greatest blunder of his life. But since he ultimately did not accept the Allies' peace terms, the result was a concentric attack under the leadership of Radetzky, head of the Austrian General Staff, and Gneisenau, head of the Prussian General Staff, who sought to annihilate him in a kind of modern encirclement strategy (*Kesselschlacht*). With Napoleon surrounded by four armies, the historic "Battle of the Nations near Leipzig" began on October 16, 1813, and ended in his defeat. In retrospect, he commented on that situation as follows:

> In the Saxony campaign I clearly saw the hour of de-
> cision coming. My star was waning. I could feel the
> reins slipping away from my hands and there was noth-
> ing I could do.

Similar to what had happened previously at the Battle of Dresden, he was now overcome by sleep in his tent, right in the middle of the turmoil of battle. He reportedly was awakened only by the ear-deafening blast of an explosion set off when, by mistake, an officer ordered a bridge to be blown too early, before the remaining half of the French army could cross. The superior Allied force won, but it could not annihilate Napoleon and his army, which still numbered 120,000 men. Exhilarated by victory, the Allies failed to pursue the defeated enemy, who was able to regroup forces for an orderly, swift retreat. So Napoleon was able to reach the Rhine on November 2nd. Then a typhus epidemic broke out and decimated his troops once again, so that he arrived in Paris on November 10, 1813, as a defeated general with a remnant of ninety thousand men.

In his blindness and lost sense of reality, he refused the generous peace offer from the Allies, although it assured him "recognition of the Bonapartist dynasty and the natural borders of France." The victors' manifesto, December 4, was certainly decisive for Napoleon's other-wise incomprehensible decision, as well as being offensive to his pride and his sense of honor. The manifesto stated to the French people that the Allies were waging war, not against France, but exclusively against that "hegemony, which the Emperor Napoleon had exercised all too long outside the borders of his own realm, to the detriment of Europe and of France." Haughtily, he declared to the French popular repre-sentatives that "France needed him more than he needed France," and he was firmly decided once again to draw from France its last reserves; for, as he said in a conversation with Metternich, a soldier like himself did not give a damn for the lives of a million men.

After the Allies were definitively convinced of Napoleon's intran-sigence and had received news of his remobilization, they decided, in December 1813, to force France militarily to make peace. But Napo-leon was not so easy to defeat in his own country. Both Schwarzenberg's army and Blücher's were defeated separately, and once again the tarnished halo of the undefeated commander shone more brightly. New peace negotiations began, but such demands were made that Napoleon

Napoleon in the year 1813. The Emperor's corpulence is already unmistakable (lithography by Wilhelm Devrient)

could not accept them; as he later stated, "merely to say them made him feel robbed of his honor." The war continued, and by March 30, 1814, Paris was in the hands of the Allies.

After the Senate assigned Talleyrand, at his own insistence, to form a provisional government, the first action of the Senate was the deposal of the Emperor of the French, so proclaimed on April 2, 1814. The news was received with approval by the citizenry, for Napoleon had always trodden the rights of the people underfoot and had unhesitatingly sacrificed hecatombs of young men for his ambitious plans to expand his personal power and satisfy his insatiable greed for glory. He at first still did not want to concede, and he attached several conditions to his declaration of abdication, but they were not accepted. Only on April 8 did he finally give up, and in a state of deep depression he made a suicide attempt, followed by a second one a few days later. Some people, however, did not believe in the genuineness of his intention to take his own life; they suspected that possibly he had ingested excessively high doses of opiates to alleviate his violent lower abdominal pains.

According to the available documents, the following must have happened: on April 12, 1814, when Marshal Alexander MacDonald, together with the Russian Count Orloff, arrived at Fontainebleau in order to have Napoleon sign the certificate of abdication, Napoleon hesitated for a long time to put his signature upon such a humiliating document; apparently he actually preferred to depart from this life. The temptation to take his own life was too obvious, since even during the war in Spain, worried that he could fall prisoner to the Spaniards, who were fanatical and known to be cruel, he had asked his personal surgeon Alexandre Yvan with the help of his court apothecary, Alexis Boyer, to prepare a poison he then always carried in a bag attached to his belt and later in a little case in his vest pocket. Presumably this poison was a mixture of *datura strammonium*, thorn-apple, deadly nightshade *(atropa belladonna)*, and opium. In the night of April 12, 1814, his servant Constant, who was standing guard in the lobby to the Emperor's bedroom, saw Napoleon take something out of a small bag, pour it into a glass of water, and drink the entire contents of the glass. When shortly thereafter he heard a painful groaning, Constant immediately notified Dr. Yvan and the Grand Marshal Duke Caulaincourt, with whom Napoleon had an especially close relationship. The

Emperor is said to have given the duke a letter for the Empress Marie-Louise with the words, "I wish that you may be happy—in a short time I will no longer be among the living."

At first it seemed as if the poison would take its full effect. The Emperor groaned and sighed constantly, his limbs became stiff and his body kept convulsing. Suddenly Napoleon began to vomit, which weakened the effect of the poison considerably, and he gradually recovered remarkably. Dr. Yvan prescribed that he should drink hot beverages, and toward morning Napoleon's condition was such that Marshal MacDonald finally could come and get the signed ratification documents around ten o'clock, to take them to Paris as instructed.

Following the final declaration of abdication, whereby Napoleon agreed "that he himself and his progeny renounced the throne of France and Italy," he was installed as sovereign of the Island of Elba, which permitted him to keep the title of Emperor, as well as a government pension of 2,000,000 francs. On April 20, he said farewell to his faithful guard regiment with a small speech. But on the journey to Fréjus, where an English three-masted ship was waiting to transport him to the island, the people pelted him with stones and shouts of scorn, such as "Down with the tyrant!" When he caught sight of a straw doll resembling himself hanging from a gallows, he finally decided to slip into a disguise as a safety precaution, in order to reach the harbor safely.

Napoleon's personal surgeon
Alexis Boyer (1757-1833)
(after a painting by I. Boilly)

Napoleon's second surgeon Alexandre Urbain Yvan
(1765-1839) (after an aquarell by Bucquoi)

"My health is excellent," he informed his spouse Marie-Louise, who meanwhile had completely written him off, unlike the Polish Countess Walewska, who visited him on Elba with his illegitimate son. While Napoleon began to establish a small model state on the tiny island kingdom, the princes at the Vienna Congress were attempting to readjust the revolutionary changes made by the "man of the century," as Klemens Metternich apostrophized the former Emperor of the French, in the sense of the eighteenth-century Monarchist ideas.

They restored King Louis XVIII, "very fat and so-to-speak deprived of the use of his legs," according to a German report of that time; and the old inequality and class privileges were quietly restored, although they had been the reason for sending the king's brother to the guillotine. The dissatisfaction of the French people increased day by day and an opposition began to form.

The man on Elba read and heard all this with mounting hope; already, a bold plan to return to France by a secret operation was beginning to form in his mind. "I am counting on surprise," he told someone confidentially. "The bewilderment of the mind is great under the impact of a bold deed. I am the cause of France's misfortune. I must heal it." The last impulse to his adventurous deed—whereby he wanted not only to save the French nation, but also to win back his royal throne because of the expected flight of the cowardly Bourbon king—was the news that they wanted to kidnap him and banish him to an island far away in the ocean.

So on February 26, 1815, he left the island of Elba with scarcely a thousand men and was carried on his supporters' shoulders to the Tuileries which had quickly been abandoned by Louis XVIII. But the stormy enthusiasm that had accompanied him on the way to Paris quickly began to cool after a pompous ceremony on June 1, when he announced the beginning of a constitutional monarchy. Little credence was given by the French citizens to his message, and Napoleon's later explanation proved how right they had been; for in retrospect he later candidly admitted that the concession of a constitutional monarchy, necessary after his return from Elba, would have been abrogated the moment his throne had been appropriately secured. The people sensed that the Emperor once again had in mind not peace but a new war.

Napoleon returns from Elba (based on a painting by Steubner)

Since the allied powers in Vienna were not willing even to enter negotiations with the "throne-robber" and expressed their determination to make Napoleon innocuous once and for all by military means, Napoleon hastily conscripted about three hundred thousand men, an emergency measure which lost him further sympathy among the people, who were not ready to make further sacrifices for him. Napoleon was completely aware of this change of attitude. One of his intimate circle wrote: "He was worried, the self-confidence of his discourse, the tone of authority had disappeared." His secretary Baron de Méneval reported upon returning from Vienna:

> The Emperor's speech was overcast with a quiet sadness and so resigned that it moved me deeply. I found him no longer certain of victory, and it seemed as if his belief in his good fortune, which had buoyed him up on the march to Paris, had now left him.

No doubt, the news that Marie-Louise despised the Emperor and that she was having a love affair with Count Neipperg played a role in this report.

In this depressed mood and without feeling supported by his French countrymen, Napoleon had to go into battle against a superior force of the combined military forces of Europe. He later described what he had felt as follows:

> My assurance was gone. Had the magic of my career turned pale in my own eyes, in my own imagination? In any case I had a feeling something was missing. There seemed to be nothing left of my good fortune that had previously always accompanied my enterprises and overshowered me with its best gifts. What loomed ahead was only a relentless destiny, from which I could violently tear one favor or another—but it would immediately avenge itself. For strangely I could no longer achieve an advantage without it being immediately followed by a disadvantage.

Nonetheless, he at first succeeded in separating the enemy armies by a powerful forward thrust. But when on June 16, 1815, he withstood Blücher and even forced him to retreat despite Gneisenau's help, though without having defeated him completely, it turned out that his ability to make rapid decisions was no longer present. Instead of

Napoleon fleeing after the battle of Waterloo (painting by Guido Sigriste)

pursuing him, he hesitated and remained standing for a whole day without finishing the half-fought victory, assuming that he could on the next day defeat the English under Wellington just as he had defeated the others on the previous day. Allegedly he was suffering strong pains in the lower abdomen, which badly impeded his concentration, and actually at this critical juncture he is said to have sunken into an exhausted sleep. Even on June 18, the morning of the historical battle near Waterloo, he hesitated to charge against Wellington's army until noon; this wasted half-day was to destroy him. Meanwhile the Prussians had time to regroup and come to Wellington's assistance, so that Napoleon and his forces ended up having to fight on two fronts and were crushingly defeated.

Closer details became known only later when his servant Constant's memoirs were published, and they could explain the reason why Napoleon, despite his excellently elaborated battle plan, lost those six valuable hours by his delayed signal to attack, which enabled Wellington to receive the much needed support from the Prussian troops under General Blücher just in time. For on that memorable day Napoleon was suffering almost unbearable pains caused by an acute inflammation of his greatly prolapsed hemorrhoidal veins. In the preceding days, that was

why he could not get into the saddle; riding in a wagon gave him hell-
ish pains as it jolted along over uneven terrain. Even on foot he could
move only toilsomely with widely outspread legs! So it came that in
the late morning hours of June 18 after the command was finally given
to attack, his soldiers passed by Napoleon's headquarters with the cry
"Vive l'Empereur," while he himself sat astraddle on a chair with his
legs outstretched, his head supported on his hands which gripped the
back of the chair; contrary to his usual habits, he could not direct the
battle from his horse.

Napoleon understandably did not like to talk about his hemorrhoidal
ailment because that was often a topic of mockery at the time. We
know, however, that during the Italian campaign he already suffered
considerably from hemorrhoids; leeches were applied—a method which
he later once recommended to his brother Jerome, who labored under
this same ailment, just as did other members of the Bonaparte family.

In his last hour as commander, he endured the sight of his fleeing
army and indeed he too was compelled to leave the battlefield in headlong flight, covered only by his mounted grenadiers. In spite of his
severe pains in the lower abdomen, he had to continue on horseback
until five o'clock in the morning, when he finally found an old wagon
in which to rest for a few hours.

On June 22, the day after his arrival in Paris, parliament
gave him the ultimatum to abdicate, as he then thought, in favor of
his four-year-old son:

> I sacrifice myself to the hatred of France's enemies....
> My political life is over, and I proclaim my son Em-
> peror of the French under the title Napoleon II.

Meanwhile, the Allies had already decided to again raise the Bourbon,
Louis XVIII, as King on France's throne. When Fouché made it clear
to his former Emperor that France had no use for him, neither in the
army nor anywhere else, he went to Rochefort, hoping to get to America
and there start a new life. However, his departure was blocked by
British ships, and on land he had been declared a wanted man by the
Allies; he saw only one way out: to ask the British for asylum. On the
English ship "Bellerophon" he sailed to England, where, in the harbor
of Torquay, the populace gaped and stared at him as though he were a
wonder of the world.

While his vanity was flattered no little by the considerable attention his appearance provoked, the decision of the English government,
in agreement with the Allies, was communicated to him: in order to be

*Napoleon says good-bye to France forever (painting by
Eugène A. Guillon)*

certain in the future that peace in Europe would never again be endangered by him, he was to be banished to the remote island of
St. Helena in the South Atlantic for the rest of his life. Despite all his
protests, on August 7, 1815, one week after the announcement of this
sentence, he was taken to the English ship-of-the-line "Northumberland," which was to put him ashore at Jamestown harbor, together with
a retinue of barely twenty persons, on October 15.

In Dr. Paul Ganière's extensive biography, *Napoléon à Sainte-
Hélène*, one learns that Professor Corvisart was asked before Napoleon's
departure to choose a doctor to accompany the Emperor. He first chose
Dr. Pierre Maingault, a former pupil of Corvisart who gave his consent
only under the assumption that Napoleon would go into exile in America,
where he himself intended to emigrate with his family. When Maingault
learned about St. Helena, he immediately withdrew his offer and was

replaced by the former ship's doctor of the "Bellerophon," the Irish physician, Barry O'Meara. This doctor was entrusted with Napoleon's medical care and, like the generals who accompanied him, he tried to maintain a kind of court ceremonial at the residence of the deposed Emperor. As permanent quarters, an old farmhouse by the name of "Longwood House," located on a desolate and inhospitable plateau, was furnished rather haphazardly, and Napoleon was obliged to move there on December 10, 1815. Cold winds alternated abruptly with oppressive heat, and throughout the whole year, damp fog settled over the island. In the bedroom, a dark narrow corner, the wallpaper showed large saltpeter stains; the dining room was sparingly lit by a glass door.

Napoleon suffered most from the restriction of his freedom of movement and from the constant strict supervision by the English governor of the island, Sir Hudson Lowe. This minor official regarded his assignment to guard the prisoner of war, who was for him only General Napoleon and not Emperor, as the most important task of his life; he seemed to derive pleasure from his quarrelsome humiliations. However, the statement of some biographers that the English wanted to undermine Napoleon's health by the unhealthy climate on the rough high plateau of the island is certainly false. The English government was, on the contrary, very intent on making sure that no blame at all could be ascribed to it, in case of the prisoner's early death. An official report of Governor Lowe to the Foreign Office in London speaks in this sense:

> I will arrange it so that he can go riding out again; otherwise, he could die of a stroke and that would be an embarrassment to us. I consider it better for him to disappear from a long-lasting sickness, so that our doctors could determine a natural cause of death.

Affecting Napoleon more than the climate of the island were the many little annoyances ordered by the Governor, which he felt to be humiliations. The inability to endure humiliations was one of his main characteristics, as he himself admitted: "I am a man whom one kills but does not insult." Probably his exaggerated sense of honor was a factor that provided a certain counterbalance to his fundamentally deeply amoral basic feeling.

What no one could guess upon Napoleon's arrival at St. Helena was that the banished man was by no means the healthy, energetic person he liked to portray. He had always claimed to be fit and healthy

German popular portrayal of Napoleon's arrival on the rugged island of St. Helena.

and boasted of his life-long overflowing health, portraying an image that served merely for the personal glorification of a man who was convinced that he was bound for historic immortality.

In his vocabulary the word "impossible" did not exist. His unbending will lifted his existence to a heroic level and he actually believed that he could overcome even death by his will. Once when he was flung out of his carriage in St. Cloud, a boundary stone on which he fell almost smashed his abdomen. Later he told the story:

> I felt as if my life was leaving me. I had just enough
> time to tell myself I did not want to die—and I lived.
> Anyone else would have died in my situation.

This portrayal given during his exile period is an example of how even as a man condemned to a slow death on St. Helena, he still tried to transform incidents from his life so that his constitution would seem heroically strong—as was proper for a historical personality from the ranks of world-historical heroes.

William Warden, the ship's doctor of the "Northumberland," who cared for him during the ocean passage, was promptly convinced of the truth of his descriptions, for he later wrote:

He had good reason to be proud of his health. And if one takes into account the various climates he had been exposed to and the work he had done in the last twenty-five years, then the excellent health he had enjoyed and still enjoyed is astonishing. He claimed to have needed to consult a doctor only twice in his whole life. The first time he had to take a laxative for his sickness, and the second time during an inflammation of the lungs they applied a blistering plaster.

SUFFERINGS ON ST. HELENA

Napoleon's state of health on St. Helena is documented by detailed reports of his doctors and several extensive descriptions by persons from his entourage, so that we have a graphic picture of the events that occurred there until Napoleon's death. A critical evaluation of the various statements, however, leads us to the conviction that they are not always historically accurate or that they were amended later. The reports of the Emperor's two valets, Louis Marchand and Louis-Etiénne St. Denis, also contradict the very carefully composed memoirs of General Count Charles-Tristan de Montholon (1783-1853), written many years later. The notes of General Count Henri-Gratien Bertrand (1773-1844), deciphered by Fleuriot de Langle, are distinguished by the greatest objectivity. However, the most informative source proves to be the collected reports to Governor Lowe, which were preserved in the British Museum, and his commentaries, as well as the private letters of the prisoners and of the officer corps intercepted by the Governor. These original documents were first evaluated critically by Octave Aubry and summarized in the monograph *Sainte Hélène*, till now the most careful study of a historian on the physical and mental state of Napoleon during his exile. From a medical viewpoint J. Groen's study, *La dernière maladie et la cause de mort de Napoléon (Napoleon's Last Illness and Cause of Death)*, published a short time later, has a similar great significance, although the diagnostic conclusions are not free of a certain bias.

On arriving at St. Helena, Napoleon apparently was feeling very well. He used to go out riding regularly, and he began writing his memoirs. The only ailment worth mentioning is a frequently recurring bronchitis, which must have been caused by the moist, foggy and windy

*Sir Hudson Lowe, governor on
St. Helena from 1816 to 1821*

climate with its abrupt temperature changes. On October 1, 1816, he complained about a toothache, and two weeks later Dr. O'Meara, who was taking care of him, discovered pale, swollen gums that bled on the slightest touch; in view of the lack of vegetables and fresh fruit, this symptom was associated with a mild form of scurvy, a sickness caused by a vitamin C deficiency. Apart from that, no signs of skin-bleeding could be discovered, as would be part of the clinical picture of a case of scurvy, but the further course of the illness also spoke against this diagnosis. For on October 23, a distinct swelling of the left cheek appeared and a few days later numerous painful blisters sprouted on the gum and the side of the cheeks, accompanied by increasingly painful and difficult acts of swallowing. Dr. O'Meara's description matches the classical clinical picture of a *stomatitis aphthosa*, which is favored by the presence of carious teeth, vitamin-poor nutrition, and generally speaking, reduced resistance of the body.

In the summer of 1816, Dr. O'Meara was more worried by his patient's feverish state, accompanied by colic, since, on the small island, barely twelve square kilometers, many cases of dysentery—probably caused by amebas—were observed that year. Indeed, it befell the majority of the population living there, including Napoleon's entourage, one of whom died of it. The assumption was therefore probable that the Emperor, too, was stricken with it. From that time on, his vitality clearly began to diminish; he became apathetic, had a tired, almost sleepy facial expression, and noticeably began to lose weight.

On May 26, 1817, in the context of a new feverish bronchial catarrh, he again had a swelling of the gums and cheek, this time on the right side. Dr. O'Meara recommended urgently that the lethargic state of the patient be alleviated by a good deal of movement in the open air and that his diet be revised to contain more vitamins. But the worsening of his general condition could not be prevented even by that. On September 26, 1817, he began to complain about a heavy feeling in his distinctly swollen legs, so that by pressing a finger above the ankle a clear depression remained—a finding already determined in a milder form in November of the previous year. To want to explain these swellings of the legs as the effects of regular habitual hot baths or by a protein deficiency, in the sense of starvation edemas (as could be observed in the prison camps during and after World War II), therefore seems untenable, because the swelling was already registered by his doctors in 1812, during the Russian campaign. These leg edemas were certainly statically conditioned, that is, by the slowed backflow in the veins because of varicose widening of the veins or, respectively, insufficient functioning of the valves in the veins. In such cases, with the position of the legs in dangling position for hours, as can so often be observed today after long-distance flights, a considerable swelling of

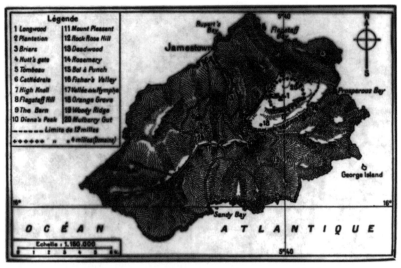

Saint Helena (from Octave Aubry, Sainte Hélène, Paris 1935)

*Napoleon in the circle of his loyal followers on St. Helena (Lithograph by
N. Maurin)*

the legs results; and it is actually recorded that Napoleon at that time
was spending the greater part of the day in a seated position.

October 1, 1817, marks an important caesura in Napoleon's medical biography. On the morning of that day, Dr. O'Meara reported of a
dull pain below the right costal arch [of the ribs]; this pain radiated
toward the right shoulder and was intensified considerably by coughing. Soon fever, combined with lack of appetite, set in. To alleviate
the pain somewhat, Napoleon pressed his hand instinctively against
the costal arch. A few days later, Dr. O'Meara, on palpating below the
right costal arch, discovered a clear swelling painful to the touch; he
diagnosed the beginning of hepatitis, that is, an inflammation of the
liver, and he was inclined to associate this causally most probably with
an amebic infection. Such an amebic hepatitis, which is still often
found today on that island, is not necessarily accompanied by dysentery, so it can easily be overlooked or misinterpreted. However, since
Dr. O'Meara knew that Governor Hudson Lowe would vehemently
deny any sickening of the prisoner that could be connected causally
with the geographic or local conditions of the imprisonment, he wrote
cautiously in his official report only:

> As a consequence of the patient's tendency to corpu-
> lence I could not determine whether this swelling is
> located in the liver or above it.

Since that day the dull feeling of pressure in the right upper abdomen remained continuous. During the night the pains became more intense, while they diminished somewhat at daybreak. A prescription of rub-downs and sea-water baths, as well as the so much-loved mercury-containing calomel brought no improvement. Not meant for the Governor, but only confided to his own notebook, Dr. O'Meara spoke of periods of stubborn constipation, which alternated with flu, diarrhea, in which "copious, gall-colored and slimy quantities of excrement were emptied." Count Montholon noted in his diary under November 27, 1817:

> The patient's skin and sclera of the eyes are colored yellow. The Emperor complains about severe bloating of the stomach. His appetite has disappeared. He feels a constant pressure in the pit of the stomach; it is impossible for him to lie on his left side; and he has a burning sensation in the area of the right upper abdomen. He suffers from an upset stomach and nausea and occasionally vomits slime and bitter gall.

Napoleon felt progressively weaker, complained of headaches and insomnia, and showed a heavily coated tongue. During the fever, which began regularly at night, he constantly suffered from thirst. His skin was dry and warm and the pulse rate, which formerly stood mostly at below 55 per minute, now was almost double that. As dawn approached he often had strong fits of sweating, followed by a phase of recovery.

On the basis of this image—quite clear to the modern clinician—with its spells of fever and profuse sweating in the night, permanent burning or dull pains radiating up to the right shoulder, pains in the right upper abdomen aggravated by coughing, palpable resistance in the right upper abdomen sensitive to the touch, yellow sclera of the eyes and periods of slimy, partly gall-discolored, flu-like bowel movements, accompanied by nausea and vomiting, Dr. O'Meara became convinced that the patient had an inflammation of the liver in the aftermath of a previous intestinal infection. He spoke of a "*hepatitis tropica*," which today would correspond to an amebic hepatitis, although this diagnosis of Dr. O'Meara's could not be an exact naming of the sickness; prior to the microscopic discovery of the ameba by the Prague pathologist Lambl—which did not occur till 1859—amebiasis understandably was lumped together with other kinds of infectious dysentery,

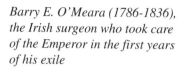
*Barry E. O'Meara (1786-1836),
the Irish surgeon who took care
of the Emperor in the first years
of his exile*

although a few doctors in the colonies even then excelled in making precise observations of the peculiarities of certain tropical forms of dysentery.

Napoleon's illness lasted for two full years, during which phases of improvement alternated with phases of exacerbation. Under normal circumstances, such a patient would naturally have had to be taken immediately to a region with more favorable climatic conditions. But the Governor, as well as the English government, was convinced that Napoleon's allegedly severe illness was just a pretext to enable him to escape from the island. When Hudson Lowe, on intercepting some letters of Dr. O'Meara to his friend Finlaison (who was supposed to forward them to the English admiralty with the intention of informing them about Napoleon's true state), discovered that they also contained remarks about the Governor's strange behavior, Dr. O'Meara's days on the island of St. Helena were numbered. Contrary to the ban on his visiting Napoleon again, Dr. O'Meara nonetheless said farewell to his patient in person and departed from the inhospitable island on August 2, 1818. (Incidentally, Napoleon left him a sizable sum of money in his will.) Since, as a punishment, he was discharged from service immediately upon his arrival in England, he resolved to act as Napoleon's advocate in England from then on. He published a series of brochures sharply attacking Hudson Lowe and called to the English government's attention Napoleon's serious state of health. His sincere efforts were, however, in vain; the congress of the Allies in Aix-la-Chapelle in 1818 took no notice of these reports and refused to make the slightest change in the conditions of his arrest.

Meanwhile, Napoleon's fate ran its course. He fell unconscious on January 6, 1819. Then, on the night of January 17, the most severe pains occurred beneath the right costal arch; this time, however, they were so severe that he hardly dared to breathe. About one hour after the attack of pain, he was overcome by a severe dizziness and finally fell completely unconscious again. Since the patient had been without medical assistance since Dr. O'Meara's departure, an urgent call was made for a doctor. Hudson Lowe's choice fell on a certain Dr. Verling, whom Napoleon, however, strictly rejected. Finally, in reply to General Bertrand's urgent note, the naval doctor Stokoe (incidentally, a friend of Dr. O'Meara's) was sent to the seriously ill man.

The result of the examination, which was published by Paul Frémeaux only later, confirmed Dr. O'Meara's suspicion. Based on the pale-yellow discoloration of the skin, the care-worn and sunken facial features, and the extremely pressure-sensitive region in the right upper abdomen, Dr. Stokoe, too, diagnosed a chronic inflammation of the liver; in his official report, in view of the patient's worrisome state, he demanded that a doctor who could be reached at all times be provided at Longwood. In Dr. Stokoe's report, not only were high fever and strong acceleration of the pulse noted, but attention was also called to the presence of a pressure-sensitive swelling beneath the right ribcage. This can be gathered from the conversation between Napoleon and his doctor about the further course of the sickness and its prognosis of a cure, as quoted by Frémeaux. Dr. Stokoe answered Napoleon's question unambiguously with the words:

> If the tumor that has developed empties into the intestine, that could mean healing. But if the purulent masses pour out into the abdominal cavity, then a fatal outcome is certain.

Worried that Napoleon's headaches could be a sign of an imminent stroke, he undertook a bloodletting, which caused the fever to decline and the breathing to come more easily but did not reduce the pains.

Meanwhile, the aggressive medical solicitude which Dr. Stokoe had for his patient seemed inappropriate to the Governor; when the doctor suggested to him the presence of an abscess that was about to rupture and alluded, moreover, to the climate of this inhospitable island as unfavorable for the further course of the sickness, Dr. Stokoe had to leave St. Helena as early as January 30, 1819, on orders from the Governor. Then Hudson Lowe saw to it that this conscientious doctor, on top of everything else, had to face a court martial. On the grounds that he had discussed nonmedical problems with Napoleon and had written tendentious reports about the prisoner's state of health and, moreover, had addressed him not with the title "General Bonaparte" but by the appellation "patient," he was thrown out of the British Navy after twenty-five years of faithful service; his pension was reduced to only one hundred pounds per year.

Meanwhile, Napoleon had survived the severe crisis without medical assistance, although now a deep depression settled on his spirits. Completely discouraged and apathetic, he closed himself in his rooms at Longwood, spent hours in bed, shaved only seldomly, neglected his exterior appearance, and could not summon the energy to continue writing his memoirs. How coldheartedly, indeed almost maliciously, the Governor took note of this change, is shown by his answer to Count Bertrand's urgent pleas to permit medical help for the Emperor. As can be read in the "Lowe Papers" of August 18, 1819, Hudson Lowe answered sarcastically: "There is no one on this island who is known by the name of Emperor."

Finally, the Bonaparte family in Europe got permission to send a clergyman, a doctor, and a kitchen worker to St. Helena. Instead of Dr. Foureau de Beauregard, who had already treated Napoleon on the island of Elba and who was a great admirer of the Emperor, Napoleon's uncle, Cardinal Joseph Fesch, had preferred Francesco Antommarchi merely because of his Corsican ancestry, despite the fact that Beauregard would have brought along far more medical experience. Dr. Antommarchi was an excellent pathological anatomist, who was employed as senior anatomist at the Medical Faculty in Pisa, but he had nearly no experience as a clinical doctor. Moreover, he must have had very dubious moral qualities, as was shown by his preference to stay in the capital Jamestown, so that he was seldom reachable when urgently needed. No wonder then that, according to Bertrand, Napoleon's opinion of this doctor was not very high, and probably for that reason he did not leave him a cent in his will.

When Dr. Antommarchi examined the patient on September 23, 1819, three days after his arrival on the island, he noted an apathetic, dull look, as well as a swollen body and edematous legs. Like his predecessors, he also found a distinct hardening and pressure sensitivity in the region of the right upper abdomen. Otherwise, in the first period he had little to do medically. Despite the ongoing dull pains in the right upper abdomen, Napoleon's mental state gradually improved to the point that in the first half of 1820 he began to interest himself again in various things. Above all, the arrangement of his little garden gave him visible joy—this is referred to as his "garden period." He began to lay out garden beds and fountains. He also would ride out on horseback or in a carriage, and on October 4, 1820, he even arranged a pleasant picnic in the shade of trees, so that hope arose of a final and permanent cure. But the people around him noticed a strange change of his entire behavior; for instance, he picked up a musket and shot wildly at anything that moved—chickens, rabbits, goats, and cattle. Another time he ordered a newly arrived officer of his staff guards to take a bath together with him in his bathtub, in order to make the man appear ridiculous. His closest intimates were especially embarrassed by peculiar erotic reminiscences, in which Napoleon confided to his circle the most delicate intimacies with Josephine and Marie-Louise.

But soon this renewed vitality had run its course. He again went out rarely, seldom took a carriage ride, and lost all pleasure in his garden. The second period of illness at St. Helena began in October 1820 and can be clinically delimited from the first one (which had lasted from October 1817 to November 1819). Toward the end of October, violent pains in the upper abdomen began, and this time they could be clearly localized in the region of the stomach. He now could tolerate only light foods, served warm, consisting preferably of noodle dishes, meat in aspic, a West Indian arrowroot sauce, and bread and milk, as his valet reported. On his own initiative, Napoleon now took frequent small meals throughout the day, indeed, even during the night, because usually the pains were especially intense at night, and a perceptible alleviation could be attained by eating food as well as by laying warm compresses on the abdomen.

As Montholon reports, an alarming pallor developed, in which the mucous membranes of the mouth, the lips, and the fingernails had lost almost all color. At the same time his hands and his legs felt ice-cold; his legs were practically without feeling up to the upper thigh, although the attendants repeatedly tried—in vain—to warm them by wrapping them in warm cloths. The least physical effort exhausted him immediately, so that General Count Montholon worriedly noted on December 5, 1820:

Francesco Antommarchi (1780-1838), Napoleon's doctor on St. Helena since 1819

The Emperor's illness has taken a turn for the worse. He has become so weak that he cannot do anything that is part of life without feeling extreme exhaustion.

Even one of the English officers guarding him wrote in his report dated January 26, 1821:

General Bonaparte's face is as white as a sheet of paper. He is very weak and his stride looks uncertain. His posture is bent, but he is still corpulent.

The very satisfactory state of nourishment, to which Hudson Lowe had referred in writing on the occasion of meeting Napoleon in a carriage on November 8, 1820, stood in crass contrast to his severely run-down state of health and was noted repeatedly with surprise in the next months. Even on March 6, 1821, two months before his death, Napoleon was described by an English officer as a tired, bitter, morally destroyed man with a pale, sunken face and deep-set eyes; but, at the same time, reference was made to his corpulence and the huge size of his stomach.

The pains in the upper abdomen now occurred periodically, at ever shorter intervals, and were at times so intense that when the pains began during a carriage ride the horses had to go at a slow pace, since in this condition, he could not bear the swaying and bumping of the carriage. Dr. Antommarchi, who like his predecessors also believed that a

Forgotten by the whole world: the Emperor in exile

chronic inflammation of the liver was the cause of these spells of pain, advised cupping-glasses on the upper arm, but he applied them so unskillfully that the skin was burned; Napoleon preferred his valet, rather than the doctor, for the medical application of this unnecessarily imposed complication.

THE DEATH OF THE EMPEROR

Since the beginning of 1821, Montholon noted with surprise that Napoleon's memory had manifestly declined and that he repeatedly contradicted himself, apparently a consequence of his extreme anemia and the resulting inadequate supply of oxygen to the brain. The same cause probably accounts for his increasing tendency to fall unconscious. On March 17, 1821, while trying to take a short stroll in the garden, he suffered an especially dramatic fainting spell. After he was quickly taken into the house, he began to experience violent stomach pains and vomiting of a "coffee-dregs-like" substance, followed by bowel movements of pitch-black color. The medical examination of the patient, who was shivering with cold and covered with sweat, showed an extremely bloated and distended abdomen. From that point on, even fluid nourishment was tolerated poorly, since it was vomited again after the shortest time; the vomit was occasionally reported to be colored with blood.

On the evening of March 19, Montholon wrote to his wife that in his opinion the Emperor would die soon. Every evening the fever rose and was followed toward morning by a profuse outbreak of sweat. Dr. Antommarchi, who could not even be found during the severe blood circulation collapse on October 17 and who returned from Jamestown only many hours later, was strictly forbidden to leave Longwood. When on March 21 massive vomiting again occurred, after examining the vomit he wrote *"febris gastrica remittens,"* that is, repeated spells of stomach fever, a nonspecific, nebulous diagnosis. Incomprehensibly he prescribed for the patient, who was no longer able to retain food anyway, the administration of *"tartarus emeticus,"* that is, an emetic. The results were terrible. The whole following night, Napoleon rolled about in his bed with pain, until on the next day some alleviation finally occurred. Unbearable thirst, accompanied by a debilitating continuous *singultus* (hiccups) increasingly tormented the patient, who was already very weakened by the fever spells and the outbreaks of sweat.

Count Charles-Tristan de Montholon (1783-1853)

Worried that even greater damage could be done through Dr. Antommarchi's incompetence, Count Montholon asked the Governor for a medical consultation, to which the regimental surgeon Archibald Arnott finally was sent. On his first visit on April 1, 1821, he did nothing more than take the patient's pulse and touch his skin. After a second examination on the following day, he reported to the Governor that General Bonaparte's weakness could be explained by a fever that was present. In order not to incur the Governor's displeasure, he tried rather to trivialize the patient's condition. In reality, Dr. Arnott must, however, have been fully aware of the seriousness of the situation, for in his diary one finds the following entry for April 2, 1821:

> He complained of nagging pains with constant nausea and vomiting. Seldom did an emptying of the bowels take place without the help of an enema. We recommended to our patient that he should immediately take some medicine for this purpose. We also prescribed gelatins and other light food, which his stomach would best be able to bear. At first he refused all medicine, but finally we got his conditional consent for him to take some laxative....When we visited him again in the evening, we found that he had not taken the medicine prescribed that morning, nor could we get him to do so, and, since he had not had any bowel movement for forty-eight hours, we prescribed an enema.

Dr. Arnott's reports to the Governor, incidentally, do not always agree with his views expressed later, which he published in book form only after knowledge of the autopsy findings, enabling him to correct some of his earlier errors. Thus, one can read in his book that, after a thorough examination, he came to the conclusion that the stomach showed no signs of an inflammation and that the pylorus also was all right, but especially that the liver showed no pathological finding. The pain was, in his opinion, caused only by constipation, that is, a blockage of stool, as well as by severe distentions. The only anomaly mentioned by Dr. Arnott was the patient's extreme pallor.

Meanwhile, Dr. Antommarchi realized ever more clearly that Napoleon had a serious, indeed life-threatening, condition; therefore his reports were written with increasingly greater alarm. Dr. Arnott always saw the patient only in the morning, when the worst symptoms were over: the violent pains, the upset stomach and nausea during the night, and the fever followed by spells of sweating. So he considered Dr. Antommarchi's reports exaggerated and tendentious. Indeed he even went so far as to diagnose "hypochondria" for General Bonaparte, for which the patient's corpulence may have excusably deceived him— a shameful misjudgment in view of the fact that Napoleon already lay dying, which was not mentioned at all in Dr. Arnott's book, published only after the autopsy report became known. From the daily reports to Hudson Lowe, it is at any rate perfectly clear that the honorable military surgeon was completely befuddled by Napoleon's sickness. As late as April 23, 1821, he still reaffirmed his view that General Bonaparte's case was one of hypochondria, since not a trace of an organic disease could be found.

One cannot avoid the impression that by such reports he was seeking to gain the Governor's favor, since the reports sent to Hudson Lowe do not accord with his diary entries. Thus the entry for April 10, 1821, states:

> The stomach again rejected everything he had eaten. His strength seemed to be sinking rapidly....The sick man tended to sleep, and when he was awake, he complained about a choking feeling. His whole body was cold.

Finally on April 27 he noted: "I had not been sitting long at his bedside, when he was again plagued by terrible choking and vomiting," and on this occasion he pointed out expressly that "the vomit that came from his stomach was a very black fluid that resembled coffee grounds and smelled horrible. This vomiting lasted until three-thirty in the afternoon." Dr. Arnott, in view of these symptoms described by himself, probably could not seriously have believed in the existence of a hypochondria.

The vomiting that began on April 10 lasted undiminished until his death. At night, he was plagued by it as many as five times, together with the outbreaks of sweating, so that in the night of April 13 Count Montholon and the valet Marchand had to change the bedsheets a total of seven times, because they were wet through and through. After that terrible night, Napoleon summoned Montholon and with his last ounce of energy he dictated his will to him, while Montholon repeated the words of his dictation. The composition of this twenty-page testament lasted until three o'clock in the afternoon, with two interruptions due to violent vomiting. In order to prevent the will from being contested later, he tried zealously to write as clearly as possible. Another will, sent to his son in case he should some day ascend the throne of France, was dictated on April 17.

Napoleon's attitude during the last days of his life was admirable. With clear understanding, he looked calmly toward death. To his favorite sister Pauline he sent a bulletin with the following content:

> The Emperor certainly hopes that Your Highness will communicate the situation to influential Englishmen. He is dying, abandoned by all, on this horrible rock. His death struggle is terrible.

Since he could not convince Dr. Arnott of his false diagnosis, he asked him most urgently to have an autopsy made after his death, in order finally to determine the true nature of his ailment. He directed the same request to Dr. Antommarchi, asking this doctor with training in pathological anatomy to pay particular attention to the condition of his stomach. Therefore, on April 27 he gave the following instruction:

> After my death, which cannot be far off, I wish that you open my body. I further wish, indeed, I demand of you, the promise that no Englishman should touch my corpse. If, however, you need someone for that, then I give you permission to use only Dr. Arnott. It is also my wish that you take my heart, store it in alcohol, and send it to my dear [Marie-] Louise in Parma. Tell her that I loved her tenderly and never have stopped loving her. Tell her also everything you have observed, everything related to my situation and my death. I recommend to you particularly that you examine my stomach most precisely, write a report about it, and send this to my son. Tell him how he can assure himself in advance and at least protect himself from the fear that has seized me....The uninterrupted vomiting leads me to think that my stomach is the sickest organ and I am not far from believing that it is the same ailment that took my father to his grave; I mean cancer of the stomach.

Napoleon could not know that his "Dear Louise," who, meanwhile, had been elected Duchess of Parma, could care very little for his heart preserved in alcohol, since for years she had been having an affair with the Count Neipperg and had married him after the Emperor's death.

The doctors continued to limit themselves to symptomatic treatments, such as aloe-pills and magnesium sulfate against constipation, the application of enemas, and tincture of cinnamon against vomiting. From April 27 on, when he vomited the viscous lumps that resembled coffee grounds, his condition degenerated rapidly. Lucid intervals alternated more and more frequently with phases of dulled awareness, in which he seemed to perceive nothing of his surroundings and mumbled incomprehensible words to himself. On April 30, a further symptom was manifested, which tormented him infinitely and persisted stubbornly until the hour of his death, namely, an incessant hiccuping, which the doctors tried to mitigate with doses of opium tincture. That evening the cold shivering began, during which his pulse could hardly be felt and his breathing took on a threatening character, but in the night a slight improvement seemed to be detectable. The patient asked for sweetened water mixed with wine to quench his consuming thirst.

But now something happened that led to a swift aggravation of his condition: namely, because of his distended and extremely bloated stomach and the stubborn intestinal paralysis, Dr. Arnott prescribed the laxative calomel; from a medical point of view, this was incomprehensible, indeed unforgivable. Although Napoleon tried to refuse and decidedly rejected this proposal, the valet Marchand was instructed by Dr. Arnott, supported by the two doctors Thomas Shortt and Charles Mitchell, to administer 600 milligrams to the patient secretly, together with the sugar water. The consequences of this irresponsible measure were ghastly. According to Dr. Antommarchi's information, that night there were eight emptyings of pitch-black masses, during which Napoleon was no longer able to keep the defecations under control. At first the dirty bedclothes were constantly changed, and finally even that had to be abandoned. The diarrheas and the constant vomiting intensified his thirst and, as a result of the massive loss of fluid, worsened the condition of his circulation. Exhausted by incessant hiccuping, and further weakened by the excessive nocturnal sweat outbreaks, he lay in the following days mostly unconscious in his bedclothes, filthy from the vomiting and the involuntary defecations, pitied by the few loyal followers standing around him.

After a terrible last night, on the morning of May 5, they heard him say his last words, muttered feverishly: *"France—Tête d'armée"* [France—head of the army]. Outside, fog, mist and rain blew around the house, and Dr. Arnott, together with Dr. Antommarchi, tried in a macabre fashion, in the last hours of the dying Emperor's life, to postpone his death with cataplasms and mustard-plaster poultices attached to the soles of the patient's feet. Shortly after five o'clock, a stormy southeastern tradewind rose howling and uprooted two little trees in front of his house, which had been planted by Napoleon himself in better days.

With his lower jaw fallen back, his eyes open as if staring to heaven in deep thoughts, he lay on his back, motionless, now barely breathing, until at eleven minutes before six in the evening death released him from his sufferings. The tropical sun began to sink into the sea just at the moment when the heart of the Emperor of the French stopped.

A few weeks earlier, he had dictated to Count Montholon the news of his own death to Governor Hudson Lowe, with the date left open. In this military report he said:

> Sir Governor! The Emperor Napoleon died on _____
> as the result of a long and painful sickness. I have the
> honor to inform you of this. I ask you to let us know
> what arrangements are prescribed by your government
> concerning the transportation of the corpse to Europe
> and also with regard to the persons in the Emperor's
> retinue.

NAPOLEON'S AUTOPSY

At the post-mortem examination of the corpse, which was scheduled for May 6, at two in the afternoon, seventeen persons in all were present, all crowded into a room measuring only five by six meters and scantily illuminated by two side windows. They pressed around the billiard table on which Dr. Antommarchi undertook the autopsy, which was awaited with suspense. General Sir Thomas Reade, who was the Governor's official representative, was accompanied by two staff officers and seven British doctors, constituting the English group. On the French side, the two generals, Bertrand and Montholon, as well as three servants, Marchand, St. Denis, and Pierron, were present. Finally two Corsicans attended the gruesome scene, namely, the Abbé Vignali and, as main actor and dissector, Dr. Antommarchi.

After a few moments, it was evident that the diagnostic clarification of the ailment leading to Napoleon's death was awaited by this heterogeneous crowd of gentlemen, less for objective medical facts,

Idealized portrayal of Napoleon's death (painting by Horace Vernet)

than to satisfy the respective political intentions of the two parties by the appropriate medical constructs. The British were very interested in not having Napoleon's death interpreted as the result of unfavorable conditions of his incarceration or of the inhospitable climate on the island of St. Helena; the French, on the contrary, wanted to put the blame on the English for their Emperor's premature death by detecting an illness contracted on this island. Embittered controversies arose during the autopsy, which resulted in the "medical grotesque" that no less than five different autopsy reports exist.

The official British report was written by the chief military physician, Dr. Thomas Shortt, who instructed Dr. Walter Henry to write down the discovered findings precisely. A second British version is Dr. Henry's report, demanded by the Governor Sir Hudson Lowe in 1823, based on Dr. Henry's own notes from 1821. This report was published in his book *Trifles from My Portfolio*, published in Quebec in 1839, and again in his book *Events of a Military Life,* published in London in 1843. Dr. Antommarchi as the examiner wrote two reports, a shorter one written on May 8, which he gave to the two French generals from Napoleon's retinue, and a second essentially more detailed one, in which Dr. Shortt—at the Governor's request—made a few changes or omissions in the text. So the total is five autopsy reports which display several deviations from one another, as could be expected.

The external description of the corpse was recorded most precisely by Dr. Henry, stressing the unusually peaceful facial expression of the deceased man, which deeply impressed all doctors who participated in the autopsy, and incidentally even surprised the bystanders in 1840, upon the exhumation of the corpse.

> The face presented a remarkably placid expression, indicative of mildness and even sweetness of disposition, which afforded a most striking contrast with the active life and moral character of the Deceased. The features were regular and even might be considered beautiful. The head was not opened. It was of large size and must have been disproportionate to the body even in youth. The forehead was very broad and full....The whole surface of the body was deeply covered with fat....Indeed the whole body was...effeminate. There was scarcely any hair on the body and that of the head

was thin, fine and silky. The pubis much resembled the *Mons Veneris* in women....The penis and testicles were small in development.

The description of the organ data by Dr. Henry corresponds broadly with the text of the official autopsy report, which was written and signed on May 6, 1821, by the British doctors, Thomas Shortt, Matthew Livingstone, Archibald Arnott, Charles Mitchell and Francis Burton.

This official autopsy report reads:

> On a superficial view the body appeared very fat, which state was confirmed by the first incision down its centre, where the fat was upwards of one inch thick over the sternum, and one inch and a half over the abdomen. On cutting through the cartilages of the ribs and exposing the cavity of the thorax, a trifling adhesion of the left pleura was found to the pleura costalis. About three ounces of reddish fluid were contained in the left cavity, and nearly eight ounces in the right. The lungs were quite sound. The pericardium was natural and contained about an ounce of fluid. The heart was of the natural size but thickly covered with fat....
>
> Upon opening the abdomen the Omentum was found remarkably fat, and exposing the stomach that viscus was found the seat of extensive disease, strong adhesions connected the whole superior surface, particularly about the pyloric extremity to the concave surface of the left lobe of the liver, and on separating these, an ulcer which penetrated the coats of the stomach was discovered one inch from the pylorus sufficient to allow the passage of the little finger. The internal surface of the stomach to nearly its whole extent was a mass of cancerous disease or scirrhous portions advancing to cancer; this was particularly noticed near the pylorus. The outermost extremity for a small space near the termination of the oesophagus was the only part appearing in a healthy state. The stomach was found nearly filled with a large quantity of fluid resembling coffee grounds.

The convex surface of the left lobe of the liver adhered to the diaphragm. With the exceptions of the adhesions occasioned by the disease in the stomach, no unhealthy appearance presented itself in the liver. The remainder of the abdominal viscera were in a healthy state.

A slight peculiarity in the formation of the left kidney was observed.

In Dr. Henry's supplementary report from 1823 one finds in addition to this statement the additional remark:

A very general expectation was entertained that the Liver would be found in a diseased state, the illness of the Deceased having been so confidently referred to an enlargement and chronic inflammation of this Viscus. In consequence when the Liver was next examined the countenances of the Spectators indicated much anxiety. When M. Antommarchi made his first incision into it he expected to see a flow of Pus from the abscess which had been anticipated in its substance, but no abscess, no hardness, no enlargement, no inflammation were observed. On the contrary the Liver was of natural size and perfectly healthy in its internal parts.

This last sentence corresponded to the Governor's intentions, but not to the truth. Dr. Shortt, who because of his age enjoyed the highest degree of authority among his colleagues who were present, said namely that he found the liver significantly enlarged. But since he had to yield to the objection of the Governor's representative, Sir Thomas Reade, who demanded an exact distinction between "large" and "too large," Dr. Shortt finally corrected his statement and dictated: "The liver is perhaps larger than normal."

The political background of the two British autopsy reports is obvious: they wanted to let the world know unmistakably that Napoleon was well treated during his exile and sufficiently fed. Therefore it was important to point out especially that at his death despite his serious illness he still displayed considerable fat accumulation. But the rumor also had to be refuted that he had contracted a liver disease during his exile on the tropical and inhospitable island of St. Helena. Rather the autopsy report must show clearly that Napoleon died a natural death as a result of his incurable chronic ailment which had no connection of any kind with the conditions under which he was kept prisoner.

This at first seemed to have succeeded promptly with Dr. Shortt's official report of May 1821, in which the cause of death was given as a stomach carcinoma, which was said to occur frequently in Napoleon's family. For this autopsy report clearly showed that the patient's life had been prolonged because of the natural closing of the stomach perforation by the adhesion of the outer stomach wall to the surface of the left hepatic lobe, since, otherwise, the pouring of the stomach contents into the open stomach cavity would have caused immediate death, whereas the liver itself was completely healthy.

To be free of any suspicion, the Governor, as a precaution, even had the compliant Dr. Shortt strike the objectionable sentence: "The liver was perhaps a little larger than natural" and replace it by the words: "With the exceptions of the adhesions occasioned by the disease in the stomach, no unhealthy appearance presented itself in the liver." Dr. Shortt, however, added this note to the original report: "The erased words were suppressed on Sir Hudson Lowe's orders," in order to rehabilitate himself in the eyes of posterity from this alteration of the text that was imposed on him, in violation of medical ethics.

Under the circumstances it is understandable that Dr. Antommarchi refused to sign this official British record. In his later memoirs, he gave the reason for this with the annoyed words:

> Suddenly I saw the Doctors Shortt, Mitchell, and Burton coming out of the apartment of the ordinance officer and approaching. The gentlemen had, as I already mentioned, attended the autopsy without participating in it. Now it suddenly occurred to them to write the report. They had already written it and brought it for me to sign. I did not accept. What did I have to do with this English document? I was Napoleon's doctor, I had done the autopsy, and so it was up to me to report about it. I could conceal nothing, keep nothing secret, I therefore offered them a copy of my report, but they did not want to know anything about it.

So he presented to the two executors of the will, Bertrand and Montholon, his own short report which for the most part agrees with the text of the British doctors, except that the liver is explicitly called "very large and distended."

Dr. Antommarchi's autopsy finding, of course, merits greater significance than that of the British, because of his professional qualification and because they only attended the event as observers. Apart from the fact that in his report, too, political motives are recognizable and that he formulated his statements less dogmatically, unfortunately his report also lacks the desired clarity. It must also be considered, however, that all pathological-anatomical descriptions then were made only by external observation and without the help of histology. Moreover, it must be considered that the standard detailed description of stomach ulcers was not done until ten years later by Jean Cruveilhier. If in his first short report, Antommarchi assented to the official version of a stomach carcinoma, it was surely because he knew only too well the vindictive reactions of the Governor from the example of his predecessors. For, after arriving in Europe, he implied that it was the British doctors who had insisted on the diagnosis of stomach cancer. In reality, Napoleon had not died of this family ailment, but from the consequences of a "gastrohepatitis," a term which unfortunately says nothing and permits no sharp conclusions. How uncertain he was in forming his opinion is shown by the circumstance that, in his detailed autopsy report published in 1825, he joined the general opinion after all and, likewise, diagnosed a stomach carcinoma as the cause of Napoleon's death; this description is, however, noticeably less convincing and cogent than the official British report.

The extensive report written by Dr. Antommarchi reads, in somewhat abridged form, as follows:

> The Emperor was noticeably thinner than at the time of my arrival on St. Helena. His body weight was less than one-fourth what it had once been. The face and body were pale, his facial features were beautiful, the eyes closed and one did not have the impression that the Emperor was dead, but much rather as if he were sunken in a deep sleep. His mouth kept a smiling expression, only the left side was slightly twisted in a "sardonic grin." The body showed on the left arm an ulcer like a fontanelle [a purulent ulcer that arose from

a blister artificially induced by a cupping-glass] and several scars [from war injuries]. Neck a bit short, chest cage wide, stomach strongly protruding and distended. Hands and feet perhaps a bit small, but well formed.

I first opened the chest, and the most remarkable appearances it exhibited were the following:

The sac formed by the costal pleura of the left side contained about a glass of fluid of a citrine color. A slight coat of coagulable lymph [according to the view then current that pleural effusion came from burst lymph vessels] covered part of the surfaces of the costal and pulmonary pleurae corresponding to the same side.

The left lung was slightly compressed by the effusion, and adhered by numerous bridles to the posterior and lateral parts of the chest, and to the pericardium. I carefully dissected it, and found the superior lobe covered with tuberculae and some small tuberculous excavations.

A slight coat of coagulable lymph covered part of the surfaces of the costal and pulmonary pleurae corresponding to that side.

The sac of the costal pleura on the right side contained about two glasses of fluid of a citrine colour.

The right lung was slightly compressed by effusion, but its parenchyma was in a healthy state. Both lungs were, generally speaking, firm (crepitans), and of their natural colour. The mucous membrane of the trachea-arteria and of the bronchiae was tolerably red, and lined with a rather considerable quantity of pituitous matter, thick and viscous.

Many of the ganglions of the bronchiae, and of the mediastinum, were rather enlarged, almost degenerated, and in a state of suppuration.

The pericardium was in a healthy state, and contained about an ounce of fluid of a citrine colour. The heart, which was rather larger than the fist of the subject, exhibited, though sound, a rather abundant proportion of fat at its base and on its ridges. The aorta and pulmonary ventricles, and the corresponding auricles, were in a state of proper conformation, but pale, and contained no blood.

The abdomen exhibited the following appearances:— Distension of the peritonæum, produced by a great quantity of gas. A soft, transparent, and diffluent exudation lining the whole extent of the internal surface of the peritonæum. The epiploon was in a state of proper conformation.

The spleen, and the liver, which was hardened, were very large and distended with blood. The texture of the liver, which was of a brownish red colour, did not, however, exhibit any remarkable alteration of structure. The vesica fellis was filled and distended with very thick and clotted bile. The liver, which was affected by chronic hepatitis, closely adhered by its convex surface to the diaphragm; the adhesion occupied the whole extent of that organ, and was strong, cellular, and of long existence.

The concave surface of the left lobe adhered closely and strongly to the corresponding part of the stomach, particularly along the small curve of that organ, and to the epiploon. At every point of contact, the lobe was sensibly thickened, swelled, and hardened.

The stomach appeared, at first sight, in a perfectly healthy state; no trace of irritation or phlogosis [inflammation], and the peritonæal membrane exhibited the most satisfactory appearance: but, on examining that organ with care, I discovered on its anterior surface, near the small curve, and at the breadth of three fingers from the pylorus, a slight obstruction, apparently of a scirrhous nature, of little extent, and exactly circumscribed. The stomach was perforated through and through in the centre of that small induration, the aperture of which was closed by the adhesion of that part to the left lobe of the liver.

The volume of the stomach was smaller than it is usually found. On opening that organ along its large curve, I observed that part of its capacity was filled with a considerable quantity of matters, slightly consistent, and mixed with a great quantity of glairous substances, very thick and of a colour resembling the sediment of coffee, and which exhaled an acrid and infectious odour. These substances being removed, the mucous membrane of the stomach was ascertained to be sound from the small to the large cavity of this organ, following the great curve. Almost the whole of the remainder of the internal surface of the stomach was occupied by a cancerous ulcer, whose centre was in the upper part, along the small curve of the stomach, whilst the irregular digital and linguiform borders of its circumference extended both before and behind that internal surface, and from the orifice of the cardia to within a good inch of the pylorus. Its rounded opening, obliquely cut in the shape of a basil [bezel] at the expanse of the internal surface of the organ, scarcely occupied a diameter of four or five lines inside, and at most two lines and a half outside. The circular border of that opening was extremely thin, slightly denticulated, blackish, and only formed by the peritonæal membrane of the stomach. An ulcerous, greyish, and smooth surface lined this kind of canal, which, but for the adhesion of the liver, would have established a communication between the cavity of the stomach and that of the abdomen. The right extremity of the stomach, at the distance of an inch from the pylorus, was surrounded by a tumour, or rather a scirrhous annular induration, a few lines in width. The orifice of the pylorus was in perfect state. The lips of the ulcer exhibited remarkable fungous swellings, the bases of which were hard, thick, and in a scirrhous state, and extended also over the whole surface occupied by that cruel disease.

The little epiploon was contracted, swollen, very much hardened, and degenerated. The lymphatic glands of that peritonæal membrane, those placed along the curves of the stomach, as well as those near the pillars of the diaphragm, were in part tumefied and scirrhous; some even in a state of suppuration.

The digestive canal was distended by the presence of a great quantity of gas. I observed, in the peritonæal surface and in the peritonæal doublings, small specks and patches of a pale red colour, of various dimensions, and scattered at some distance from each other. The mucous membrane of this canal appeared to be in a sound state. The large intestines were covered with a substance of a darkish colour and extremely viscous.

The right kidney was sound; that on the left side was out of its place, being thrown back upon the lumbar vertebrae: it was longer and narrower than the other; in other respects it appeared sound.

The bladder, which was empty and much contracted, contained a certain quantity of gravel, mixed with some small calculi. Numerous red spots were scattered upon its mucous membrane, and the coats of the organ were in a diseased state.

Thus ends Dr. Antommarchi's extensive report; and it agrees on essential points with the official British autopsy report, but by describing additional details not mentioned by Dr. Shortt, it permits pathological-anatomical conclusions which were undesirable from a British perspective and so were left unconsidered. The two autopsy reports written by the English military doctors thus repressed the tubercular excavations and older tubercles, shown by Dr. Antommarchi to the bystanders at the autopsy. For this kind of finding could have allowed the suspicion to arise that Napoleon had died from a tuberculosis of the lung, a cause of death all too easily associated with the unfavorable living conditions on that inhospitable island in the South Atlantic.

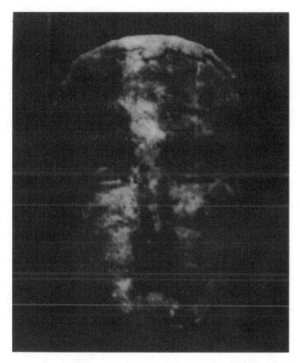

Napoleon's death mask, made by Francesco Antommarchi

Another finding in the official British autopsy report that does not agree with the Corsican pathologist's statements is the reference to the adhesions of the liver with its surroundings. Dr. Antommarchi spoke clearly of an extensive internal degenerative adhesion of the liver surface with the diaphragm, which must have existed for a long time and, associated with it, he spoke of a circumscribed degenerative adhesion of the lower surface of the left hepatic lobe with the region of the lesser curvature of the stomach where the ulcer perforating the stomach wall was located. This description was contested by Dr. George Rutledge, one of the British military doctors present at the autopsy. He referred to the description of the degenerative adhesions of the hepatic surface with the diaphragm, as well as the description of the adhesion of the liver with the stomach mentioned by Dr. Shortt, as "superficial data," which only multiply "numerous errors" with which Dr. Antommarchi's book was filled. He thus contradicted not only his colleague Dr. Shortt, but also Dr. Henry's description. Dr. Henry reported that the detachment of the adhesions was possible only with the greatest difficulty—namely, with the help of a scalpel. But since Dr. Henry had to submit to the Governor's wish to draw attention from any conceivable lesion in the liver and to relate everything only to a stomach ailment, he chose a corresponding, though medically illogical formulation by concluding:

> There was a small adhesion of the convex surface of the left Lobe to the Diaphragm which appeared to have been a continuation and a consequence of the adjoining adhesion between the Liver and Stomach.

For the experienced pathologist Antommarchi, on the contrary, the firm degenerative adhesions between the lower hepatic surface and the stomach at the site where the perforation canal opened, close to the pylorus, could only one interpretation: it had to be the consequence of an acute event in the stomach, namely, a stomach perforation with subsequent adhesion of the outer stomach wall to the adjacent lower surface of the left hepatic lobe. This extensive, wide, and firm concrescence of the hepatic surface with the diaphragm, however, could, in his opinion, have nothing to do with this event. Rather, he logically linked it with a disease of the liver in the sense of a perihepatitis, that is, an infection of the liver capsule. Dr. Antommarchi left open what liver disease it could have been, or respectively, he dismissed it with the vague term, "gastrohepatitis." Surely, no one would then have dared recall the statements and accurate prognosis of Dr. Stokoe, who was apparently experienced with the tropics, for he had considered probable an amebic abscess of the liver with the danger of a perforation into the abdominal cavity.

Unfortunately, Sir Hudson Lowe gave strict orders that Napoleon's corpse was not to be embalmed and that the organs which had been preserved in separate silver containers filled with ethyl alcohol (the heart and the stomach, removed by Dr. Antommarchi after the end of the autopsy) were to be placed in the grave. He thereby not only prevented the fulfillment of Napoleon's last wish that his heart be sent to his wife Marie-Louise, but he also impeded the possibility that a more accurate examination of the stomach, undertaken later, could gain more reliable diagnostic insights.

As the valet Marchand reports in his memoirs, Dr. Arnott was given the task of strictly guarding the corpse in its coffin during the night and watching out that nothing, especially not the two silver containers, was removed. Despite the strictest surveillance, Dr. Antommarchi nonetheless succeeded in removing two tissue samples from the dead man's intestine without being noticed, and he took them with him to Europe. Probably through contacts with Dr. O'Meara, they were sent to the English surgeon, Sir Astley Cooper, who had them stored in the museum of the Royal College of Surgeons (which he had founded). Until World War II they could be viewed there, and only after the bombing of London by the German Luftwaffe did they disappear forever.

Sir Arthur Keith, custodian of the Royal College of Surgeons of England, after a thorough examination of the tissue samples, became convinced that these were indeed from Napoleon's corpse; and when, almost a century after the autopsy, the samples were subjected to an exact microscopic analysis, suddenly a new light was cast on these lines to Sir Colonna by Dr. Antommarchi:

> I declare to you, to the whole Imperial family and to the whole world, that the sickness under which the Emperor had to suffer, arose from the climatic peculiarities.

The histological processing of the tissue fragments showed the presence of a chronic infection. Therefore, in 1913, the curator of the Royal College, Sir Arthur Keith, after consulting the precise description of Napoleon's medical history during his exile years on St. Helena, concluded that he fell sick "of an endemic fever, with the symptoms of an inflammation of the liver."

After the autopsy, the corpse was washed with eau de cologne and covered with a gold-embroidered coat from Marengo. Since the English government refused to allow the transportation of Napoleon to Europe, the coffin was buried in a ravine on the island of St. Helena, in a place where two willows cast their shade on a bubbling spring. England did only one thing in honor of the dead man, namely, it ordered that a guard be posted at the grave. This continued until the dead Emperor of the French was brought back to Paris nineteen years later.

When his death became known in Paris, Talleyrand dismissed it with the remark: "That is merely news, but no longer a major event." But this shows how very wrong he was about the mood of the people. Suddenly, the French people seemed to have forgotten everything wrong that Napoleon had done to them and to remember only the good things. To Talleyrand's surprise, a countermovement soon would form under the name Bonapartism, gathering together all the disappointed and dissatisfied persons from the most varied political camps.

NAPOLEON'S PSYCHOGRAPH

To understand Napoleon's character better, one must go back to the origins of his childhood impressions, since, to clarify individual contradictions and apparent obscurities, all stages of development that leave their mark on a developing character, starting with earliest childhood, must be included in the medical study. From this perspective, several phases of his life, decisive for his later development, can be distinguished.

First, one comes upon a strongly pronounced mother-complex that is recognizable not only in his childhood and early youth but during his entire life. This mother-complex played an important role in shaping his later ideal of women, and it was also responsible for many a distancing or rejecting stance toward females who did not correspond to this ideal, as well as for a certain timidity toward the female sex which he often felt as an adult. His love for the considerably older Josephine Beauharnais probably also had its deeper roots in this mother-complex.

Important for his later development must have been the circumstance that his strongly felt love for his mother was not returned in the way he expected it to be. His mother fought actively at her husband's side in the Corsican war of liberation, and later, because of her fearless, brave, and unbending behavior during and after the turmoils of the French Revolution, she was given the nickname "Madame Mère." She was a rather hard woman, unable to give the love-famished boy the tenderness he hoped for. Apparently little Napoleon suffered greatly under this psychic distress and when he was put in a boarding school, far away from his mother at the age of nine, lacking the least trace of caressing and pampering, the idealization of his mother and the ideal image of woman in general reached its zenith. This unquenchable longing to be loved and spoiled that had germinated in his early childhood continued to exist all his life, though mostly repressed into the subconscious; and even later it still typified the general, the politician, and the Emperor. Although he always expected unconditional obedience in all these positions, at the same time he also always wanted to be loved and honored. Understandably, this desire was expressed most clearly on the sentimental side of his life, whether in his love for the Countess Walewska or in his affection for Marie-Louise. His strongly marked need to be loved is also revealed in his notable concern for his servants and the faithful followers of his closer entourage.

At an early age, he tried to compensate for this unsatisfied longing for love and tenderness by working hard to achieve externally visible successes, in order to impress others. In this way even at school he sought to win the admiration of his fellow pupils and his teachers by brilliant accomplishments; later, this method of obtaining the recognition and affection of his fellowmen by intensive work dominated the young man's life, until finally military and political successes quenched his longing for love and admiration completely.

A strong influence on the development of his personality was exercised by his life in the military academies of Brienne and Paris. Because of his Corsican origin and his obvious poverty, he was unabashedly ostracized by his comrades who stemmed from the nobility. His weak physical constitution also made him unable to match strength with them physically. So in his ambition he looked for another way to compensate for his low status. He began to devote his leisure hours exclusively to intellectual activities and thus acquired a kind of precocious superiority whereby he could outmatch and dominate his comrades. He once told of his burning ambition: "I could not bear the thought of not being first in my class." Though this did not bring him the affection he hoped for, it did win him a certain respect from his comrades and so even in his youth his pronounced authoritarian tendencies were already emerging. Moreover, the snubbing by his noble comrades aroused in him a sort of inferiority complex that never left him, even later in his relations with the nobility.

His feelings of revenge toward the arrogant sons of the aristocracy at the military academy of Brienne were probably one of the reasons why, during the French Revolution, in the shift of power from the Girondists to the Jacobins, he adopted the ideas of the latter and offered his services to the Revolution. If at that time isolation from his comrades led to an incipient hatred of France coupled with heightened Corsican patriotism, during the Revolution his hatred was no longer directed against France, but only against the *ancien régime*. Since even as a child he had forever been hearing of the heroic Corsican freedom-struggle, at a very early age the concepts of patriotism, sense of duty, and loyalty were branded into his soul as the most important of all manly virtues, so that in combination with his later reading of the writings of Jean-Jacques Rousseau, he was mentally and emotionally quite an ideal candidate to participate in the Revolution.

A salient character trait of Napoleon's was that he instinctively felt challenged by any kind of authority. The roots of this attitude also reach back into early childhood. Like almost all boys who display an especially strong mother bonding, he also developed a kind of jealousy toward his father, with a desire to take his place. This jealousy was directed even against his older brother, which certainly must be the real and deeper cause for his strange behavior toward his family after his father's death. Napoleon declared himself to be the "chief of the family clan," not, as was customary, his older brother Joseph. He behaved very similarly toward anyone who, from his point of view, represented a kind of paternal authority—for instance, the Bourbons, royal princes, and even Pope Pius VII. Since in his view anyone who claimed a position of equality alongside him had to bend unconditionally to his yoke, whether it was one of his siblings, his generals, or reigning sovereigns, it is obvious why Napoleon could have no one as a sincere friend.

In Paris, after the end of the Revolution, he got to know the organizational and political inefficiency of the Directory from very close up, and he experienced the humiliation of being summarily dismissed without any real justification—though that dismissal was only temporary, since the Directory soon ran into difficulties. This disappointment changed the former idealist into a cold, calculating realist and cynical despiser of mankind. Because of his low level of tolerance for frustration, he felt a sense of nearly mortal insult from the marital infidelity of his wife Josephine. His originally very idealistic attitude toward women changed into a kind of cynicism toward them, so that from then on he dealt with them only with the greatest circumspection.

All these experiences increased his already notable hunger for power and stirred up his unbending will to dominate people in the future. This striving for power over people, from whom he hoped to win both love and affection, sprang from an unconscious urge to compensate for an initial frustration that lay far back in the time of his childhood, and, since such a compensation can never be complete, Napoleon remained unable to attain perfect happiness and perfect relaxation all his life, despite his spectacular successes.

Early in his cometlike career, his claims to power and his authoritarian tendencies were kept under control by his outstanding intellect and his unerring sense of reality. But as his power became greater and greater and as he began to feel as if he were indeed the Ruler of Europe, he lost his fine touch. Formerly his instinctive certainty and disciplined patience had enabled him to await the right moment for optimal success in an undertaking, but now he believed that he could bend fate to his will. Reminiscent of the phrase, "Power corrupts, absolute power corrupts absolutely," Napoleon increasingly misused his power; hand in hand with that misuse of power, his actions became ever more unrestrained and egocentric. Spoiled by his rapidly ascending career, he no longer tolerated even the slightest contradiction; and, when someone from his entourage, from whom he expected blind obedience and boundless worship, dared to resist his intentions, he fell into real fits of rage. With almost sadistic satisfaction, he convinced himself from time to time of the devotion and loving affection of his most loyal companions by intentional humiliations, in the conviction that everything was permitted to him as absolute ruler and master and that he could deal with his subjects as he liked.

This ever stronger feeling of omnipotence gave him the certainty that, like Alexander the Great, Hannibal, or Caesar, he had been chosen by fate for great historical deeds of a unique kind and was endowed with the corresponding abilities and talents. In his almost pathological delusion of power, personal destinies no longer played a role for the achievement of his ambitious plans. When he sacrificed hundreds of thousands of France's sons on European battlefields for this purpose—and these tremendous sacrifices long since ceased to serve for the glory and grandeur of France, but merely his own personal greed for more and more power—this seemed legitimate to the Emperor Napoleon, in his conviction that for him the moral boundaries of ordinary mortals did not apply. So his power-obsessed passions took on ever more psychopathic features and lured him ultimately, in boundless overestimation of himself, to Utopian undertakings. With the Spanish adventure, but above all with his ill-fated Russian campaign, he rashly challenged fate. The plunge of the fiery comet thereby became inevitable, and when he finally lay on the ground, defeated and humiliated, not only his numerous enemies, but also many of his supporters and admirers who had been faithful for many long years, breathed a sigh of relief.

Dr. Groen, in his study on Napoleon's last sickness, especially in connection with Napoleon's stomach ailments, to be discussed in more detail below, dealt with some of his character traits predisposing him for these ailments. These traits are found in the majority of people suffering from ulcers. Among these typical characteristics, a particularly important place is occupied by an outstanding intellect and a notably quick power of comprehension—these types of persons are known as "intellectual sprinters." They are usually distinguished by an exaggerated zeal and ambition; they have great organizing talent; and, because of their versatility, they plunge enthusiastically into every area of activity. They demand strict obedience and a sense of responsibility, not only from others, but also from themselves. From earliest childhood they strive for independence, and thus generally strive for leading positions in which *they* can give orders or commands. In their desire to be recognized by and to dominate over others, intrigues and patronage play no role, and ,as a rule, hatred is *not* involved in their journey upward. Personal achievement is all that counts for the attainment of their ambitious goals.

Their marked egoism demands affection, praise, and recognition and misleads them to vanity and pride. Especially typical is their intolerance of frustrations, that is, their sensitivity and exaggerated vulnerability to criticism or disparaging allusions to their person. Their strongly developed social sense also often results in their devoting themselves to social interests or working for socially oriented political groups.

This brief summary of the typical characteristics of individuals who tend to develop ulcers shows surprisingly that many analogous qualities are found in Napoleon's character. Given such psychological predispositions, it is no wonder that stressful situations in his military campaigns or in his political power struggles readily could have lead to the development of a stomach ulcer or could have triggered a recurrence. The psychogenic factors in the etiology of ulcers also clarify why his exile on St. Helena brought the final catastrophe on the long road on which this ailment had accompanied him. That island had all the harmful preconditions.

Thus it would seem indicated to submit to a more exact analysis the influence of incarceration on his psyche during the six years of exile on St. Helena. Groen has summed up the psychological stress factors contributing to Napoleon's spiritual martyrdom on that island that could be given in a somewhat abridged form as follows:

> First, there was his plunge from dizzying heights, where, a short time before, the oldest dynasties of sovereigns had bowed to him; and now he had to exchange this grandeur for life as a humiliated prisoner deprived of all rights. Abandoned or betrayed by most of his generals and ministers, who owed their position and wealth to him, abandoned and forgotten by his second

wife Marie-Louise, who was already long since involved in an affair with Count Neipperg and from
whom he never received even one word or sign of interest; and without news of his son, who was forbidden
even to mention his father's name, he lived as an exile
on the lonesome island, aware that with the restoration of the Bourbons all his efforts to create better living
conditions for the citizens of France were nullified.
Even his own family was too preoccupied with its own
interests to remember him; and his brother Louis did
not even hesitate to slur him personally in a book.

Other sources of bitter experiences and abasements were the measures taken by the English government and its extended arm,
Governor Hudson Lowe. Even on board the ship "Northumberland"
that took him to England, he had to be addressed only as "General
Bonaparte" and now it was strictly forbidden to address him as "Napoleon," not to mention "l'Empereur Napoléon." This humiliation hurt
him deeply, since he had always dealt with his defeated enemies mag-
nanimously. But in other ways, too, the English government, and
Hudson Lowe in particular, omitted no opportunity to let Napoleon
feel that he was simply a prisoner. British warships patrolled off the
coast of the island day and night, and Longwood itself was surrounded
by soldiers. If he wanted to go for a stroll in the daytime, a restricted
security boundary limited his freedom of movement, and if he wanted
to cross that boundary he had to be accompanied by an English officer.
His letters were subject to strict censorship; twice per day an English
officer had to go personally to ensure that the prisoner was still present.
He was also forbidden to speak with the inhabitants of the island.

An especially stressful component of his exile was the personality
of the Governor himself. Insofar as a diagnosis is possible, given the
details present for such a judgment, Hudson Lowe probably would have
to be classified as a neurasthenic with clear signs of a compulsive
neurosis: his narrow-mindedness, his sick pedantry, his paranoid distrust, his exaggerated show of correctness and gentlemanly behavior,
and his mania to preserve even the most insignificant scraps of paper.
His fear that the prisoner could escape degenerated into an obsession.
It is understandable that Napoleon could not bear the presence of this
low-ranking, petty-minded man; on one occasion when a visit by
Hudson Lowe was announced, he barricaded his door to spare
himself the sight of the man. Indeed, he even loaded his rifle and his

revolver to show demonstratively that he was willing if necessary to defend his right to privacy with his life.

A further burden was the island's climate. When it was not raining, it was foggy; and stormy winds swept the high plateau. The residence on Longwood was cramped and damp; the food was of poor quality and, moreover, very expensive, so that Napoleon was sometimes forced to sell silver utensils in Jamestown, the capital of the island, in order to buy food. He began to suffer more and more from loneliness, for the material for conversation with his companions had long since been exhausted, apart from the fact that several of them had long ago left the island. He was increasingly burdened with the feeling that his presence was an obstacle to the release of his faithful followers. He followed events in Europe with great interest and commented on them diligently, but everything he wrote remained without reverberation. His only satisfying activity remained his study of history, especially of his own extraordinarily eventful life. Day and night he dictated his reflections on his activities during his rule as Emperor of the French and about his great battles. But gradually he fell into resignation at the senselessness of his existence and, to his own astonishment and that of his entourage, he preferred more and more to lie in bed all day long.

Thus exile on St. Helena embodies the last phase of his psychological development. It meant not merely his personal defeat and the disintegration of laboriously constructed structures, but it made clear to him the final and unrestorable separation from the nations he had dreamed of ruling. Deprived of all his power and grandeur and devoid of all love and affection, for the rest of his life he was condemned to a slow death. Formerly it had been possible to make up for all defeats and disappointments in his life by overwhelming successes in other fields, but now the possibility of any effective compensation was taken away forever—both as a military commander and as a statesman or politician. The hesitant attempts to establish communication with the outside world, still undertaken at the beginning of his exile, brought no response, since the world had already forgotten him. So the only possibility left for him was to establish contact with posterity in the form of a message epitomizing his heritage.

The definitive disappearance of all hope meant that he had accepted his irrevocably sealed fate. Now his slogan became: "Complaints are beneath my dignity and do not accord with my character. Either I give commands or I remain silent." And he remained faithful to it until a few days before his death.

Napoleon on St. Helena (in civilian clothes in front of his house)

ANALYSIS OF NAPOLEON'S MEDICAL HISTORY

Although Napoleon always boasted of an iron constitution, this was far from the truth, although admittedly he endured only a few serious illnesses. His self-image of never having been seriously ill merely reflected an exaggerated feeling of self-worth. After all, a victorious military commander and wise statesman of the rank of a Napoleon Bonaparte was, in the eyes of his contemporaries, such a uniquely heroic figure of world history that he had to be unassailable, and even immune to disease. But he was not born with any such iron-clad health as he boasted.

Since Napoleon was put in the care of a nursemaid immediately after his birth, news of possible sicknesses in the first years of his life is rather scanty and imprecise. It is certain, however, that even as a small child he seemed extremely irritable and nervous to the people around him. And by the age of two he still was not able to hold his head straight, since it had turned out somewhat too large. He is also said to have suffered from "cramps," which from a modern viewpoint probably corresponded to the so-called "infant spasms" that were frequently observed in earlier times in the context of rickets.

Rickets was a very frequent illness in Europe until the beginning of this century and affected mainly the poorer strata of the population. It never began until the second month of life—and, very rarely, after the child was two years old. Rickets is caused essentially by a Vitamin D deficiency, which leads to disturbed calcium/phosphorus metabolism. Therefore, the illness affects primarily the skeletal system; by impeding development, it can lead to disorders in body growth and physical disproportions. Even when no visible curvatures appear, children with rickets as a rule are shorter, and the stunting of the facial skeleton makes the skull seem even larger than it is. A child with rickets may be delayed for months from learning certain static bodily functions, such as lifting or holding up his heavy head. Demineralization formerly also resulted in muscular atony, that is, a slackness of the musculature, tending to affect primarily stomach and intestinal muscles. Various typical "digestive disturbances" then followed, including the tendency to a persistent bloating of the belly—so that in the past century such children were said to have a rickety "frog or potato belly." Quite frequently the cramp-like muscular twitchings called "infant spasms" were triggered by excessive gas pressure in the body. Since such cramp attacks were accompanied by muscular twitchings lasting for a few minutes, they could resemble real epileptic seizures and were often wrongly diagnosed as epilepsy.

The existence of rickets in Napoleon's early childhood may be accepted with certainty. The demonstrably undernourished child of poor parents showed several symptoms that speak for such a diagnosis: the somewhat stunted body size, the oversized rectangular head, the short neck, the child's reported inability to hold his head erect at two years of age, clear digestive disturbances, and cramps observed at the toddler stage, which were later wrongly classified as epileptic. The slight curvature of the spine at chest-level, noticeable in various portraits, gives the impression of his neck being too short and is probably also a consequence of a late rickets case.

Dr. Groen, however, also discusses the possibility that this slight bone deformity could also be a change such as can be found in so-called thalassemia. These are an extremely variegated group of hereditary disturbances in the formation of hemoglobin in the red blood cells, such as can still be found today in the Mediterranean area and also not so rarely on Corsica itself. Since this sickness also can lead to a greater deterioration of the red blood cells, the degree of seriousness of the disturbance can, in addition to an anemia marked by noticeable pallor, also result in a mild yellow coloring of the eyeball, such as is observed in other forms of jaundice. The yellowish, olive-green complexion of the young Bonaparte—also mentioned in later years—was most impressively described by a native teamster on the occasion of crossing the Alps during the Italian campaign and would speak for Dr. Groen's version, although for lack of more precise information it can only remain a suspicion.

In the young Bonaparte, an unusual irritability and strikingly low tolerance threshold were observed at the military academy in Brienne. Even the slightest criticism of his person or the gentlest correction, if it was felt to be a humiliation, could lead to practically theatrical over-reactions. Psychosomatic manifestations were in the foreground of this symptom; for instance, after being corrected by a supervisor who ordered him to take his meal in the dining hall on his knees as a punishment, he reacted with violent vomiting and a fainting spell. Such psychosomatic reactions afflicted him in later life, too, to a greater degree in critical situations or under unusually stressful conditions, and they affected mainly the stomach or the urinary bladder. Due to his extreme mental instability, in his school years a trivial matter could make him so angry he would begin to shake as if from fever or would refuse all food— hysterical reactions, which he later also used to influence the people around him.

His unstable psyche could, however, easily swing in the opposite direction and lead to fits of depression, described by him as a sixteen-year-old second lieutenant, in a letter conveying a genuine melancholic mood of *Weltschmerz* and world-weariness:

> Since I must die someday anyway, why couldn't I just kill myself right now?...Always alone, I come home... only to abandon myself to waves of my melancholy. What is its inclination today? Death. Life is only a burden for me, I have no enjoyment, everything turns to pain.

This is a matter of a reactive depression almost resembling a pre-suicidal stage, and it reveals how very much the youth, separated from his mother, longed in vain for love and tenderness and how depressed he could be, with his withdrawn way of life, avoiding social contact with his arrogant noble comrades.

At the age of twenty, during the time he was stationed in Auxonne, Napoleon must have caught malaria, which had a rather high incidence rate in that region, and it would continue to trouble him for a rather long time. Unfortunately details are not known about this, so that this diagnosis can be made only indirectly from the few existing documents and a few clues in his medical history. The first clue is obtained from a letter he wrote to his uncle, Cardinal Joseph Fesch, on August 22, 1788, from Auxonne, where he was then serving as a young second lieutenant of artillery, in which he reported:

> I am somewhat ill. The great projects I had to com-
> plete lately are the cause of that. As you know, my
> dear uncle, the General shows me a great deal of re-
> spect and attention, and this has turned the captains
> somewhat against me....I am worried mostly about my
> health, which seems somewhat run-down.

This illness due to the unhealthy climate of Auxonne seems to have afflicted the "spindle-thin" Lieutenant Bonaparte just as it had the enlisted men and other officers. A local report from that time describes the moats surrounding the fort, built in the style of the famous Vauban, and how their brackish swamp water contaminated the city, already damp because of the frequent floods. Officers and men often suffered from "spells of fever."

Considering the local conditions in those years, the "spells of fever" could have occurred in the context of malaria. For malaria at that time was rightly called swamp fever. It especially afflicted the swampy regions of Italy and Greece, but in the first half of the nineteenth century it was also found in the estuaries of the great European rivers. So at that time the great rivers, Weichsel, Oder, Elbe, Rhine, and Danube, were the breeding places for malaria, just as were the shores of the sea with their high and low tides. But there were also regions which became malaria breeding grounds temporarily because of frequent floods or from wall and moat constructions, and this could have been the case for Auxonne.

Treatment by the regimental doctor, Bienvelot, cured Bonaparte of his spells of fever, but his general condition seemed considerably weakened for a longer time. On July 1789, almost a year after contracting the illness, he complained in a letter to his mother:

> I have no other distraction here than work. I get nicely
> dressed up only once per week. Since my illness I
> have been getting very little sleep.

No information has been handed down about the kind of treatment Dr. Bienvelot used, but, presumably, if malaria was suspected he used quinine bark, which was available by that time. Quinine bark, known by the Indian tribes of the South American Andes as an effective means for reducing fever since primeval times, was first brought to Spain in powder form at the beginning of the seventeenth century, by the Jesuit priest Barnabé de Cobo. Soon afterwards introduced into Rome, this medicine was administered free of charge for the care of "poor" patients. At first sharply rejected by Italian doctors, the use of quinine bark was strongly advocated toward the mid-seventeenth century by the famous Dr. Sydenham in England and Dr. de Barbeyrac of the University of Montpellier in France. During the construction work at the palace of Versailles, which was built in a swampy region and caused countless patients, these "everyday fever attacks" were successfully treated with quinine bark. Robert Talbot, an English apothecary, carried on a booming trade with his secret formula consisting of quinine bark. In 1679, after having cured Charles II of England and the Grand Dauphin of France of malaria, he sold the secret to the Sun-King Louis XIV for an enormous sum of money. The king then provided for the rapid distribution of this valuable medication. Presumably, in France, quinine bark was well known for treating malaria specifically, so that young Bonaparte must have benefited from this therapy.

It is impossible to know for certain whether this really was the case or how long Dr. Bienvelot continued his treatment. Probably the medicine was stopped too early, since young Napoleon evidently fell sick again with spells of fever between September 1789 and February 1791, probably a relapse into malaria which had not been completely cured. Later we no longer hear about this sickness, so a final cure can be assumed.

During the siege of Toulon at the end of 1793, Napoleon's long struggle against an annoying skin disease began. It caused unbearable itching, and various doctors have engaged in long discussions about the real nature of this ailment. He himself apparently believed this skin itch was caused by a kind of scabies, and he described how he had caught it as follows:

> During this siege I was afflicted by a terrible disease: scabies! I was in a battery with two cannons. One of the English sloops drew near shore, fired, and killed two artillery men at my side. So I grabbed a ramrod that had fallen from the hand of one of the dead men. The man had been ill, as it turned out, and a few days later I was afflicted with a kind of scabies. I used baths and was healed. Since however I took very bad care of myself, I got it again five years later in Italy and again in Egypt. When I returned from there, Corvisart [Professor of Medicine at the Charité in Paris and later Napoleon's personal physician] cured it completely by putting two blister-poultices on my chest, which induced a wholesome crisis. That is why I am always very yellow and thin. Since then, however, I have been feeling better and I have acquired a healthier appearance.

This description is surely not accurate from a medical perspective in several respects. Scabies is caused by the scabies mite and can be communicated to a healthy person only by intimate association with a scabies patient or by the use of items of laundry or clothing that have been worn by a scabious person and infested with the scabies mite. A fleeting contact with a scabious patient, such as during a medical examination, or by touching a wooden or metal object used by a scabious patient, such as the dead soldier mentioned by Napoleon, can by no means lead to an infection. Rather, the infection with scabies mites must have been caught in the sleeping shelters prevalent in the bad hygienic conditions of war, in which unlaundered bedclothes are often re-used. Bonaparte himself pointed out that this disgusting disease recurred in him later several times due to deficient hygienic care.

Doubt of the scabies diagnosis is suggested by the alleged cure Jean Nicolas Corvisart obtained by applying a blister-drawing plaster on the patient's chest, because, of course, scabies cannot be affected at all by that procedure. This merely shows that at that time scabies was not yet known to be caused by a parasite from the outside, but was blamed on a disturbance of body fluids. In light of this, it is understandable that Bonaparte, despite the alleged cure of his ailment by Corvisart, continued to be tormented by an unbearable itch until the beginning of his Consulship in 1799. As Angelo Bellini pointed out as early as 1900, this can only mean that "his doctors regarded the alleged scabies as a humorally caused disease and treated it as such." As an excuse for this therapeutic procedure, senseless as it seems to us today, it must be admitted that—as Augustin Cabanès rightly remarked in 1932—scabies "at that time was still looked upon as a dangerous disease. Even the cure, it was believed, could bring fatal consequences in its aftermath because the disease had a tendency to spread to the inner organs when driven away from the skin." Indeed, the skin rashes caused by scabies were even believed possibly to be beneficial because they allowed harmful substances in the blood—which supposedly caused various internal diseases—to leave the body. So it was not unusual for people to infect themselves with scabies intentionally in order to cure an existing, more dangerous sickness. From this perspective, one can understand why Napoleon during the Egyptian campaign covered himself with articles of clothing that had been worn by scabies patients, hoping thereby to get rid of his stomach pains, which appeared for the first time.

A further argument that casts doubt on or even refutes the statement that Napoleon had suffered from a long-lasting scabies ailment is the circumstance that his wife Josephine demonstrably never had scabies, although she had intimate relations with Bonaparte during the four months between his first visit in her home and their wedding in March 1796. Moreover, neither Josephine's two children, Eugène and Hortense de Beauharnais, nor any other member of the imperial family ever had scabies. Dr. Desclaux, therefore, in 1932, definitely denied the truth of this legend with the words: "It became classical to assume that Napoleon suffered from scabies during a part of his life." Others, such as Boris Sokoloff, continued to hold the scabies thesis.

How confusing medical opinions on this topic still were at the beginning of our century is shown by the imaginative comment of Wayne Whipple, in his book *The Story-Life of Napoleon*:

> All his life Napoleon was tormented by a substance in his blood that produced a strong itching. In boyhood age it was a kind of nettle-rash that made him irritable, nervous, wild and uncontrollable. As an adult the ailment expressed itself in a skin rash that his enemies called scabies. When the substance in the blood causing the skin rash did not penetrate to the surface of the skin, then it burned like a strange fire inside him and caused insatiable passions such as are

unknown to the normal person. This inner "hell-fire" irritated and embittered him in the most violent crises of his career. In the heat of a great battle his blood became overheated to such an extent that instead of supervising the conflict he was found under a blanket undressed down to the skin, lying on straw or on the bare floor, surrounded by his aides who scratched his quivering body until blood appeared, while he ordered them to comb him like a donkey.

This description points out for the first time the circumstance that his skin-itch became especially severe when he was under extraordinary mental stress. So during the nerve-racking moments of the "coup of Brumaire" [in November 1799, making him First Consul—TRANS.], he had such a severe skin itch that he scratched the pimples that sprouted on his face until they bled. During periods of extreme worry, he used to scratch open the skin of a declivity in the upper thigh (a scar left by a bayonet-wound suffered in the battle of Toulon), until the blood flowed. Only then did he feel mentally and physically relieved, and he thought this did him more good than any doctor's medicine. His own description shows how even he was not spared from the consequences of the humoral theory that accorded with the spirit of those times. That theory generally recommended copious bleedings to remove patho-genic substances from the blood. Dr. Antommarchi himself reported, in 1819 on St. Helena, that in time of particular mental strain the Em-peror scratched his eczema bloody and told him his opinion that "he would be healed only if he sweated or if the scar on his thigh opened."

James Kemble in 1959 was the first to interpret the itching skin ailment (from which Napoleon suffered all his life, except for a few rather long, complaint-free intervals), as neurodermatitis, that is, *der-matitis herpetiformis,* described in 1884 by Duhring, in which, as experience shows, strong psychogenic components play a great role as triggering factors. In this disease the itching tends to reappear again and again at varying intervals, either as a consequence of a previous irritation or without any clearly distinguishable cause. The disease generally begins between the ages of twenty and twenty-five, which would correspond with its first appearance during the siege of Toulon in 1789, in which, incidentally, the stress factors that trigger this ail-ment can be assumed as given. Since the course of neurodermatitis is chronic, Napoleon was never again free of crises of violent itching after the incident in Toulon and also in the following years. These crises were repeated at irregular intervals, depending on strong mental stress, until the time of his exile on St. Helena.

An additional factor must, with great probability, have been a lack of (or at least inadequate functioning of) his sweat glands in the skin, a so-called *anhidrosis,* which can become excruciating above all in a hot climate and which is well known in horses by veterinarians. This *anhidrosis* must be an essential reason why Napoleon all his life regularly took frequent, long-lasting baths and tried to explain them with a strange statement, when he said: "I live only with the assistance of my skin." Dr. Yvan, who accompanied him on his military campaigns and who knew the problems of his patient from close hand, wrote in one of his reports:

> As soon as his pores closed, whether through emotions or from atmospheric causes, more or less distinct signs of irritability appeared along with coughing or *ischuria* [retention of urine in the bladder]. All these manifestations vanished, as soon as the functioning of the skin was restored.

During the Italian campaign, Bonaparte fell ill several times with a feverish infection of his air passages, together with headaches and coughing. So he wrote on October 17, 1796, from Modena: "The day before yesterday I spent all day in the field. Fever and a violent headache prevented me from writing." Similar news can be gathered from his later letters too. On February 16, 1797, he mentioned incidentally in a letter to Josephine: "My health is somewhat weak, I still have a cold."

These cold symptoms probably were caused by a viral infection of the upper air passages, but in the year 1799 the clinical picture changed in the direction of a more serious illness. For, in addition to violent coughing, he complained about pains in his chest, aggravated by coughing or deep breathing. The First Consul Bonaparte therefore sought out a doctor he trusted, Professor Corvisart, who cured him of these complaints, though no record has been left of the kind of medications used. The later autopsy report revealed a degenerative adhesion of the two pleural layers after an infection of the pleura, but there is hardly any doubt as to the nature of this sickness. We can even accept as certain that this pleuritis in the year 1799 was of tubercular etiology, for along with the described pleural adhesions, the autopsy also found an older tubercular process in the left upper auricle of the lung, in the form of tubercles, and a few cavernous lesions, that is, hollow formations. This tubercular process must have been active in the year 1803, since he coughed up blood at that time, a symptom Corvisart associated with a blockage in the lungs. Since the appearance of a lung blockage could not come into consideration in the young, healthy-hearted First Consul, and, on the other hand, tubercular sites were proven in the left upper lung auricle, the coughed-up blood can probably have come only from such a hollow. The tuberculosis of the lungs must subsequently have taken an especially benign course, since Napoleon, despite many stressful periods during his military campaigns, never again complained about ailments in this regard.

The assumption of an active tuberculosis of the lungs occurring between 1799 and 1803 is by no means speculative. For we know that at the turn of the century, more than 90 percent of all adolescents went through a tubercular illness before reaching eighteen years of age, which the doctors of that time generally interpreted as a nonspecific infection of the upper air passages. In Napoleon's case, too, one must start with the assumption that he had undergone a primary tubercular infection in his youth, all the more so, since, based on the description of a "spindle-thin" youth, he had the right build for it. If in Napoleon's case, a renewed outbreak of tuberculosis occurred at an adult age, then it was a matter—as almost always is the rule—not of a new infection, but of the reactivation of an older infection under a reduced defensive situation of his body.

Napoleon first complained of stomach pains during the Egyptian campaign, and Paul Hillemand, in his extensive presentation in 1970 titled *Pathologie de Napoléon,* attributed them to a stomach ulcer, documented as often occurring in his family. What can be taken as a proof of this assumption is the fact that Napoleon certainly complained again and again, since 1802, of stomach pains that could be relieved by eating. So, next to his bed, he always kept tidbits to nibble on to alleviate pains when they occurred at night. Hillemand even considered the possibility, as early as 1802, of a perforation of an ulcer in the area of the lesser curvature of the stomach. It seems to me certainly not permissible to conclude, from Napoleon's typical hand position, that even then, as First Consul, he had tried to mitigate his pains by pressing his hand against the painful stomach region. Hillemand is speaking of the left hand, whereas, in the majority of his portraits, the right hand is portrayed in this pose and, in view of the way men's clothing was fitted with buttons, this surely must have corresponded to reality.

It was also discussed whether as early as 1802 the "calloused ulcer" could have led to a connective-tissue narrowing of the distal opening of the stomach, that is, to a stenosis above the pylorus, as was found in the later autopsy. To corroborate such an assumption, it is stated that Napoleon himself reported that he never took large meals and that he had his "attraction" for drink firmly under control, since he knew that his stomach promptly would reject any excess beverage. However disciplined he was in this regard, he was all the more unreasonable about the speed of his meals. Not only did he consume his food at a very hot temperature, but he also swallowed it too quickly, without first chewing it sufficiently. For this reason, Corvisart, in the year 1808, on the occasion of a complaint from Napoleon about the violent stomach pains, told him that they were caused by his bad eating habits. Certainly his stomach ailments were not always caused by an ulcer, as we can gather from a report of the field surgeon Dr. Yvan, who accompanied him on all campaigns, to General de Ségur:

> The Emperor's constitution can be designated as highly nervous. He reacted with extreme sensitivity to emotional events, with spasms that affected either the stomach or the urinary bladder.

Napoleon's complaints about the urinary bladder involved his difficulty at times in getting the flow of urine started. He was often found leaning on a tree or with his forehead pressed against a wall or a cannon and it could take minutes before the first flow of urine came. Napoleon himself once said: "My bladder is my weak point. I will perish from it someday." Although later, the autopsy found very fine stones in the bladder, so-called "gravel," these must not have been responsible for the above-described disturbances. An indication of this is that he hardly ever complained of pains in connection with his difficulties in passing water. This difficulty in urinating, appeared predominantly during times of severe mental stress and was therefore a nervous condition, so that Frank Richardson, in his extensive monograph, rightly considered it to be a manifestation of what Alfred Adler once called "organ-inferiority."

An interesting variant to explain the urinary problem was presented by Professor Wardner Ayer in 1966 in the United States. Together with other symptoms, it could be traced back to a schistosomiasis, possibly contracted by Napoleon during the Egyptian campaign. This disease, also known as Bilharzia, originates from infection by the *Schistosoma haematobium* which occurs in Egypt and *Schistosoma mansoni* which spend a part of their life cycle in fresh water snails. The released larvae, called *cercariae,* readily bore into the skin of humans who wade or bathe in such water and they pass through the blood stream into the liver and the bladder. The embryos, called *miracidia,* can then get back into the water with the urine or the excrement of the host, where they again infect snails and start a new cycle. In Napoleon's time, many soldiers of his army contracted this disease, which they called "Egyptian bloody urine." The incubation period of schistosomiasis until the appearance of definite symptoms can last up to two years; if Napoleon was infected, the first appearance of urinary passage complaints during the battle of Marengo in the year 1800 would fall exactly within this period.

The complaints were then especially bad during the battle near Borodino in the year 1812. Professor Ayer, who is employed at New York University, also considers it possible that Napoleon's skin rashes and his dry cough could have been caused by *cercariae,* since experience shows that these symptoms are often found in schistosomiasis. Although no cogent proofs can be presented for this interesting theory, it at least sounds more serious than the fairy tale disseminated by the Prussian Commissioner, Count Truchsess von Waldburg, that Napoleon had suffered from a venereal disease. This witness, who was extremely hostile to Napoleon, reported that in his presence Napoleon had taken medication for the aftereffects of a venereal disease—apparently because he was again having difficulty urinating.

In 1803 or so, a noticeable change in Napoleon's appearance and behavior took place. Formerly he had been thin, with deep-set eyes, sunken cheeks and olive-brown skin color; so now a strikingly white skin and rosy facial color were bound to be noticed by people around him, which the Countess Abrantès summed up with the words: "Everything that was bony, yellow, indeed sickly, has become round, bright and beautiful." He himself repeatedly stated: "I have always said that at the age of forty I would become very fat, and you see, gentlemen, I was right." In fact, he gradually became extremely fat, with a round unwrinkled face and thick round upper thighs, which made him look shorter than he really was. For some time his friends had begun noticing his increasingly feminine appearance with his delicate little hands and feet, his general roundness and his "full, rounded breasts, such as are not common in the male sex." As we learn from his secretary de Méneval, he himself often joked about his full breasts and on St. Helena he once said to his doctor Antommarchi, walking into the room naked from an alcohol rub-down:

> See, Doctor, see what lovely arms! What a smooth, white skin, without a single hair. What rounded breasts. Any female beauty would be proud of a bosom like mine.

This increasingly feminine appearance, called *gynandromorphism*, with the full breasts, called *gynandromastia*, the pubic hair similar to a woman's *mons veneris*, the testicles and penis described as small, the gynecoid distribution of fat, with narrow shoulders and broad, projecting hips, were already described by Hillemand as the "neuroendocrine syndrome of last century" in his life of Napoleon, the beginning of which he established to be in the year 1811. This strange syndrome was associated with mental changes that seemed peculiar to his entourage: loss of liveliness of movements, slowness of speech, and decline of energy—symptoms which had never occurred before and which astonished everyone around him. Although there still were hours of extremely industrious activity, on the whole he tended to speak rather than act. His decisiveness vanished noticeably and his self-confidence also seemed to decline visibly. On occasion, he showed signs of tiredness and he even fell asleep over a book—this was the same Napoleon who used to get by with six hours of sleep at most! This lethargy, and above all, his attacks of real somnolence, which can be understood as the so-called "Pickwick Syndrome," sometimes led to astonishing situations, such as in later years would occur even on the battlefield. A first occurrence of this sort was during the battle of Jena in the year 1806, where General de Ségur reported that the French grenadiers had to "form a protective square around the sleeping Emperor." And after the battle of Leipzig, even the ear-deafening noise from the demolition of a bridge across the Elbe failed to awaken him, so that he could not supervise the retreat of his defeated troops.

Dr. Groen understood this syndrome of obesity, reduced activity, loquacity, and somnolence simply as male menopause (*climacterium virile*), while Dr. Leonard Guthrie assumed the existence of a so-called Fröhlich syndrome, which could also involve the observed personality changes—this somewhat blurry term was replaced by Richardson with the more exact term "pituitary eunuchoidism." Today this is generally explained with changes of the *hypophysis*, that is, the pituitary gland, or respectively the midbrain (*diencephalon*), whereby one speaks of an exhausted, "burned out," glandular activity. Since the midbrain and the pituitary gland control all other internal secretion glands, including the sexual glands, this would explain all the observed physical and mental changes that began in Napoleon since about 1805. In 1953, W. R. Bett, with his "hypothalamic interpretation of history," pointed out that some important figures of world history display a medical history that suggests hypothalamic involvement as the explanation of their symptoms or peculiar behavior. For we know that the hypothalamus, located close to the pituitary gland, functions as the coordinating center of the autonomic nervous system—beginning with the regulation of body temperature, of sleep, all the way to the complicated emotional defense mechanisms. Among the best known disturbances caused by pathological changes of the hypothalamus area are, among others, the Fröhlich syndrome and *narcolepsia*, a somnolence that comes on like a seizure. A historical example of a classical hypothalamic symptom which Bett cites is the *hypersomnia* of Alexander the Great, who according to Plutarch's narrative could sleep from after supper to the next noon, indeed sometimes even the whole next day. Alexander's uncontrollable fits of rage near the end of his life are also classified by Bett among hypothalamic symptoms. Another classical example for the foregrounding of hypothalamic symptoms late in life cited by Bett is Napoleon, with the remarkable changes in his physical constitution, obesity, the spells of somnolence and the signs of a pituitary eunuchoidism, as described above.

From today's perspective the existence of a Fröhlich syndrome, which is extremely rare and not clinically defined with sufficient exactness, can most probably be excluded in Napoleon's case. A more accurate term would be a neuroendocrine syndrome, which is a matter of a hypogonadism triggered by the midbrain, whereby the genitals tend to atrophy but without loss of functioning. Accordingly, Sterpellone's suspicion that a gonadal insufficiency also impaired Napoleon's sexual life, must be relegated to the realm of pure speculation. The clinical picture that Sterpellone tried to construct of the lover and husband Napoleon also does not fit Napoleon's admissions in his correspondence about Josephine Beauharnais and his preference for everything that had his manliness and potency as content. Napoleon's sexual life apparently must have been quite normal, if not rather intensified above the norm, especially under the impact of strong stress. It was even claimed that he sometimes masturbated before a battle to at least be freed of a part of the tremendous tension and excitation. But the passionate sexual relation to Josephine also suggests this. It was almost a strange spectacle that the victorious commander and liberator of Italy, during all the military events and battles of his Italian campaign in 1796, was more and more consumed by a deep longing for his unfaithful Josephine. So on July 21, plagued with jealousy, he wrote:

> Now you will probably know Milan very well. Perhaps you found the lover you were looking for....But no, we want to have a better opinion of one another. Farewell, beautiful, good, incomparable, divine woman! A thousand ardent kisses everywhere, everywhere!

This consuming love of Bonaparte's was not returned from the first. The indifference of her feelings became known to him immediately after their wedding, since he had to discover in the very first wedding night that the marriage bed was stubbornly defended by Josephine's poodle. He described this later in these words:

> He is my rival. He was from the first the real master of Josephine's bed. I tried to drive him out but it was useless. I became friendly, but was definitely made to face the choice between sleeping elsewhere or accepting his partnership.

But the more he became aware of her indifference and emotional coldness, the more he seemed to be drawn to her sexually. The more distanced she acted and the more evidence he gathered of her marital infidelity, the more passionately he longed for her sexual charms and as can be read in one of his letters:

> Great god, how happy I would be if I could watch you again at your lovely toilette, be permitted to kiss your shoulders, your small supple bosom....A thousand kisses on your mouth, eyes, shoulders, bosom—and especially on your little black forest.

That is not how a man writes when his gonadal function is beginning to be extinguished.

If Napoleon was temporarily inclined to consent to the plan of a faked childbirth by Josephine—a plan that failed due to Professor Corvisart's determined opposition—it was certainly not from any thought of being sterile himself, but exclusively for the intention of saving his marriage by a pretended heir to the throne. Moreover, he proved his fertility later, in the marriage with Marie-Louise of Austria as well as in the intimate relation with the Polish Countess Marie Walewska, each of whom gave him a son. As early as 1806, Éléanore Denuelle de la Pleigne, a lady companion of his sister Caroline, had borne him a son, Léon.

That his sexual activity in the last decade of his life, during the incarceration on St. Helena, decreased and finally ceased completely, as he stated to one of his faithful followers, General Gaspard Gourgaud, is more than understandable in view of the desolate mental situation on that island. So it must not have been difficult for him to do without women during his exile, and actually no contacts with the female sex of any kind took place there, for otherwise even the most insignificant amorous episode would not have gone unnoticed.

Apart from a bad infection of the larynx during the Russian campaign in 1812, which prevented him from speaking for days and forced him to give his commands only in writing, these urinary difficulties and stomach pains were the main health problems that troubled him again and again, according to the doctors Mestivier and Yvan. Particularly intense stomach pains beset him in the night of October 17, 1813, during the battle of Leipzig, as his Grand Marshal Count Caulaincourt reports.

Finally, from 1796 on he was accompanied by a stubborn hemorrhoidal ailment such as often occurred in his family and at times made riding impossible. In the battle of Waterloo an unusually painful inflammation and thrombosis of the external hemorrhoids made him almost unable to walk and—in combination with excessive dosages of opium administered to him to kill the unbearable pains—possibly so hampered his power of decision as to contribute no little to the defeat.

Finally, a brief remark should be made about Napoleon's attitude toward suicide. Even at a young age he occupied himself theoretically with thoughts of suicide; and later, too, although he was always proud of his iron nerves, hours of deep depression could awaken the desire in him to put a violent end to his life. In general, however, he sharply condemned suicide. Even after losing the battle of Waterloo, he strongly rejected the idea of suicide, despite the possibility of falling prisoner. To his cabinet secretary Fleury de Chaboulon he said:

Napoleon in his house coat on St. Helena, dictating his memoirs to General Gourgaud (painting)

One should leave suicide to weak characters and sick minds. Whatever fate awaits me, I will never shorten my life even for one moment with my own hand.

And even in exile on St. Helena he exclaimed:

Suicide is the act of a gambler who has lost everything or of a man favored by fortune who is ruined. My principle was always that a man shows more courage by bearing his misfortune than if he takes his own life.

And yet this man, who expressed himself thus about suicide, acted otherwise at the moment when blow after blow was dealt him by fate. In April 1814, when he had to renounce his throne, he could not resist the temptation to lay hand on himself and make a suicide attempt, which failed, however, as described above at some length. In this suicide attempt, the idea was probably to display his deep abasement before the eyes of his army, which had been accustomed to victory, by a heroic act of self-sacrifice. Immediately after taking the poison, he said words suggesting the likelihood of this motivation to Caulaincourt, who, when notified by the valet, hastened to Napoleon's bedside right away. Napoleon told him he had an aversion to every mode of death that left bloodstains on the body or mutilated the face. If he was to be displayed in an open coffin after his death, his loyal guards should recognize on his face the calm they had so often seen amid the storms of battle.

Napoleon's Cause of Death

At the end of the 1930s, a heated discussion broke out concerning Napoleon's last illness. Whereas until then the version that he had died of a stomach cancer had been accepted as satisfactory—indeed many of the newest treatises still uncritically accept this opinion—since that time experts in tropical medicine, pathologists, and clinicians have expressed doubts about this diagnosis. First, after 1949 when Fleuriot de Langle published General Bertrand's diary with its meticulous description of the last months of Napoleon's life, it became irrefutably clear that the illness on St. Helena had two clearly distinguishable stages, as described above, which could not be identical.

The first phase of illness began on October 1, 1817, and lasted until November 1819, with spells interrupted by bearable but not fully complaint-free intervals, and was characterized by the following symptoms: in October 1816 attacks of fever lasting for several weeks were accompanied by pains in the upper abdomen and occasionally by slimy diarrhea; then on October 1, 1817, new pains appeared in the right upper abdomen which this time were more severe, radiating out to the right shoulder and intensified by taking a deep breath. At the same time fever set in; it used to decline again toward morning with strong outbreaks of sweat. Gradually, this fever led to a considerable weakening of the patient's general condition. Because of these two symptoms, namely the slightly yellowish discoloration of the sclera of the eyes and the palpable, pressure-sensitive enlarged liver, Dr. O'Meara diagnosed a liver infection which he called "*hepatitis tropica*" in view of the preceding diarrheic, slimy excrements—a diagnosis that was fully endorsed by Dr. Stokoe after Dr. O'Meara's dismissal. In his 1892 commentary, Baron Hippolyte Larrey, the son of the most important field surgeon in Napoleon's army, also interpreted the medical history on St. Helena as a chronic hepatitis, such as was endemic on that island. Finally in 1913 the Irish doctor J. Knott expressed a similar opinion when he accepted as a given fact that Napoleon's illness was a long-lasting hepatitis, which he labeled "St. Helena sickness." Sir Arthur Keith concurred with this diagnosis, based on the microscopic examination of tissue samples taken by Dr. Antommarchi during the autopsy and preserved in his institute. Together with Sir William Leishman, an outstanding specialist for tropical medicine, the two doctors in 1913 suspected that the disease could have been *brucellosis*—an infectious disease that can be communicated to humans from sheep or goats. The autopsy finding of a normal-sized spleen, however, speaks strongly against this assumption. Indeed, this diagnosis is dubious, in view of the severe decline of health caused by spells of fever lasting for weeks, since brucellosis hardly affects the general health.

The highest degree of probability goes to the suspicion that the disease in question was an amebic infection, which we know is found endemically on that island. Dr. Guy Godlewski, during an on-site inspection on St. Helena, examined in the Jamestown archives the lists of all the soldiers who had died on the island during their military service, and he discovered that the mortality rate always went up when their military unit was stationed for six months on the high plateau of Longwood where Napoleon was housed. Godlewski's inquiries showed that both Napoleon's residence and the military camp drew their water from a brook that was channeled along a street in a conduit made of bricks and from which the soldiers, the predominantly Chinese workers, and all Napoleon's house personnel drew their drinking water. Contamination of this water seems absolutely conceivable as the source of infection.

During his on-site inspection, Godlewski established that amebic dysentery must have been previously unknown on St. Helena and was first brought to that island in 1816—that is, the first year Napoleon was incarcerated there—probably by imported Chinese laborers and servants. Just a short time later, about a hundred persons on a ship full of prisoners, docked at Jamestown to load up on water, fell ill. At about the same time, almost the whole crowd of Napoleon's retinue was seized by an amebic dysentery, which even cost the *major domo* Cipriani his life. It therefore seems more than probable that Napoleon, too, was not spared by this disease.

Since the *Entamoeba histolytica* was first identified in 1913 as the cause of an endemic dysentery involving the liver, Dr. J. Knott, as well as Sir Arthur Keith, or respectively Dr. William Leishman, could not yet refer to it in their statements. So it is explainable that not until 1931 did the Belgian physician, Dr. de Mets, a remote relative of Dr. Antommarchi, call for a clear determination of the case and the simultaneous rehabilitation of Dr. Antommarchi. These efforts were supported mainly by Dr. Abbatucci, who later became Physician General of the French colonial army and accumulated copious experiences in the field of tropical diseases. In a publication on August 3, 1933, he agreed fully with the version presented by Dr. Pullé (in October 1932 before the Medical Society in Rome), which stated that Napoleon did not die from a stomach cancer, but from an amebic abscess of the liver that had bored through the stomach wall. This was how Abbatucci interpreted Dr. Antommarchi's description given in a manuscript written in 1822, a year after Napoleon's death and authenticated in London by Professor Vittorio Putti of Bologna, in which he spoke of a major enlargement of the liver with tissue lesions at the dissected surface.

As can be seen from a letter located in the archives of the Princess Pauline Borghese, written by Dr. Antommarchi on March 17, 1821, to a friend, he, too, drew a causal link between the hepatic lesions and the unfavorable conditions on the tropical island of St. Helena:

> Since July 1820...His Majesty's state of health has grown worse from day to day, to such an extent that six months ago it reached the bile-ducts, so that the liver functions are fully disturbed....To fulfill my responsibility, I hereby declare openly to the Imperial family and to all Europe that the development of His Majesty's health and the accompanying symptoms must be rated as very serious and that they were caused directly by the climate here. Nothing can be undertaken against the effects of this climate and if the English government does not hurry to take him out of this destructive atmosphere, the Emperor will soon leave this mortal body.

Dr. Abbatucci concurred with this interpretation, which had already been expressed by Dr. Stokoe in 1819, and he felt certain that Napoleon had died of a suppurated hepatitis resulting from an amebic infection. The abscess in the liver, which first caused a circumscribed peritoneal inflammation with wide adhesion to the stomach, opened up, in his opinion, into the stomach cavity, whereby at first a fatal peritoneal infection was impeded. The hepatic abscess, in Abbatucci's view, was not discovered in the autopsy because it was small and already mostly emptied, since approximately fifty days had passed between the rupture and the death. In addition, the defect was largely concealed by reparative processes. Besides, Abbatucci was not certain whether an adequate search had been made for such an abscess. That it actually probably had not been, can be seen from a line in the report of the Governor's official representative, Sir Thomas Reade, who was present at the autopsy:

> At my urgent wish to be able to see the organ from close up, he [Dr. Antommarchi] took his knife and made a cut from one end of the liver to the other with the remark: "It is normal, perfectly healthy, and without any striking features."

According to this, only one single cut was made through the organ.

In his 1935 monograph, *The Riddle of Napoleon,* the high-ranking military doctor, Raoul Brice, named his colleague Abbatucci as the one who first gave a credible portrayal of Napoleon's "liver disease"; and to support this thesis he pointed out that the amebic dysentery was endemically widespread on the island. From the present-day perspective, however, one cannot agree completely with Abbatucci's portrayal, insofar as he suspected the cause of Napoleon's death to have been the rupture of an amebic abscess of the liver into the stomach, as will be shown below. On the other hand, the version which held that Napoleon probably caught an amebic infection as early as 1816, which led to the formation of an amebiasis of the liver and dominated the clinical picture from 1817 to 1819, must have been right after all. This certainty gained ever sharper contours as our knowledge of this disease was deepened and broadened. To show how very much the description of the clinical symptoms in Napoleon from 1817 to 1819 actually coincides with those to be expected, according to the present state of medicine, concerning an amebic infection of the liver, the following material on the subject is abstracted and summarized from the most recent edition of the standard work on this subject: *Diseases of the Liver* edited by the world-famous American hepatologist, Professor Leon Schiff, in the section describing hepatic abscess and hepatic amebiasis by Michael E. DeBakey and George L. Jordan, Jr.:

> We know today that amebiasis is endemic in the United States and other nontropical countries. The most common site of amebiasis outside of the intestine is the liver, where it leads to dysenteric symptoms. The liver infection can manifest itself under the clinical picture of an amebic hepatitis, that is, without suppuration, or of a liver abscess. The clinical symptoms are extraordinarily varied. They can appear in the first weeks during an amebic dysentery, but sometimes also only years later. Moreover, in a high percentage of cases a dysenteric stage with diarrhea is completely absent.

> The clinical symptoms of hepatic amebiasis may be classified into generalized and local complaints. Generalized symptoms, in order of frequency, are fever, weight loss, weakness, chills and profuse sweating, nausea, general discomfort, and loss of appetite. The fever generally has the form of an intermittent fever, and almost regularly appears in an amebic hepatitis, that is, still without purulent complications, whereas in the later stages of abscess formation it is less pronounced. Chills and perspiration are encountered in both amebic hepatitis and in the amebic abscess of the liver. In the chronic form of the disease the development of conspicuous pallor is typical, while jaundice is rather seldom observed.

> Among the local symptoms of hepatic amebiasis, the earliest and most common are pain and tenderness in the right upper abdominal area. The pain is described variously and can be felt as dull, sharp, or stabbing. It can radiate toward the right armpit or to the right shoulder and may be intensified by deep breathing, which is a sign of involvement of the right lower pulmonary area. Such pain radiating toward the right shoulder is a strong sign of the presence of an amebic abscess in the

liver. Another typical symptom is a distinct enlargement of the liver, which is present in almost all cases
of amebiasis. Sometimes it is hard to demonstrate the
enlargement of the liver by palpation, due to the extreme tenderness and the reflex tension of the
abdominal muscles in the right upper quadrant.

Initially true amebic abscesses are bacteriologically
sterile.

Among the complications, a secondary infection of the
amebic abscess with pyogenic [pus-producing] organ-
isms is most common. When that occurs, the clinical
manifestations become more severe and septic temperatures with high jagged peaks of fever result. The
second most frequent complication is the pleuro-
pulmonary involvement under rupture or direct
extension of the abscess in the liver, whether by rupture of the abscess through the diaphragm into the lung,
or by spreading via the lymphatics that pass through
the diaphragm. Most liver abscesses in amebiasis are
located just under the surface of the right lobe of the
liver, and the adjacent diaphragm is invaded readily.
With rapid spreading of the abscess an inflammatory
reaction of the pleura, located just above it, soon results, producing obliterative adhesions in this area, so
that the abscess readily ruptures into the pleural cavity
but not into the lung. Finally, the third of the complications is the rupture of the hepatic abscess into the
abdominal cavity, an event observed in less than one-
tenth of such patients today because effective treatment
is available. If the abscess develops slowly, peritoneal
adhesions form along the inferior surface of the liver.
This can localize the process and prevent the extru-
sion of pus into the abdominal cavity. Rupture of the
abscess into the stomach or intestine is extremely rare.

This precise description of the typical symptoms of a liver attack
in the framework of an amebic infection agrees astoundingly with the
clinical picture given to us by the doctors treating Napoleon: O'Meara,
Stokoe, and Antommarchi. At the present state of our medical knowledge, we must therefore assume, with probability approaching certainty,

that in the described phase of disease from 1816 to 1819 it was a matter of the consequences of an amebic infection which led to the formation of one or several abscesses in the liver. These must, as is so typical for this sickness, have been located close to the surface of the right liver lobe and either by way of a lymphogenic spreading or as a consequence of a rupture through the right peritoneum have lead to an infectious reaction of the pleura above it, with final broad degenerative adhesion at that spot.

The apparently missing link in the chain of proof for the description just presented is the circumstance that Dr. Antommarchi, at the autopsy, could not detect any liver abscess. Professor Schiff expressly stressed that there are no specific anatomical changes in the liver in amebiasis and that this diagnosis therefore cannot be guaranteed by the proof of abscessed liver. Moreover, it must be admitted that Dr. Antommarchi, during the autopsy, as can be seen from the existing documents, made only one cut through the whole organ and that it did not reveal any peculiarities. We do not know whether, in view of knowledge that did not yet exist about this clinical picture, he considered it unnecessary to make several cuts or whether he was intimidated from investigating the liver further for abscesses, by the presence of ten British observers who followed his activity with hostility.

In any case, it is clear that under such circumstances one or several abscesses lying scattered in the liver, if they were present, had to escape the scrutiny of the autopsist. A lack of typical lesions at the only dissected surface cannot therefore cogently be presented as a counterargument against the diagnosis of an amebiasis of the liver any more than can the report of a prior period of diarrheic, slimy stool, but not of certain clinical signs of an amebic dysentery. Since it is certain today that the majority of patients with amebiasis show no intestinal symptoms and the full clinical picture of an amebic dysentery in an amebic abscess of the liver is rather the exception, this question has become irrelevant.

From a current medical perspective, the question must certainly be answered in the affirmative that Napoleon became ill of an amebiasis of the liver, with spreading of the abscess processes through the right diaphragm to the pleura, where it left extensive degenerative adhesions. Still, Abbatucci's and Brice's thesis that a liver abscess led to Napoleon's death as a consequence of a rupture into the stomach and an acute peritoneal inflammation caused thereby remains improbable. Apart from the fact that such an event is unusually rare in this sickness, the second stage of Napoleon's sickness on St. Helena, starting in October 1820, shows a completely different behavior that is medically clearly definable.

On October 4, 1820, violent stomach pains suddenly started, accompanied by vomiting and gradually leading to the complete cessation of all bodily activities. The pains had a stabbing character, appeared more strongly at night, and were typically mitigated by food intake and by local applications of heat. The further course was not continuous, but typically a week-long painful crisis was followed by an almost complaint-free remission, in which he could stand all foods again without complaint and livened up mentally.

As we can gather from a report of Bertrand's, his appetite held until the last days of his life and for the further appraisal of the nature of this disease it is important to emphasize that Napoleon in the last months of his life even often asked for particular delicacies and showed a special preference for various meat preparations. Accordingly, even at the advanced stage of this disease, there was absolutely no loss of body weight, as a few informative sketches from that time clearly show. An island-dweller who saw him in this last phase of life, described this meeting with the nasty words: "I saw Napoleon a few months before his death as fat and round as a Chinese pig."

If it is recalled that Napoleon, since his Egyptian campaign, complained again and again of stomach pains, which mostly began with mental stress and whose nightly occurrence he was able to alleviate by taking small quantities of food, then the diagnosis of a stomach ulcer is evident. The typical symptoms, no loss of appetite, no aversion to meat foods, and no loss of weight, which were confirmed for us by Clarke Abel, among others, who on a trip back from China visited Napoleon in Longwood during a brief stopover on St. Helena, are absolutely incompatible with the diagnosis of a cancer of the stomach. Dr. Héreau, doctor of Napoleon's mother and of his second wife Marie-Louise, was the first to express, as early as 1819, justified doubts of the diagnosis of a carcinoma of the stomach. Rather, he believed in a chronic gastritis made worse by the climatic inclemency of the island and the many personal humiliations during the last years of Napoleon's life. This unwholesome effect of living conditions on the prisoner's state of health was also pointed out by the young, intelligent Irish physician, Dr. O'Meara, in his letter to General Bertrand, which he sent after his transfer from the island:

Two years of inactivity, a murderous climate, the pitiful rooms with their unhealthy air, the shameful
treatment, the loneliness and solitude—all that can
destroy his spirit and worsen his state of health so that
one must fear the worst.

This acute worsening, the decisive turning point in Napoleon's
medical history announcing his approaching end, occurred on March 19,
1821: after violent pains and severe vomiting he was suddenly covered with cold sweat. He presented the signs of most extreme circulatory
weakness, which immediately led to unconsciousness as soon as he
even attempted to get up. Exhausting outbreaks of sweat, a variable
fever, severe pains in the area of the upper right quadrant with repeated
vomiting, as well as a mightily swollen body because of generally lamed
intestinal activity, and, finally, in the last days of life, ever more tormenting *singultus* (debilitating hiccups): for a modern-day doctor, all
these symptoms leave no doubt of the diagnosis of the perforation of a
stomach ulcer. The final coffee-dregs texture of the vomit and the
appearance of tarry stool, moreover, prove also that bleeding had occurred from a stomach ulcer such as is frequent even without a
perforation. Finally, the weeks-long vomiting, even of liquid and mushy
foods, points to the existence of a narrowing in the area of the distal
opening of the stomach (near the pylorus)—in such a case, one speaks
of an hour-glass stomach.

For a doctor today, these unmistakable facts speak a clear language.
But for doctors in those days, to whom the clinical picture of a stomach
ulcer was still unknown, it presented a riddle in many regards. Occasionally by the end of the eighteenth century, doctors did discover
"gastric ulcers," that is, ulcers in an inflamed stomach lining—for instance Matthew Baillie in the year 1799—but it was reserved for the
great French clinician Cruveilhier in 1830 to give a more precise description of the clinical picture of a stomach ulcer and to elaborate the
difference between the ulcerlike carcinomas and gastric ulcers, so that
even today the ulcer rightly gets its name from the lesser curvature of
the stomach. In this light, Dr. Antommarchi cannot be blamed for
diagnosing "cancerous ulcers" in the autopsy of Napoleon's corpse.

It was not till 1892 that Hippolyte Larrey expressed doubt of the
theory that Napoleon had died of stomach cancer. Others who similarly expressed themselves critically were Edward L. Andrews from
the United States in 1895, Baudouin in France in 1901, and de Mets in
Belgium in 1931, the latter basing himself mainly on the detailed

studies of the Napoleon case by Dr. Hartmann and Dr. Paoli. The real impetus for the final revision of the "cancer-myth" was first given, however, by Dr. Dale from Oklahoma who stated outright in 1952 that the "Emperor certainly did not die of a stomach cancer, as is generally assumed." He was also the one who finally opened a discussion of an *ulcus* perforation, that is, the rupture of a stomach ulcer; and he was supported energetically in 1957 by Dr. Guy Godlewski. The arguments presented in support of this thesis were so convincing that the American author Ralph Korngold felt justified to say in 1961: "Modern pathologists are as good as certain that Napoleon did not die of cancer."

That this stomach rupture, which was prepared by previous progressions of an obviously penetrating ulcer, reaching deep into the stomach wall up to the peritoneal layer, did not lead immediately to the outpouring of the stomach contents into the abdominal cavity and to a fatal diffused peritoneal infection, was due to the circumstance that a localized adhesion between the outer stomach wall inflamed at the perforation site and the abutting lower surface of the left lobe of the liver led to a spontaneous closure of the opening of the perforation canal. However, this process of a self-healing attempt did not, of course, go without symptoms, since a circumscribed peritoneal infection developed, which was responsible for the intestinal blockage and the resulting huge swelling of the intestinal loops as well as the tormenting hiccups.

When the autopsy report speaks of a "cancerous ulcer" and "cancerlike ulcers" on most of the inner surface of the stomach, that does not mean the existence of a real carcinoma in the modern sense. Since they did not know of *ulcus* ailments, the pathologists of those days—moreover working solely on macroscopic findings—could not differentiate a carcinoma. Therefore, chronic, "calloused" ulcers with their hardened and raised borders as in Napoleon's case were as a rule interpreted as cancerous ulcers. Something similar is true for the gastritis accompanying a stomach ulcer, in which sometimes thick lumpy mucous membrane folds—a so-called "giant-fold gastritis of the Ménetrier type"—were found, which gave Dr. Antommarchi the impression of cancerlike ulcers distributed over the entire inside surface of the stomach.

The autopsy findings, however, also provide us with direct signs that exclude with certainty the presence of a carcinoma perforating the stomach wall. Dr. Antommarchi set particular value on describing the perforation canal and its surroundings. According to him, the perforation site was round inside and the perforation canal, which bored through the stomach wall at an angle and narrowed to the outside like a funnel, was covered on the outside with a pale-gray and smooth wall. Such a macroscopic finding is unthinkable in a carcinoma or a degenerated carcinomatous stomach ulcer, as the Finnish doctor Tano Kalima and Dr. de Mets suspected at the beginning of the 1930s, just as the very place of perforation, namely, just above the pylorus, would represent a rarity for a carcinoma penetrating into the abdominal cavity. Above all, in the case of the presence of stomach cancer that already pervades the whole stomach wall, a smooth adhesion of the outside stomach wall with the lower surface of the liver is impossible and completely unthinkable, given the complete absence of metastatic lesions in the adjacent liver as well as in the regional lymph nodes, as this was distinctly noted in Dr. Antommarchi's macroscopic description as well as in the later microscopic examination of the autopsy tissue samples preserved in London.

Finally, the description used in the autopsy report of a "scirrhous hardening" just above the pylorus needs an explanation. For the term "scirrhous" then meant not the presence of a malignant process, but it was used for hardening of tissue with various etiologies. One must therefore not equate a scirrhous process of "almost the whole of the remainder of the internal surface of the stomach" mentioned in the autopsy finding with today's concept of a scirrhus of the stomach, a particularly malignant form of stomach cancer—apart from the fact that we know no combination of an ulcerous type of carcinoma with a scirrhus of the stomach.

Thus, consideration of the historical medical particularities even of Dr. Antommarchi's autopsy findings leaves no doubt today that Napoleon did not die of a stomach cancer. We should rather with certainty accept the fact that he suffered for many years from a stomach ulcer, for whose origin there was a marked predisposition based on his typical characteristics and which was aggravated by the interpersonal conflicts on St. Helena. In view of the long duration and frequent spells of his ulcerous ailment over the years, there developed a chronic, so-called "calloused" ulcer that was located just above the pylorus on the lesser curvature of the stomach. Its surroundings were characterized by a greatly altered hypertrophic texture of the stomach lining—which can reach the thickness of a finger. The scarred changes above the pylorus led to the formation of shrinkage similar to connective tissue, an "hour-glass stomach"; and this, in turn, caused the frequent vomiting by obstructing the emptying of the stomach due to excessive narrowing.

The ulcer finally penetrated the stomach as far as the left liver lobe, which sealed off the perforation in the stomach like a cork and prevented the immediate death of the patient. Death only weeks later was prepared by the effects of the local peritoneal infection on the one hand and the obstructions to the emptying of the stomach on the other; and it finally ensued from massive bleeding in the stomach with final total failure of the blood circulation.

For the sake of completeness, we should now deal with the theory that Napoleon's was a case of death by poisoning. Dr. D. Wallace from Australia, at the beginning of the 1860s, suspected merely an intoxication resulting from unintentional medical use of arsenic-containing medications. But the book published by the Swedish surgeon Dr. Sten Forshufvud under the title *Who Killed Napoleon?* brought the poisoning theory swiftly into the limelight. In this treatise, which represents a model of brilliant detective work, the author based his case on the significantly elevated concentrations of arsenic which Dr. Hamilton-Smith and Dr. Lenihan in Glasgow found in the hairs taken from Napoleon's head between the years 1816 and 1821.

Based on this surprising discovery Hamilton-Smith, as well as Forshufvud, believed that the symptoms of disease described during the exile years on St. Helena could be more credibly ascribed to arsenic poisoning than to the much-disputed stomach carcinoma. Those who held the poisoning theory were not lacking in suspects who could come in question as the perpetrators. A particular suspect in this connection was Count Montholon, one of Napoleon's closest companions on St. Helena. The role he was suspected of playing was as an agent in the service of the Bourbons.

Forshufvud even believes that Napoleon was already given small doses of arsenic as far back as the battle of Leipzig, in order to do away with him. Basically this idea would not be completely far-fetched, because after the great losses in that battle in 1813, surely many Frenchmen were no longer ready simply to accept the tremendous bloodshed in the service of the insatiable striving for power of a ruthless autocrat who seemed not to learn from his failures, and perhaps some got the idea of seeking the violent removal of Napoleon—much as did the conspirators from the German Officers Corps against Hitler in 1944. But assuming this, it would be hard to imagine why they waited until 1821 to send the completely powerless prisoner on St. Helena to his maker.

de nos Rois, est inspiré par la reconnaissance autant que par le devoir.

___

Paris , le 6 juillet.

BULLETIN DE LA COUR.

Saint-Cloud, le 6 juillet.
Le Roi a travaillé pendant la matinée avec son Exc. le marquis de Lauriston, ministre de sa maison, et successivement avec M. le duc de Richelieu, président du conseil des ministres.
S. A. S. Mme la duchesse de Bourbon est venue faire sa cour au Roi.
S. M., qui devait aller aujourd'hui à Versailles, a différé cette promenade ; ses équipages sont rentrés à trois heures aux écuries du château de Saint-Cloud.
S. A. R. MADAME, duchesse d'Angoulême , est sortie à deux heures, S. A. R. devait rentrer à cinq.

___

On a reçu par voie extraordinaire les journaux anglais du 4 du courant.
La mort de Buonaparte y est officiellement annoncée.
Voici dans quels termes le *Courier* donne cette nouvelle :
« Buonaparte n'est plus : il est mort le samedi 5 mai à six heures du soir, d'une maladie de langueur qui le retenait au lit depuis plus de quarante jours.
» Il a demandé qu'après sa mort son corps fût ouvert, afin de reconnaître si sa maladie n'était pas la même que celle qui avait terminé les jours de son père, c'est-à-dire un cancer dans l'estomac. L'ouverture du cadavre a prouvé qu'il ne s'était pas trompé dans ses conjectures. Il a conservé sa connaissance jusqu'au dernier jour, et il est mort sans douleur.
» Voici l'extrait d'une lettre que nous avons sous sous les yeux ; elle est datée de Saint-Hélène , le 7 mai :
» Buonaparte est mort samedi 5 , après une maladie de six semaines, qui n'avait pris un caractère sérieux que dans la dernière quinzaine. Le cancer qui lui rongeait l'estomac avait produit une large ulcération.
» Il a été exposé depuis hier au soir , après que l'amiral, le gouverneur et autres autorités eurent visité le corps.
» Quoique sa maladie ne se fût pas prononcée d'abord d'une manière alarmante , il sentait qu'il n'en pouvait revenir. Bientôt les médecins en furent eux-mêmes persuadés.
» On dit que cinq ou six heures avant de mourir , il a donné des instructions relativement à ses affaires et à ses papiers. Il a demandé à être ouvert, afin que son fils pût être informé de la nature de sa maladie. L'ouverture a été faite par son propre médecin.
» Nous croyons qu'il a laissé un testament, qui, avec tous ses autres papiers , sera envoyé en Angleterre.
« Les dépêches concernant cet événement ont été apportées par le capitaine Crokat, du 20e régiment. Elles ont été aussitôt communiquées à tous les ministres et aux ambassadeurs , qui ont sur-le-champ expédié des courriers à leurs cours respectives. »

___

Aux noms que nous avons déjà donnés, des personnes désignées par S. M. pour assister , avec M. le duc de Grammont, ambassadeur extraordinaire , au couronnement du roi d'Angleterre, on doit ajouter celui de M. le marquis de Perignon , pair de France.

Most representatives of the poisoning version therefore thought of environmental factors which could have led to arsenic poisoning. The most plausible theory for some seemed to be the idea that the "Paris green" curtains in Napoleon's bedroom probably contained arsenic and copper, which could have led to his repeatedly breathing arsenic-containing vapors volatilized by the moist, steamy atmosphere of his bedroom. But first of all, today the proof of arsenic in a person's hair is diagnostically no longer ascribed probative value because of the widespread occurrence of arsenic in nature. Secondly, the Institute for Nuclear Medicine in Toronto was able to prove by re-examination of a lock of Napoleon's hair that, contrary to earlier assertions, its arsenic content was only slightly above the norm. However, the antimony content, which experience shows was contained in numerous drug-mixtures of the eighteenth and early nineteenth centuries, was significantly heightened. Therefore, if any

"Le Moniteur universel" [The Universal Monitor] announces the Emperor's death on July 6, 1821

poisoning conceivably took place, it was the result of the methods of treatment customary at that time.

Forshufvud also held such an interpretation, namely, that Napoleon's doctors, from a modern perspective, could themselves have contributed to a poisoning by senseless, indeed almost criminal, therapeutic procedures. He pointed out that Dr. Arnott, who stood completely under the influence of the British Governor and was professionally very incompetent, shortly before Napoleon's death administered to him the unusually high dose of three grains of calomel, that is, triple the customary dosage, together with almond milk. In this way, Forshufvud believed, the poisonous mercury cyanide could have come from the mercury chloride, and that could have ultimately caused death.

All these criminalistic scenarios are perhaps not uninteresting; but they have meanwhile become obsolete, since today we are able diagnostically to explain Napoleon's diseases and, above all, the one that led to his death with a probability approaching certainty, based on available documents and with the help of current medical knowledge.

RETURN TO FRANCE

Whereas Bourbon France received the news of Napoleon's death without particular interest, in England it stirred waves of emotion. Lord Byron's poem to Napoleon, from the year 1822, as well as the first biography by Sir Walter Scott, which appeared in 1827, are eloquent examples of this. Not only the public, but official England, too, seemed to have felt touched under the impression of the words Napoleon finally said to his British physician, Dr. Arnott:

> I, who am now dying on this horrible rock-bound island...leave my death as a disgraceful spot on England's ruling dynasty.

When the all-too dutiful governor of this island, Sir Hudson Lowe, who contributed no little to Napoleon's final catastrophe by his unnecessary chicanery and humiliations, returned to England, he was received extremely coolly. Instead of being recognized by the government with praise, he was transferred to a subordinate post in Ceylon, from where he later returned to his homeland, old, bitter, and forgotten. Fate even saw to it that he should live to see the triumphal return of the mortal remains of his former prisoner on St. Helena to Paris and that he should have to note bitterly that "General Bonaparte," meanwhile, had again risen to be the "Emperor Napoleon."

Napoleon's return to Paris in December 1840 was celebrated with a thundering cannon salute over the city like the triumphal journey of the "Emperor Napoleon" returning victoriously after a great battle. Before the burial ceremonies, Dr. Guillard was permitted to open the coffin and examine the corpse for a few minutes. Dr. Arnold Chaplin, in his monograph *The Illness and Death of Napoleon Bonaparte*, published in 1913, described the brief report of this inspection. The excellent preservation of the corpse was surprising, and this was attributed to the tropical climate on St. Helena. According to Guillard's report:

> ...his beard seemed to have grown after his death. The cheeks were full and the skin of the face felt soft and supple. The Emperor's features were so little changed that his face was immediately recognized by those who had known him when alive, and on the whole he gave the impression of a person just recently buried.

This kind of mummification of a corpse is familiar to experienced forensic doctors, but for many people it was surely a further mysterious contribution to the legends surrounding this comet-like phenomenon. Unfortunately, the two silver containers which still contained Napoleon's heart and stomach in unchanged position were left inside the coffin when it was closed. So this last existing possibility for a precise and objective medical examination of the organ which was to blame for Napoleon's death was lost forever.

After the coffin was resealed and the gates of the Dome of the Invalides were opened wide, a herald proclaimed in a loud voice audible to the crowd: "The Emperor!" Then the King and his whole retinue watched the solemn state burial of their Emperor just as reverently and deeply moved as was the large pressing crowd.

Long ago, during his coronation as Emperor in the cathedral of Notre Dame, he had whispered to his brother Joseph: "If only our father could see us now!" That ceremony had been the glorious external zenith in his life; now his triumphal return from exile to Paris closed his unusual career with a zenith of another kind, amid the accolades of his French people. Many of those present commented with the words: "If only he could have lived to see this triumph himself!"

With similar satisfaction he would, however, also have experienced how nobly and effectively England in 1900 also rehabilitated him and fulfilled the prophecy proclaimed in his will: "I am dying prematurely, executed by the English oligarchy and its hired killers. The English

Transferring Napoleon's coffin in Cherbourg on December 10, 1840, from a large oceanic sailing ship to a river steamboat, during transport from St. Helena to France

people will not hesitate to avenge me for it." With the formal accusation of the English government of 1821, Napoleon's accusation before the tribunal of history was finally taken into account in 1900 by Prime Minister Lord Rosebery; Napoleon's prophecy that someday the English people would avenge him was fulfilled.

So, not only the French, but the English, too, apparently largely forgave Napoleon only a few decades after his death for having plunged millions of people into misfortune or driven them to their death for his selfish, ambitious plans. Like Hitler later on, Napoleon made France and the world believe that he wanted peace, while in reality his ambitious mind was already soaring far beyond the present looking for ways to realize his world-spanning dreams of power. Napoleon used the enthusiasm of the French people with cool calculation to pursue his vain, purely personal goals and rise to the position of "Ruler of the World," as he confided to his brother in 1800 while First Consul. Like Hitler, he abandoned himself to fantastic strategic dreams of following in the footsteps of Alexander the Great, and he, too, was inclined to embellish his political prophecies with a touch of superstition:

Opening of the coffin after Napoleon's exhumation, Paris 1840 (lithography by N. Maurin)

Nothing has ever happened to me that I had not first foreseen…and I have a similar intimation of the future and know for certain that I will attain the goal I set before me.

Posterity, nonetheless, was not too hard on the Emperor of the French for his vainglorious ambition, his personal greed for power, and his brutal wars of conquest with their hecatombs of human victims, calculated without the least qualms of conscience. The reason probably was that, despite all the cruelty of his military campaigns, his activity, apart from a few individual cases of arbitrariness, was free of violations of human rights on the greatest scale and of criminalistic mass murders, including genocide, such as have to be charged against the National Socialist and Soviet potentates and their leaders Hitler and Stalin.

Besides courage, hardness, and will power, the maxims of his behavior were guided also by concepts such as love, honor, and chivalry. Napoleon remains in our memory as a great personality with a humanistic sense of law and tolerance and an emotional world capable of love. So even today, hardly anyone visiting the Dome of the Invalides will pause before Napoleon's sarcophagus without a certain reverence.

ADOLF HITLER

All that you are, you are through me,
And all that I am,
I am through you alone.

The Führer to his people,
January 30, 1936

The highly complex phenomenon of Adolf Hitler as a world-historical event will probably never be completely understood. Some like to speak of an unprecedented, powerful burst of energy, shattering everything that had existed before and enabling Hitler single-handedly to transform himself, if only for a short time, from a poor and nameless vagrant to the absolute master of Germany and almost all of Europe. He had an astounding capacity to sense the mentality, fears, and hopes of the people of that era and to explain to them clearly and sharply the political circumstances responsible for their sufferings. He was also able to convince the masses that his own feelings coincided exactly with their frustrations and complaints, and so he came to be regarded as representative of all contemporary thinking in Germany. This talent must be seen as an essential element of his development to "historical greatness," if the term is interpreted in the sense of Jacob Burckhardt's words in his *World-Historical Meditations*: "The definition of greatness seems to be that it implements a will that transcends the individual." Burckhardt was alluding mainly to a "mysterious coincidence" between the egoism of a single individual and the will of the whole society.

From this aspect, Adolf Hitler indeed represents all the moods of the time, simmering below the surface of everyday life, which he brought into focus like a magnifying glass and forged into an effective, almost "magical" instrument of power. His political adroitness, as well as his demonic charisma as a popular orator, enabled him to unleash unimaginable collective forces and to apply them to his revolutionary goals. Since his political objectives all served to realize his monomaniac, fixed delusionary ideas—the destruction of Bolshevism, the extermination of the Jews, and the coercive expansion of German Lebensraum (living space) toward the East—he succeeded in channeling the concentrated and constantly recharged energy of an entire nation toward the outside. And this, in turn, enabled him to keep the forces he had unleashed under his own control, at least for quite a long time. In the course of history, revolutions, as a rule, have swallowed up their own children, but Hitler escaped this fate, for he was, as Hugh Trevor-Roper expressed it, the Rousseau, Mirabeau, Robespierre and Napoleon of his revolution "all in one person."

While Alan Bullock spoke of Hitler's "moral and intellectual cretinism," such a loose application of terms contributes little to a better understanding of the myth surrounding this person. As little as the moral dimension within which Hitler moved needs to be discussed at all, still such an oversimplified devaluation of the man's intellectual capacities seems problematic, for at least until the beginning of World War II he was able to appraise a number of political situations very logically, realistically, and objectively. Although Tucholsky, who like many domestic and foreign politicians dangerously underestimated Hitler, wrote, "The man does not exist at all; he is only the noise he produces," it was a rude awakening for many when after 1933 this man "turned out to be a very energetic, inventive, and efficient manipulator," as Sebastian Haffner put it. Yet Hitler's intellectual abilities must not be overestimated. It should, rather, be taken into account that his domestic and foreign policy from the end of the 1920s to the start of the war were almost never achieved against a strong opponent and that much had already begun to crumble before he appeared on the scene.

Hitler's spectacular accomplishments, which astonished the world from 1933 to 1938, have led some who forever cling to the past to believe that basically Hitler started off all right, but later went decidedly too far. Had he settled for his successes up to the annexation of Austria, indeed, perhaps even up to Poland's defeat—they like to argue—today he would certainly be praised as the most eminent politician and statesman of German history; for he would have realized Bismarck's dream of creating a "Great German Reich." Whoever thinks this way shows, however, that he has not at all understood Hitler's personality structure and psychological drives, which strove to attain rigidly pre-established objectives that determined all his actions. For the war with Russia was pre-programmed in his monomaniac delusions from the first. Likewise, the destruction of Marxism and the eradication of the Jews in Europe were essential components of his ideological system, for he saw them both as the greatest obstacle to realizing the "historical mission assigned to him by Providence."

For a deeper understanding of the phenomenon Hitler, it is not enough to study the countless more or less objective biographies that have appeared since then, even if his political rise to absolute ruler over the life and death of millions of people is described in them as meticulously imbedded in the political context of all Europe. The man himself, his reality and his myth, which, according to Joseph Stern, remain the most significant single phenomenon of their time, can hardly be understood by the traditional kind of biography, even when a more detailed treatment of psychopathic characteristics is presented here and there. It seems worthwhile, based on a careful biographical retrospection, to examine with a magnifying glass, from a purely medical point of view, Hitler's abnormal personality structure, his particular psychic traits, and his actions, which can hardly be fitted into a humane catalogue of norms. Such a study can be based on a whole series of valuable prior studies by eminent psychologists, neurologists, psychohistorians, and psychiatrists, dealing with the influence of pedagogical formative factors by family and school, with identity-finding and personality formation, and with the "human destructiveness characterizing Hitler's inner life" or the possible effect of his later Parkinson's disease upon various of his actions; finally, such a study can also be based on de Boor's extraordinarily seminal criminal-psychology analysis in order to reach the decisive question: What actually was Hitler—"human, "superhuman, or subhuman"?

Although a medical attempt at such an overall perspective hardly will bring new aspects to light, at least one can hope to present a more rounded, less stereotypical picture and to contribute to a deeper understanding of this eerie, ephemeral apparition on the horizon of world history. Since the years 1989/90, events of the Russian *perestroika* (restructuring) and the resulting disintegration of the Soviet Empire have brought the historical epoch of World War II, which is inextricably linked with Hitler's name, vividly back to the forefront of world attention. Many people who still remember that apocalyptic epoch, but above all the majority who did not experience it and for whom Hitler's emergence seems as far back in the past as Napoleon's, now have a stronger desire to learn more than mere slogans about this weird phenomenon called Hitler.

BIOGRAPHICAL SURVEY

FAMILY ORIGIN AND EARLY CHILDHOOD

Rarely has any other historical personality tried so intensely and consistently to withdraw from any human contacts and warily to conceal anything intimate and personal behind an impenetrable veil, as did Hitler throughout his life. This begins with the genealogy of his family, which he never wanted to discuss in any detail. It was supposed to be left in mysterious darkness like the ancestors of a mythical figure. The deeper reason must have been not merely his constant striving after a high stylization of himself, but rather a well-grounded fear that investigations into his family background could unearth some unpleasant surprises for this loudly self-proclaimed "apostle of pure Germanhood."

Strange facts turn up in the entries of the Catholic baptismal register of the city of Braunau concerning the birth on April 20, 1889, of a rather weak, dark-haired, and strikingly blue-eyed boy, who was given the first name Adolf. The entries made by various generations of Catholic priests under the names of the child's parents, Alois and Klara Hitler, née Pölzl, do not correspond to the whole truth, because the father, Alois, came to the world extramaritally as the son of Maria Anna Schicklgruber. Since, from a documentary standpoint, this was a defect, the justifiable question later arose: What was Adolf Hitler's real ancestry? As early as the summer of 1921 vague rumors were circulating among leaders of the newly formed NSDAP [National Socialist German Workers Party] about an alleged Jewish lineage of their Führer, and since, in 1925, Hitler gave no clear answer to the question of his parents' ancestry in the first volume of his book *Mein Kampf*, a kind of strictly guarded mystery soon arose about that topic.

The first clues to a possible Jewish origin of Hitler came from the manuscript "In View of the Gallows," written in his Nürnberg cell by Hans Frank, the notorious governor-general of Poland, while under a death sentence. In that work he revealed:

> Hitler's father was the illegitimate son of a woman with the last name Schicklgruber from Leonding near Linz, who worked as a cook in a Graz household.... This cook called Schicklgruber, Adolf Hitler's grandmother, was employed in a Jewish household by the

name of Frankenberger when she gave birth to her child. And this Frankenberger paid child support to Fräulein Schicklgruber on behalf of his approximately nineteen-year-old son for the period from the child's birth until his fourteenth year of age. There also was correspondence for years between these Frankenbergers and Hitler's grandmother, the overall tenor of which...was that Fräulein Schicklgruber's illegitimate child had been conceived under circumstances that made the Frankenbergers responsible to pay child support....Accordingly, Hitler himself was one-fourth Jewish.

Although this report has since been proven incorrect, the results of Frank's research, as well as the essentially similar findings of an investigation ordered by Himmler in August 1942, were reason enough for Hitler himself to have serious doubts about his purely Aryan origin.

Nor could the newest documents, unpublished until recently, clarify the situation with absolute certainty, but the facts collected with real astuteness by Werner Maser and the conclusions he draws from them at a distance seem to come closest to the actual truth. First of all, these investigations decisively contradicted the allegation that Hitler's grandfather was Jewish. Since Alois Schicklgruber was born on June 7, 1837, a Jew named Frankenberger would have had to be living in Graz in 1836, and Maria Anna Schicklgruber would have had to have been employed in Graz in that same year. Both preconditions, however, are untrue. Neither in the registry books of the Jewish synagogue nor in the "birth records" of other religious communities of Graz is a Frankenberger to be found. An Alois Frankenberger appears for the first time in 1900; but since he was much younger than Alois Schicklgruber, he naturally is out of the question as Alois' father. The case is similar with Maria Anna Schicklgruber, who was recorded neither in the Graz "domestic register" nor in the "municipal register" for the time in question, which was impossible, anyway, since she was living in Waldviertel in Lower Austria as a subject of the "Counts of Ottenstein."

The most recent genealogical studies have cast additional light on the identity of Hitler's grandfather. These studies show that the illegitimate child Alois, whose family name Schicklgruber was not officially changed to Hitler until 1876, was never acknowledged as his own child by his alleged father Georg Hiedler—a variant spelling was Hüttler—even when Georg married Maria Anna Schicklgruber in 1842. This rejection of paternity was understandable since Hitler's real grandfather happened to be not Georg but his brother Johann Nepomuk Hüttler. Nepomuk, a wealthy married man, had apparently, by means of adequate subventions, convinced his brother Georg to marry the mother of his illegitimate child Alois, because this made it possible for him to bring up the little Alois as a child in his household without arousing the suspicions of his unsuspecting wife. This also readily explains why Alois spent his childhood and early youth not in his mother's house, but in that of his "uncle" Nepomuk Hüttler. It also explains how after Nepomuk's death in 1888 Alois Hitler's financial situation took such a sudden turn for the better. For, as Maser at least tried to make plausible, after the legitimation of the name Hitler in 1876, Alois, as sole heir, apparently inherited his "uncle" Johann Nepomuk's entire fortune.

This grandfather of Adolf Hitler's on his father's side enters Hitler's family tree in yet another way. Nepomuk Hüttler had a pretty granddaughter called Klara Pölzl, whom Alois liked very much and therefore

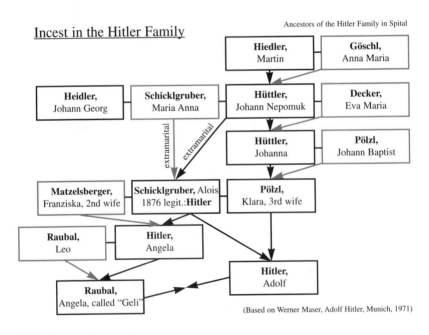

Hitler's genealogy

Klara Hitler, née Pölzl, Adolf Hitler's mother

employed as a domestic servant in his home in Braunau after his first wife had died of consumption and while his second wife was away in a sanitarium being treated for a serious lung disease. At first, Klara Pölzl merely served in the household as a servant girl and baby-sitter for Alois and Angela, the two children from the second marriage, but soon she became the man's mistress. In 1884, after his second wife's death, Alois married Klara, who was probably already pregnant at the time.

But now it turned out that to contract this third marriage a dispensation of the Catholic Church was required due to "consanguinity in the second and third degree," and this was finally granted from Rome. Adolf Hitler, who was born of that marriage, was thus a product of inbreeding because of the close blood relationship of his parents, since

Johann Nepomuk Hüttler was not only Adolf's grandfather on his father's side, but also at the same time his great-grandfather on his mother's side, since he was Klara's grandfather. At some point, Adolf Hitler was informed about the inbreeding in the Hitler clan, so his later repeatedly stated refusal to have children of his own is understandable. He had reason to worry that his incestuous origin might cause the birth of a mentally or physically handicapped child. This discovery also provides a plausible explanation for Adolf Hitler's own sexual relations with his niece "Geli" Raubal; for genealogists confirm that such a series of incestuous relationships is a relatively frequent and typical occurrence.

Among all the determining factors, the parents' character exerts the strongest influence on the development of a child's personality. Therefore, the question seems warranted whether Adolf Hitler's parents could have contributed to his later developing into a "monster," as Erich Fromm phrased it. In attempting such an analytical interpretation, the mother's role will be examined first, since it is critically significant for the most sensitive phase, earliest childhood.

Most biographers rate his mother's influence in the formation of Hitler's character positively. Bradley Smith, who is considered the most reliable source on Hitler's childhood, reports that everyone who knew Klara "agreed that it was in her love and devotion for the children that Klara's life was centered. The only serious charge raised against her is that because of this love and devotion she was over-indulgent and thus encouraged a sense of uniqueness in her son." Since three of her children born before Adolf died within a single year—Otto immediately after birth and Gustav and Ida of diphtheria—it does not seem unusual that all her care and love were conveyed on her fourth child, Adolf. For she lived in understandable fear of losing this child, too. Although, according to a house servant, the boy had always been "very healthy and cheerful," his anxiously caring mother considered him especially illness-prone and therefore nursed him at her breast for more than three years. This exaggerated pampering by his mother made Adolf the coddled center of the family and—as one often reads—a very strong bond was formed between her and her son. However, Alice Miller, in her psychoanalytical study, regards this seemingly plausible simplification as questionable and sees Hitler's later cold, distanced way of relating to people, especially his rather peculiar relations to women (including perverted sexual inclinations) as evidence that in his early youth Hitler must have experienced no real love from anyone.

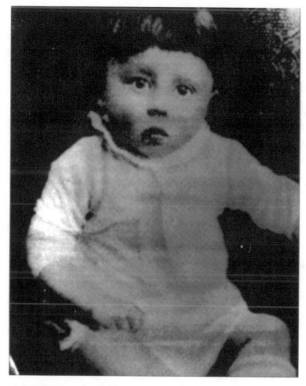

Adolf Hitler as a baby

If the events preceding Adolf's birth are considered, in the shortest span of time Klara endured the birth and death of three children and in the very year her little daughter Ida died she was pregnant again—then it can be assumed that she still had not gotten over her grief for her deceased children and must have feared that death could also snatch away her fourth child, who had just been born. These harrying experiences must have caused dreadful anxiety in the mother. The infant on whom this mother's fearful state of anxiety was transmitted during this early, symbiotic phase can hardly have received a feeling of calm, happiness, and pleasant security.

In Hitler's case, however, there is an additional factor militating against the assumption of most biographers that in his childhood he had been showered with a superabundance of maternal love. Although most existing documents attest that Hitler loved his mother sincerely and warmly and always carried her picture with him until the end of his life, it must not be overlooked that as a child he also had feelings of disappointment and some bitterness, which were repressed into the subconscious. For again and again he experienced, with painful disappointment, that his mother did not provide him the least assistance against the often very severe punishments inflicted by his father; but rather, she looked on in silence, without doing a thing, while he was being humiliated and punished. In his eyes this no doubt meant that she shared the responsibility, and it made her appear to be in solidarity with his stern father's actions.

This experience of his mother as a blindly devoted, subservient handmaid of her husband's, whom all her life she dared address only timidly as "Uncle Alois," must have given rise to Hitler's later contempt for women and hidden "deep-seated antifeminine affect." His mother, however, also seems to have given him the model of female nature which he had in mind in his characterization of the masses in *Mein Kampf*, when he wrote:

> The psyche of the broad masses is not receptive to anything halfway and weak. Like a woman, whose psychic feeling is determined less by reasons of abstract rationality than by an indefinable emotional longing for a complementary strength, and who therefore prefers to bow to the strong than to rule over the weakling, so the masses love the ruler more than the requester and feel internally more satisfied with a doctrine that tolerates none other beside itself than by the approval of liberal freedom; for they generally can make little of it and even feel slightly abandoned. The shamelessness of their mental terrorization comes as little to their consciousness as the outrageous abuse of their human freedom, for they have absolutely no intimation of the intrinsic nonsense of the entire doctrine. They see only the relentless strength to which they finally submit forever.

His submissive mother could not be characterized more clearly; for by her disappointing behavior during his childhood she confirmed for him that one can be victorious only by ruthless brutality.

His perverted sexual inclination also led to the conclusion that he hardly can have had a serene and warm intimacy with his mother. For it seems almost inconceivable that a man who had as a child experienced his mother's tender love could be subject to such sadomasochistic compulsions as will be described below.

The bonding with his mother as a result of her unlimited pampering certainly contributed most strongly to the development of Hitler's extreme narcissism and his typical passiveness. By never reprimanding him and always giving him her boundless admiration, she instilled in him at an early age the conviction of "being wonderful without having to exert himself at all." Any wishes he had were fulfilled by his mother without any effort on his part; and if she ever acted reluctant, he knew that he could quickly bring her back into line by adroitly throwing a temper tantrum. Such excessive solicitousness often gives a child the feeling of being trapped and losing his independence, and it can cause him to respond by a withdrawal tactic and by retreating into his shell; and we know that such a relationship with the mother obstructs the differentiation and integration of the personality appropriate to each age level. In extreme cases, even so-called "wishes to kill" aimed at a violent release from the mother can arise and leave in the child deep unconscious guilt-feelings, leading to aggressive defensive actions, repression mechanisms, and projections of various kinds, such as we later find in several of Hitler's primary character traits.

This phase of spoiling came to an end in 1894 with the birth of his brother Edmund, who displaced the five-year-old Adolf from his position as his mother's sole favorite. Erich Fromm has tried to explain the fact that, contrary to the usual assumptions, the child Hitler did not experience this event as a competitive challenge but on the contrary "fully enjoyed the year after his brother's birth," by his hypothesis of an early "malignant incestuousness" with his mother. This thesis, by establishing a causal linkage between Adolf's being spoiled by his mother's love and his development into an ice-cold, destructive, and highly narcissistic character follows from his well-grounded assumption that:

> Hitler's fixation to his mother was not a warm and affectionate one up to the age of five; that he remained cold and did not break through his narcissistic shell; that she did not assume the role of a real person for him, but that of a symbol for the impersonal power of earth, fate—and death. If this was so, one could understand why the birth of a brother would not have been the cause for his withdrawal from mother. In fact, one could not even say that he withdrew from her, if it is true that affectively he had never felt close to her. Most

importantly, one could understand that the beginning of Hitler's later manifest necrophilous development is to be found in the malignant incestuousness that characterizes his early relationship to his mother. This hypothesis would also explain why Hitler later never fell in love with motherly figures, why the tie to his real mother as a person was replaced by that to blood, soil, the race, and eventually to chaos and death.

These remarks can be made more understandable if it is pointed out that an "incestuous attachment," in which the child feels sexually attracted to his mother, is a perfectly normal process showing that the mother has become a person, namely, a woman, in the eyes of the little boy. Such an incestuous attachment takes on pathological import only when it is not disengaged at the time of puberty. In such a neurotic development, the adult man remains dependent on his mother or a substitute figure all his life.

While this type of incestuous fixation of the child on his mother is very frequently found, there is a much rarer variant of vicious, malignant incestuous fixation, which Fromm sees as one of the roots of necrophilia. Typically, such children never develop warm erotic and, later, sexual feelings for their mother, nor do they long to have an especially close relationship with her. Later, they also do not fall in love with maternal substitute figures, but for them the mother is a phantom-like figure rather than a real person—the mother becomes a symbol. Children with such a "malignant incestuous bonding" to their mother remain cold, narcissistic, and incapable of genuine emotional reactions all their lives. This view coincides with R. Binion's thesis that the significance of the early childhood relationship between Adolf and his mother Klara resides in the fact that, for Adolf Hitler, Germany later symbolically took the place of his mother.

While Hitler's mother apparently was a simple, uneducated, probably rather disappointed but on the whole pleasant enough woman, his father was a far less attractive individual. Born as an illegitimate child and having grown up in the house of his supposed "uncle" Johann Nepomuk, he moved far away at the age of thirteen to learn the shoemaker's trade. But by 1855 he had managed to improve his social position considerably by becoming an employee in the Finance Office. That without adequate schooling and solely by autodidactic work he could be promoted only five years later to the rank of "Austrian Tax Department Official" in Braunau on the Inn is a sign not only of his

His father Alois Hitler in the uniform of an Austrian customs official

extraordinary intelligence and unusual eagerness to learn, but also of his extraordinary determination and persistence. This invites comparison with the later development of his son Adolf, but other strikingly similar qualities of the two are also evident:

> Both were...markedly dominant natures and had unusual charisma....[They] were unwavering, impatient, and restless, dominated others coldly and calculatedly, knew how to acquire and manipulate power as well as to impress and lastingly convince the world around them, which they looked down upon.

Apparently the grandfather, Nepomuk Hüttler, also displayed similar traits which were passed down to his descendants. The handwriting analysis mentioned by Maser could be interpreted in this sense;

without knowing their origin or name, a graphologist analyzed the handwriting of two of Hüttler's descendants and came to the same conclusion: "Great determination, irritability, strong aggressive willpower, urge to dominate and ambition, nervousness and derangeability"—characteristics that strikingly match those of Adolf Hitler.

Erich Fromm appraised the father as a man who loved life, believed in duty and a sense of responsibility, and was not at all a fear-inspiring figure who could have terrified his son, in other words not a tyrant but only an authoritarian person. But this opinion is in many respects diametrically opposed to the image we get from the existing documents on the father's role in Adolf Hitler's youth. For the boy, namely, the image of his father must have been anything but exemplary. Alois Hitler was quarrelsome, irritable, and brutal; and his violent behavior was at times directed even against his wife and against the innocent dog of the house, which "he beat so long that it curled up and wet the floor." His physical chastisements with a hippopotamus whip—an instrument which Hitler later liked to carry with him during the time of struggle—show that he regarded cruel physical methods of training as the only effective ones for a child's normal psychic development. The one who had to suffer most drastically under this cruelty, as John Toland reports, was Adolf's stepbrother, Alois Jr., who was once so mistreated with the whip that he lost consciousness. But, as Adolf's sister Paula later testified, he, too, had been administered "his proper share of beatings every day" by his father. Statements by Franz Jetzinger show that Adolf was beaten not only as an older boy but even as a child of less than four years. Even harder than any physical punishment, the son was affected more by humiliating and debasing experiences, as he himself later admitted to Helen Hanfstaengl.

Alice Miller refers to the harmful influence of that kind of "black pedagogy" in Adolf's case by the example of a few of his criminal actions. His father's tyrannical educational methods forced Adolf to live under constant threat and anxiety; and since his father accepted no excuses for violations that might possibly not even have been committed, lying remained the only chance for avoiding further mistreatment and saving a pitiful remnant of one's dignity. What an undignified, slavishly obsequious figure Adolf must have seemed in his father's eyes is illustrated by Rudolph Olden with the words:

> Adolf in particular could not understand it. He tyrannized him. To summon the boy, the former noncommissioned officer whistled on two fingers.

This humiliation of being whistled at like a dog rather than being called by his first name, Miller compared with the later defenseless and nameless status of the Jews in the Third Reich, exposed to every arbitrary torment. Anyone of Jewish origin was subjected to the most shameful degradations, and neither special achievements and merits, nor brave conduct during World War I provided any alleviation—a phenomenon for which there is no comparable example in all history. Alice Miller sees this as an unconscious reenactment of Hitler's own childhood drama, whereby he transposed his own childhood family trauma to the entire German people:

> Just as the Jew had no chance, so formerly the child Adolf could not escape his father's blows, for the cause of the blows was the father's unsolved problems...and not the child's own behavior. Such fathers often pull their sleeping children out of bed when they cannot deal with a mood of their own, and they beat the child in order to reestablish their own narcissistic harmony.

This psychological viewpoint attempts to draw an analogy between the constant threat to the Jews in the Third Reich and Adolf's childhood situation, for whom, likewise, "continuous blows were assured. No matter what he might do, it could have no effect on the daily blows. The only recourse available to him...was self-denial and identification with the aggressor."

Another circumstance from Hitler's childhood was bound to affect his later behavior. As a child, he was forced to conceal from the outside world his daily fear and the threat posed by his father, not merely out of fear of the possible consequences but, more importantly, because probably no one would have believed him. For who would have believed that this honorable and dignified higher official in the tax office, who set great value on his external appearance and proudly paraded his uniform on official occasions, was capable of being a tyrannical, brutal head of family. Even later biographers, such as Joachim Fest, regarded some of Adolf's reports about his father as childish exaggerations, and Franz Jetzinger, too, in his book about Hitler's youth, considered the strict father to be a thoroughly progressive-minded man, whose blows "the disobedient and obstinate lad genuinely deserved." At any rate, it does not seem far-fetched that Hitler, later as Reichschancellor, must have unconsciously emulated his father's conduct

when, in the presence of foreign guests, he acted like the perfect statesman with peaceful and honorable-sounding views, while within the
state he was ruling with an iron fist.

Since Adolf apparently never experienced any signs of affection
from his father even at intervals, his hatred toward him developed con-
tinuously until the moment when he later freed himself from it by
creating a distinct image of the enemy (*Feindbild*), which finally "allowed him to hate permissibly." The figures in this image of the enemy
were at first the enemy soldiers in the World War, later the "November
criminals," and finally the Jews, on whom he subsequently transferred
all his suppressed hatred.

Although Hitler himself reported very little about his childhood,
during which essential elements of his nature were being formed, he
does provide one important source of information for describing the
atmosphere in which he grew up as a child. As anyone who is writing
an autobiography, as a rule, involuntarily reveals a lot about his earliest
childhood, Hitler, too, in *Mein Kampf,* without having been aware of it,
betrays the true situation of his home where he grew up. Since, even as
a child, he was taught to "obtain his parents' support only at the expense of a complete disguising and denial of his true feelings," it is not
surprising that with the few lines describing his parental home he wanted
to show that he had grown up in well-ordered family circumstances,
with a father who was a "dutiful state official" and a mother who "was
totally occupied with the household and was, above all, devoted to the
children with unremitting, loving care."

But how he really must have experienced his childhood can be
gathered from those passages in his book which describe the miserable
conditions of a worker's family around the turn of the century, from
which unmistakably a close relation to his own childhood experiences
can be read. There it is stated:

> In a cellar apartment consisting of two dreary rooms
> lives a six-member worker's family. Among the chil-
> dren is also a boy, say, three years of age....The very
> closeness and crowding of the room does not lead to
> favorable conditions. Quarreling and strife will very
> frequently result in this way....But when this struggle
> is being fought out between the parents themselves,
> indeed almost every day, in forms that often leave noth-
> ing to be desired in inner crudity, then—however

slowly—the results of such visual instruction must finally show up in the children. Of what kind they must be when the mutual discord takes the form of crude outrages of the father against the mother and leads to drunken abuses, it is hard for a person to imagine who does not know such an environment. At the age of six the small pitiful boy has misgivings which an adult can feel only with horror....What the little fellow hears at home does not strengthen him or lead him to respect the dear surrounding world....But it ends badly when the husband from the first goes his own ways and the wife, precisely for the children's sake, opposes this. Then there is quarreling and strife and to the extent that the husband is now more alienated from his wife, he draws closer to alcohol. Finally when he comes home drunk and brutal Sunday or Monday night...scenes often take place, merciful God! I have experienced all this myself in hundreds of examples.

If it is recalled that until the time of writing his book, Hitler had but few friends and contacts with families, then it seems practically impossible that he could have experienced hundreds of such scenes. More likely, he was describing his own childhood home, all the more so since the depiction is strikingly similar to various eyewitness accounts.

What a baneful influence such a situation and family structure, which is virtually a model of a totalitarian regime with a sole brutal dictator in the form of the father at its head, can have on a talented boy's development, is demonstrated impressively by the example of Adolf Hitler. He must himself have been fully aware that a father's character is an especially decisive factor in the formation of a boy's character, for he later admitted that this first, most important phase of character formation is that age "in which a child's first impressions come to his awareness. In talented children, marks of memory from this time of life are still found at an advanced age." If, from this perspective, many of Hitler's primary personal qualities become understandable as to how they developed, for Bradley Smith it still remains unclarified, how "Hitler's [former] weakness became strength and a romantic escapism was transformed into a quest for power and a demand for extreme solutions."

Psychoanalysis replies with the classical attempt at an explanation in the form of an oedipal conflict. Such an Oedipus complex can, of course, be constructed relatively simply with the "overprotective mother" and the brutal "castrating" father. Hitler's guilt-ridden wish for incestuous relations with his mother or with a substitute for her in the form of his half-niece Geli Raubal can be fitted without constraint into this oedipal pattern. Even the sexual perversions reported by Norbert Bromberg, which, incidentally, have not been flawlessly documented, could be explained by a fear of castration and early sexual overexcitation through excessively close ties with the mother. Above all, even Hitler's tremendous aggressiveness could be explained in this light as stemming from his early experience with his brutal "castrating" father and resulting in the never-ending wish to compensate for his inner weakness by a relentless hardness and iron determination.

A radically different interpretation of the development of Hitler's character in connection with his earlier childhood and his family and social environment comes from the psychoanalyst Erich Fromm, who sees the role of his two parents completely differently, posing the question:

> How can we explain that these two well-meaning, stable, very normal, and certainly not destructive persons gave birth to the future "monster" Adolf Hitler?

Fromm also studied Hitler's preoedipal phase. Instead of the customarily discussed psychoanalytic aspects, however, he placed in the foreground his above-mentioned hypothesis of a "malignant incestuousness" with the mother and in this way arrived at the profile of a man motivated by a primary malignant destructiveness that must be classified under the concept of necrophilia. This term "necrophilia" is understood in the characterological sense as "the passionate attraction to all that is dead, decayed, putrid, sickly; it is the passion to transform that which is alive into something unalive; to destroy for the sake of destruction; the exclusive interest in all that is purely mechanical. It is the passion 'to tear apart living structures.'"

In his youth, according to Fromm, Hitler was able to live out his necrophilia only in the realm of his fantasy. In support of this view, Fromm alludes to the fact that in Hitler, as early as the age of six, definite traces of a narcissistic character were already recognizable; it was expressed, among other things, in his extraordinary longing for freedom. This longing for "irresponsibility, lack of constraint, and most importantly 'freedom from reality'" led later to the "defective sense of reality" so typical of Hitler. If this thought is pursued further, then one notices how readily this thesis helps to explain his entire later conduct. His contempt for school and its teachers or later his disdain for the professors of the Academy of Arts, whom he blamed for his own failure, thus emerging from his repeated setbacks with an unbroken narcissism. "The more he failed in life, the greater his narcissistic wound became; the deeper the humiliation he suffered, the more relentless became his decision for revenge."

The transition from early childhood to school age occurred abruptly. As a result of the early retirement of his father, who purchased a farmstead with nine acres of land in Hafeld near Lambach, the family had to move to Hafeld, where little Adolf attended the nearby village school in Fischlam. For the father, who was relatively inactive as a farmer, retirement meant that he could now devote himself entirely to his beloved beekeeping. But his family, meanwhile enlarged by a daughter, Paula, born in 1896, seems to have increasingly become a psychological burden on him, causing him to become ever more quarrelsome and irritable. Adolf submitted, at least externally, to his demands and moods, but Smith comments on this: the boy had reservations. "He was still able to manipulate his mother to a degree, and his temper could explode at any time against anyone." At school, which he attended with his half-sister Angela, the two children made a good impression on the teacher, who later recalled that Adolf was very bright, obedient, but also very vivacious. Yet even at that early age he displayed traits that would stay with him all his life, namely, his rigid obstinacy and his overtly insurmountable reluctance for any form of regular disciplined work. He felt that the strong elements of regimentation to which the school rules subjected him, over and above his father's stern hand, were an intolerable restriction of his freedom. He compensated for this by engaging enthusiastically in the soldiers-and-Indians games with other boys, and he swiftly developed into a "little ringleader." In this role, he first displayed the tendencies that later would be increasingly noticeable in him, namely, the need to dominate others and an inadequately developed sense of reality.

A short time later, when Alois sold the property he had purchased so recently, Adolf entered a comparatively more modern grammar school, where he continued to do well. In this Lambach cloister school, over whose portal, incidentally, was located the coat of arms of the abbot Theodor Hagen in the form of a swastika, he was bombarded by new impressions that probably left formative traces on his soul. Because of his beautiful singing voice, he was accepted into the boy's choir of the monastery, and soon he also became an altar boy. So he began more intensely "to revel in the solemn majesty of the extremely magnificent church festivals." This went so far that he seriously hoped, like a few fellow pupils, to pursue an ecclesiastical career and become an abbot—after all, what else could the goal of his plans be? Decisive for this ambition must have been the dominant figure of the preacher who with his powerful words could cast a spell over the dull masses of believers. This impressed him greatly. Hence he used to like to play the role of an eloquent preacher. Wearing a priest's costume, he "got up on a chair and held long fiery sermons." Apparently, he showed a remarkable oratorical talent, as his former fellow pupils, without exception, later confirmed, and this ability also came in handy in the various "war games" for which he continued to have a special preference, as is stated by Balduin Wiesmayr, his fellow pupil and later abbot of Wilhering. According to his portrayal, the pupils frequently had to wage war with one another on Adolf's initiative. He himself led the troops and even then managed to apply his charismatic power over others to good advantage.

In November 1898, his father bought a house in Leonding, a suburb of Linz, where his brother Edmund died of the measles in February 1900 and his stepbrother Alois left the parental home. From then on his strict, ambitious father's entire hope was concentrated on this one son Adolf, thus aggravating even more the ever-latent conflict between father and son. Adolf's wish to be allowed to enter an artistic career ran counter to the ideas of his father, who had a secure government career in mind for him. In order to avoid a possibly violent confrontation, Adolf, without revealing his plans, pretended to accept voluntarily the pursuit of a high school education determined for him by his father. This entry into the public Realschule of Linz, however, marked a decisive break for the eleven-year-old boy and in subsequent years reinforced the preconditions for his "malignant development," to use Erich Fromm's term.

What first stood in the foreground was his disastrous failure in high school, which he later tried to interpret as an intentional protest expressing his inner rebellion against his father. This story was, however, just a badly contrived legend, as is evidenced by the fact that after his father's death on January 3, 1903, nothing changed in Adolf's

Adolf Hitler (top row, center) as a pupil in the 4th grade of the grammar school in Leonding (1900)

performance as a high school student. His failure had other causes. Although in elementary school he had excelled his fellow pupils because of his superior intelligence and had obtained excellent grades without particular effort, in high school the average intelligence was higher so that one had to work hard to succeed. But because of his deep aversion to regular systematic tasks, he was unwilling and perhaps unable to do the required amount of work. Drastic failures were pre-programmed, so to speak: repetition of the first year, promotion to the second year only after passing special examinations, and finally transfer to the third-year class at the non-classical secondary school (*Oberrealschule*) in Steyr, where he quit after finishing the fourth year, thus giving up on a regular school graduation.

This bitter experience of a catastrophic failure after having succeeded without effort in grade school must have been a shocking eye-opener and a challenge to his extremely narcissistic attitude. Yet instead of applying all his energies to overcoming this crisis, he immersed himself more and more into his fantasy world. He withdrew from people and was no longer even interested in getting good grades at least in German History—a subject that had formerly fascinated him. From now on, his only real interest was confined to war games. In his leadership role, these games gave him a chance to persuade and dominate others, thus further reinforcing his narcissism. Since the parameter of the games stemmed from his own vivid imagination, he was able to withdraw more and more from reality and operate almost exclusively with unreal persons and events.

How much this narcissistic, introverted young Hitler moved in an unreal fantasy world, playing the role of an unconquerable leader and fighter, can be seen from an event reported later by Kubizek, a friend of his youth, namely, Hitler's almost ecstatic reaction after a performance of Wagner's opera "Rienzi." Even years later, he had confided to his friend how he identified with the fate of Cola di Rienzi, whose anachronistic revolutionary action as a tribune of the people in the late Middle Ages inevitably collapsed from the lack of understanding on the part of the world of his time.

Had he admitted to himself that his failure was his own fault and could be overcome by stronger efforts—for he had talent enough—then the consequences would have been avoidable. But since his immoderate and unassailable narcissism blocked such an insight, the situation arose, as Erich Fromm states, that:

> [Hitler was] not able to change reality, he had to falsify and reject it. He falsified it by accusing his teachers and his father of being the cause of his failure and by claiming that his failure was the expression of his passion for freedom and independence. He rejected it by creating the symbol of the "artist"; the dream of becoming a great artist was for him reality, and yet the fact that he did not work seriously to achieve this aim showed the phantastic character of this idea. Failure in school was Hitler's first defeat and humiliation, followed by a number of others; it is safe to assume that it must have greatly reinforced his contempt for and resentment of anybody who was a cause or a witness

of his defeat; and this resentment could very well have constituted the beginning of his necrophilia had we no reasons to believe that its roots are to be found already in his malignant incestuousness.

Helm Stierlin casts a different light on the mother's role in connection with Hitler's mental processes during his adolescence and his conflict with his father. Stierlin holds the view that despite the father's domineering status and his unreservedly autocratic style of governing the family, he nonetheless probably did not represent "the stronger parental reality" for Adolf, but rather, the weak mother, helplessly subservient to her husband, was the one he regarded as the parental figure immediately above him. In fact, conceivably she looked upon her vivacious and strong-willed son and saw a chance to use him as her accomplice in her hopeless resistance to her husband. In this way, as Stierlin sees it, Adolf was to advance as her "loyal delegate" with the task of helping her stand up to her husband and perhaps also to make her future life more meaningful and interesting through her son's successful enterprises. But surely, as an adolescent, the contribution he could make on his mother's side in the married couple's conflicts had to be scanty enough and could at most involve a kind of passive resistance to his father, as expressed in his school failure or in the refusal to take up a career in government. Had this been the case, then with his father's death this role would have lost its meaning, and the hour of freedom to realize his future plans would have arrived. But nothing of the sort took place. He lived exactly as before and was, as Smith formulated it, "little more than a composite of pleasant games and dreams."

His father's death led to notable changes. With the cessation of the authoritarian style in the family, Adolf felt more free to devote himself undisturbedly to the construction of his dream world. When not dreaming, he was reading or drawing, and he could get very annoyed and angry if anyone disturbed him at these activities. His former class director, Professor Dr. Eduard Huemer, who in 1923 on the occasion of the trial after the failed putsch [a secretly plotted and suddenly executed attempt to overthrow a government] in Munich had been asked to give a description of Hitler's character from his point of view, gave the following description of his former pupil:

> He was distinctly talented, although somewhat one-sided, but he lacked self-discipline, being generally regarded as obstinate, high-handed, intransigent and

fiery-tempered. His teachers' instructions and admo-
nitions were often received with ill-disguised repug-
nance, whereas from his fellow pupils he demanded
absolute subordination and enjoyed the role of leader.

Only his history teacher Dr. Leopold Pötsch is said to have been able to
fascinate the "gaunt, pale lad" with his colorful depiction of the ancient Teutons.

In the public secondary school in Steyr, his teachers noticed not
only that Adolf had difficulty fitting in with his classmates, but also
that he gave an impression of being sickly. In his autobiography, he
claimed that after always having been healthy, apart from a measles
infection and the surgical removal of his tonsils, he now contracted a
"severe lung ailment":

> Then an illness suddenly came to my aid and decided
> in a few weeks about my future and the persistent point
> of contention in my paternal house. My severe lung
> ailment caused a doctor to advise my mother most ur-
> gently not to allow me…under any circumstances to
> work in an office later on. Attendance at the high
> school likewise had to be postponed for at least a year.

Klara Hitler, who lacked her husband's vitality and who was, moreover, filled with great worry for her admired son, consented without
hesitation to the doctor's recommendation, convinced of the necessity
for her son to leave school. Herself no longer quite healthy, she trav-
eled with Adolf to her relatives in Spital in Waldviertel, where he was
treated by Dr. Karl Keiss from Weitra. He drank a lot of milk, ate
abundantly, and recovered rather quickly. But he established almost
no contact with his relatives nor with the young people of the village,
but limited himself to sketching, painting, and long walks during which
he observed his relatives working in the fields.

Later, his story about having had to leave the school for ill health
was often suspected of being just a white lie. But the statements of a
few eyewitnesses from those days militate against this theory. Thus a
neighbor later reported that the sixteen-year-old boy "had had to give
up attending school because of a lung disease that caused him to spit
blood," a statement also confirmed by Paula Hitler. She later asserted
that her brother suffered from "bleedings." It was, then, probably the
manifestation of pulmonary tuberculosis in the form of a reinfection

following a tubercular primary infection that he had contracted earlier, such as could be found in the vast majority of young people in those days. This assumption is also supported by the circumstance that he labored under this lung ailment for a rather long time, for a friend of his youth remembered this period with the words:

I know that he was still plagued long afterwards by coughing and colds, especially on damp, foggy days.

Afterwards, no one could deter the young man from going his own way, however much his mother repeatedly admonished him to take life a little more seriously. Despising all authority, "mother's darling son" enjoyed doing nothing and "the hollowness of a comfortable life," as he himself later called it. Besides sketching and painting, he avidly read one book after another, designed unreal, fantastic architectural plans, and exhilaratedly attended performances of Wagner operas in Linz, not skipping a single one. Basically this lifestyle was an escape from harsh reality to a dream world in which he enjoyed, since the autumn of 1905, endless conversations with August Kubizek, son of a wallpaperer in Linz and the only person with whom he came into closer contact. Their conversations generally centered on music and art, to

House where Hitler's mother was born in Spital near Weitra, in the Gmünd county of Lower Austria

which in the future he wanted to devote his entire life, for—as he confided to his friend—he had no need to earn a living at a "humdrum job."

Again we come across this inclination to idleness and aversion to regular, not to mention strenuous, work, so often found in adolescents with a strong maternal bond. These young people feel they have absolutely no need to contend with gainful employment since their mother will take care of their welfare anyway, as she always has. They live, so to speak, in a "paradise where nothing is expected of them and everything is done for them."

As a matter of fact, Adolf's mother did try energetically to remove all difficulties from his way. Since he liked to dress elegantly, she even paid for the clothes which, as Smith says, "turned him into something of a dandy, perhaps in the hope that this would serve as a bridge to wider social horizons. If that was her plan, it failed completely. The clothes merely served as symbols of independence and self-sufficient isolation." His mother, however, tried seriously to arouse his interest in something or other, for during this period he was interested in absolutely nothing; nor was he willing to exert himself for anything. He was satisfied with having found in August Kubizek an audience he apparently so urgently needed even then: someone willing to listen patiently to his endless discourses, which were accompanied with lively gestures and, in part, seemed to have the force of "volcanic eruptions." August soon began to admire and revere him ardently and thereby gave him a second gift, unconditional admiration. His mother and his sister Paula must have provided a similar audience, for he gave them similar "rhetorical lectures on historical and political topics," which, according to Paula, sometimes soared to visionary heights.

In her justified concern for Adolf's future, his mother sent him to the Academy of Arts in Munich, hoping this would help him attain his dreams, but after a few months he returned from there without having achieved anything. A four-week journey to Vienna, which she financed for him, had a similar result. Meanwhile, his mother was beginning to show signs of a serious illness. She consulted the Jewish doctor, Eduard Bloch, M. D., who was considered to be a "poor man's doctor," and he diagnosed a sizable tumor in the chest and sent her to the Merciful Sisters Hospital in Linz, where she was operated on in January 1907 by the chief surgeon, Karl Urban. The histological examination showed a *"sarcoma musculi pectoralis minoris,"* that is, an especially malignant tumor in the area of the smaller chest muscle. Klara Hitler survived this operation, but she had only a short span of time left, during which she lived in the tormenting certainty that her son would relentlessly "continue on his way as if he were alone in this world."

THE VIENNA YEARS

After Klara had recovered somewhat under Adolf's care, she gave him the financial resources to move permanently to Vienna to study painting at the Academy of Arts. But his poor results in the admissions examination were a shock to the young Bohemian, who had grown up in his own dream world. The director of the Academy of Fine Arts explained to him in no uncertain terms that he was not suited to be a painter and that his abilities lay "manifestly in the field of architecture." He himself later wrote: "I was so certain of success that the notice of my rejection hit me like a bolt out of the blue." This was the penalty for his premature departure from the Realschule; for successful graduation from a Realschule or a Bauschule (technical building arts school) was an indispensable requirement for admission to the School of Architecture. But instead of striving to make up for this omission as quickly as possible, he did nothing or exactly the opposite of what he boastfully claimed in *Mein Kampf*:

> I wanted to become a master contractor, and obstacles are not there for one to capitulate to them but for one to break them down. And I intended to break down these obstacles.

Bradley Smith summarized the result of Hitler's disastrous failure at the Academy of Arts in Vienna as follows:

> His personality and his way of life prevented him from acknowledging his errors and accepting his rejection as a sign of the need for any change. His escapism was reinforced by his social affectations and his scorn for work which seemed dirty, degrading, or tiring. He was a confused and snobbish young man who had indulged himself for so long that he would neither work at an unpleasant task nor consider anyone except himself and the manner of life he enjoyed. His solution to rejection by the Academy was to go back to the Stumpergasse and settle down as if nothing had

Dr. Eduard Bloch, the Jewish doctor of the Hitler family, in his office in Linz

happened. In this sanctuary, he resumed what he grandly called his "studies," doodling and reading, with excursions around town or to the opera.

This was possible for him only because his inheritance from his father and the pension the government paid to orphans of its officials relieved him of worry about financial support for a rather long time. Dressed like a young idler, he hoped with his black, ivory-knobbed cane to be mistaken for a university student. He hoodwinked everybody, including his friend August, into thinking he was an art student at the Academy. But the news that his mother lay dying tore him abruptly out of these dreams. This was the second, even harder blow of fate for him that year.

When he consulted Dr. Bloch on October 22, 1907, the doctor told him that his mother had apparently been operated on too late, for her pleura was already permeated with metastases. The only possible treatment Dr. Bloch could prescribe was a daily local application of iodoform on the open wound; and this was done regularly starting on November 6.

As the family doctor stated, Klara Hitler bore the pains, which became increasingly more severe, "bravely, undauntedly, and without complaint." Adolf cared for his mother very touchingly in those weeks, sleeping next to her bed and cooking for her. When she died early in the morning on December 21, Dr. Bloch found the son sitting by her deathbed with a pale face, holding a drawing of his dead mother in his hand. The Jewish family doctor later described this moment: "In my entire career I have never seen anyone so filled with grief as Adolf Hitler."

Whereas Erich Fromm, with his thesis of "malignant incestuousness," holds the view that Hitler enclosed himself coldly and egoistically in his narcissistic shell as a reaction to Klara's excessively solicitous care and therefore faced his mother's fatal illness quite unfeelingly, the notes of Dr. Bloch, the Hitler family's doctor, which have, meanwhile, been deciphered and evaluated, describe the situation differently. As Rudolph Binion rightly stresses in his psychohistorical study, *Hitler und die Deutschen*, these documents clearly show that during the last phase of his mother's fatal illness from cancer Hitler was not, as Fromm believed, dallying unconcernedly in Vienna, mostly forgetful of his dying mother, but, rather, was at her bedside in Linz nursing her.

Moreover, Binion, in his effort to interpret the later Hitler's personality, tried to attribute a central role to the person of Dr. Bloch as the Jew who treated his mother. For Binion believes that Hitler, although he himself urged the family doctor to use all possible therapeutic means to alleviate Klara's pains and constantly assured Dr. Bloch of his gratitude, which was visibly shown, among other things, by enabling him to emigrate to the USA in 1940, nonetheless, in his helpless and vengeful pain, saw the Jewish doctor as the man who had poisoned his mother and even had drawn a financial profit from her suffering. This idea, unconsciously dormant in him, had, according to Binion, been catapulted eruptively to the surface of his consciousness by Germany's defeat in 1918, and since he thought he saw the Jews as the real "November criminals," Hitler from now on saw Germany as a kind of ersatz-mother, whose destruction needed to be avenged. Binion also interprets in this way the perhaps unconscious hints recalling his cancer-ridden mother's operation. For instance, when Hitler gave his gruesome order for the systematic, organized mass-murder and final extermination of the Jews, he spoke of the necessity to "remove, excise, and extirpate the Jewish cancer from the body of the German people."

From this new viewpoint, Binion undertook to do better justice to the fundamental idea of the Oedipus complex by associating it with the role of the Jewish family doctor:

> The hatred Hitler directed at the Jews is now fed by the rage which he unconsciously felt for the Jewish physician, Dr. Bloch, his mother's money-hungry destroyer. This rage, in turn, relates back to the rage his "castrating" father had once unleashed upon him, and which Hitler later transferred to Dr. Bloch.

At the same time, Binion's view should also expand the possible meaning of the early childhood relation between Adolf and his mother by the thesis that Germany later took his mother's place and that the urge for revenge and retaliation grew from this imaginary intertwinement.

Stierlin came to this same interpretation when he spoke of a symbiosis with the new maternal symbol "Germany." His starting point is Hitler's apparently ambivalent relationship to his mother, who by spoiling him gave him a feeling of uniqueness, while because of his overly strong attachment to her, she stood as an impediment to his personality development. This resulted in an ambivalent wish for constant symbiotic closeness and for a simultaneous liberation from her, a conflict that reached its culmination at his mother's death. He felt an infinite fear of losing her, yet at the same time, subconsciously, also the liberating idea of being free at last from her depressing embrace. This inner conflict gave rise to distressing guilt feelings, which he was able to mitigate, but not completely eliminate, by lovingly nursing his fatally ill mother. Only after Germany's defeat in 1918, which he found so depressing, does a possibility to finally overcome his separation conflict seem to have come to his mind, analogously to Binion's idea, by "transferring to Germany all the feelings that bound him unconsciously to his mother" and in this way making "Germany his sole bride."

However his mother's death may have influenced his later actions, the shock of this loss, which was certainly hard for him, by no means led him to look reality more squarely in the face. After taking care of the formalities, he returned to Vienna without delay to immerse himself in the security of his fantasy world. Although he twice failed the entrance examination for the Academy of Arts and spent the first year in Vienna roaming aimlessly around the streets of the city, drawing and redrawing sketches of the façades of buildings, he continued to assert to Kubizek that this activity was enough to enable him to obtain the necessary qualifications for the profession of architect.

Georg von Schönerer (1842— 1921)

This unwavering confidence that he was on the best road to be-coming an important artist is one more proof of his total lack of a sense of reality. And yet he must have felt deep down that he was a failure, on top of it all, in every single field where he had hoped for a great future as a talented artist. His only justification was to reproach the professors of the Academy as inept and arrogant and to put the whole blame for his failure on them. His hatred of the faculty, and also of society in general, was the only thing preventing the collapse of his narcissistic dream world, into which he now withdrew completely. He even broke off his only personal tie, namely, with August Kubizek;. during a short absence of his friend, he precipitously abandoned the room they rented together, without leaving him a forwarding address.

During this self-chosen total isolation, he plunged enthusiastically into reading books and various pamphlets of political, racist, and anti-Semitic content, such as were circulating in the ideological groups represented quite copiously in Austria at that time. Incapable of mas-tering the "identity crisis of his youthful years," he chose a "career aside from bourgeois happiness and economic security" and his hatred of life and of the ruling circles of society necessarily drove him into the arms of two personalities who dominated middle-class German Vienna of the turn of the century, namely, Georg von Schönerer and Dr. Karl Lueger, who thus became two important figures of Hitler's formative years.

Georg von Schönerer (1842-1921), became an avowed model for Hitler, first, by his thesis that the Jews were the driving force and cause of all evils of the world and, second, by his radical slogans aiming to influence the masses by trivial and primitive arguments. Dr. Karl Lueger (1844-1910), the anti-Semitic leader of the Christian Socialist Party, was admired by Hitler in *Mein Kampf* as "the most powerful German Bürgermeister of all times." Lueger made a tremendous impression on young Hitler, with his Machiavellian leadership style and his art of demagogically influencing the masses. So Hitler was drawn into the wake of the widespread anti-Semitic attitudes of the population of Vienna at that time. Inevitably, this avid reader also became an adherent of the swindler and runaway monk, Lanz von Liebenfels (1874-1954), whose mixture of occult and erotic ideas were widely disseminated among the people in the journal *Ostara*. Thus, Hitler pursued the utopian goal of "preserving the European master race from destruction by maintaining racial purity through the practical application of anthropological research." In his Vienna years, Hitler did not prepare for the career of artist for which he had originally strived; but instead, through a hurly-burly mixture of anti-Semitism, racism, nationalism, and socialism, he laid the actual foundation for his later path as a political leader.

Although the money from his inheritance enabled him to attend the opera and the theater regularly and to maintain the outward veneer of a student, gradually this perpetual idler's financial reserves dried up, until by the fall of 1909 they finally were exhausted. Hitler's "hard apprenticeship years," as he later called this phase, now began. Unable to continue paying the rent, he was forced to sleep on park benches like a homeless tramp, begging for a plate of hot soup at a monastery and eking out a livelihood with part-time jobs as a luggage porter or hired hand. How much he retained his incontestable hunger for education, even during this crisis period, and refused to give up his unreal dream world as an artist who had failed through other people's fault is illustrated by an event described in Rosa Albach-Retty's memoirs from those days. As she tells it, one day a mason's helper, working on her villa in Döbling, came to her door with the polite request to please lend him two volumes of Nietzsche's works. Since this "mason's helper," on returning the books, left a handwritten calling card between its pages, she also knew his name: it was Adolf Hitler!

In December 1909, he was forced to seek admittance into the homeless shelter in Meidlin, "an admission of his extreme defeat," as Smith

Sind Sie blond? Sind
Sie ein Mann?
Dann lesen Sie die „Ostara", Bücherei
der Blonden und Mannesrechtler!

Nr. 65
Rasse und Krankheit, ein Abriß.
der allgemeinen und theoretischen
Rassenpathologie
von J. Lanz-Liebenfels

Abb. 47.
Gesäßformen: A. der niederen,
B. der höheren Rasse.

*Examples of race-theory excesses in Lanz von Liebenfels' "Ostara"
booklets. The texts read: (top) Are you blond? Are you a man? Then read
the "Ostara" library of blonds and men's rights advocates! (middle) Nr. 65,
Race and Disease, a Survey of General and Theoretical Race-Pathology.
(lower) Forms of Buttocks: A. of the lower, B. of the higher race.*

says, and finally he did move permanently into the men's home in the
Viennese quarter of Birkenau. Although this men's home, whose
"luxury" was decried in some bourgeois circles, contained a small library, a recreation room, and even a "study," still this shelter must have
seemed an unspeakable humiliation to a young man who had previously considered the private sphere to be sacred. That this man, with
his highly narcissistic disposition and bourgeois origins, did not break
down under this deep humiliation, but even emerged strengthened by
it, proves his astonishing stability and his hermetic narcissism, which
apparently nothing could break. His own description can be understood in this sense:

> I owe to that time the fact that I have become hard and
> can be hard. And, moreover, I praise it for tearing me
> free of the hollowness of the comfortable life.

Even then he showed his enormous inner willpower, which later was an important precondition for his incredible political success.

In the men's shelter, he proudly called himself an "academic painter" and later occasionally also a "writer," and began in the house's study room to produce drawings based on photographic originals in postcard format. When he befriended the trained illustrator Reinhold Hanisch, an older tramp of bad character, his situation improved considerably, since for a commission Hanisch would sell the watercolors and oil paintings to art dealers and other interested persons, thereby providing Hitler a small income. However, Hanisch was taken into custody by the police, because Hitler had reported him for fraudulent practices; Hitler then continued this trade on his own and developed into a kind of businessman with a modest but steady income. This enabled him to advance to the small privileged group of permanent residents of the men's home. Soon the more intelligent of this group became aware of Hitler's artistic activities, and it was not long before the "study" became a kind of discussion forum where, at first, music, literature, and art were debated. Soon it also became the scene for carrying on political polemics, in which Adolf Hitler, as the dominant spokesman, began to inveigh more and more vehemently against the corruption of the ruling classes of society and against the mounting activity of the Social Democrats, without neglecting tirades in favor of Pan-Germanic ideas.

This kind of political polemic accompanied by wild gesticulation also brought him a first reproof in Vienna, when two sturdy workers gave him a sound thrashing, then dumped him back "at Valhalla" with minor injuries, a bruise on his right arm and a bump on his head. From this experience Hitler gained the insight that in political discussions the audience's opinions and reservations must be taken into account, unless one wishes to turn them into enemies. The men's home thus became the first training ground for his later career as a political demagogue.

Various scholars have tried to research the psychological reasons why Hitler stayed in the men's home. Though at first the wish to submerge into anonymity after his failure at the Academy of Arts may have been predominant, soon other motives were added. In the men's home, not only did he have the possibility to overcome his loneliness

One of the residences where Adolf Hitler temporarily resided: Vienna 10, Humboldtgasse 36

by establishing contact with other people, without having to surrender his intimate private sphere through excessively close ties, but he also found there the audience so important to him, distinctly inferior to him in intelligence and offering him over-awed admiration and respect, such as he had formerly gotten from his friend Kubizek. He needed all this very urgently to confirm his narcissistic ego. Such extremely narcissistic persons face only one outcome if a humiliating defeat, such as Hitler experienced in Vienna, is not to plunge them into a psychosis with the severest mental consequences—an outcome which Erich Fromm says is open only to the most gifted:

They can try to change reality in such a way that their grandiose fantasies are proved to be real. This requires not only talent but also historical circumstances that make it possible. Most frequently this solution is open to political leaders in periods of social crisis; if they have the talent to appeal to large masses and are shrewd enough to know how to organize them, they can make reality conform to their dream. Frequently the demagogue on this side of the borderline to a psychosis saves his identity by making ideas that seemed "crazy" before appear to be "sane" now. In his political fight he is driven not only by the passion for power, but also by the need to save his sanity.

At first, all his hatred was directed at Vienna, the metropolis of the Danube monarchy with its patchwork quilt of nationalities, which he blamed for his failure to fulfill the illusions and dreams he had cherished since childhood. The extent to which, in his narcissistically structured dream world, he continued to see himself as a misunderstood and rejected genius can be gathered from a letter written at that time, in which a tone of something like a sense of mission is first sounded:

> Without arrogance I still believe that the world lost a great deal because I could not attend the Academy and learn the technical aspects of painting. Or has fate destined me for something else?

He repeatedly tried to explain his personal failure to himself and the world by the specific socio-political characteristics of Vienna, which intensified his feelings of rejection of and aversion to this "melting pot" of the most varied nations and races, and he directed his entire thinking and aspirations more and more to Germany as his true "fatherland." As he later wrote, by a kind of autodidacticism concerning the society and social conditions in contemporary Vienna, he had gotten to know the shady sides of this magnificent capital, which at first had attracted him like a magnet, and he had elaborated his "world view" based mainly on these Viennese experiences. Vienna had not only intensified his German nationalism, which was already anchored in him before he ever stepped foot in the Austrian capital, but, in his opinion, it had helped him identify the three main enemies that threatened the existence of the German master race in its very foundations,

"Schlier Lake." Oil painting by Adolf Hitler, painted in 1913.

namely, the "racially inferior" Slavs, the Marxists, and the Jews. The decisive step to a correct evaluation of the "Jewish question" had been, according to his own statements, the discovery that the Jews are not, as he had formerly believed, Germans with Jewish religion, but a separate race. This race-concept, first conceived in Vienna, later occupied a key position in his ideology, corresponding closely to the social Darwinism he had adapted from Lanz von Liebenfels, that in the eternal struggle for existence only the most capable can emerge as victor.

All in all, in Vienna Hitler remained an unusually narcissistic person living in a twilight atmosphere between reality and fantasy, not really sympathizing with anybody and with no genuine interest in anything, who was inspired by the pipe dream of subjecting the world to himself, though at first without any concrete ideas about how to realize these ambitious plans. However, he also remained a man full of hatred and vindictiveness for all the humiliations he blamed on human society and its incompetent representatives. These pent-up aggressions were directed at just about everybody, including doctors, as one can gather from a letter of the time, which also shows for the first time the extraordinary susceptibility of the man's vegetative system [pertaining to involuntary body functions, especially the the digestive system]:

> It was certainly nothing more than a stomach colic, and I am now trying to cure myself by a diet (of fruit and vegetables), after discovering that the doctors are all idiots. I find it simply ridiculous to speak of a nerve ailment in my case.

This passage from a letter shows a tendency that later became almost a general rule: his impatience to correct the competent statements of experts in a know-it-all fashion. It also shows his touchy sensitivity to statements possibly injurious to his narcissistically configured self-image. As Erich Fromm noted, the intensity of such a narcissism stands in direct ratio to the degree of a person's sense of mission, as so often can be observed precisely in political leaders. Even in their young years, such individuals generally lay claim to infallibility and insist that others acknowledge their absolute priority and unrestricted power— elements which in Adolf Hitler soon would come sharply to light.

OVERCOMING THE IDENTITY CRISIS

When Hitler suddenly decided, in May 1913, to leave Vienna and move to Munich to apply for admission to the Academy of Art, he suffered a second defeat when admission was denied him there, just as it had been in Vienna. As Smith reports, in order to earn a living he was forced to go about selling his pictures from door to door or in beer halls. As in Vienna, in Munich, too, he lived the life of an eccentric loner and is reported by his landlady Frau Popp to have radiated his "Austrian charm," but he really made no effort to come into closer contact with anybody. When not occupied with painting and reading books and magazines, he could be found in taverns, where he took every opportunity to engage in political discussions. His audiences even then noted the convincing power of his language, underscored by the enthusiastic gesticulations of this otherwise notably awkward, insecure, and introverted man. Later eyewitness accounts agree that Hitler's behavior showed clear psychopathic symptoms: his exaggerated need for recognition, his impulsive, aggressive reactivity, his shifting moods, his obstinacy, and his opinionatedness. The ideas he presented, often immeasurably distorted as they were, and his fantastic-sounding plans for the future were heard partly with amusement, but often enough they also left a certain bewilderment and dismay. He always meticulously avoided making known his lack of knowledge or signs of weakness; he was assisted in this by experiences from his youth, in which he had learned how to consciously exploit the weaknesses of others, while himself remaining a coldly observant young man.

On January 18, 1914, he was urgently awakened from his dream world when arrested on the charge of having evaded Austrian military service. However, he managed to make such a pitiful impression on the Austrian Consul in Munich that he was allowed to report for duty at the more closely located recruitment station in Salzburg rather than at his originally assigned post in Linz. How little trouble he had in convincing the General Consul and the military authorities of his complete innocence is significant, and also how geared to arouse sympathy; he wrote of his sufferings in the Austrian capital in his justification letter:

> I was a young inexperienced person...having to rely on myself without any support, the few crowns, often my last penny, barely sufficed to pay for a place to sleep. For two years I had no other lady friend than care and hardship, no other companion than unquenchable hunger. I never knew the beautiful word "childhood." Even today after five years I still have reminders in the form of frost blisters on my fingers and hands and on my feet....Despite great hardship, amid an often more than dubious environment, I always remained honest and I kept an absolutely clean record before the law except for failure to report for military duty, which I knew nothing of at the time.

In truth, Hitler had confided to his friend Kubizek in late summer 1908 that he did not want to serve in the same army as Czechs and Jews, nor to fight for the Habsburg state, whereas he was ready anytime to die for the German Reich. With the cooperation of the General Consul, whom he told of his "severe lung ailment" during his youth and who therefore in his approval document added the remark, "Is supposedly afflicted with an ailment," he had obtained the desired assignment to Salzburg. On February 5, 1914, he was classified as "unsuitable and too weak for military and auxiliary service."

Unwilling as he was to serve in the Austrian army, at the outset of World War I he enlisted enthusiastically as a volunteer with the IInd Bavarian Infantry Regiment #16 as early as August 16, 1914. Two weeks earlier, on August 1, the day the German Kaiser announced a

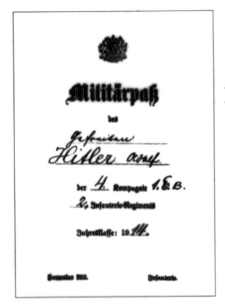

Military passport of lance-corporal Adolf Hitler

general mobilization, he had expressed his enthusiasm—an enthusiasm shared with Ludwig Thoma and Thomas Mann—with his typical dramatic exaggeration. He later wrote that, inspired by blind fanaticism, "he had fallen to his knees thanking heaven with an overflowing heart." According to Lange-Eichbaum, the famous psychiatrist of that time, this typically psychopathic affect of Hitler's came about "through the relentless strength of his emotional life, greater irrationality, as well as lack of self-control with all its consequences." No doubt, Hitler's overflowing enthusiasm can be understood mainly from his ardent German nationalism, but another factor just as certainly contributed, though possibly subconsciously. The outbreak of the war fell chronologically exactly in that phase of his life when his failure as an artist was brought to his consciousness definitively and irretrievably through his rejection by the Academy of Art in Munich. Like a magic wand, the news of war released him from oppressive worry about what direction he should give his future life now that his dream of becoming an artist had come to an abrupt end. In such a depressing situation, didn't he have to regard it as a decree of heaven to be suddenly relieved of such a difficult decision and to be given the chance to exchange the sad existence of an ill-fated and humiliated loser for that of a proud, self-confident soldier with a responsible task in the service of the German army? A short time ago, he had felt marginalized by society; now he was a respected and valued member amid his comrades, contributing to the defense of Germany and to nationalist values, and now for the first time he could feel like a proud, brave hero instead of a humiliated and ignored failure.

So it is not surprising that Hitler was described as an extremely conscientious soldier, decorated for bravery with the Iron Cross First and Second Class, who enjoyed the respect of his superior officers. A short time before, he had been an idler and drifter; now he proved to be a disciplined, correct, and responsible soldier, in short, a completely different person. Yet even during the war years he preserved his typical characteristics without change. Rated as an intellectual by his comrades at the front, he associated with them rather reservedly, and he liked to demonstrate his mental superiority by reading in Schopenhauer's *The World as Will and Idea*, so far as the situation permitted. Since he used to engage in a great deal of polemics even in the trenches, his comrades increasingly got the impression of him as a pompous babbler and ridiculous braggart. Indeed, sometimes they actually doubted his sanity, for example, when he formed figures out of clay at the edge of the trench, set them up, and held speeches to them, promising them the creation of a free people's republic *(Volksstaat)* once victory was won.

On the other hand, the fact that he had repeatedly escaped death, in ways bordering on the miraculous, was also noticed; and this confirmed him in his conviction that "Providence" must have destined him to be the savior of his people. Inspired by this feeling, he once proclaimed ominously to his comrades the prophecy which most of them probably found incomprehensible: "You will be hearing a lot from me yet. Just wait till my time has come."

Such words are uttered only by a person who feels chosen and is filled with a virtually messianic sense of mission. Apparently he was even then occupying his mind with tasks that would await him in Germany after the war was won. That is probably also why he wrote in a letter to the assessor E. Hepp, dated February 1915:

> Each of us has only one wish: to settle scores soon
> with that bunch once and for all...and that those of us
> who will have the good fortune to see our country again
> will find it purer and more cleansed of alien influ-
> ences...so that through the river of blood flowing here

day after day against an international world of enemies,
not only will Germany's foreign enemies be crushed,
but also internationalism within our own borders.

The war also gave Hitler the opportunity to indulge his thirst for destruction and annihilation to the full. Because of his complete faith in the validity of social Darwinism, the war's gruesome excesses of death and destruction did not cause him disgust and nausea, as any normal-feeling person would have to think, but a deep sense of satisfaction. Indeed, later he seriously avowed that the years spent in the war had been the happiest time of his life.

In October 1916, Hitler suffered a wound in the left thigh from a grenade fragment, but by December 1 he was already transferred back to the front where he continued to show a great deal of courage as a corporal. The reason why he was not promoted to sergeant during his entire service at the front despite his proven courage was, strangely, according to a superior officer's statement, that one "could not discover the appropriate qualities in him." In mid-October, 1918, Hitler fell victim to a British gas attack and, therefore, had to be sent to the Pasewalk military hospital in Pommerania. On November 29 he wrote:

In the night from October 13 to October 14, 1918, I
got a very serious mustard gas poisoning in the course
of which I at first became totally blind.

According to the narrative of General von Bredow, who later conducted an investigation of this incident by order of Schleicher, this blindness, from which he had completely recuperated after three weeks, was supposed to have been an "hysterical blindness," since it was associated simultaneously with a temporary speech impairment and since no objectively demonstrable lesions could be detected, either by the ophthalmologist or by the neurologist.

This diagnosis made after the fact has caused some confusion. Based on extant documents and eyewitness accounts, what happened was, from a modern perspective, the following: according to Dr. Solleder's deposition, Hitler was sent to the hospital as "sick from gas" together with other comrades after the aforementioned gas bombardment near La Montagne. "Under the fear of being permanently blinded" he had for a moment been so shocked that he temporarily could not speak a word, a condition interpreted as hysterical dumbness in G. Dalma's psychiatric study published in 1944. Today we can say with certainty that his gas poisoning was a very severe infection and

Adolf Hitler (left) together with fellow soldiers on the Western front (photo from the year 1915)

swelling of the conjunctiva and eyelids which made sight impossible. This condition cleared up relatively quickly, so that Hitler could be convinced not to have sustained permanent damage to his eyes. But then in the Pasewalk field hospital, the shocking news of the German capitulation reached him and he reacted to this news by a "relapse into blindness," as he himself described it. This time the ailment was a psychogenic blindness, conditioned purely by the mind. This psychogenic or hysterical blindness diagnosed by Professor Forster of Greifswald was confirmed by a psychiatric opinion of Dr. Wilmann, Professor of Psychiatry at the University of Heidelberg, as well as by Professor Bumke, director of the psychiatric clinic at the University of Munich.

Hitler's unfortunate decision to become a politician was probably made during his stay at the Pasewalk field hospital. In the hypnotic sessions initiated as treatment for this psychological blindness, Professor Forster gave him the order to save Germany and to eliminate the disgrace of the November capitulation, an order which Corporal Hitler, trained to unconditional obedience as a soldier at the front, then translated into a kind of assigned mission. Since such ideas transmitted during a state of hypnotic trance become firmly anchored in the depths of the psyche, the affected person develops "a feeling of unwavering certainty immune to any criticism"; and de Boor therefore suspects that this must have been the real foundation of Hitler's indomitable sense of mission.

In any case, World War I certainly penetrated into Adolf Hitler's personality vacuum as the dominant formative factor. After a definitive attainment of personal identity had failed during the "formative years" of the Vienna era as a result of various identity crises, this war was the decisive "great positive formative experience" that triggered the belated maturation process and helped Hitler's previously "amorphous gestalt" gradually to develop perceptible individual contours.

At first, the outbreak of the war had seemingly laid the loser Hitler to rest once and for all and relegated the time of failures and humiliations to the past; but the end of the war with the German army's defeat and the victory of the revolution in his homeland was a new deep humiliation. Even the military defeat was an unbearable thought for him; but the revolution was felt to be an attack on himself personally, since he had arrogantly identified himself completely with Germany. Also hard to take was the circumstance that several influential leaders of the putsch in Munich were Jews, who now had the nerve to endanger his nationalist and racist ideas. In his eyes, this deep humiliation could be erased only by relentlessly destroying all persons responsible.

So Hitler's urge for destruction received its definitive form. Since in this way he could transform his personal humiliation into a national defeat, this time it was not a matter of a personal failure but a failure of Germany, his only "bride":

> By avenging and saving Germany he would avenge himself, and if he wiped out Germany's shame, he would be wiping out his own.

For Erich Fromm, the way in which Hitler planned to encounter a putsch like that of 1918 is a classical early example of his rage for destruction and killing, whereby "he would immediately kill all leaders of opposing political currents, also those of political Catholicism, and all inmates of concentration camps. He figured that in this way he would kill several hundred thousand people." Although the total number of his victims would have been only minimally "increased" compared with the slaughter of the Jews, Fromm deduces from this urge to kill, the following proposition:

To be sure, it is correct to say that Hitler was a Jew-hater…but it is equally correct to say that he was a German hater. He was a hater of mankind, a hater of life itself.

It is strange that Hitler, despite his stored up hatred of all Social Democrats, Bolshevists, and Jews, whom he simply lumped into one and the same category, remained an indifferent spectator in the camp during the turbulent and bloody days of the Munich revolution, while grizzly deeds were occurring during the Communist takeover and units of the Reichs-Army and the volunteer corps were massacred in their counteroffensive to remove the "council" regime. He was first induced to participate actively on the political scene by his military superior, Captain Karl Mayr, who ordered him to enroll in a "re-education course" which national-minded professors were conducting at the University of Munich. Afterwards, he was transferred to an "educational squad" assigned to educate the returning German prisoners of war, who were, in part, infected with Spartacist ideas, and to put them back on the right track, the anti-socialist patriotic one. Here he began to practice his oratorical talent and eloquence on such themes as "The November Criminals" or "The Jewish-Marxist World Conspiracy." And soon he was said to be "a born popular orator, who absolutely compels his audiences to take heed and agree with him by his fanaticism and charismatic demeanor," as one of his listeners later reported.

However, the race hygienist Professor von Gruber, who observed Hitler during a meeting, formed an overall negative impression of this orator:

> Face and head [show] bad race, a half-breed receding forehead, ugly nose, wide cheekbones, small eyes, dark hair. A short brush of mustache, only as wide as the nose, gives the face an especially repugnant look. The facial expression is not that of a man in full command of himself but of an insanely excited one. Repeated twitching of the facial muscle. At the end an expression of elated self-esteem.

For Hitler himself, however, along with the "experience of a political awakening" caused by Germany's defeat and the victory of the revolutionaries in his homeland, the discovery of his oratorical talent, along with the possibilities it offered, was the decisive experience. It gave him the happy feeling of having a reason to live and it must have essentially solved his identity problems. From the moment he decided in 1919 to become a politician, he always had a clear goal in mind. But the deficits in his quest for identity, beginning in early childhood and unresolved during the long series of frustrations until 1918, could no longer be fully compensated at this point in time. Therefore, as de Boor states, Hitler always "remained an ego-weakling, who never could arrive at a complete identity, at a harmony between inner and outer world, a correspondence that is the necessary prerequisite for successful, but at the same time normative living."

BEGINNING OF HIS POLITICAL RISE

In his next role as "political informant" for the Munich Group Surveillance Unit, which had the task of ferreting out the growing number of indefinable rightist radical associations in Bavaria, in 1919 he met the railroad mechanic Anton Drexler, who had founded the German Workers Party. From his very first appearance in this circle, he was able to virtually electrify his audience and to impress them so much that they invited him to join their Party. After hesitating briefly, he accepted and immediately took charge of the propaganda agendas on the executive committee. A short time before, he had characterized his hopeless situation at the end of the war with the words:

> What was depressing was the complete disregard under which I then most suffered.

Now, however, he had a leadership function and a welcome field of experimentation for testing his oratorical talent, an instrument by which he was preparing himself for a meteoric rise as a politician.

Hitler's membership card in the German Workers Party with #7

Exaggerated as Adolf Hitler's facial expressions and gestures seem today, it was hard to escape his demagogic genius.

But what was the really unusual thing about his oratorical talent? On reading Karl Tschuppik's comments, Hitler's rhetorical art in the early 1920s—the art of analyzing and constructing—still seems to have been quite modest:

> Rhetorically weak, intellectually about zero, the most effective element of Hitler's discourse remains merely the ability to transmit emotions....Perhaps Hitler believes the things he says; at any rate, it is the tone of emotional conviction that brings him success. That is the most primitive stage of oratory.

Now, of course, Hitler was not interested in the least in impressing the "liberal intellectuals and ink-riders," as he called them. Rather, his concern was to match his ideas, borrowed from the petit-bourgeoisie, with those of great parts of the German middle class. Those ideas of his may have been thoroughly mediocre, but they were "representative," for they expressed the fears and hopes of many of his German contemporaries. Moreover, he intentionally struck tones intended to appeal not just to the destructive instincts of a defeated nation, but also to call attention to the importance of restoring traditional German values, threatened with extinction by the defeat of Kaiser Wilhelm's German Reich. Anti-Semitism was also inserted purposefully into this line of thinking, for even before World War I it had been a fundamental tenet of right-wing extremist movements in Germany, and it also fit into the preoccupations of contemporary society.

In the last phases of the war, Hitler engaged in discussions in which he openly proclaimed his boundless hatred of the Jews, as his former company commander Wiedemann later testified. With Germany's military defeat and the deep narcissistic injury associated with it, Hitler's hatred of the Jews—but also of the Bolshevists and all other participants in the "November crime"—was intensified to such an extent that his former Reichs-Press Secretary Dietrich could define him in no other terms than as a "demon possessed with populist delusions." It is worth noting that, as early as September 1919, Hitler, in his first political manifesto, laid out the unavoidable treatment of the Jewish problem from his point of view. There he wrote:

> Anti-Semitism for purely emotional reasons will find its last expression in the form of pogroms. The anti-Semitism based on reason, however, must lead to the

systematic legal battle for eliminating the privileges
of the Jews....But its ultimate goal must adamantly be
the elimination of the Jews in general.

In his speeches, Hitler used yet another element that was bound to
affect the masses, who still could feel the horrors of World War I in
their bones, namely, the concept of the "authentic inner experience,"
as Joseph Stern called it. The strongest trump in his hand which he
played repeatedly, his own personal "front-line experience," was supposed to convince the masses that every word the man said was the
expression of his sincere feelings. This "front-line experience" functioned as substitute for a real program or an ideology and represented
an appeal to the feelings of the masses that he could use effectively
again and again in countless variations.

Here is my experience, here are my firm convictions,
my representative experience of the world. This is the
sanctifying source of my love and my hatred.

A fanatic who presented his cause so convincingly was a "highly attractive figure" in so insecure a time as Germany of the 1920s. Amid
the social and political chaos he could easily be stylized into a kind of
"savior." Hitler's greatest talent, of using his oratory to move, influence, and persuade other people, was based partly on his ability to use
his voice consciously as an instrument to achieve the desired effect in
optimal fashion. For this purpose, when necessary, he used wild outbreaks of hatred in his speeches to whip up the passions of his audience,
but, as Erich Fromm says, despite the genuineness of his hatred, these
sorties were by no means uncontrolled, but were planned with cold
calculation.

Hitler's career as a politician began with this unusual oratorical
talent, and he was even then called the "drummer" because of the sensational effect of his propaganda. On the occasion of the first mass
assembly in the festival hall of the Munich Hofbräuhaus on February 24,
1920, he succeeded, despite tumultuous disputes, in changing the party's
name to National Socialist German Workers Party (NSDAP) and immediately presenting to it an "unchangeable" twenty-five-point
program. He left the armed forces, to which he had still belonged until
then, and devoted himself exclusively to political agitation from then
on. When protests were lodged in his own ranks about his kind of practices, he threatened to resign on the spot unless he were granted the

office of first chairman with dictatorial powers. The real founder, Drexler, was promptly removed from his previous position and Hitler was appointed in his place. The reason given was:

> The committee is ready, in recognition of your tremendous knowledge...and your rare oratorical skill, to grant you dictatorial authority and most joyfully welcomes your taking this office.

These "Byzantine tones of later deification practices" must have added fuel to Hitler's still latently slumbering sense of mission.

This identification of the movement with Hitler's own person created the myth of a charismatic leader responsible only to himself. Understandably, it appealed primarily to a particular group among the lower middle-class population, whose orientation was "rather vulgar, chauvinistic, and hostile to foreigners, authoritarian and with an eye for crude manliness, anti-intellectual, and, above all, anti-Semitic." Sebastian Haffner, incidentally, rightly recognized that Hitler's decision to be chosen as Führer resulted not only from the fact that he "discovered his hypnotic ability to take over a collective subconscious whenever available" but conversely that he recognized how enormously stimulating the masses were to him. This experience of a formerly rather withdrawn and reclusive eccentric now suddenly rediscovering himself transformed into an intoxicating dominator of the masses strengthened his self-confidence immeasurably, but at the same time it also fed his inclination to arrogance and his feeling of being chosen, which had been slumbering latently since his youth. The masses, whom he knew how to manipulate and influence quite masterfully—probably not least of all through his earlier study of Gustav Le Bon's *Psychology of the Masses*—could not know that their idol had a low opinion of them and, indeed, despised them.

For further reflections, it is important to point out that even at the beginning of his political career Hitler's deep-seated hatred of the Jews had already degenerated to a pathological fixation. Eloquent testimony of this is a report by retired Major Josef Hell, to whom Hitler in 1922 stated in a kind of fit of fanatical candor that if he ever really were in power, he would "set up as many gallows as the traffic permitted on Marienplatz in Munich. Then the Jews would be hanged, one and all, and they would be left hanging...as long as the principles of hygiene permitted. As soon as they were taken down, it would be the next ones' turn, and that would continue until the last Jew in Munich is wiped out." This sick, irreconcilable hatred of the Jews made even some close friends in the Party uneasy and some even said: "The man is simply crazy." But what were they really supposed to think when, as Dietrich Eckart reported, their Führer, having returned from Berlin, described conditions there and, with a hippopotamus whip in his hand as the symbol of paternal chastisements, said:

> I almost felt like Jesus Christ when he came to his Father's temple and found the money-changers there.

With a snap of the whip he then cried out that it was his mission to come over the capital like the Lord and punish the godless.

In general, even in those early years, his sense of mission assumed dubious forms, as Helen Hanfstaengl told us:

> Hitler now had strong Napoleonic and Messianic allures; he stated that he felt in himself the calling to save Germany and that he would be given this role, if not now, then later. He also drew a series of parallels with Napoleon.

In mid-October 1923, Hitler decided that the time for a new revolution had come. The Rapallo Pact of the German foreign minister Walter Rathenau, who was murdered in June 1922 by members of the Free Corps, the occupation of the Ruhr by the French in January 1923, and the reparation demands, which were senseless in the face of a rampant inflation, necessarily had a destabilizing effect on the German population politically and psychologically and created a seemingly very opportune situation for Hitler. During the conflict between the central government in Berlin and the right-leaning state government in Bavaria, as early as the autumn of 1923, preparations for a revolt and for a march on Berlin were being made. When on November 8 a major convocation of the rightist associations took place, attended by the Bavarian minister president von Kahr, together with General Lossov and the Munich police president Seisser, as a kind of triumvirate, Hitler barged into the hall accompanied by armed SS-men, herded the members of the government into a side room, and declared them deposed, while triumphantly proclaiming to the baffled audience the simultaneous deposition of the Reichs-president and the Stresemann government. But that same night, the triumvirate managed to escape; the next day the Bavarian government, conjointly with Berlin, declared Adolf Hitler's putsch to be high treason, and the planned revolution was struck down.

When Hitler learned of the failure of his plan, he suffered a nervous breakdown—despairing fits of rage alternated with crippling indecision. For the first time, Hitler's weakness of will was displayed in his hesitation and doubt, as can be observed in many people who lack strong will when they are forced to make a decision.

Later, too, Hitler would frequently tend to let events come to him until the resulting situation made it unnecessary to decide. Incapable of making a decision, he locked himself in the Bürgerbräukeller, a tavern, and General Ludendorff, whom Hitler had intended for the position of a leader of the reorganized national army, had to take control and organize a demonstration march toward the center of the city. This demonstration came to an abrupt end in front of the Feldherrenhalle, after the police had opened fire and killed fourteen demonstrators. While General Ludendorff marched on and was arrested on the spot, Hitler joined the headlong flight of his followers, after first having been knocked to the ground by a mortally wounded fellow fugitive. In the fall, he suffered a dislocation of the left shoulder and a fracture of the upper arm socket.

When he was discovered by the police two days later hiding out in a country house that belonged to Hanfstaengl, he lost all composure for a moment and tried to shoot himself with a revolver. This failed suicide attempt, which was repeated again in 1931 on the occasion the suicide of his niece Geli Raubal, accords with Hitler's tendency to depressive moods, always associated with a triggering event and therefore

The Hanfstaengl family. This couple supported and promoted Hitler in his "time of struggle."

Adolf Hitler as a "nameless person" amid a group of decorated World War I officers and prominent privy-counsellors, in a somewhat pompous pose ("German Day" celebration in Nürnberg, September 2, 1923)

definitely classifiable as reactive. Sebastian Heffner explains Hitler's tendency to feel the need to throw away his life without hesitation by the fact that his personal life was always too empty for him to consider it worth keeping when adversity struck.

Incarcerated in Landsberg Fortress, the convict Hitler at first refused all food and brooded by himself in deepest despondency. He was bothered psychologically not only by the failure of the revolution, but above all by the mockery and contempt with which the press inundated him, reporting disdainfully of "a miniature revolution from the beer cellar" and a "brawling lieutenant of Ludendorff's." For a man who considered himself chosen by Providence to be Germany's savior and was convinced of the narcissistically and assiduously preened uniqueness of his appearance, the worst thing was to be exposed to public ridicule. Seen this way, the two-week hunger strike in the framework of his depressive state once again takes on a suicidal color.

As was strongly emphasized in an affidavit by the prison doctor Brinsteiner, dated January 8, 1924, this "strong reaction with its temporary pathological depression after Hitler's failed putsch" was completely overcome by the prisoner after ten weeks. Nor probably did the pains in the area of his left shoulder and arm after his injury from the fall last very long, since Dr. Brinsteiner's medical affidavit, dated December 19, 1923, already reports:

> The pains in the left arm of Adolf Hitler, a prisoner awaiting trial, which are traceable to a traumatic irritation of the nerve, have improved very considerably in recent days, and his sleep is normal again.

In biographies, but also in the notes of Hitler's doctors, the indication is found persistently that after the abortive putsch he suffered from a "shaking neurosis" for a rather long period. Maser bases his statement to that effect on the testimony of Alois Ott, who was employed as a teacher in the prison and claims to have observed "that both Hitler's left arm and also his left leg trembled." Since, in all Dr. Brinsteiner's medical affidavits this alleged trembling during his prison stay never appears, this "trembling," which was mentioned by Hitler himself, must surely have been an intensified physiological tremor such as can appear in any person under great psychological stress.

When Maser claims to see in two photographs from February and December 1924 a cramped stiffness of the left hand, in which Hitler seems to be pressing his hat close to himself with his arm tightly against

Adolf Hitler, Erich Ludendorff, and Ernst Röhm before the People's Court-house, Munich I, at the beginning of their trial for high treason

First session of the Munich putsch-trial against Hitler, Erich Ludendorff and others. The indictment is read in the hall of the Infantry School on May 6, 1924

his body, in order to hide his "trembling neurosis," this posture should rather be connected with a stiffened shoulder-joint socket. Experience shows that, after a dislocation of the shoulder-joint and the subsequent immobilization, as a rule, there results a kind of shrinkage of the shoulder-joint socket that leads to a considerable limitation of the movement of the affected arm and can be overcome only gradually by a consistent program of physical therapy. This assumption is supported by an account given by Hitler on March 31, 1945, in a conversation with his personal physician Dr. Morell, in which he said his left arm had been "paralyzed" for a rather long time in 1923, but had become "completely utilizable again through the most strenuous exercises."

At any rate, when Hitler was transferred to the Munich detention prison on February 22, 1924, he was again in best shape both physically and mentally; and quite a few observers during the subsequent trial considered him the real rhetorical and political victor after all. But he was sentenced to five years in prison, which the public considered to be a ridiculously mild judgment. After the sentence was pronounced, he again fell into a depressed mood, but he quickly regained faith in his "mission," as the words noted in his diary on April 1, 1924, show:

> The trial by bourgeois stupidity and personal vindictiveness is over—today marks the beginning of "my struggle" (*mein Kampf*).

It also marked the beginning of the most successful but least read bestseller in the world.

A few days after Christmas in 1924, Hitler was already released from Landsberg Fortress on parole. And after the state of emergency was revoked by the Bavarian minister president on February 16, 1925, and the NSDAP became legal again, the very first issue of the *Völkischer Beobachter* (Popular Observer) boasted Hitler's editorial under the headline "A New Beginning." The attitude he presented was of a new Adolf Hitler, determined to enter the political struggle, henceforth, only by legal means and ready for compromises. But it became evident only too soon how dangerous to state security he continued to be as an orator. So he was banned from speaking anywhere in Bavaria; and soon this ban was adopted by most other German states, including Prussia. Surprisingly, he accepted this renewed coerced retreat from

Adolf Hitler before the barred window of his cell in Landsberg on the Lech (1924)

public life with the same indifference as his previous imprisonment and used this constraint to establish closer contact with important Party functionaries and to concentrate on long-range political strategy.

On February 14, 1926, at a meeting in Bamberg he presented the first Party program drafted by himself in 1920 as the "founding document of our religion and world view. To undermine this would mean treason against those who died believing in our idea." Faithful to his earlier conceived messianic sense of mission, "National Socialism was now a religion and Hitler was its savior—crucified at the Feldherrnhalle and resurrected again in Landsberg," as Toland so well formulated it.

That spring, Hitler had finally achieved absolute control of the whole NSDAP, which at the same time meant the end of any democratic cooperation and complete subjugation under the Führer-principle. As every kind of movement whose political loyalty takes the form of a confession of faith seems unable to do without a kind of Bible—think of Stalin's *Foundations of Leninism* or Chairman Mao's "Little Red Book"—Hitler's *Mein Kampf* became mandatory reading for all Party comrades. He had dictated the first part of it to his secretary Rudolf Hess while in prison, and it was published in 1925, while the second part, written in his house in Obersalzberg, was published in 1927. Unfortunately, politicians in Germany and abroad learned much too late that this book already contained in absolutely unchangeable form all of Hitler's ideas, which he later implemented. The "second book" of *Mein Kampf,* written in 1928 and never published for tactical reasons, became known in 1958 as a typed manuscript and was even more clear. Nor was the slightest trace of the edifice of his ideas altered at all in the coming years.

The most important demands of his "world view," which he expounded for the reader, were the conquest of new living space (Lebensraum) in the East for the German people and the uncompromising implementation of National Socialist racial policy. To prepare the masses for these projects, targets had to be created on which the disgruntled comrades could focus their aggressiveness and hatred. And in his eyes these targets were, along with the annihilation of so-called "life not worthy of life," especially the "racially inferior" Slavic peoples and, most of all, the Jews. In this connection, his "second book" already delineated the clear outlines of his planned genocide and spoke openly of eradicating the "breeding places for miscegenation" and the "purulent cells" in which the international Jewish "maggot of nations prospers." Presumably, he forbade the publication of this book to prevent an attentive reader from discovering in such passages his plans for mass murder.

It has repeatedly been asked whether this pathological hatred of Jews is accessible to a psychological explanation and whether an exact date can be given for the beginning of this aggressive anti-Semitism. That Hitler's anti-Semitism, which certainly began to germinate already in Vienna, cannot have been so crass at first is proven by his own statements on this topic:

> I still saw in the Jew only his religious affiliation and, therefore, for reasons of human toleration in this case, too, I rejected an attack on religion. So the tone sounded mainly by the anti-Semitic press seemed to me unworthy of the cultural tradition of a great nation. I was depressed by certain events in the Middle Ages and really did not want to see them repeated.

Under the influence of anti-Semitic propaganda in Vienna—from Lueger and Schönerer to Lanz von Liebenfels—and the nationalist slogans before and during the time of World War I, putting the whole blame for the misery of the German people on the Jews and the Jewish-dominated Bolsheviks, his aversion to Judaism, latently present since his youth, now blossomed into that "boundless hatred of the Jews," reported by eyewitnesses from the last phase of the war and blatantly expressed in his first political manifesto from the autumn of 1919.

A real tactical element may have played a role in Hitler's hatred of Jews, since history taught him how uniquely he was thereby legitimated in Western tradition, that is, how successfully hatred of the Jews had been used for ages by ruling Christian sovereign houses, as an effective means of manipulation, to promote their respective interests. Indeed, the Jewish people had been persecuted even by the highest ecclesiastical authority since the beginnings of Christianity, so that, for the likes of a politician like Hitler, even according to moral principles, the Jews seemed particularly well suited for the "legitimation of an unpermitted hatred." Yet it must be unique in history how disgustingly Hitler worked himself up into this pathological hatred of Jews in the following years. Eberhard Jäckel once collected phrases apparently intended for a public that could, like himself, indulge in such perverse fantasies; they give a look into the frightful spiritual morass of this fanatic:

The Jew is the maggot in the rotting body, a pestilence worse than the black death of yore, a bacillus-carrier of the worst sort, the eternal fissioning fungus of mankind, the drone that infiltrates into the rest of humanity, the spider slowly sucking blood out of one's pores, a pack of rats fighting one another bloodily, the parasite in the body of other nations, a freeloader who spreads more and more like harmful bacteria, the eternal bloodsucker, the vampire of nations.

Given such a hatred of Jews branded into the masses, it was only a matter of time until the stored-up destructive aggressions could be given free rein without punitive consequences, and that time was no longer far away.

Hitler and Women

I am so infinitely happy that he loves me so much
and I pray that it will always remain so.
I never want to be to blame
if he should ever not love me any more.
Eva Braun in her diary, February 18, 1935

Hitler's disturbed ability for human contact and his personal inaccessibility were manifested all his life, among other things, by the fact that he was unable to make friends. Johanna Wolf, employed as his private secretary since 1929, later reported: "I don't know of him ever having had a friendship. He was very reserved." This applied even to his old military comrades; he avoided personal contact with them too, especially after seizing power in 1933, probably in order not to "allow the significance of his historical greatness to be diluted in profane lowlands"—a human inadequacy which, according to Eitner, characterizes the "typical hypersensitive narcissist, at an irresponsible distance from his fellow man."

The same lack of empathy, genuine affection, tenderness, or even love was also expressed in Hitler's relations with women. Erich Fromm observed very accurately when he distinguished two categories of women who attracted Hitler's interest. Essentially, he defined them in terms of their social rank, namely, "respectable" women who came from wealthy or influential circles or were prominent actresses, and ordinary women who stood socially and intellectually "below him."

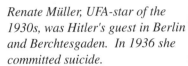

Renate Müller, UFA-star of the 1930s, was Hitler's guest in Berlin and Berchtesgaden. In 1936 she committed suicide.

Among the women of the first group were older, wealthy ladies of the upper social class who donated sizable gifts to him or his Party and whose admiration he greatly enjoyed. They represented for him mother figures who did not attract him erotically but to whom he was occasionally devoted in a purely masochistic way. Behavior of a kind that points to Hitler's masochistic submission under a woman's scepter in situations of an intimate tête-à-tête was later reported by Hanfstaengl's wife. During one of Hitler's visits to the house located near Munich, her husband happened to leave the room for a few minutes, and Hitler fell to his knees before her, calling himself her slave and bemoaning fate for having given him the bittersweet experience of knowing her too late. As he buried his head in her lap, she thought he was acting like a little boy, and she later said "it would have been terrible if anyone had come into the room. Humiliating for him."

This masochistic disposition was shown even more clearly in a scene that occurred in the thirties in the Reichs-chancellory and is supported by a document located by Walter Langer in 1972. It describes an evening that the famous film actress Renate Müller spent in the Chancellory, the details of which she confided to her director A. Zeissler. He wrote in 1943:

She was certain he would have intercourse with her; they had both undressed and were apparently about to go to bed when he threw himself on the floor and told her to kick him. She protested, but he continued urging her, calling himself unworthy, heaping accusations upon himself, and contorting himself before her in a self-tormented manner. The scene became unbearable for her, and so she finally gave in to his request and kicked him. This excited him very much, and he kept begging her for more and more, constantly repeating that even this was better than he deserved, for he was not worthy to be in the same room with her. The more she kicked him, the more excited he became.

Apparently put under pressure by Hitler, Renate Müller committed suicide in 1936 by jumping out of a window.

It is remarkable that several women close to Hitler committed suicide or tried to. The first known case was sixteen-year-old Maria Reiter from Berchtesgaden. Her love for Hitler, who was twenty years her senior, reached such a "flood of passion" that in 1927, on being informed that he wanted to live with her but not marry her, she tried to hang herself; but the attempt was discovered at the last minute, just in time to save her. Others who later made similar suicide attempts were the Viennese woman Susi Liptauer, Lady Mitford, and Martha Dodd,

Maria Reiter met Hitler in 1926 in Berchtesgaden and became his mistress for a short time. In July 1927 she made a suicide attempt in desperation.

The Englishwoman, Lady Unity Mitford, was an enthusiastic follower of Adolf Hitler. When war broke out in 1939, she shot herself in the temple with a pistol.

the daughter of the American ambassador in Berlin. Apart from the suicide of the former actress Inge Ley in 1943, who, before leaping out of the window, left a letter for Hitler which is said to have moved him deeply, there are no clues that such events affected him emotionally.

Inge Ley, the wife of Robert Ley, leader of the German Workers' Front, committed suicide in 1943. Her farewell letter was addressed to Hitler.

The readiness of several women with closer ties to Hitler to commit suicide is somewhat bewildering, since Hanfstaengl and Speer inform us that even in later years he displayed a marked shyness toward women. By his own report, he was extremely shy in his youth and generally was wild about pretty blond girls, such as Stefanie, a girl from Linz whom he ardently loved only in secret and from a distance. Even in Vienna, he reportedly was still very bashful and never mustered the courage to make any advances. In another passage, however, he informs us that during his time in Vienna before 1913 he had "met many other beautiful women." So it can certainly be assumed that during his Vienna years he made various contacts with female persons to satisfy his sexual desires. Before the beginning of World War I, 75 percent of the young men polled in Vienna experienced their first sexual contact with prostitutes and about a further 20 percent with housemaids and waitresses, so that Hitler's statement of March 1942 speaks in a quite unequivocal language that he "learned from many girls, mostly waitresses, only after the fact" that they had given birth to illegitimate children.

After the war, too, like so many of his former comrades, he tried to make up for missed occasions of sexual contacts. Indeed, in the early twenties in Munich he even had the reputation of being a regular Don Juan to whom friends occasionally referred as "the King of Munich," because the most beautiful and wealthiest women allegedly had lain at his feet. The *Münchner Post* of April 3, 1923, had reason to report that "women infatuated with Hitler" lent or even gave him money and "did not always make their subventions only in cash."

The second group of women in Hitler's life were those whom he neither admired nor respected, but who subordinated themselves to him. He had sexual relations only with this type of women, among them mainly Geli Raubal and Eva Braun. Beyond this, Hitler was a sincere admirer of female beauty, a tendency which was supported after 1933 by Goebbels, who adroitly arranged various private meetings, for example with Gretl [Margarete] Slezak, Leo Slezak's daughter, and with the actress Mady Rahl. To what extent this resulted in sexual contacts must be left undecided.

Angela Raubal, who was usually called "Geli," was the daughter of Hitler's stepsister, who took care of his country villa in Obersalzberg and who permitted her daughter, meanwhile twenty-one years of age, to live with her uncle in Hitler's comfortable nine-room apartment, which he had acquired in 1929, for the purpose of continuing her

Margarete Slezak, the daughter of Leo Slezak, often came together with Hitler through the mediation of Magda and Joseph Goebbels.

studies in Munich. This paved the way for an incestuous relationship, which was also to become Hitler's only great love. Geli was, according to the photographer Heinrich Hoffmann's description, a "likable young woman who charmed everybody with her natural and carefree manner," and according to the description of Hoffmann's daughter, Henriette (von Schirach), she was "charming, full-bosomed, a bit

The film actress Mady Rahl. She too was rumored to have had an affair with Hitler.

ironical, and quarrelsome." Hitler was drawn under her spell from the
first. Outwardly retaining the role of uncle, he soon no longer made
any serious effort to hide his courting of her favor from the public. He
always "followed her like a lamb" and strove zealously to read her
every wish from her lips. If she wanted to go swimming in Chiemsee,
"this was more important to him than any conference, however important" and he even let her talk him into accompanying her on a small
shopping spree. In his absence, he assigned two guards to follow her
everywhere like her shadow. To Hoffmann's discrete hint that sooner
or later such a restriction of her personal freedom was bound to make a
vivacious young lady like Geli unhappy, Hitler answered gruffly:

> I am determined to watch out that she does not fall
> into the hands of some adventurer or swindler...I love
> Geli and I could marry her.

As opposed to other relationships of Hitler's, for instance with Maria
Reiter or later Eva Braun, in the discreet affair with his niece Geli he
was always the jealous partner who accommodated her obligingly in
all things.

Hanfstaengl's later description of Hitler's relations to women reveal a few things about his sexual life, although we do not have enough
facts to be able to give a detailed picture of his sexual practices. But
with Erich Fromm we may assume that the "sexual interests of a cold,
timid, sadistic, and destructive man like Hitler were mainly of a perverse nature...and his sexual desires...were largely voyeuristic,
anal-sadistic with the inferior type of woman..."

This can be documented concerning Hitler's incestuous relation to
Geli Raubal by a few clues and eyewitness statements: Geli herself
made a revealing remark to a girlfriend: "My uncle is a monster. No
one could imagine what he asks of me!" And a remark by Franz Xaver
Schwartz, the former Party treasurer, gives some idea of the nature of
her uncle's monstrous demands. Schwartz stated that Hitler was black-
mailed by a man who had gotten hold of some pornographic drawings
Hitler had made of Geli showing her in poses and positions "such as
any professional model would reject." Hitler seems later similarly to
have morally offended Eva Braun, for she complained in a letter to a
girlfriend that now and then she had to model nearly obscene poses for
her Führer. In Geli Raubal's case, however, Hitler's perverse lusts
seem to have gone beyond the observation of compromising positions
of her body, if Norbert Bromberg's disclosure can be believed.

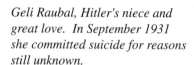

Geli Raubal, Hitler's niece and great love. In September 1931 she committed suicide for reasons still unknown.

According to him, "in order to reach full sexual satisfaction, Hitler had to observe a young woman squatting over his head, as she urinated on his face." This mortifying sexual practice would medically be the so-called "urolagnia," a form of sexual perversion in which there is a heightened interest in everything connected with the emptying of the bladder. Sadism and masochism are always complicatedly interwoven with this perversion.

Walter Lange, in his psychological study of Hitler, already pointed out such a shift of the sexual instinct to organs which had earlier given sexual stimulation. If the eye becomes an ersatz-organ, then looking develops into a sexual action, and this seems to have been the case with Hitler. In fact, according to various testimonies, even at the beginning of the time of struggle, he liked to have young girls brought to Berchtesgaden for him to observe them naked, and even later he could not feast his eyes enough on naked dance performances, which he used to follow with an opera glass.

Bromberg tried to trace back the development of Hitler's perversions on the basis of what could be discovered about the causes of his sexual anxieties and his typical defense mechanisms. The reason why he preferred sight rather than action and was excited more by the rear view than by the front view of the female vulva was his strong castration anxiety and fear of the female genitalia. The remarks which Röhm is supposed to have made once in Hitler's presence could also be understood in this sense:

> He thinks of the peasant girls standing in the fields and bending down over their work so that one can see their behind. That is what he likes, especially when they are big and round. That is Hitler's sex life. What a man!

Geli Raubal apparently confided her shocking experiences with Uncle Adolf not only to her friend, but also to a few other persons she trusted, such as Hitler's ally in the early struggle, Otto Strasser. In her despair at her jealous uncle's strange propositions and exaggerated protectiveness that made it almost impossible for her to meet other acquaintances, she began an intimate affair with Hitler's chauffeur Emil Maurice, which was soon detected by her observant uncle. Maurice countered Hitler's threats with the warning that he would contact the press (the *Frankfurter Zeitung*) if necessary and inform it of the private life of the Führer, who presented himself to the public as so ascetic and moral. Maurice was then paid 20,000 marks to keep silent, and with this money he set himself up as an independent shop owner, whereby Hitler then considered the whole matter closed. But the tensions between Geli and her uncle seem to have continued to escalate, and they ended on September 17, 1931, with a violent quarrel, whose cause is given various interpretations, and with Geli taking her own life the next day by a pistol shot through the heart.

Geli was, apart from Hitler's mother, the only person in his life whom he had ever really loved, and her loss affected him so deeply that in his depressive despair he allegedly would have put an end to his own life if Rudolf Hess had not interfered at the last moment. Plagued with strong self-reproaches of having caused Geli's act of desperation by his jealous possessiveness of her young life, he felt emotionally unable to attend her funeral in Vienna. He visited her grave incognito only a few days later and is said to have decided to renounce animal protein in the future and to have become a vegetarian as a kind of self-punishment.

Now the time had come for Eva Braun, an attractive seventeen-year-old girl whom he had met as early as 1929 in Hoffmann's studio and with whom he took frequent outings and visits to the theater even while Geli was still alive. By her cuddly nature and her devoted love

Eva Braun, born in 1912, first met Hitler at Heinrich Hoffmann's in 1929. From 1932 on, she was Hitler's mistress. She became his wife on April 29, 1945.

she soon attained her desired goal of winning him all to herself and becoming his mistress, which happened at the beginning of 1932. At least since that time, we also have from Eva Braun's diary written proof that, contrary to other statements, Hitler was indeed sexually potent. Speculations to the effect that he was incapable of physically loving a woman and having normal intercourse are based on rumors that he had only one testis. Although Maser denied such allegations as fabricated, relying incomprehensibly on dubious statements by Dr. Morell, Hitler's personal physician, the fact remains that this rumor had a real basis in the form of an unambiguous finding by the Munich urologist, Professor Kielleuthner, from the 1920s, which states the following: "Hitler had only one testis but I was not able to help him since he was too old." Thus Hitler actually did suffer from a so-called cryptorchism, in which one testis remains stuck in the inguinal canal during a boy's development—a finding which, incidentally, could be confirmed later at the autopsy of Hitler's corpse. Such a deformation can be corrected relatively simply in early childhood but no longer at the age of thirty-three, as was the case with Hitler at the time of this urological examination.

Otherwise, such a deformation, which is not rare, is unconnected with any disturbances of sexual activity. Eva Braun's diary also agrees with this, when she wrote for instance in the entry for March 1935:

> He needs me only for certain purposes...it is not pos-
> sible otherwise....When he says he loves me, he means
> it only at that moment.

With this note, she was at the same time describing Hitler's attitude toward women in general. For in later conversations he repeatedly expressed the opinion that a "great man"—which he of course considered himself to be—could keep a girl for the satisfaction of his sexual desires and it was all right for him, without any heartfelt affection and without any sense of responsibility, to treat her as an immature child, practically without rights. And as Albert Speer later confirmed, that is exactly how he treated Eva:

> In general he had little concern for her feelings. Hitler
> took little notice at all of her presence. Quite without
> embarrassment he spoke his opinion about women in
> her presence: "Very intelligent men should take a
> primitive and stupid wife."

Given this attitude, it is understandable why he married Eva Braun only a few minutes before his death, to a certain extent symbolically as the epitome of the apocalyptic drama of his downfall. His aversion to entering a marriage no doubt had several reasons. One of them was concern that he might lose much of his charismatic aura with the female electorate and thus make his political course unnecessarily more difficult, as he himself confirmed in conversations:

> Many women are devoted to me because I am unmar-
> ried. That was especially important in the time of
> struggle. It is like with a movie star: if he marries he
> loses a certain something with the women who idolize
> him and then he is no longer quite so much their idol.

Another reason was, once again, his pathologically egregious narcissism, which categorically rejected anything that could in his eyes cast even the slightest shadow on his self-glorified personality. That could apply to the most secondary matters; for example, he refused to be seen in a bathing suit, even by Geli, for fear that he could be compromised and lose some of his dignity. And for similar reasons he consistently avoided every kind of sports activity, whether it were winter sports, horseback riding, or any kind of gymnastics.

But the very thought of a possible marriage seemed to frighten him worst of all, as can be gathered from his own words:

The Führer resting from his exertions; on the right,
Eva Braun (photo from Eva Braun's collection).

You see, if I ever had a wife, she could meddle with
my work! I could never marry. If I had children, what
problems! In the end they would try to set my son as
my successor. Besides, someone like me has no prospect of having a capable son. That is almost always
the rule in such cases. You see, Goethe's son, a quite
useless person.

Eva Braun seemed to be just the right mate for such a man, the
kind of mistress he wanted to allow "only to outstanding men" and
from whom he expected submission, as he avows in a conversation on
January 25, 1942:

It must be possible for a man to put his stamp on any
girl. That is exactly what a woman wants.

That is exactly how Eva was: dedicated to him for better or worse. In
letters to her sister, she always reported about her lover by the respectful title of Führer and she always carried out his desires in anticipatory
obedience—for instance, aware of Hitler's preference for full-bosomed
women, at first she had padded her bras with handkerchiefs to simulate
ample forms!

How unhappy this young woman was under the cold affective relationship of her lover, who treated her before all the world without
any consideration for her feelings, can be seen from entries in her diary.
Thus, under March 11, 1935, it says:

I wish for only one thing, to be very sick and to know
nothing of him for at least a week. Why doesn't something happen to me, why must I go through all this. If
only I had never seen him. I am in despair. Why
doesn't the devil come and get me? It surely is nicer
in hell than here.

Similar complaints are also found in later entries of her diary; and on
May 28, 1935, she announced a second "absolutely sure" way of ending her life, but this second suicide attempt was also foiled.

ON THE ROAD TO POWER

At the end of March 1930, Heinrich Brüning was nominated Reichs-
chancellor and in September 1930, on Reichs-president Hindenburg's
request, he formed the first so-called "presidential government" of the
Weimar Republic. At the very moment when Brüning was taking office, "Black Friday," that tremendous crash within the world economic
crisis of October 24, 1929, was beginning to make itself felt with full
force in postwar Germany. A race began between the government and
the crisis. In July 1930 the Reichs-president set in force Article 48 of
the Weimar constitution, which gave the Reichs-president special powers in case of an extreme state emergency. The parliamentary majority
responded by voting to abolish the emergency regulations, thus precipitating a parliamentary crisis and forcing Hindenburg and Brüning
to call for new elections immediately.

In an electoral campaign, the likes of which had never before been
seen in Germany, the NSDAP managed to win 107 seats in the
Reichstag, unleashing a veritable political landslide. On that date, September 14, 1930, the NSDAP's concerted attack on parliament and on
the parliamentary system began with the surefire means of impractical
bills and reckless demagogic agitation. Unemployment, following upon
the bank collapse in the early summer of 1931 and, meanwhile, spreading in great waves, gradually radicalized the political climate in
Germany toward conditions similar to a civil war, to which the militant
battalions of the Communist Party and the NSDAP's battle brigades
contributed most strongly. It was mainly to the latter right-wing radical influences that Hindenburg became more and more accessible, and
finally they persuaded him to instruct Brüning to reorganize his cabinet with a turn toward the right.

Even in those years of political activity, Hitler displayed an explosive temper and a lack of control of his emotional outbursts and he seems already to have used them on purpose to achieve his wishes more easily, as Otto Strasser, a colleague who had fallen into disfavor, reported:

> One day he became aware of the crushing effect of his fits of rage. From that moment on, anger and screaming served him as weapons.

The description of his fits of anger in the years 1929 to 1932 given by the former SS chief of staff, Dr. Otto Wagener, who also had been expelled, sounds similar:

> In such cases he could work himself up into indignation and anger, so that the veins on his forehead from the stem of the nose to the hairline swelled with rage and turned almost frightfully blue, and his voice cracked, so that you could believe you had to fear for his life—but also for your own.

The police president of Berlin, Jakob Diel, who was installed in 1933 after the Nazi seizure of power, once witnessed such an unrestrained and hate-filled state of excitement:

> With fleeting breath, he abandoned himself to wild fantasies with a mixture of pathetic declamation and panting groans.

Some witnesses may, however, have strongly overdrawn Hitler's explosiveness, and this led to various legends, such as that he threw himself down on the floor and chewed at the carpet. Such a description came from Hermann Rauschning, the former president of the Danzig senate, whom historians have suspected of exaggerating:

> What I saw with my own eyes and was told by acquaintances was the expression of unrestraint to the point of a total breakdown of the personality. His screaming, raging, and foot-stamping, all the outbreaks of his irascibility, those tantrums of an ill-behaved, spoiled brat: despite his grotesque and hair-raising manner this was not insanity. Although it is questionable when an adult pounds on the wall, kicks at the chain like a horse in the stable, or throws himself on

the floor....Apparently the period was then beginning
in which he would throw the world around him into
confusion by calculated fits of rage and make them
willing to capitulate. People were beginning to fear
his unpredictable behavior.

Albert Speer, too, said: "Some seemingly hysterical reactions that are
reported may well be attributable to this kind of playacting." But not
one of these portrayals mentioned his "biting the carpet," as did an
article by the Italian psychiatrist Dalma in 1944 in a professional journal, referring to the Rauschning incidents with the term "Mangiatappeti"
(chewing the carpet), and this notion was taken up uncritically by other
authors like Langer or Sterpellone.

In any case, Hitler must have used all the registers of his tactical
and rhetorical possibilities during his truly gigantic operation in the
election campaign for the Reichs-presidency, running against the aged
Hindenburg. Although in the last weeks prior to the election scheduled
for March 1932 he was struggling with his last reserves of energy, he
tried outwardly to hide any sign of tiredness, not to mention exhaustion, in order to demonstrate his strength and vitality to everyone.
However, Albert Krebs, at that time Gauleiter of Hamburg, also experienced him in those days from quite a different side. In a personal
conversation, he learned of Hitler's "hypochondriac fears for his health"
and of various so-called psychosomatic ailments such as stomach
cramps, sweat outbreaks, and states of excitation in which his limbs
began to tremble. Hitler was especially alarmed by stomachaches,
because he considered them to be forewarnings of cancer signaling
that he had only a few years left to complete his work. This fear led, in
Sebastian Haffner's view, to one of the most unusual and momentous
decisions of his life, namely, the future subordination of his policies
and his political time-schedule under what Hitler believed would probably be the short duration of his earthly life.

Hindenburg emerged victorious from the presidential election, but
Hitler, too, was satisfied with the results. For the election results of
April 10, 1932, brought him a sensational gain of two million votes.
The Papen and Schleicher cabinets, which followed, strike us today in
historical retrospect as a planned preamble to Hitler's seizure of power.
Von Papen, who was nominated as the new Reichs-chancellor in May,
yielded the field as early as December 3 to General Schleicher, who
then finally convinced Hindenburg to raise the leader of the strongest

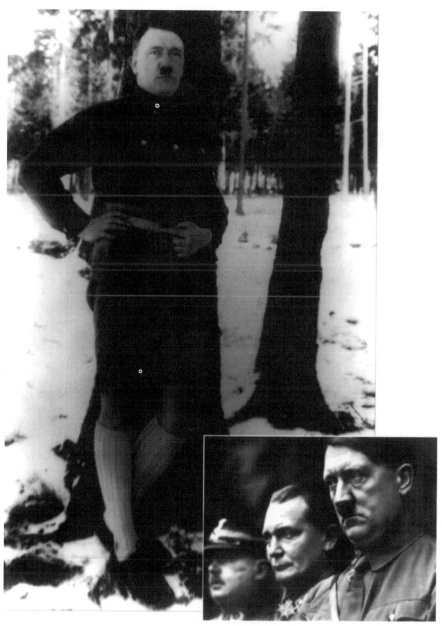

Hitler poses for his photographer Heinrich Hoffmann in leather trousers (ca. 1930). Inset Photo: In power at last—the Führer with Hermann Göring and Ernst Röhm taken on November 19, 1933 (Memorial service for the victims of the 1923 putsch)

Reichs-chancellor Adolf Hitler conversing with his Vice-chancellor Franz von Papen and his Defense Minister Werner von Blomberg (March 21, 1933)

party, Adolf Hitler, to the post of chancellor, even though in the last election, on November 6, 1932, the NSDAP had relinquished more than two million votes.

This setback affected Hitler all the more because, in the midst of the foregoing election campaign, he received the news that Eva Braun had tried to take her own life by shooting herself through the throat with her father's pistol. A letter to Wagner's wife from those days shows that the political defeat and Eva's suicide attempt aroused renewed thoughts of suicide in him, too. In this letter he hinted that he had given up all hope, and as soon as he was certain all was lost he would end his life with a bullet.

This depressive phase was of short duration and quickly gave way to new energy when on January 30, 1933, Hitler was named Reichs-chancellor, but his so-called "seizure of power" did not yet occur with this cabinet formation. This first came about only in the following month as the work of an unwavering, persistent man obsessed with power and his policies. His regime began legally and without bloodshed,

Ein feierlicher Augenblick von der Grundsteinlegung zum Haus der deutschen Kunst.

Der päpstliche Nuntius Vasallo di Torregrossa spricht eben zum Führer:

**„Ich habe Sie lange nicht verstanden.
Ich habe mich aber lange darum bemüht.
Heute versteh' ich Sie."**

Auch jeder deutsche Katholik versteht heute Adolf Hitler und stimmt am 12. November
mit:

„Ja"!

National socialist 1933 election poster highlighting
Hitler's favorable attitude toward the Church:
A festive moment at the cornerstone ceremony of the House of German Art.
The papal nuncio Vasallo di Torregrossa is just saying to the Führer:
"For a long time I did not understand you.
After having given it a lot of thought, today I understand you."
and every German Catholic today understands Adolf Hitler
and on November 12 votes YES!

fostering in the middle class the reassuring hope that the revolutionary element of the NSDAP would from now on fade into the background and that Hitler himself would change from a revolutionary agitator to a wise and benevolent statesman. But the events of February 27, 1933, would show that this hope was a naive dream. Although it has been proven that the fire which erupted at the Reichstag in Berlin on that day was set neither by the Communists nor by the National Socialists but by Marinus van der Lubbe, acting alone, for purely personal motives, Hitler reached the edge of hysteria with fear that a revolution from the left could sweep him out of the office he had just obtained with such great effort. After Hindenburg had invoked the emergency regulation on February 28, then Hitler, with his Empowerment Law of March 24, 1933, hastened to initiate the process of abolishing democratic constitutional government *(Rechtsstaat)* and to secure his position of absolute power in the Reich.

In his paranoid fear of personal enemies who could be a damper on his newly created position, he did not stop short even of his closest collaborators, as the Röhm affair of June 30, 1934, most crassly showed. Ernst Röhm, as the leader of the powerful SA (Brownshirts), seemed to him increasingly like a dangerous rival whom it was best to eliminate. Therefore, with the assistance of Heydrich, Goebbels and Göring, he staged a disgusting play of intrigue in which Röhm was accused of seeking to murder his Führer. The executions of several of Hitler's own comrades and associates, which he ordered himself on that day, allowed him to give free rein to his sadistic tendencies for the first time against an entire group, this time of his own followers. A later report literally lets one sense his Satanic delight in murder and destruction:

> I gave the order to execute the main instigators of this treason, and I also gave the order to cauterize the ulcers of our inner well-poisoning down to the raw flesh.

Words spoken openly in 1932 just before the seizure of power should have caught one's attention:

> We have to be cruel. We have to give a good conscience back to cruelty. Only thus can we drive out of our people their softness and sentimental bourgeois mentality.

But the executions of June 30, 1934, were a gruesome foretaste of his future crimes, cruelties, and barbaric acts. At the same time they also showed that his unparalleled indifference to human fates applied not merely to the Jews, Gypsies, and Slavs, but equally to German civilians, soldiers, and even his own Party comrades, who in his opinion belonged to the Aryan race. How little the lives of young German men were worth in his eyes can be seen from Hitler's own admission, made in 1934, in anticipation of the great war he was planning:

> Someday when I shall command the war, I cannot have any reservations about the ten million young men I will be sending to their death.

The Röhm putsch did not concern the aged Hindenburg very much, although it brought death before the firing squad to hundreds of men without a trial, merely to arbitrarily protect the position of the anxious and distrustful Führer. But the "execution" of General Schleicher and his wife in their private apartment by two of Hitler's stooges filled Hindenburg with indignation and he demanded an investigation. How pitifully weak this old president's position was by this time is shown by the fact that he could not enforce this demand but instead signed a congratulatory telegram to Hitler, the text of which was drafted by functionaries of the NSDAP, expressing his thanks to the Reichs-chancellor for having saved the German people from a grave peril. While Hindenburg was no longer able to recognize Hitler's total lack of moral principles, some of the Führer's former ardent supporters now saw through him. For instance, Hein Rick, who later played an important role in Otto Skorzeny's commando action to kidnap Benito Mussolini, stressed that from that day on, in his eyes and those of his friends, Hitler was finished as a human being. Foreign countries, too, were watching events in Germany with some concern. The sharpest attacks came from Italy, especially after the murder of the Austrian Chancellor Dollfuss during an attempted putsch by the National Socialists in July 1934. Mussolini prophesied to Vice-Chancellor Starhemberg literally the end of European civilization if this country of "murderers and pederasts" should overrun Europe, and he then went so far as to call Hitler a despicable, sexually perverted man and dangerous fool.

Meanwhile, Hitler, since Hindenburg lay dying, drafted a law that amounted practically to a *coup d'état*, stipulating that from now on the offices of Reichs-president and Reichs-chancellor were to be combined in one person. Hitler had thus appropriated the title of "Führer and Reichs-chancellor" and on August 19, 1934, somewhat more than two weeks after Hindenburg's death, the German people voted for this law by an "overwhelming majority."

In the following years, a whole series of Hitler's positive achievements caused the mood in Germany, on the whole, to show a clear upward trend in his favor, which seems incomprehensible to the present generation in historical retrospect. What stands first among his positive achievements at that time is surely, as Sebastian Haffner correctly remarked, his so-called economic miracle, which strictly speaking was not to Hitler's own credit but was due to the skillful finance minister, Hyalmar. In January 1933, there were six million unemployed in

Germany; by 1936, full employment was attained, moreover, without inflation and with stable wages and prices. From a current standpoint it is, of course, clearly recognizable that this was possible only for a dictatorial regime with its concentration camps in the background and with a mandatory system of fixed wages and prices. For the people living in Germany at that time, this was, however, not so evident, apart from the fact that the masses of unemployed were really absolutely indifferent as to how this "miracle" came about. Today the objection is frequently made that, just by reintroducing universal military conscription in the context of Germany's military mobilization and rearmament, a hundred thousand unemployed vanished from the streets and that additional hundreds of thousands found work through enormous munitions contracts. Whereas in 1933 Germany had an army of only one hundred thousand men and no air force at all, by 1938 it had advanced to the strongest military power and air force in Europe. Sebastian Haffner disagrees; in his critical study on Hitler, he pointed out a fact often ignored by historians, namely, that the preponderant majority of the originally six million unemployed had, by 1936, found reemployment, not in the armaments industry, but "in completely normal industries."

To recognize the seeds of the future catastrophe latent in these indubitable and astonishingly successful achievements even then, would have required extraordinary insight on the part of the German people—insight which, as is known, even expert diplomats and politicians of foreign countries completely lacked at the time. For, although foreign countries regarded Adolf Hitler as an anti-democratic and extremely nationalistic statesman, at the same time, in their shortsightedness, they quite disastrously believed him to be a politician capable of appraising situations realistically and of promoting his objectives moderately and without endangering the peace. To give that impression, Hitler resorted to his typical art of camouflage and talent as an actor and was able to sell his lies and treacherous plans in the garb of a peaceful dove.

He used similar methods to remove intraparty tensions such as arose near the end of 1935. Early the next year, he convoked all the Reich- and Gau-leaders to a conference, urging them with tearful eyes to maintain solidarity with him and to swear continued absolute devotion and loyalty to him, since otherwise the great goals he had charted for the future could not be achieved. If they did not give him solid support, he threatened, as he had done in the dark times at the end of 1932, then he

Hitler's personal physician
Dr. Theodor Morell (1886-
1948). From 1936 on, he was
responsible for the Führer's
medical care.

would unhesitatingly take his own life. This hysterically announced suicide threat attained its purpose; they all left deeply moved and ready to follow him to the death with unswerving loyalty.

In foreign policy, 1936 was a successful year, although what was achieved cost Hitler nothing. It began with the invasion of the Rhineland without any concerted foreign reaction being mounted. Hitler, enormously strengthened in his already pronounced sense of mission, proclaimed with proud words:

> I am walking with a sleepwalker's certainty on the path
> Providence has called me to go.

Yet, the uncertainty before starting the whole enterprise seems to have created in him tremendous tensions that affected him psychosomatically, especially in the form of stomach cramps, and resulted in heightened irritability and insomnia. Shortly before Christmas, Hitler fell into a depressive mood, as he usually did in this season which reminded him of his mother's death. Moreover, an eczema had formed on his lower left thigh and made it almost impossible for him to wear boots. So, on December 25, 1936, on recommendation of his personal photographer he sought out Dr. Theo Morell, a fashionable physician and dermatologist with a lucrative practice on the Kurfürstendamm in Berlin, who from then on was to function as Hitler's personal physician.

Why he chose precisely this doctor, who was considered negligent and hygienically unclean among his colleagues, to be his personal medical caretaker cannot be clearly known. Probably the friendship that had developed between Mrs. Morell and Eva Braun played a role. Morell, at any rate, interpreted the eczematous skin lesions to be the result of a digestive problem and he gave his patient Mutaflor capsules, an emulsion of *E. coli* [bacteria typically found in the digestive tract] popular at the time "to regulate the altered intestinal flora." In addition, for Hitler's flatulence the so-called Dr. Köster anti-gas pills were prescribed, which contained, besides atropine, slight quantities of strychnine. Finally, Morell associated Hitler's stomach cramps with his extremely one-sided vegetarian diet, which supposedly led to an irritation of the intestinal membranes.

Dubious as these measures may have been, Hitler believed in them; when after less than a month the painful eczema had disappeared, he declared Morell to be a miracle doctor who had saved his life. In view of the prior unsuccessful treatment by the famous Professor Gustav von Bergmann from the Charité Hospital in Berlin and Dr. Ernst-Robert Grawitz, director of the Red Cross, he enthusiastically gloated:

> Grawitz and Bergmann had me starving. They allowed
> me only tea and melba toast. I was so weak I could
> hardly work at my desk. Then along came Morell and
> cured me.

With an elated feeling, effusive self-satisfaction, and a strong sense of the mission assigned him by Divine Providence, on January 30, 1937, Hitler appeared before the Reichstag completely revitalized with a speech celebrating the fourth anniversary of his chancellorship, in which he announced to the people with pathetic words:

> I must humbly thank Providence whose grace enabled
> me, a once unknown soldier of the World War, to win
> back their honor and decency for our people.

A few months later, he hinted at the kinds of means he intended to use to attain this goal, namely, the brutal eradication and destruction of people who thought differently. This was in a speech at the opening of the House of German Art in Munich, where the jury had made its selections in line with purely artistic criteria and therefore logically included many modern paintings. Since Hitler considered such art degenerate, in his opening address he asserted that in the future such artists

A propaganda photograph from 1936: the Führer as a fatherly friend...

would have to be eliminated, and he proclaimed threateningly the methods whereby that would have to be done, namely, either to sterilize them or to have them prosecuted as criminal violators. He cynically declared:

> If they actually were able to see reality only in that way, then it would have to be investigated whether their optical defect had come about mechanically or by heredity. In the first case, it was deeply regrettable for those unfortunate wretches; in the second, it was important for the Reichs-Ministry of the Interior, whose duty it would be to deal with the question of at least curtailing any further inheritance of such horrid optical malfunctioning. But if a certain other cause brought modern art to the public, then such an offense falls within the jurisdiction of the penal code.

Seldom in history has the megalomanic mind of an arrogant, narcissistic, and objectively totally incompetent dictator manifested its delusions more gruesomely.

His arrogance and pride would, however, turn out to be capable of even greater inflation. In February 1938 he made known to the commanding generals his surprising decision to assume the supreme command of the armed forces in person. The first goal envisaged by Hitler in his preparations for the predetermined plan of a future great war was the incorporation of Austria, his "homeland," into the German Reich, as he stated with his usual messianic feeling:

> I have a great historical mission and I will fulfill it because Providence has destined me for it....I believe that it was also God's will to send a lad from there into the Reich, to let him grow up and raise him to be the Führer of the nation, in order to make it possible for him to bring his homeland back into the Reich.

Cardinal Innitzer, the head of the Catholic Church in Austria at that time seems also to have perceived this "will of God," since he greeted Hitler with the sign of the cross and assured him of the loyalty of Austrian Catholics. Although Hitler was quite assured of Chamberlain's appeasement policy, he seems not to have been in perfect health during the invasion, as is proven by his stomach cramps during the triumphal ride to Vienna, which were especially intense during the brief stopover in Linz. But perhaps it was just his excessive joyful excitement that sedimented into psychosomatic complaints.

Adolf Hitler and Joseph Goebbels making the rounds at the opening of the German Art Exhibition on July 10, 1938

During the subsequent annexation of the Sudetenland and the immediately following occupation of Czechoslovakia in the fall of 1938, Hitler worried that the Western powers might intervene after all; he saw himself compelled to get the approval at least of his only ally, Mussolini. But during the railroad trip to Rome, Hitler's tremendous psychic tensions and fear that an unintentional war with the West might endanger his fixed plans for conquest in the East triggered such a stomachache that he spent several hours writing a last will and testament. But his ailments soon cleared up again, once he had purchased Mussolini's loyalty by ceding South Tyrol to Italy and once Mussolini had pledged to go along completely with Hitler's "unshakable decision to wipe Czechoslovakia off the map."

Hitler had been complaining for a long time about a persistent throat infection and increasingly hoarse voice. According to the *Times* of November 14, 1938, Hitler had supposedly visited Professor Heinrich Neumann, director of the University of Vienna's laryngological clinic in the fall of 1935 for similar ailments, because this doctor was considered to be especially skilled in that field. But Neumann, an orthodox Jew, had politely but firmly turned down this request. This time, in

*Adolf Hitler during his entry into his native city of Braunau, Austria, on
March 12, 1938*

May 1935, Hitler went to Professor Karl von Eicken, director of the
University Clinic for Throat, Nose, and Ear Diseases in Berlin, who
discovered a nonmalignant polyp of the vocal cords and removed it
with a minor surgical operation, performed in Hitler's apartment in the
Reichs-chancellory.

Meanwhile, the pogrom-mood in Germany was given an unexpected boost by the murder of Ernst von Rath, a member of the German
embassy in Paris, by a young Jew, Herschel Grynspan, on November
8, 1938. With Hitler's explicit approval, Goebbels incited the SA units
in the entire Reichs-territory to the plundering, murderous excesses
that were called by the macabre and euphemistic title of the "Reichs
Crystal Night" because of the countless smashed panes of glass. On
the night of November 9, two hundred and fifty synagogues were burned
down and more than twenty-five thousand Jews were hauled off to
concentration camps.

The radical phase of Hitler's anti-Jewish policy began on that day.
Once again, nothing was done by any foreign countries to try to stop
this base and criminal activity, at least through diplomatic channels.
However, the conviction was gaining ground that this Hitler was capable of the wildest exaggerations and of practically insane ambitions,

as François-Poncet phrased it. Sigmund Freud, who had managed to escape to London, summed up this characterization with the terse statement: "You can never know what a crazy man will do next."

While this turn of public opinion in England and France destroyed Hitler's credibility as a partner for negotiations once and for all, in his extreme narcissism (which made it impossible for him to admit a mistake), he regarded the other countries' reactions as just a temporary loss of his reputation. The Catholic Church also seems to have been of this opinion, for on April 20, 1939, even the Pope sent his congratulations to Hitler on his fiftieth birthday, which the German bishops dutifully seconded with their prayer "for God's blessing on the Führer and the people," and they prayed for the Almighty's continued help "to the Führer and Reichs-chancellor, the enlarger and preserver of the Reich."

Hitler spent the summer of 1939 at the Berghof in apparent idleness, which made his opponents somewhat uneasy. In reality, he had completed all preparations to implement the annexation of Danzig and to create an extraterritorial link to East Prussia right through the Polish corridor. With advance knowledge of the provocative actions worked out in detail by the Germans, he threatened "to crush Poland without warning upon the least incident." The decision for military intervention was all the easier for him, since in his non-aggression pact with

Scene from March 1939 of Jews forced by the SS-men to clean the sidewalk with their toothbrushes while the crowd laughed

Russia on August 23, 1939, he had in a secret codicil already arranged for the future partition of Eastern Europe, and Poland, in particular. So now he was ready with open eyes to challenge his destiny, despite his own prophecy made in *Mein Kampf* that any German-Russian pact would inevitably lead to a military conflict, which "means the end of Germany."

THE SECOND WORLD WAR

How far Hitler's megalomania had developed by this time and how low the limit of his self-critique had sunken is shown by a speech he gave to his generals on August 22, 1939, a few days before the war began. Permeated with his solitary greatness, he justified his decision to attack with the words:

> In all modesty, a further factor is my own personality. Essentially it depends on me, on my existence, because of my political abilities. Then there is the further fact that probably no one will ever again have the confidence of the whole German people. In the future, there will probably never again be a man who has more authority than I. My existence is thus a great value-factor.

In the blitzkrieg that began on September 1, 1939, introducing a new era of future military science, the Polish air force was completely wiped out after only two days, and another two days later Poland's thirty-five divisions were either encircled or in frantic disarray. On September 17, units of the Red Army crossed the Polish border and, while the Russians were just beginning to occupy Eastern Poland and the Baltic countries, Hitler had already transformed the rest of Poland "into a slaughterhouse." These atrocities, ordered by Hitler personally, were accompanied by the ruthless expulsion of more than a million Poles—the Soviets, incidentally, with their usual zeal tried to keep pace. Then immediately after the end of the Poland campaign, the first transports of Jews to the East began. Intoxicated by these orgies of annihilation and destruction, Hitler no longer had the least inhibitions to overcome in order to give his criminal drives free rein and realize his delusionary ideas. An eloquent example of this is the horrible "Führer's order" of September 1939, to kill all incurable or mentally ill German citizens as "superfluous eaters." About five thousand children and a hundred thousand adults fell victim to this directive to eliminate the mentally ill and other forms of "worthless life."

Together with his order to murder millions of Jews and other nationalities whom he called "subhuman," because he believed them to be racially worthless, this directive ranks among his very worst crimes. Hitler's so-called "euthanasia program" of course had nothing to do with the concept of euthanasia, that is, the assuagement of the end of a human life already in the process of being extinguished, certainly and painfully. Rather, it was an extreme case of the mass-killing of life "not worthy of life," the likes of which cannot be found in all history. Alice Miller believes she has discovered a motive, grounded in depth psychology, for the conception of that gruesome secret order of Hitler's. Her speculation is that Hitler's Aunt Johanna Pölzl, who was hunchbacked from birth and later became sick with schizophrenia, represented for him an unprocessed nightmarish childhood trauma. Daily contact with his crippled, mentally ill aunt and her peculiar and alarming behavior in his early childhood would then be partly responsible for his later decision to mercilessly wipe out the mentally ill, cripples, and other forms of "life not worthy of life." Interesting as such reflections of a depth psychologist may be, they are quite unsatisfactory as an explanation. Why should such a childhood trauma—which, after all, many people have to endure—in Hitler's case have led to a total lack of inhibitions in realizing his criminal drives? Dietrich, his longtime press secretary, later put this into words:

> In his choice of means...he lacked any feeling of good
> and evil, or for the moral imperative.

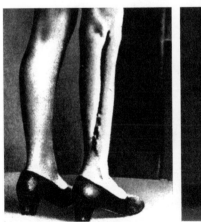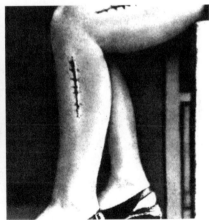

Two examples of experimental operations performed on female concentration camp prisoners.

De Boor regards this complete leveling of the structural barrier as the most essential cause for the issuance of that gruesome euthanasia-edict.

[This total lack of inhibition to aggressive reactions] qualified Hitler as a prototype of the dangerous violent criminal who displays a tabula rasa from a moral standpoint, whereas other violators of the law still show at least a remnant of their former structural barriers. From a criminological standpoint, the loss of the structural limit is one of the most momentous phenomena known to empirical criminology. Only in a mass murderer does the extinguishing of normative substance occur on a similar scale.

Outraged by the Führer's abnormal actions, some resistance groups began to form in Germany to remove the dictator, but their planned coups d'état, such as that of Colonel Oster, could not be realized. Later attempts to assassinate Hitler had similar outcomes; for instance, that of the cabinetmaker Georg Elser, on November 8, 1939, in the Bürgerbräukeller in Munich, failed by pure accident. When Hitler learned of this abortive assassination attempt, he was tremendously confirmed in his sense of mission, as can be gathered from his words delivered in a voice hoarse with emotion:

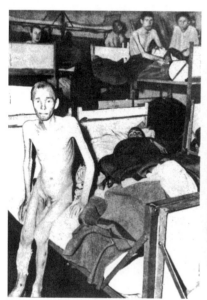
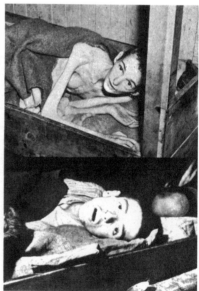

The "sick ward" in Flossenbürg concentration camp

Now I am completely calm! That I left the Bürgerbräukeller earlier than usual is a confirmation that
Providence wants me to achieve my goal.

He voiced this opinion in a tone of deep conviction. Cardinal Faulhaber
of Munich apparently agreed, for immediately after the assassination
attempt he sent a telegram to Hitler and had a *Te Deum* sung in the
Frauenkirche in Munich "to thank Divine Providence in the name of
the diocese for the fortunate saving of the Führer's life."

More than ever convinced of his leadership qualities and his destined mission, on May 10, 1940, Hitler launched the Western offensive,
which came to a successful end as early as June 25, due to a better
strategic conception, threefold air superiority, and an unprecedented
massive deployment of armored troops. The day Hitler was informed
that France had asked for a truce, almost hysterical with joy, he performed before the amazed eyes of his generals a veritable St. Vitus
dance, which was captured on film. Virtually hypnotized by his own
military and political successes, his narcissistic superstructure knew
no bounds. In his megalomania, he told a Party functionary that he
was the first and only mortal ever to have risen to the "status of a superman." Therefore, his being should henceforth be regarded as "more
divine than human," as standing "above the law" and no longer subject
to the conventions of human morality.

The mass of the German population was bewildered by all the developments leading to the outbreak of war, and many felt absolutely
betrayed. Had they known their Führer's true character traits more
precisely, they would have been even more perplexed. A handwriting
analysis of texts that Hitler wrote on May 2, 1938, during his journey
to Rome to see Mussolini, and which Maser in 1970 submitted to the
German graphologist Sigurd Müller (without revealing the writer),
would even then have revealed Hitler's characteristics, which Müller
summarized as follows:

> Wrong ideas, limited critical and judgmental ability,
> volatility and unreliability, strong determination with
> a tendency to speculation, ability for human contact
> hampered due to idiosyncratic dogmatism, crass lack
> of consideration and tendency to exaggerate in con-
> nection with the urge to expand his living space.

As to his health, a medical examination in January 1940 showed a tendency to high blood pressure. However, an assertion publicized by some journalists that Hitler had caught syphilis during his time in Vienna, and therefore was later suffering from a progressive paralysis, could not be verified. Such speculations are probably based on hints by the Finnish masseur Kersten, who took care of Himmler and is supposed to have been told confidentially by him that Hitler had caught that venereal disease during World War I. Contrary to Maser's opinion, the negative results of the serological examination made on January 15, 1940, does not exclude an earlier luetic infection, but it does speak with certainty against an untreated progressive paralysis; and this was confirmed by the ophthalmologist's normal diagnosis, made by Professor Löhlein of the Charité in Berlin.

Despite repeated English warnings, the powerful German army that moved out against Russia on June 22, 1941, found the Soviet Union completely unprepared. In his instructions for this operation called "Barbarossa," Hitler saw the most urgent task as first to occupy the Baltic states, then to conquer Leningrad and break through southward to Kiev as far as the Dneiper, since this would deprive the Soviets of their most important agricultural and industrial resources. His ultimate goal was a Reich extending eastward from Archangelsk on the Arctic Ocean to Astrakhan on the Caspian Sea. But from a "discussion of the situation" dated February 17, 1941, we know that Hitler's immoderate hunger for power and land was striving beyond that to a kind of world rule; for its realization, he wanted a study prepared on a future invasion of German units into Afghanistan, with the ultimate goal of conquering India and then destroying the British Empire.

However, his strategic plan was modified in its early stage. In the summer of 1941, in the swampy region where he had his headquarters, the "Wolf's Lair," he fell ill with a feverish diarrhea, probably caused by a dysenteric infection; his generals tried to cancel the original plan and launch an armored thrust at Moscow. At the end of July, Hitler showed signs of coronary and circulatory problems, as is reported in connection with a loud dispute with Ribbentrop, his foreign minister. In the midst of the violent discussion he suddenly turned as pale as a corpse and grabbed his heart as he sank back into a chair; then after a rather long, oppressive silence he said: "I thought I was having a heart attack." Probably he actually had suffered a considerable rise in blood pressure during the strong excitement, as was repeatedly observed by his personal physician Dr. Morell. Then a set of symptoms similar to angina pectoris led to a temporary deficiency in the oxygen supply to the coronary arteries. Corresponding changes in the coronary blood vessels were described at the time by Professor Alfred Weber, director of the Heart Clinic in Bad Nauheim, based on an electrocardiogram sent to him by Dr. Morell (without the patient's name revealed), for his expert opinion.

Another event casts some light on the state of Hitler's circulation at that time. One of Morell's notes dated August 7, 1941, shows that after a rather long flight his patient complained of dizziness associated with ear noises on his left side and a "peculiar feeling" over the left temple, during which a distinctly higher blood pressure was measured. This time the trouble was a temporary circulatory disorder in the area of the blood vessels of the brain, wrongly interpreted as a "mild stroke" by Nicolaus von Below, the air force adjutant accompanying Hitler, in his later memoirs.

A large quantity of film material from a total of eighty-three news reels was systematically analyzed and evaluated in sharp detail by Ellen Gibbels, from a neurological viewpoint. These films register poor associated movements of the left arm as well as "slightly impeded total mobility" around the middle of 1941—pathological symptoms not previously observable, but which became more and more apparent in the following years. These impairments were accentuated even more, especially on high official occasions, by Hitler's almost ponderous movements, due to his inflated feeling of self-importance.

With Hitler's surprise attack on Russia, his structural barrier, that is, that socio-cultural imperative which prevents more serious aggressive reactions even under the strongest emotional build-up and in extreme cases is the most effective inhibitive mechanism against killing, had broken down totally. Strictly speaking, it already had failed during the election campaign for the Reichstag in March 1933, in which fifty-one political opponents had been murdered in cold blood. Fifty concentration camps were put into operation in that same year, as reported by Eugen Kogon. With the beginning of the Russian campaign, however, Hitler was able to give full vent to his uninhibited urge for brutality, cruelty, and destruction. In an OKW-instruction dated September 8, 1941, he denied all Russian war prisoners, whom he considered racially inferior, any claim to be treated as honorable prisoners of war. Therefore, every German had the right to resort "to the

*Major General Heinz Guderian
(1888-1954) was dismissed by
Hitler in March 1945*

most ruthless measures" against them. This inhuman edict is to blame
for the fact that in February 1942, of the four million Soviet soldiers
who were taken prisoner, only one million survived.

Hitler's absolute cold-bloodedness applied even to his own soldiers. He once warned Guderian, his best armored general, who had
called attention to the inhuman condition of the front-line troops:

> You have too much pity on the soldiers. You ought to
> distance yourself more. Believe me, from a distance
> one sees things more clearly.

And when the ability of the home front to hold out came under discussion, he said, unmoved:

> Even in that regard I am ice cold. If the German people
> are not ready to risk everything for their own self-
> preservation, then they ought to perish.

The invasion of Russia was simultaneous with preparations for the
planned mass murder of the European Jews. By the beginning of July
1941, he boasted:

> I feel like a Robert Koch of politics. He discovered a
> bacillus and showed new ways to medicine. I have un-
> masked the Jews as the bacillus that disintegrates society.

Contrary to the exonerating portrayals that are still being bandied about, it was definitely he alone who had personally ordered this most unparalleled process of annihilation in history. Both Rudolf Höss, the notorious camp commandant of Ausschwitz, and Adolf Eichmann later testified that "the Führer had ordered the physical destruction of the Jews," as well as the entire "final solution of the Jewish question."

Although, by the end of 1941, the military situation did not exactly look overwhelmingly positive for Hitler, since the German troops were retreating with heavy losses from overextended forward positions and a turning point was fast approaching in the North African theater of war, he was at first unaffected, either mentally or physically, by these setbacks. Until 1939 Hitler had been able to grasp domestic and foreign policy realities with remarkable speed and accuracy; but, in general, the year 1942 marks the beginning of an unstoppable process of failure to recognize reality. This "blocking out of undesirable facts" must be seen as the reason for a whole series of coming failures on a catastrophic scale and there is no doubt that his own self-image as a "superman" in the Nietzschean sense of the term left absolutely no room for the idea of any misjudgments on his part, not to mention wrong actions. Hitler's saying, handed down by Eitner, is quite à propos:

> For almost twenty years, time was almost my slave in the form of incredible tangible successes and for me it corroborated my infallibility as a unique genius of mankind.

And he said something similar in the winter of 1941/42 to one of his secretaries:

> My genial, world-revolutionizing creative ideas ripen in the distant view across the Berchtesgaden and Salzburg landscapes, quite detached from everyday life….In those moments I no longer feel bound to mortal men.

The generals, above all, General Field Marshal Keitel—often mocked as "Lakeitel" [Hitler's little lackey]—bear a great deal of the blame for Hitler's high stylization of himself into a kind of demigod and unique strategic genius. They actually believed that their supreme commander was a "mighty, mystical superman." This was also the reason why they punished with merciless harshness any denigration or derision of their "leader," as exemplified horribly by Hitler's former fellow pupil Eugen Wasner. While serving in an infantry unit in the southern sector of the Eastern front, Wasner told his comrades a humorous anecdote about the eight-year-old Adolf Hitler. The episode, more closely described in a chapter, "A Youthful Prank in Leonding," written by Wasner's later defense attorney, Dr. G. Güstrow, was told in court as follows: Among other provocative statements, Wasner had said to his comrades:

> Ah Adolf! He was loony since childhood when a he-goat bit off half of his testes!...Yes indeed, I was there myself. He made a bet, Adi did, that he would piss into a Billy-goat's mouth. When we ridiculed him, he said: "Come with me, we'll go to the meadow where there's a Billy-goat." In the meadow I held the goat firmly between my legs, another friend pried the goat's mouth open with a stick and Adolf pissed into the goat's mouth. Just as he was doing it, the friend pulled out the stick, the goat snapped up and bit Adolf in the testes. Adi then screamed terribly and ran away crying loudly.

Eugen Wasner was called to account for this harmless story from Hitler's boyhood; he was taken to the military prison in Spandau, and there, despite desperate efforts by his defense lawyer Güstrow, he was condemned to death for "perfidious slander of the Führer and undermining the army." The poor fellow swore to the end by "Jesus and Mary" that he had told the sacred truth, but he still was executed. This lack of ability to accept humiliating insults without reacting aggressively is one of the typical characteristics of socially immature individuals; indeed, this intolerance of frustration often serves the criminologist as an important clue to better explain a lawbreaker's deviant behavior. This example raises the suspicion that Hitler's toleration of frustration was diminutively developed from the first; that is, a high potential for aggression was inherent in him even on a biological plane.

Destructive misuse of power had almost completely eroded Hitler's internal inhibitive mechanisms. The law enacted on April 26, 1942, also removed the last external formal hindrances that had restrained Hitler in the full enjoyment of his absolute power and impeded his feeling that he was a quasi-divine being, entitled to decide over life and death. This law stipulated, among other things:

> The Führer, in his capacity as leader of the nation, supreme commander of the army, head of government,

and supreme wielder of executive power, must be able if necessary to require every German...to carry out his duties by whatever means seem suitable to him and, after conscientious deliberation, to impose appropriate penalties without consideration of so-called vested rights.

This criminalistic law, which exposed every individual of the German population to the moods and whims of an all-powerful dictator, was reason enough for the spread of fear and unrest. But the notorious Wannsee conference of January 20, 1942, which decided upon the "final solution to the Jewish question" not only for German Jews but also for all European Jews, signaled the start of mass destruction with a factory-like systematicness until total extermination. Thus began the most frightful mass slaughter known to history, a genocide to which more than six million Jews fell victim and which is designated by the term "holocaust" in Israel and in the English-speaking world.

From the spring of 1942 on, Hitler's physical and mental state by no means matched the "Führer's iron constitution," as the media tried to portray it to the outside world. Violent headaches repeatedly befell him, and people around him began to notice, for the first time, a diminution of his highly praised memory. Shortly after the Führer's headquarters were transferred from the "Wolf's Lair" in East Prussia to Winniza in the Ukraine, he fell sick with a "severe head cold," as Dr. Morell expressed it. In Winniza on July 22, 1942, during a temporary phase of elevated blood pressure, he suffered a severe frontal headache and a brief impairment of his vision in the right eye, but this ailment quickly subsided. Finally at the end of 1942, after the catastrophe in Stalingrad, for which he had to assume sole responsibility, some symptoms which had started in mid-1941 began to worsen again; and they were to develop progressively until his death, namely, limitations of mobility in the left arm, accompanied by poor associated arm movements and expressive movements, as well as a tremor of the left hand. Linge, his servant of many years, describes this in his memoirs *Till the Downfall*, published in 1980, as follows:

At the end of 1942, when the battle around Stalingrad had reached an ominous stage, his left hand began to tremble. He had a hard time to repress and conceal this tremor from strangers.

Dr. med. S. Rascher   München, den 17. Februar 1943
SS-Hauptsturmführer

An den Reichsführer
und Chef der Deutschen Polizei
Herrn Heinrich Himmler
Berlin SW 11
Prinz-Albrecht-Str. 8

Hochverehrter Reichsführer!

In der Anlage überreiche ich, in kurze Form gebracht, eine Zusammenstellung der Resultate, welche bei den Erwärmungsversuchen an ausgekühlten Menschen durch animalische Wärme gewonnen wurden.
Zur Zeit arbeite ich daran, durch Menschenversuche nachzuweisen, daß Menschen, welche durch trockene Kälte ausgekühlt wurden, ebenso schnell wieder erwärmt werden können als solche, welche durch Verweilen im kalten Wasser ausgekühlten. Der Reichsarzt SS, SS-Gruppenführer Dr. Gravitz, bezweifelte diese Möglichkeit allerdings stärkstens und meinte, daß ich dies erst durch 100 Versuche beweisen müsse. Bis jetzt habe ich etwa 30 Menschen unbekleidet im Freien innerhalb 9–14 Stunden auf 27°–29° abgekühlt. Nach einer Zeit, welche einem Transport von einer Stunde entsprach, habe ich die Versuchspersonen in ein heißes Vollbad gelegt. Bis jetzt war in jedem Fall, trotz teilweise weißgefrorener Hände und Füße, der Patient innerhalb längstens einer Stunde wieder völlig aufgewärmt. Bei einigen Versuchspersonen trat am Tage nach dem Versuch eine geringe Mattigkeit mit leichtem Temperaturanstieg auf. Tödlichen Ausgang dieser außerordentlich schnellen Erwärmung konnte ich noch nicht beobachten. Die von Ihnen, hochverehrter Reichsführer, befohlene Aufwärmung durch Sauna konnte ich noch nicht durchführen, da im Dezember und Januar für Versuche im Freien zu warmes Wasser war und jetzt Lagersperre wegen Typhus ist und ich daher die Versuchspersonen nicht in die SS-Sauna bringen darf. Ich habe mich mehrmals impfen lassen und führe die Versuche im Lager, trotz Typhus im Lager, selbst weiter durch. Am einfachsten wäre es, wenn ich, bald zur Waffen-SS überstellt, mit Neff nach Auschwitz fahren würde und dort die Frage der Wiedererwärmung an Land Erfrorener schnell in einem großen Reihenversuch klären würde. Auschwitz ist für einen derartigen Reihenversuch in jeder Beziehung besser geeignet als Dachau, da es dort kälter ist und durch die Größe des Geländes im Lager selbst weniger Aufsehen erregt wird (die Versuchspersonen brüllen (!), wenn sie sehr frieren).
Wenn es, hochverehrter Reichsführer, in Ihrem Sinne ist, diese für das Landheer wichtigen Versuche in Auschwitz (oder Lublin oder sonst einem Lager im Osten) beschleunigt durchzuführen, so bitte ich gehorsamst, mir bald einen entsprechenden Befehl zu geben, damit die letzte Winterkälte noch genützt werden kann.

Mit gehorsamsten Grüßen
bin ich in aufrichtiger Dankbarkeit
mit Heil Hitler
Ihr Ihnen stets ergebener
S. Rascher

Cynical report from a concentration camp doctor in Dachau. The English translation of the report appears on the following page.

Hypokinesis, lack of mobility in the area of the right arm, also set in, as Gibbels was able to establish clearly from motion pictures, as well as impairment of the formerly upright position of his upper torso.

Today it can hardly be doubted that after the Stalingrad disaster Hitler no longer believed in victory. Nonetheless, he rejected every possibility of ending the war because he now regarded his own survival as his only worthwhile goal. Consequently, from then on his strategic decisions were oriented not so much on victory, but rather on a tenacious holding action, for the purpose of gaining time. Since he now apparently realized that he had failed to achieve his primary

S. Rascher, M. D.   Munich, 17, February 1943
SS Main Storm Leader

To the Reichsführer
and Head of the German Police
Mr. Heinrich Himmler
Berlin SW 11
Prince Albert St. 8

Very Honored Reichsführer!

Enclosed I send you in abridged form a summary of the results which I have obtained in experiments at warming deep-cooled humans by means of animal warmth.

At present I am working to prove by human experiments that people who are deeply cooled by dry cold can be warmed up again just as quickly as people who are deeply cooled by an immersion in cold water. The SS Reichsdoctor, SS-Group Leader Dr. Gravitz, however, strongly doubted this possibility and believed that I first had to prove it with 100 experiments. To date I have cooled about 30 humans kept naked outdoors for 9-14 hours down to 27-29 degrees [F]. After a time equivalent to one hour of transportation I laid the experimental persons in a hot bath. In each case until now, despite hands and feet frozen partly white, the patient was completely warmed up again within an hour at most. In some experimental persons a slight lassitude with a mild rise in temperature occurred on the day after the experiment. Till now I have been unable to observe any fatal outcome of this extraordinarily rapid warming. I have not yet been able to carry out the warming by a shower as you commanded, highly honored Reichsführer, since in December and January the water was too warm for outdoor experiments, and now the camp is quarantined because of typhus and I am not permitted to bring the experimental persons into the SS-showers. I have had myself inoculated several times and am personally continuing to carry out the experiments in the camp despite typhus in the camp. It would be simplest if I, soon to be transferred to the Weapons-SS, would drive to Ausschwitz with Neff and there quickly clear up the question of persons frozen on land in a large-scale experiment. Ausschwitz is in every respect better suited than Dachau for such a large-scale experiment, since it is colder there and, because of the size of the terrain in the camp, less attention is aroused (the experimental persons scream loudly (!) when they are freezing very much).

If, highly honored Reichsführer, it is your intention to carry out as fast as possible these experiments, which are important for the Army, in Ausschwitz (or Lublin or any other camp in the East), then I ask you respectfully to send me an order to that effect soon, so that the last cold of winter can still be utilized.

                                 With most obedient greetings
                                 I am with sincere gratitude
                                 with Heil Hitler
                                 your ever devoted
                                 S. Rascher (signed)

political goal, namely, the expansion of German territory across all Europe, he now wanted to turn his total efforts, as Haffner concluded probably rightly, to the realization at least of his second goal, namely, the extermination of the Jews. If from a Jewish perspective an improvement of their situation was expected when Hitler's military setbacks began early in 1943, they must have experienced a bitter disappointment. Instead of slowing down the machinery of destruction against the Jews, which had been operating at full speed since the Wannsee conference, Hitler ordered the opposite, to intensify the Satanic annihilation process and drastically increase the number of Jewish victims to be eliminated each day. His murderous frenzy and fanatical hatred were so extreme that occasionally the mass murders even ran counter to his own political or military interests.

With his methods of eradicating the Jews, Hitler showed his true character as a monster, such as could hardly be found again in world history. What makes him fundamentally different from Alexander the Great, Friedrich the Great, or Napoleon, with whom he so liked to compare himself and in whose wars of conquest, likewise, an infinite amount of blood was spilled, is the fact that Hitler was responsible for the killing of millions of innocent, harmless people, from the infant to the elderly, not for military reasons, nor even for power politics, but merely out of personal vindictiveness and a Satanic delight in exterminating people whom, in line with his subjective delusion, he classified as "of little value." He had all this killing done with sophisticatedly designed technical and rational factory-like procedures; this fact stamps him for all time as what Haffner called "quite simply a mass murderer."

In February 1943 at his headquarters in Winniza, Hitler again became sick with a "grippe-like infection." The people around him were well aware that he had slowed down and that his general health seemed to have greatly deteriorated. With his dull, protruding eyes, his rigid stare, his extremely quick excitability, his crooked back and his forward-leaning posture, he looked severely run-down. When in March 1943, a few weeks before the final collapse of the North African campaign, he returned from Winniza to the Wolf's Lair in East Prussia, his staff thought that they were looking at an old man. With his senile obstinacy and his lack of strategic ideas, he drove his general staff more and more to despair. Nor could this diminished general condition be altered by Dr. Morell's medical treatments: he administered glucose, high dosages of vitamins, and to alleviate his depressive mood an extract of seminal vesicles and prostate gland tissue.

To recover, Hitler therefore spent the spring of 1943 in his mountain castle in Berchtesgaden. On his arrival Eva Braun was horrified by the changes in his external appearance, and she confided to Hitler's secretary, "He has become old and gloomy." As she reported, his knees sometimes began to tremble when he had to stand for a long time. He absolutely rejected the doctors' advice to do more physical exercise, to sleep longer, and to be massaged, although Dr. Morell must have told him that a recent electrocardiogram showed a worsening heart condition. His distrustfulness, which counts among his primary personal characteristics, increased so much even toward his immediate entourage that two SS-men standing behind him had to act as food-tasters before he himself would take a bite of the food prepared in the kitchen of the Dr. Werner Zabel Sanitarium.

The year 1944 began dismally for Hitler. In February he suddenly felt a sharp pang in the right eye and subsequently he saw everything as if through a veil. In an eye examination at the Charité in Berlin, Professor Dr. Walther Löhlein diagnosed a severe clouding of the right eye, caused by a hemorrhage that had occurred in the vitreous humor; this was treated with radiation and Homotropin eyedrops. Toward the end of March this bleeding was mostly reabsorbed and gradually the diffused veil before his eye disappeared again. On this occasion, Löhlein prescribed bifocal glasses, which were then still a rarity. Hitler had needed glasses much earlier, but this did not become known for a long

The Führer's lunch menu:
Orange juice with linseed slime
Rice pudding with herbal sauce
Crisp bread with butter
Nut-paste

7. Juni 1943
============

Orangensaft
mit Leinsamenschleim

--

Reispudding
mit Kräutertunke

--

Knäckebrot D mit Butter
Nuxo - Paste

time because he never showed himself in public with glasses, and so the text of some of his speeches had to be prepared with extremely large letters on special "Führer typewriters." For reading maps or texts during military conferences, he used a strikingly large magnifying glass to take in a larger field of vision.

The Allied invasion in Normandy on June 6, 1944, made it clear to everyone that the German defeat was ultimately sealed. Hitler's declaration that he was not ready to decide for peace depended primarily on the fact that he clasped the fate of the German people more and more tightly to his own pitiful life; and to him, no sacrifice on the part of other people seemed too great if only it could prolong his own life, even just for a few months. He was able to get others to make this sacrifice willingly because he still inspired in them, and probably in himself too, an unshakable certainty of victory, though all the facts pointed to the contrary. This hope was probably grounded in his deeply rooted belief in the omnipotence of the will. This ability to use his will to convince other persons or to pull them out of discouragement, with an almost demonic persuasiveness, is repeatedly documented. Franz Halder, the head of the general staff until September 1942, once said that Hitler had been practically the "incarnation of brutal will" and Christa Schröder, Hitler's private secretary, confirmed this during her interrogation by the Allies:

Hitler reading a news item with a powerful magnifying glass (in 1944)

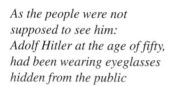

As the people were not supposed to see him: Adolf Hitler at the age of fifty, had been wearing eyeglasses hidden from the public

He labored under the delusion that an iron will can do anything....He was a monster of willpower.

Under the influence of Nietzsche and Schopenhauer, who regarded the will as an instrument of natural law, Hitler declared the will to be something absolute. At the same time, this was a ruse to conceal his subjective ego behind an objective principle. How this transformation of the subjective expression of will into an objectivity affects a demagogue and his hearers, was described impressively by Nietzsche:

> In all great deceivers, a process to which they owe their power is noteworthy. In the very act of deception, amid all the preparations, the pathos in voice, expression, gestures, amid the appropriate scenery, they are overcome by belief in their own self. This is what then appeals so miraculously and cogently to the persons around them....For people believe in the truth of what is obviously strongly believed.

In his knowledge of the will, Hitler probably always strove to preserve his strength of will from any deleterious influences. His brusque rejection of all reports on troop strengths or on the state of the enemy's armaments production shows this. It is shown, too, by his stubborn refusal to review, with his own eyes, the catastrophic conditions at the front or the devastating destruction of the bombed German cities. Even his later isolation in the bunker of the Berlin Reichs-chancellory served the purpose of warding off the soberingly terrible reality, in the hope that his will to hold out would not collapse.

Although German officers had banded together into a resistance group against Hitler as early as the fall of 1938 and a total of seven assassination attempts were initiated in 1943 alone, they all failed. The opposition movement's first real chance of succeeding came with Count Schenk von Stauffenberg, a charismatic, strong-willed personality. However, on July 20, 1944, this meticulously planned action also failed, this time because, for no apparent reason, Hitler left his seat in the conference room of the Wolf's Lair and went to the opposite side of an oak table just before the bomb went off, and this protected him from the main impact of the explosion.

Once again Hitler had escaped with his life by the failure of an assassination attempt, and once again his conviction of being under the special protection of Providence and therefore a Chosen One was again confirmed, as can be seen from his words to Dr. Morell: "I am invincible. I am immortal"—words of which Mussolini, who was there on a visit, also was fully convinced, as an Italian who tended to believe in miracles. But objectively this attempt had quite far-reaching medical effects. Hitler's SS-personal physician von Hasselbach, who bandaged his wounds and put his right arm in a sling, discovered as first examiner that the explosion had propelled numerous wood splinters into the skin. More than a hundred had to be removed from his legs alone. His right elbow and left hand showed some bleeding and the right wrist was sprained. The face had minor cuts, the forehead had a scratch and the hairs on the back of his head were mostly singed. Blood flowed out of the ear passages, and Hitler complained of a taste of blood in his mouth. Dr. Giesing, the military doctor, diagnosed an injury to the eardrum in both ears, and so he had to cauterize the edges of the wounds "without anesthetic, as Hitler wished." Besides a severe earache, there was temporary deafness in the right ear, while the left ear retained merely limited hearing.

If even at the beginning of the Russian campaign his generals had felt his "sick, boundless distrust," now it increased dramatically, as General Guderian later reported:

Benito Mussolini, during his prescheduled visit on July 20, 1944, is escorted by Hitler into the heavily damaged barracks to show him the effect of the bomb and his "marvelous saving."

In accordance with his character, the deep distrust he already felt for mankind in general and for the General Staff Corps officers and generals in particular, now became profound hatred....He believed no one anymore. It had already been difficult enough dealing with him; it now became a torture that grew steadily worse from month to month.

Besides the mental effects of the assassination attempt, the eardrum injury and the hearing impairment associated with it also had a pejorative effect, as we learn from his servant Linge:

Hitler now accepted medications only from my hand. His distrust had reached the maximum. By early October he was again able to hear whispered conversations from five or six paces away, but that did not diminish his suspicions, which now made life a hell not just for himself.

This extreme distrust also increased his aloofness, interpreted by de Boor as a form of social autism. Signs of this were known even in his childhood, and it clung to him until death. This strange aloofness always contrasted sharply with his remarkable ability to influence individuals in his immediate circle as effectively as the masses.

Another effect of the assassination attempt on Hitler's psyche was a clearly recognizable decrease of his ability to control his emotional outbursts. Previously his irritability threshold, anchored in his primary personality, had been low and weakly developed, and therefore repeatedly gave way to "immeasurable excitement," "frenzied ranting," "the most severe rebukes and pathological reactions to momentary impressions" and "indescribable fits of rage," as his generals later testified. After the assassination attempt, Hitler went even more out of control. "He often lost his self-control and let himself go more and more in his choice of epithets," said General Guderian. General von Choltitz, who went down in the history books as the "savior of Paris," described this tendency even more graphically:

> Finally Hitler came to speak of July 20. I experienced this outburst of a hate-filled soul….He talked himself into a senseless frenzy; spittle literally ran out of his mouth. His entire body trembled, so that the desk he was clinging to started to vibrate too. He was bathed in sweat and his excitement rose even more as he shouted that those generals would "hang." The certainty came over me that I had a madman before my eyes.

This impression of madness was strengthened even more by the shocking spectacle of his sadistic vindictiveness after the execution of the generals who had been linked with the planned assassination. He had a movie film made of the executions, in which the condemned men were hanged from meathooks with piano strings while their pants were simultaneously pulled down; and he repeatedly watched this movie with great pleasure. The film material of the negotiations during the show trials, which took place under the chairmanship of the notorious "bloodhound," Roland Freisler, before the "people's court," gives a vivid idea of the inhuman abasements to which the accused were helplessly exposed. Unmoved by these gruesome scenes he wrote at the same time to his dear "Tschapperl" [sugar roll], as he often called Eva Braun, that he was well except for a mild exhaustion:

> I hope to come home soon and to be able to rest in
> your arms. I have a great need for rest.

To Hitler it seemed almost like a miracle that the violent blast of the explosion caused the tremor of his left arm and leg suddenly to disappear. But this apparent improvement turned out to be very temporary, and the tremor in the left side of his body soon returned. On the contrary, compared with before, he began to have disorders of balance, with unintentional deviations from the vertical, and his stride showed the first signs of dragging that would become more pronounced later. Immediately after the attempt on his life, he was almost euphoric, since he had emerged from the inferno relatively unscathed, and so once again he felt confirmed in his sense of mission. But a few weeks later, he fell into a sort of depression. Dejectedly he announced, in a statement on August 31, that the many failures and personal disappointments had made his life into a torment at many an hour, and in a crestfallen voice he added:

> If my life had ended on July 20th, it would have been
> for me personally...only a liberation from cares, sleep-
> less nights, and a severe nervous ailment.

On the whole, then, it is impossible to agree with Trever-Roper's assessment that "the events of July 20" had "little physical significance in the life of Hitler." They had decisive importance for his generals, many of whom, since those days, felt nothing for their supreme commander but contempt and disgust, such as were voiced by the desert general Rommel, who was respected throughout the world, on September 6, 1944:

> This pathological liar has now become completely in-
> sane; he has directed his real sadism against the men
> of July 20, and we have not yet seen the end!

THE END APPROACHES

Meanwhile the Western front collapsed under the impact of the powerful forces marshaled by the American offensive in Normandy. Hitler wanted to go there to lead the military operations himself, but this was strictly forbidden by his doctors. For his persistent headaches in the frontal areas, Professor von Eicken prescribed the administering of cocaine drops in the nose to cause the swelling of the membranes to go down and to give some alleviation. On September 12, according to a report of Dr. Giesing, the doctor who was treating him, such a local cocaine application led to a brief incidence of a so-called near syncopal episode with a dimming of vision and reeling dizziness, so that Hitler had to grab a table to keep from falling. This condition, accompanied by a strong acceleration of the pulse, lasted only ninety seconds, but similar attacks on September 14 and 16 were accompanied by outbreaks of cold sweat. The headaches were joined by extreme toothaches, so that Professor Dr. Hugo Blaschke, who had been his dentist since 1933 was called and a tooth had to be extracted. Hitler's dentition had already been in very poor condition for years. The few remaining yellowish natural teeth were complemented by crowns and bridges—in all, ten of the fifteen teeth in the lower jaw were artificial and in the upper jaw there were nine teeth made of porcelain or gold. This tooth chart of Dr. Blaschke's was later to play an important role in identifying Hitler's corpse.

On September 17, 1944, Hitler was desolated by the news of the Allied landing near Arnheim and Nimwegen. He suffered a heart attack that forced him to keep the strict bedrest ordered by his doctors. In addition to the already known impairment of the coronary blood supply to the heart, the electrocardiogram done on September 24 this time showed symptoms that Hitler had suffered a myocardial infarction [heart attack]. This probable diagnosis made by Professor Dr. Alfred Weber, to whom the EKG was sent in Bad Nauheim, could not be confirmed with absolute certainty, however, since only the readings for the extremities but not those from the chest wall are available. But the accompanying collapse of circulation, the cold outbreak of sweat, and the general frailty and weakness during this heart attack are symptoms that seem to support the diagnosis. Now Hitler, who was still suffering from violent and persistent pains in the area of the frontal cavities and was no longer able to sleep through any night, showed himself ready to be transported to the field hospital in Rastenburg for an x-ray of his skull. The x-ray plates showed the existence of an inflammation in the area of the left maxillary antrum and the left ethmoidal cells of the sinuses, which was causing the painful headache.

The alarming news from the Western front affected his stomach and intestinal tract, which, since his time in Vienna, had recurrently given him considerable trouble whenever he was under strong mental

The Berlin throat specialist,
Professor Karl von Eicken,
operated on polyps on Hitler's
vocal cords in 1935 and 1944.

pressure. He refused all food, did not want to see anybody, and described his intestinal colic as "so violent that I sometimes would like to scream loudly." His personal servant Linge said that under such violent body colics he drew in both legs to ease the pain. Occasionally cramplike twitchings of the facial musculature even resulted. In such situations Dr. Morell saw himself forced to prescribe alkaloids, such as Eucodal, in addition to the usual cramp-relieving medications. The

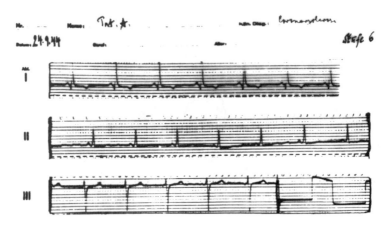

The extremity readings from Adolf Hitler's last electrocardiogram record
(September 29, 1944)

people around the Führer agreed they had never before seen him so weak and apathetic, even about the critical daily reports from the front. The reason for this extreme weakness and exhaustion was no doubt an additional illness he had contracted, namely, an infectious inflammation of the liver, which was also affecting countless soldiers in that war. Jaundice of the skin and the conjunctiva was first registered by Dr. Giesing on September 25, and now the doctors had a medical explanation for the lack of appetite, which within three days led to a weight loss of three kilograms [approximately 6.7 pounds], and for the noticeable lack of energy.

Hitler's feebleness and depressive, apathetic mood must not have been the result of his organic ailments alone. What contributed perhaps more to his mental decline than headaches, intestinal colics, and jaundice were certain documents that had meanwhile come to his attention, revealing that far more officers of the supreme command of the army had had foreknowledge of the July 20 conspiracy than was first assumed. He therefore increasingly felt surrounded by secret opponents and traitors; and this crisis of confidence included not merely the circle of his closest colleagues, but gradually also his doctors. What triggered this crisis was the recent discussion that had arisen about the medical justification of the "anti-gas pills," which Dr. Morell had been prescribing for years against Hitler's flatulence. Dr. Giesing, and also Dr. von Hasselbach and Dr. Brandt, the SS-doctors who tended him at headquarters, considered the chronic use of these pills inappropriate and perhaps even dangerous, since they contained strychnine in addition to atropine. This amounted to a disavowal of Dr. Morell's and Dr. Giesing's own methods of treatment. From today's standpoint this objection of the doctors, who apparently were professionally not very competent, was unfounded since the percentage of strychnine in those pills was so slight that a feared strychnine poisoning was out of the question, even with a dosage of sixteen pills per day. Ellen Gibbels pointed out that Dr. Morell with his undoubted misuse of the anti-gas pills, must unknowingly even have caused an improvement of the hand tremor, since that preparation contained the same dosage of atropine as the medication "Homburg 68," called at that time the "Bulgarian cure," which was prescribed for Parkinson's disease.

These debates led Hitler for a time to doubt the integrity of the man who had been his personal physician for many years; but Morell soon won back the upper hand and his patient's complete confidence.

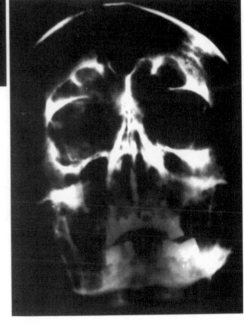

Hitler in the fall of 1944, looking very aged and rundown

X-ray photograph of Hitler's skull (September 19, 1944)

The SS-doctors, Dr. Brandt and Dr. von Hasselbach, on the contrary, fell into disfavor and were dismissed. Even Dr. Giesing, to whom Hitler owed gratitude because of his successful otorhinological treatment measures, ultimately lost a lot of his previous position of confidence, since he had been the real instigator of the "anti-gas-pill affair."

In Dr. Giesing's last action on October 1, 1944, the day on which the Allies had already reached Reichs-territory, an incident occurred during the cocaine treatment, which Giesing described as follows:

> Then Hitler said: "Would you please have another look at my nose and put in that cocaine stuff. My larynx is somewhat better, but I still feel hoarse." I treated the left nostril with the 10 percent solution of cocaine... with the patient lying down. Afterwards I examined his ears again and the larynx. Some moments later Hitler said: "My head is almost clear again now and I feel nearly well enough to get up. But I feel...very weak what with all this colic and eating so little." A few moments later I noted that Hitler's eyes were closed and that his face, previously rather flushed, had turned pale. I took his pulse which was rapid and weak. The pulse rate was about 90 and the quality seemed to be very much softer than at other times....I asked Hitler how he felt and received no reply. He had obviously suffered a slight collapse and was not responsive. Linge had gone to open the door that led into Hitler's small sitting room, because someone had been knocking on it....I can only have been alone with Hitler for a very short time since I was still treating the left nostril with cocaine when Linge returned. Linge stood at the foot of the bed and asked how much longer the treatment would take. His question startled me. "I've almost finished," I said. Just then Hitler's face grew even paler and for a moment his features twitched convulsively as he drew up his knees. Seeing this, Linge murmured: "The Führer's getting colic again. Better leave him alone. He probably wants to sleep now." Making as little noise as possible, we packed up my instruments and quickly left the bedroom.

*SS-doctor, Dr. Karl Brandt
(1904—1948, executed).
Until September 1944, he was the
doctor accompanying Hitler in the
headquarters.*

Whether Dr. Giesing had really intended, as he later testified, to use the few short moments alone with Hitler to administer a fatal dose of cocaine must surely remain unanswered. In any case, Dr. Giesing was no longer called in after October 7, and Hitler dismissed him after first having Martin Bormann hand him a check for 10,000 Reichsmarks. On October 31, Dr. Ludwig Stumpfegger, on Himmler's recommendation, began his assignment at the Führer's headquarters, and he quickly won Hitler's trust and persevered in the bunker of the Reichschancellory to the bitter end.

On November 16, 1944, with the Ardennes offensive, Hitler tried once more to risk everything on a single card. Despite his bad physical and mental state, he decided to take the military operations into his own hands, and so he moved to the Führer headquarters at the "Eagle's Nest" in Taunus, which had been constructed back in 1939. On the journey there, in a heavily guarded special train, he made such a downcast and absent-minded impression on everyone around him that they were all perplexed. His secretary Traudl Junge later reported:

> His voice was now merely a soft whisper; his eyes were staring either at his plate or at a spot on the white table cloth. The atmosphere was so depressing that we all were filled with strange and dismal forebodings.

*Hitler's secretary, Martin Bormann
(1900-1945)*

Apparently, the reason that Hitler was in such a downcast mood was his fear that he might lose his voice because of a recent operation to remove another polyp from his vocal cords, performed by Professor von Eicken. The operation had been successful and he recovered quickly. Then he tried in his customary manner to reassure his officers of the feasibility of this military operation by pretending to be an energetic, healthy Führer once again.

On closer inspection, however, Hitler looked quite different, as General Hasso von Manteuffel's description shows:

> He was a broken man, with unhealthy complexion; his demeanor showed exhaustion, his hands trembled. He sat there as if the burden of responsibility were pressing down on him; and compared with the appearance he had presented during the last conference at the beginning of December, his body seemed even more feeble. He had become an old man.

His physical changes were also noticed by other eyewitnesses. Both Guderian and Linge observed his slow movements and his dragging gait, and Skorzeny especially noticed the dragging of the left leg. Besides the bent posture, a tremor or trembling was most noticeable. After December 1944, the tremor also went over to the right arm. As is typical for Parkinson's disease, this tremor appeared more strongly in times of heightened mental stress, as was the case before the start of the Ardennes offensive. The changes in Hitler's voice were probably also connected with this same underlying illness, since it causes a reduced tension of the vocal cords, resulting typically in a gradual loss of speech volume and tone, as was noted by the people around Hitler since the middle of 1944.

The initial successes of the Ardennes offensive sufficed to restore his self-confidence and endurance so that he temporarily managed to revive his commanders' faith in him which they had almost totally lost. Professor von Eicken, who went to give him a physical examination in the "Eagle's Nest" on December 30, 1944, was surprised at Hitler's recovered health, his reacquired speech, and his confidence. But just three weeks later, the battle in the Ardennes was lost. A devastated land and more than seventy-five thousand dead were the price for this gruesome experiment of a fanatic lashing out with blind fury in all directions, when his pathological compulsive notions and schemes had long since left the ground of reality.

On November 24, in view of the rapid advance of the Russian armies, he gave Himmler the order to close down the deathcamps in the East and level them to the ground, in order to make it impossible for the enemy and the entire world public to see the unimaginable horror of the diabolical annihilation machinery that had been used for the systematic eradication of the Jews. The assignment was carried out

Corpses of Jewish prisoners in the Ausschwitz-Birkenau concentration camp (after liberation of the prisoners by the Soviet armed forces)

with the exception of Ausschwitz, which was liberated by the Red Army on January 27, 1945, as the SS-cadre were trying in vain until the morning of that very day to explode the gas chambers and crematoria in time. Because of the incomplete destruction, at least in Ausschwitz, the incontrovertible proofs for the abominable events of a factory-like mass murder of Jews were preserved for all time in the form of heartrending photographic documentaries.

Despite all military setbacks and the unimaginable sufferings of the civilian population, the main actor of the drama which now unfolded in Germany remained ice-cold, and was zealously concerned only with maintaining the myth of his historical mission that he himself had established. The only way his imagination could continue to cling to this unshakable belief in himself and the mission assigned to him by Providence was with the idea that defeat, if it came, resulted only from the failure of others and from disgraceful treachery that made it impossible for him to accomplish his tasks. General Halder gave an accurate characterization of this ice-cold man, alienated from reality, driven by compulsive ideas, and misanthropic:

> For him, when he stood at the peak of power, there was no Germany, no matter how often the word crossed his lips; for him there were no German troops for whose welfare and suffering he felt responsible; for him there was only one greatness that dominated his life and to which his demonic power sacrificed everything: his own ego.

In this light, his life could not possibly have ended differently than it did at the beginning of 1945, after Berlin had been transformed into one big heap of rubble. He barricaded himself obstinately with a small crew of faithful followers under concrete walls many meters thick, for the sole purpose of eking out his life at least for a few months or weeks. Yet this could not prevent fate from mercilessly continuing its work of destruction on his emaciated body. When Dr. Giesing, who had not seen him since the beginning of October 1944, met him again in February, he was appalled at Hitler's transformation since he had last seen him:

> When I saw Hitler's face now I was astonished at the changes. He seemed aged and even more bent than before. His complexion was immutably pale and he had large bags under his eyes. His speech was clear

Hitler six weeks before his suicide in the bunker of the Reichs-chancellory, physically aged and looking exhausted and psychologically broken.

but very soft. I immediately noticed a strong trembling of his left arm and hand, which always became stronger when the hand was not resting on something, so that Hitler always kept his arm on the table or supported his hands on the bench....I got the impression he was quite absent-minded and no longer able to concentrate. He seemed to be absolutely exhausted and distracted. His hands also were very pale and the fingernails empty of blood.

In early February 1945, Hitler decided to dictate a political testament to his secretary Martin Bormann, so that if he died, posterity would know how close he had come to realizing the plan assigned to him by

Providence. This "justification legend" put the blame for World War II exclusively on the Western powers and restated for history that in his mind the most important goal of the war had been the eradication of the Jews. He regarded this sick compulsive idea as a kind of inner voice prescribing the way for him, the Chosen One, to achieve his providential mission. Since this delusionary idea naturally left no room for universally valid moral principles, he was absolutely convinced that "the world of the future would be eternally grateful to him" for having massacred the Jews by the millions.

The lucidity with which he dictated this "political testament" speaks against the total breakdown of his intelligence during the last weeks of his life and stands in crass opposition to his physical state. An older staff officer assigned to the Führer's headquarters at the end of March 1945 was at first appalled at the appearance and condition of the man who still decided arbitrarily about the life and death of millions of people:

> Before I drove to the Reichs-chancellory for the last time, I was told by a staff officer that I must be prepared to see Hitler as a completely different man than the one known to me in photos and films or perhaps at a former meeting: a worn-out old man. The reality exceeded the warning by far. I had seen Hitler previously only twice: in 1937 at a state ceremonial before the monument honoring the fallen soldiers of World War I and again at his birthday parade in 1939. The old Hitler had no resemblance whatever to this wreck of a man I reported to on March 25, 1945, and who offered me a weak, trembling hand....Physically he presented a horrible picture. He dragged himself toilsomely and ponderously from his apartment to the bunker's conference room, casting his upper torso forward and dragging the feet behind. He had lost a sense of balance. If he stopped along the short way, he had to sit down on one of the benches arranged along the two walls for that purpose or lean on his conversation partner....His eyes were bloodshot; although all the documents intended for him were written on special "Führer typewriters" with triply magnified letters, he

was able to read them only with strong glasses. Spittle often drooled from the corners of his mouth—an image of misery and horror....Mentally, Hitler was still fresh, compared with his physical decline. Sometimes he showed signs of weariness, but often he still displayed a remarkable memory....From the enormous number of reports brought to him, which were often contradictory, given the variety of sources, he recognized the essential, and keenly sensed the dangers which had barely begun to materialize and reacted to them.

Nor does Hitler's power of concentration seem to have been essentially impaired during the last phase of his life, according to the testimony of the doctors who were interrogated by American officers after the war. Evidence of this is an impromptu speech lasting several hours given by Hitler to his officers just four months before his death, as well as the description by General Field Marshal Kesselring, who was astonished at Hitler's "mental acumen" as late as mid-April 1945. Finally, the impromptu dictation of his personal testament in the night before his suicide excludes a diminished power of concentration shortly before his death.

Faced with the increasingly catastrophic gravity of the situation, in March 1945 Hitler worked himself up into a state of mind characterized by spite and anger, as Albert Speer wrote later:

Hitler's fits of rage became more frequent. Sometimes he became very loud, ranted, screamed and scolded.... Despite all that, however, I often had the occasion to admire his self-control.

Albert Speer considered this ability of self-control to be "one of Hitler's most amazing qualities." Actually all those present during the last days of his life were impressed by the "composure with which he faced the approaching end" as well as by his "cool and unemotional" decision to stay in Berlin until the end, a decision probably also based partly on his still functioning strategy of self-deception, whereby he consistently continued to repress awareness of his opponents' military strength. As late as January 1945, he was still alluding to reports of the enormous power of the Soviet units attacking Berlin as "the greatest bluff since Genghis-Khan."

The more hopeless the situation became, the more ruthless his choice of means, which was shockingly evidenced in some of the most brutal acts of violence. Apparently, his brain was now filled only with hatred and the desire to avenge, murder, and destroy. One example of this is the threat made in March 1945, to terminate the Geneva Convention's rule protecting prisoners of war and to have all POWs and detainees in the concentration camps exterminated before the enemy troops arrived. Albert Speer recognized extremely late that by such a command "Hitler was consciously committing high treason against his own people." Speer therefore did not implement this order nor the insane "Nero Command," whereby Hitler, as his last warlike defensive measure, called for the destruction of all industrial plants, means of transportation, and news media in his own country, in order with this "scorched earth" policy to leave nothing useful for the enemy. To what extent his lack of social conscience toward human society was developed and how absolutely he lacked all empathy for his fellow human beings, is shown by his justification of the Nero-like command to Albert Speer:

> If the war is lost, the people will also be lost. There is no need to take into consideration the foundations which the German people needs for its most primitive survival...for the people has proven itself the weaker one. Anyway, what will be left after this struggle will be inferior, for the good have fallen in battle.

Nothing could demonstrate better than these words his boundless egocentricity and relentless egoism at the moment of the collapse of his dream of solitary greatness and unlimited power. The degree of his moral baseness was shown, shortly before his suicide, by the insane command that made mockery of all humanity, in April 1945, to prevent the advance of Russian soldiers through the subway tunnels by opening the floodgates of the Spree river, whereby he would without the least remorse have exposed thousands of wounded German soldiers and civilians to death by drowning.

Since mid-March 1945, Hitler spent day and night in his Führer bunker located fifteen meters under the garden of the Reichschancellory together with Eva Braun, who meanwhile had joined him in Berlin. When on April 22 he heard of the failure of the last counterattack in Berlin by General Steiner, on which he had set some hope, he fell into a rage, and in the presence of his generals spoke of nothing

One of the last briefings with Göring and Keitel shortly before the end

Last photograph of Hitler on April 20, 1945. Together with his adjutant Julius Schaub, he inspects the ruins of the former Reichs-chancellory.

The SS-doctor, Dr. Ludwig Stumpfegger took care of Hitler during the last days. On May 2, 1945, he committed suicide.

else but the liars and traitors he had surrounded himself with. He called them all too mediocre to be able to understand his great mission and now even Dr. Morell, his personal physician for many years, fell into disfavor. He suspected Dr. Morell of secretly wanting to give him morphine in the recommended injections of Vitamultin-forte, so that he could be removed from Berlin against his will. This medication, manufactured since 1944 especially for Hitler, to "build up the Führer's resistance," contained, among other things, caffeine and pervitin. Morell, who suffered an attack of faintness on hearing the news of his dismissal without notice, was flown out of the besieged Reichs-capital, so that at the end only Dr. Ludwig Stumpfegger, a surgeon and SS-doctor, functioned as Hitler's personal physician. After this last fit of rage, Hitler sank back exhausted into his chair and, with chalk-white face and tremulous voice, finally said aloud what had long since been clear to everyone: "The war is lost." Resignedly, Eva Braun wrote to her friend Herta Ostermayr: "He has lost faith." General Alfred Jodl later reported:

> Hitler had made the decision to stay in Berlin to lead the defense there and to shoot himself at the last moment. He said that for physical reasons he was unable

to fight, nor would he fight in person because he could not risk the danger of perhaps being wounded and falling into enemy hands.

After Hitler had learned that Heinrich Himmler, his Reichs-leader of the SS, had begun negotiations with the Swedish Count Bernadotte to capitulate with the West, in the night of April 28, 1945, he decided to put an end to his life. Between two and three in the morning [actually April 29], the civil marriage with Eva Braun was performed in the presence of a lawyer, with Goebbels and Bormann as witnesses. Hitler's personal testament, dictated just before, said:

> Since in the years of struggle, I did not believe I could responsibly enter a marriage, I have now decided before the termination of this earthly career to take as my wife that girl who after long years of loyal friendship entered this almost beleaguered city of her own free will to share her fate with mine. She goes to her death at her own wish as my wife….I myself and my spouse choose death, in order to avoid the shame of deposition or capitulation. It is our will to be cremated immediately in the place where I performed the greatest part of my daily work in the course of a twelve-year service to my people.

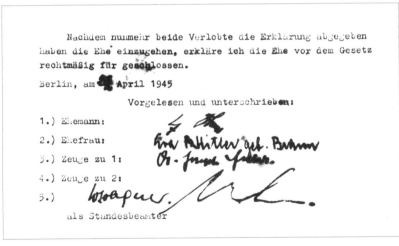

Eva and Adolf Hitler's marriage certificate dated April 29, 1945. The marriage was performed after midnight, and the date was changed after the fact.

Even at that hour, as can be seen from his "political testament" dictated just a few hours before his death, his fanatical hatred of Jews remained unchanged and alive, when he urged his followers:

> Above all I enjoin the leaders of the nation and their followers meticulously to maintain the racial laws and unmercifully resist the world poisoners of all nations, international Jewry.

His chauffeur Erich Kempka reports in detail about Hitler's last hours in the bunker. Toward noon on April 30, 1945, he said good-bye to all persons present and thanked them for their loyalty to him. He gave his adjutant, Otto Günsche, the express order to have enough gasoline ready to cremate his corpse and his wife's, an action which he justified with these words: "I don't want to be exposed in a Russian wax museum after my death." Between 2:30 and 3:00 p.m., Hitler and his wife said farewell to the Goebbels family, Bormann, and a few other closest colleagues, then withdrew to their private quarters. Otto Günsche's eyewitness report on the last minutes in the lobby to their private chambers says:

> When toward 3:30 Bormann, Linge, and I opened the double doors, we saw Adolf Hitler sitting in the armchair that stood by the left wall before us next to the divan. He had slumped over and hung over the right arm of the chair. Blood was dripping out of his right temple. A pool of blood had already formed on the rug and floor. He had shot himself, as was immediately evident, in the right temple, with his own PPK 7.65 mm pistol, which he had taken out of the drawer of his night table on April 22, 1945, after a turbulent discussion of the situation and since then always carried with him loaded and with the safety on....Whether Hitler bit through the poison capsule simultaneously with the pistol shot is unknown to me. But I consider it possible.

As Erich Kempka further reported, Hitler's corpse and that of Eva, who had poisoned herself, were carried outside in front of the entrance to the bunker, soaked with gasoline, and burned. But total incineration was impossible, since the incessant artillery bombardment of the area made it impossible to resoak the uncarbonized remnants of the body parts with gasoline and to re-ignite them until everything was consumed. In the evening, the remnants of the two corpses were pushed onto a tent canvas with a spade and, as Otto Günsche later told, lowered into a nearby shell crater and covered with earth, which was leveled out with a wooden tamper. Thus Hitler was buried under the rubble of the Reich that was supposed to have lasted a thousand years. Countless millions of people had lost their lives because of it, but now it ended ignominiously after so few years of existence in a defeat unparalleled in all history.

RIDDLE OF THE FÜHRER'S CORPSE

Werner Maser, near the end of his book in 1971 said that Adolf Hitler "vanished without a trace from a world which, because of him, would never be the same again to the lasting detriment not least of his own country. Where the ashes are interred is today a no man's land." This legend can no longer be maintained. An affidavit dated May 5, 1945, states that members of a Soviet intelligence team, after occupying the abandoned Führer-bunker on May 3, came across the strongly carbonized remains of a man and a woman in a shell crater next to the

Shell-crater where the incompletely burned corpses of Adolf and Eva Hitler were found on May 5, 1945, by a Soviet intelligence team. To the left, the gasoline cans used for the cremation.

bunker's emergency exit, in which two dog cadavers also lay. This site where the discovery was made matches exactly with Otto Günsche's testimony, so that even then it was hoped that a positive identification could be made with the autopsy done on May 8. Contrary to expectations, however, this could not be achieved with absolute certainty, so that soon the most scurrilous speculations were voiced about Hitler's whereabouts.

From the autopsy report, whose complete text was reproduced by Hans Bankl, at first only the following conclusions could be drawn:

1. The corpse was that of a man 165 cm. [5' 5"] tall, between fifty and sixty years of age.

2. The left testis could be found neither in the scrotum nor in the inguinal canal nor in the pelvis.

3. The most important evidence for identifying the person was the dentition, which showed many artificial bridges and teeth as well as crowns and fillings. The upper-jaw bridge taken from the corpse, consisting of nine teeth, as well as the charred lower jaw with an additional fifteen teeth were compared with the description of the state of Hitler's dentition written by Katherina Heusermann, Professor Blaschke's dental assistant. Her description coincides with the anatomical data about the mouth cavity of the unknown man whose burned corpse was dissected.

4. On double-checking the shell hole where the corpse was discovered, they also found the part of the cranium listed as missing in the autopsy report. The left parietal bone showed a craterlike defect whose larger diameter was on the outside and thus was typical for an outward-bound gunshot. The localization of the defect as well as its form and the size of the exit shot make it possible to identify the shot as coming through the mouth or the right temple. Since several small splinters could be found in the inner plate of the left skull bone, it must be assumed that the shot, which came upward from below and backward from right to left must have been fired at very close range. The

interpretation of these data established with probability verging on certainty that the shot was fired by a medium caliber weapon with the right hand into the temple region.

5. The presence of the remnants of a broken glass ampoule in the mouth cavity, the marked odor of bitter almonds emanating from the corpse and the proof of cyanide compounds on the inner organs led the commission to assume that death in this case was caused by poisoning with a cyanide compound. The same finding was made concerning the female corpse.

6. As for the two dogs, the death of the German shepherd was caused by cyanide of potassium, that of the second dog by a shot into the head and one in the stomach.

Although the age, the lack of the left testis, the state of the dentition, the shot in the right temple, and the evidence of potassium cyanide in the body of the burned male corpse agree with data attested in Hitler's lifetime or, respectively, with reports of eyewitnesses who saw the corpse immediately after his suicide, this was not sufficient for an absolutely certain identification and for the definitive removal of all doubt about his death. The Bavarian District Court in Berchtesgaden therefore did not dare to declare Hitler officially dead until October 25, 1956. So the legend which arose that Hitler had vanished from this world without a trace was far from refuted. This refutation was successfully accomplished only in the years 1972/73 by Professor Reidar Sognnaes of UCLA and Ferdinand Ström from Oslo, who by carefully comparing the smallest details from five different sources, finally were able to make a definitive identification. These sources were x-ray plates of the skull which had been taken after the July 20, 1944, assassination attempt, photographs of the upper and lower jaws of the autopsied corpse, the autopsy report with the exact description of the state of the teeth, as well as the sketches of the dental prostheses and Professor Blaschke's description of Hitler's dentition. The identification of the corpse autopsied on May 5, 1945, by these comparative studies of two specialists working independently of one another became possible only three decades after Hitler's death, because the x-ray plates were in the

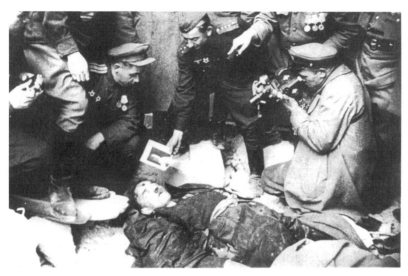

*An announcement to the world—a mock-up of a simulated dead Hitler,
arranged on Stalin's orders, to disprove rumors that Hitler was still alive.*

hands of American agencies, while the photographs of the jaws were in
Russian files. So, at last, the legend of Hitler having disappeared from
this world without a trace could be laid to rest forever.

ADOLF HITLER, THE PATIENT

In his monograph *Patient Hitler,* Professor Dr. Ernst Günther
Schenck has evaluated in detail, from the point of view of internal
medicine, the recollections available in existing memoirs as well as the
statements of the physicians, Dr. Morell, Dr. Brandt, Dr. von Hasselbach
and Dr. Giesing, and the diagnostic reports of Professors Dr. Löhlein
and Dr. von Eicken, and has with great precision assembled the available symptomatic data and the medicines administered. Yet, in my
opinion, a few additions which seem important to me should be included; above all, the neuropsychiatric aspects require a broader
portrayal, because only that can make it possible to delineate Hitler's
psychograph. Moreover, knowledge of Hitler's primary-personal characteristics has great significance for deciphering his psyche and
revealing its forensic-psychiatric properties, in order to get a closer
picture of the "psychological and psychiatric riddle of this uncanny
mover of world history."

For internal medicine, his frequent stomach and intestinal ailments that accompanied him all his life since his youth stood decidedly in the foreground. We first hear of them in his Vienna years when he reported in a letter of "a slight stomach colic." Apparently, this was not an organic disease, since the doctors interpreted his complaints as the expression of a "nervous illness" —an interpretation which, incidentally, he strongly resented. In 1932, under the mental stress during his candidature for the office of Reichs-president, along with various psychosomatic conditions and "hypochondriac anxieties about his health" came renewed violent "stomach cramps," which he saw as heralds of impending cancer. These hypochondriac fears, concentrating mainly on a possible cancerous disease, were of ominous significance for the fate of the German people because Hitler in his constant fear of not having long to live, thought he had to realize these ambitious plans of world domination within a few years. His hypochondria also expressed itself in a constant, exaggerated fear of a venereal infection and here again mainly of syphilis, as in general his hypochondriac worries extended mainly to bacilli and parasites of various kinds. These phobias also explain his compulsive handwashing and his strict instruction not to allow persons with colds to come near him.

Since December 1936, these abdominal colics were treated by Dr. Morell, to whom he had entrusted himself for treatment of a painful eczema on the lower left thigh and who interpreted his complaints as a stomachache or as an irritation of the gastric mucosa. Medically, however, all evidence points to its really having been the typical symptoms of irritable colon which, in a person with a certain vegetative disposition under conditions of severe mental stress, frequently leads to colic-like abdominal pains. The extraordinary tendency to flatulence with often uncontrollable gas release, from which Hitler increasingly suffered, especially during the last decade of his life, and which often could lead to very embarrassing situations, can also be understood in this sense. No doubt, his strictly one-sided vegetarian diet, whose observance he had imposed on himself as a kind of self-punishment after the tragic death of his niece Geli, contributed to this flatulence. His personal physician treated the stomach and intestinal ailments with Mutaflor capsules and with the so-called Dr. Köster anti-gas-pills, and they seemed to bring some relief. In March 1938, the abdominal colics came back again with particular intensity during his triumphal ride to Austria; and during the railroad trip to Rome on the occasion of his visit to Mussolini they reached such intensity that, fearing the start of cancer, he even wrote a last will. Similar painful attacks were repeated subsequently depending on the extent of his mental stress. For instance, in September 1944, when he received the news that the Allies had landed in Arnheim, almost unbearable colics began and put him totally out of commission.

Another internal ailment that made its first appearance in early 1940 was the incipient high blood pressure, which could under mental stress climb as high as 200. In Western industrial countries, that kind of essential hypertension is, with a prevalence of almost 20 percent, the most frequent disease of the cardiovascular system and is clinically most significant because it marks a heightened risk of suffering a heart attack or a stroke. Most urgently significant is the thickening of the wall of the left cardiac chamber because it can lead to coronary heart disease, an atherosclerotic narrowing of the coronary arteries, which can precipitate an impending heart attack. In Hitler, clinically recordable symptoms first arose in July 1942 when after an excited debate, probably within the framework of a considerable rise in blood pressure, an attack similar to a short-lasting myocardial infarction resulted. An electrocardiogram made at that time showed the signs of myocardial damage in the left area of the heart as a result of an insufficient supply of oxygen to the heart muscle due to the narrowing of the coronary arteries. A routine medical checkup in the spring of 1943 showed a worsened electrocardiogram. Then on September 17, 1944, the day of the Allied landing near Arnheim, a heart seizure occurred, probably signaling a heart attack. The accompanying collapse of circulation, the cold sweat, as well as the rundown general physical condition, point in that direction; and the electrocardiogram he was then given supported this probable diagnosis. The question arises, then, whether the development of coronary artery disease in Hitler might not have been caused partly by his earlier considerable use of cigarettes in addition to his high blood pressure. By Hitler's own account, during the years 1907 to 1913 in Vienna, he smoked twenty-five to forty cigarettes per day; but he was forced to give up this habit for financial reasons and therefore "he had thrown his cigarettes into the Danube and never reached for them again." This later portrayal, however, was made for reasons of prestige, since understandably a German folk-hero could under no circumstances be a smoker. In truth, he gave up smoking much later; for Lumnitzer, the inaugurator of "technical emergency aid" in Munich, reported as late as 1923 that he had noticed "Hitler for

his horrid irrepressible loquacity" and also for his "worst, uncontrollable chain-smoking of cigarettes." Consequently for sixteen years, if
not longer, Hitler was a heavy smoker, which must no doubt have had
a negative impact on the coronary vessels. But it is known with certainty that after taking power in 1933 he never again touched a cigarette
and consistently saw to it that no one smoked in his presence.

From the numerous memoirs, biographies and, above all, careful
analyses of Hitler's mobility, such as that done by Professor Ellen
Gibbels based on studies of more than eighty sequences of German
newsreels, today the diagnosis of Parkinson's syndrome can be made
with certainty. The disease began in mid-1941 and from the first affected the left side more strongly; but subsequently it showed a
progressively more distinct set of symptoms and a broader general diminution of mobility, while still retaining the left-side accentuation. It
affected not only the involuntary associated movements, including the
facial expression, which later presented almost the total image of the
so-called "mask-face" of Parkinson's disease, but also voluntary actions. The typical tremor while at rest was noted by eyewitnesses as
early as 1941, while the body position with the upper torso lightly
stooped forward, so typical of Parkinson's disease, first became clearly
noticeable only in 1943 and the dragging stride, likewise so typical of
this disease, not until mid-1944. Finally, a comparison of Hitler's sig-
natures in the period from 1938 to 1945 shows a progressive diminution
of the size of the letters, the "micrography" so typical of patients with
Parkinson's disease. Contrary to a few exaggerated depictions, Hitler's
Parkinson's syndrome toward the end of his life must be classified, at
most, as an ailment of moderately serious gravity. By 1945, however,
the symptoms became so pronounced that the director of the University Neurological Clinic in Berlin, Prof. de Crinis, was able to make
the diagnosis with certainty without ever having examined Hitler personally. The many misinterpretations by the doctors tending him, as
well as by his biographers, can be explained by a lack of expertise; for
the vacillations in the intensity of the trembling of the hands, and especially their dependence on stressful and unstressful situations,
necessarily led to unsolvable difficulties in the medical diagnosis.

As for the cause of this Parkinson's syndrome in Hitler, arterio-
sclerotic processes in the blood vessels of the brain can probably be
excluded. Reports that at the end of July 1941 and again at the beginning of 1945 he had suffered a "mild stroke" are purely speculative
observations by laymen. Above all, the normal finding for the back of

the eye noted by Prof. Dr. Löhlein in March 1945 indicates with certainty that Hitler could have had no mentionable arteriosclerosis of the small blood vessels of the brain. Even if one wanted to suppose an arteriosclerosis of the blood vessels of the brain, it could not, on the basis of our present knowledge, be used to explain his Parkinson's disease, since that disease can be found approximately as often in people with perfectly healthy blood vessels. A connection with vascular processes would exist only if syphilitic changes were present, but even in that case exclusively in connection with a set of symptoms in the framework of a syphilis of the brain. But as Gibbels emphatically stresses, given the fact that Hitler's Parkinson's syndrome progressed over many years and that during that period not the slightest neurological focal symptoms developed, syphilis can be excluded with a probability bordering on certainty.

Since other symptomatic forms of the Parkinson's syndrome, particularly those produced by drugs, also can be excluded, the only possibility left is the choice between the so-called idiopathic, genetically conditioned *morbus Parkinson* and the so-called post-encephalitic parkinsonism, as it was described in 1917 by Constantin Economo following the terrible pandemic of the "Spanish flu," which often progressed under the image of an inflammation of the brain called "encephalitis lethargica." After this epidemic, which rampaged in Europe between 1915 and 1925, a considerable number of patients actually came down with Parkinson's syndrome, sometimes only after an interval of years or even decades. Such a possibility was also considered in different ways by two different groups of researchers to explain Hitler's *morbus Parkinson*.

Johann Recktenwald was the first to try to trace back all of Hitler's noticeable mental and organic peculiarities to an epidemic of encephalitis allegedly contracted when he was twelve years old. This hypothesis assumed that Hitler's brother Edmund died in 1900 not from measles but from an epidemic influenza and that Adolf likewise had fallen ill of that same influenza. Recktenwald interprets the decline in Adolf's school performance after entering high school and his "monster stage" (*Unholdstadium*) of the following years as typical post-encephalitic "pseudo-psychopathic" symptoms; and consequently he associates the wild gesticulations and impulsive emotional outbreaks observed later during Hitler's speeches, as well as Hitler's piercing, rigid stares, with pathological compulsions and fits of rage.

J. Walters and, above all, P. Stolk, on the contrary, argued essentially more cautiously and transferred the suspected influenza infection
to a later time, namely, around 1920. Although for this point in time
the biographical record provides no clue that would indicate such an
encephalitic infection in Hitler, still the possibility of a causal connection with his later Parkinson's syndrome cannot be excluded for certain,
since even cases that go absolutely unnoticed clinically sometimes can
develop a Parkinson's image after a symptom-free interval lasting for
years. Ellen Gibbels, however, rejected the possibility of such a post-
encephalitic form for the reason that in such patients, as experience
shows, the impeded mobility stands completely in the foreground, less
a tremor than rather tic-like motions are observed, the legs tend to suc-
cumb first, and the decreased performance of the cerebrum becomes
observable early—phenomena documented for Hitler neither in medical reports nor by eyewitness testimony. Thus everything points to the
existence of a classical idiopathic Parkinson's disease, including the
lack of any family recollection of such an illness. In this idiopathic
form, an increasing diminution of the number of ganglia cells in the
core areas of the brain stem occurs as a rule essentially earlier than
would be the case in the age-conditioned degenerative processes.

Much more significant than the etiological considerations about
the origin of this set of symptoms, however, is without a doubt for
everyone the question to what extent Hitler's Parkinson's disease may
possibly have influenced his mental modes of behavior and thus also
his political and military decisions. For we know that chronic organic
psycho-syndromes actually are observed in the majority of patients
with Parkinson's disease, and it is surprising that very few psychiatrists have dealt with this question in judging Hitler. This theme was
treated in most detail by Recktenwald, who pointed out that among the
chronic aftereffects of an Economo post-influenzal encephalitis occurring at a young age, various changes of character and disturbances of
the drives are in the foreground, and that the latter can be manifested in
sexual disorders. Interesting in this context is the suggestion that even
juveniles damaged only moderately often have difficulties fitting in
socially because apparently "precisely the central, evaluative, guiding,
significative, and goal-setting authority that is required for social adaptation and successful action" is insufficiently developed. From this
point of view it is not surprising that these intensified drive tendencies
and disturbances are no longer tolerated by society and quite often even
lead to criminality. A study dealing with the later fate of such patients,

with severe post-encephalitic character changes, actually shows that about 40 percent became criminals and came into conflict with the law because of violent acts, vagabondage, or prostitution. In Hitler's case, Recktenwald identifies the signaling sharp behavioral change as the decline of his scholastic achievements after transferring from grammar school to high school in the spring of 1900, and he believes that all of Hitler's psychic particularities which appeared later, including that of the "monster stage of the childhood form," can be characterized within such a post-encephalitic syndrome.

Recktenwald sees the rightness of his thesis as supported by the following clues: Hitler's "late parkinsonism," the above-described fits of rage often accompanied by "compulsive ideas in reiterative think-ing," and finally his sleep disorders. However, except for the fits of rage, all these psychic phenomena enumerated by Recktenwald could not be verified by the American officers through the detailed interroga-tion of the doctors who had treated Hitler for many years; and therefore, de Boor, who has presented the most complete analysis of all Hitler's mental phenomena to date, became convinced that "a post-encephalitic character-transformation in Hitler must be excluded." For Gibbels, however, the question still remained open: whether or not it was con-ceivable to regard "Hitler's youthful behavior as the prototype of a person affected by a monster stage of the childhood form of an epi-demic encephalitic aftermath condition and to speak of a processual psychotic occurrence in the wake of which a character decay, equiva-lent to moral insanity, takes place, with pathological lack of moral judgment, absolute egoism, emotional coldness, and a high degree of unscrupulosity." The starting point for such reasoning is not an or-ganic psycho-syndrome present since childhood, but Hitler's extraordinarily complex primary personality arrayed with numerous abnormal traits; and the attempt is made, by comparing the documents available to us from the pre-morbid phase of his life, that is, prior to the beginning of his Parkinson's disease, with the documents from the last four years of life, in order to deduce a possible illness-conditioned "heightening" of certain primary personal characteristics. Such height-ened primary personal traits that then lead to personality changes have repeatedly been described in patients with Parkinson's disease with various etiologies.

Summarizing Gibbels' minutely detailed analysis, then, the most we can say about Hitler is a vague suspicion of an organic psycho-syndrome in the sense of a "heightening" of a few primary personal traits. This conclusion is confirmed by the famous Swiss historian and politician Carl J. Burckhardt, who, after reading the "Bormann dictations," that is, Hitler's political testament, spoke of a "strange fascination." For in comparing these dictations with the impression he had gotten during a personal meeting with Hitler in 1939, he came to a conclusion that is remarkable in many regards: "At beginning and end exactly the same man, the same brain." With a probability bordering on certainty, Hitler's political and military decisions thus must not have been influenced during the last four war years by personality changes, such as have been very well described in patients with Parkinson's disease. The suspicion expressed occasionally, here and there, that he was only limitedly accountable for his actions, at least during the last months of his life, must therefore be modified into the forensic conclusion drawn by de Boor. He concluded that, even for the last phase of Hitler's life, clues could be discovered "for an impairment neither of his criminal responsibility nor of his business and legal capacity."

A PSYCHOGRAPH OF HITLER

PLEASURE IN KILLING

Certainly Hitler's most notorious character trait is his necrophilic character, which Erich Fromm defined as "the passionate attraction to all that is dead, decayed, putrid, sickly; the passion to transform that which is alive into something unalive; to destroy for the sake of destruction." The objects of his urge for destruction were cities and men, and the most extreme expression of his frenzy to destroy for the sake of destruction was his decree calling for a "charred earth" policy on September 1944, whereby in case of the occupation of German soil by the enemy, he wanted to expose Germany to a grizzly annihilation, as Speer expressed in detail in 1970:

> Not only the industrial installations, the gas, water, and electric plants, and the telephone centers were to be totally destroyed, but everything that is necessary to support life; furthermore food supplies were to be destroyed, farms burned down and cattle killed: the architectural monuments, the castles, palaces and churches, the theaters and opera houses were likewise destined for destruction.

As Henry Picker wrote, Hitler's destructiveness was also displayed in his plans for the future fate of Poland. The Poles were to be culturally castrated and to merely eke out their lives as cheap labor slaves. The first human objects to fall prey to his destructive urge were the incurably ill, and a further early destructive act of vindictiveness was the treacherous murder of Ernst Röhm and several hundred other SA-leaders. But the Jews and Slavic peoples occupied the central role in his destructive frenzy; in his hatred for Jews, yet another necrophilic element of his character played a role, namely, the idea that the Jew would poison Aryan blood. This fear of poisoning, dirtying or infection with dangerous pathogens occupies a great deal of space in the imagination of a necrophilic person and was manifested in Hitler in the form of a compulsion to wash and in his conviction that syphilis was "the most important vital question of the nation." The culmination point of his blind addiction to destruction was reached with his own end, which had to be accompanied by his wife's death and—if it had been up to him—the death of all Germans and the destruction of their living space.

If Hitler's extremely pronounced destructiveness was perceived neither by the German people nor by most foreign statesmen and politicians, the reason was, on the one hand, the repression of his destructiveness by rationalizations of every kind, which imputed noble intentions and sacred duties to these orders for annihilation, and, on the other, the dazzling performance he gave as a perfect liar and brilliant actor. This deceitfulness and disloyalty, both in the human and in the political arena, was one of his particularly repugnant character traits. As exemplified in the "night of the long knives," he spared not even his closest friends and most faithful followers when his own personal advantage was at stake. His dishonest and hypocritical behavior also applied to the Catholic Church. At the same time as he was signing a concordat with it, he was already planning a "final solution" for the Church at a later time:

> A moment will come when I will settle accounts with them without any long beating about the bush....Every century that continues to burden itself with this cultural disgrace will no longer be understood in the future. As the belief in witches had to be eliminated, this relic too must be eliminated.

But even Hitler's entire foreign policy was geared solely toward betrayal and deception, for which the Munich Conference of September 1938 is a sad example.

SADISM AND PATHOLOGICAL SELF-LOVE

Along with Hitler's necrophilia and destructiveness, another of his peculiar character traits is his sadomasochistic authoritarianism, described very accurately by Fromm as early as 1941. It not only determined to a great extent his sexual relations with women but was displayed repugnantly in many other examples. Krausnik, for instance, told of a remark of Hitler's after a Nazi Party meeting that casts light on his entire sadistic hatred of the Jews:

> They should get out of all professions back into the Ghetto, cooped up somewhere or other, where they could perish as they deserve while the German people looked on, the way one stares at wild animals.

A particularly shocking example of his sadistic vindictiveness is his reaction to the sight of the corpses of the generals involved in the July 20, 1944, assassination attempt. Hitler, who otherwise could not stand the sight of corpses, ordered a movie made of the torture and execution of the generals and of their corpses hanging on meathooks with their pants down, and he had this film played for him. He then repeatedly watched this movie with sadistic satisfaction and as the peak of poor taste he even had a photograph of this gruesome scene placed on his desk. This loathsome image of a sadistic person cannot be mitigated or even glossed over by the fact that once in a rare while he could simulate sentimental emotions. for instance, by pretending not to be able to stand the sight of wounded or even killed German soldiers, or when, as is sometimes remarked almost as exculpating him, he personally could not attend a murder or execution, such as that of Röhm and many other fellow combatants from the ranks of the SA whom he treacherously killed. Such reactions did not stem from genuine, empathetic feelings, but were merely the expression of a phobic defense mechanism to keep him from recognizing his own indescribably destructive and sadistic disposition, awareness of which he sought to repress. Through such deceptive maneuvers one must always keep in mind that "a deeply destructive person often displays a facade of friendliness, courtesy, love for family, children and animals, that he often speaks of his ideals and good intentions," and this behavior can easily lead to false evaluations of such a man. As his former admirer Rauschning wrote:

> Hitler could cry when his canary died, but at the same moment he could be having a political opponent cruelly murdered.

A further especially prominent characteristic of Hitler's was his extremely marked narcissism with all its typical symptoms, which Fromm described as follows:

> He is interested only in himself, *his* desires, *his* thoughts, *his* wishes; he talked endlessly about his ideas, his past, his plans; the world is interesting only as far as it is the object of his schemes and desires; other people matter only as far as they serve him or can be used; he always knows everything better than anyone else. This certainty in his own ideas and schemes is a typical characteristic of an intense narcissism.

There are eyewitness accounts impressively illustrating the full image of such a narcissism in Hitler, for instance, when Hanfstaengl described Hitler's behavior on hearing a tape-recording of one of his speeches:

> Hitler then threw himself in a large Morris chair and enjoyed his own voice, as it were, in a kind of complete narcosis—a counterpart of the Greek youth tragically in love with himself, who in admiration of his own reflection on the water's surface met his death in the waves.

This sick self-love showed up during his imprisonment in the Landsberg Fortress, where the prison instructor spoke of his "prima donna vanity"; and his later enthusiastic devotion to Bayreuth, likewise, served less the cult of Richard Wagner, as he always pretended, than rather his narcissistically stamped cult of his own splendid self-representation before the Festspiel guests, who brought him their homage with respectful devotion. How little he really cared about Bayreuth's significance is shown, according to de Boor, "by his order for the execution of Gauleiter Wächtler in March 1945, when the latter, to preserve the art treasures and architectural monuments of this city, offered to surrender to the American troops without a struggle." This conduct of Hitler's corresponds completely to Nietzsche's simile that every great talent is like a vampire whose visionary world therefore often resembles a rubble field of human existences and hopes. Hitler, too, felt this way. He was "completely occupied with directing his gigantic theater, in which people were for him merely actors and extras who had to follow the director's orders or let themselves be sent to their death." Only such extremely developed narcissism in a person with a deeply destructive character can explain the almost self-murderous decisions made by Hitler during the Russian campaign, with a total absence of any feeling of guilt to achieve a visionary ideal. Joachim C. Fest described them as a "strategy for a grandiose downfall and his will for an all-embracing catastrophe."

All biographies speak of Hitler's unbending will, and he himself was absolutely convinced that this was one of his strongest advantages. Erich Fromm was the first to point out that "what Hitler called his will, was nothing else but his passions that fired him up and drove him mercilessly to realize them." Albert Speer, too, said that his will had been as uncontrolled and unpolished as that of a six-year-old child. Thus it could more accurately be said that he was driven by his impulses and was incapable of accepting frustration. How little genuine willpower he had was shown even in his adolescent years. He was an idler without a trace of self-discipline, who, even in the critical phase after his rejection by the Academy of Arts in Vienna, did not muster the strength to make up for missing qualifications by greater efforts than before to achieve his dream-goal of becoming an architect. If the political situation after World War I had not turned out to his advantage, he probably would have continued his shiftless existence and settled for a modest life.

Hitler's weak will continued to show itself later in his noticeable hesitation and doubt whenever a decision was required of him, for example in the failed putsch-attempt at the Bürgerbräukeller in Munich. He was always inclined to let things come his way, so that a decision became unnecessary. To comprehend the apparent contradiction between this indecision as the expression of a weak will and his unflinching decisiveness when applying his "iron will" to attaining a goal, one must be clear on the different concepts of the "rational" and the "irrational" will. By rational will, Erich Fromm understands "the energetic effort to reach a rationally desirable aim: this requires realism, discipline, patience, and the overcoming of a self-indulgence." The irrational will, on the contrary, incorporates "a striving, fed by the energy of irrational passions that lacks the qualities needed for the rational will." In apply-ing this psychological knowledge to Hitler, then, one comes to the result that, in fact, he did have a very strong will, if an irrational will is meant, but, on the contrary, his rational will was very weakly developed.

Another of Hitler's qualities was his disturbed sense of reality. His lack of contact with reality appeared in his childhood, for his dream of becoming an artist had very little to do with reality. Even the people he dealt with and who were generally just tools in his hand, were almost never real for him. One must not, however, imagine that he lived only in a fantasy world, for when necessary he even had a remarkable sense of reality, for instance, when it was a matter of correctly assessing the motivation of his opponents. On the other hand, in his strategic plans, Hitler seemed to lack all sense of reality and therefore was incapable of an objective appraisal of the real situation. Percy Ernst Schramm, who dealt most exhaustively with this problem, therefore said that Hitler's strategy had been a "prestige and propaganda strategy" and that his lack of a sense of reality made him totally oblivious to the fact that waging war and spreading propaganda are subject to totally differ-ent laws and principles. Especially toward the end of the war his reflections moved only in an unreal world, so that even Joseph Goebbels, who admired him beyond measure and was slavishly devoted to him, got the impression "as if Hitler were living in the clouds."

A fundamental trait of Hitler's personality was his strongly marked distrust, which had become apparent, in the late 1930s, to the High Commissioner of the League of Nations for the Free City of Danzig: "He distrusts everyone and everything, accuses everyone of being in contact with his enemy or being about to change over to the other side." This extreme distrust reinforced his reclusiveness since his youth and remained with him to the end of his life.

Other qualities firmly anchored in Hitler's character were his strong irritability and his penchant to violent, at times almost explosive, emo-tional outbursts—classic symptom of an unusually low tolerance for frustration. His often-cited fits of rage contributed to a stereotypical idea, especially widespread in other countries, that Hitler was constantly angry, always shouting, and never able to control his fits of anger.

The stereotype does not accord with the truth. His fits of rage could, indeed, be extremely violent, especially toward the end of the war, but they were rather the exception. Contemporary witnesses agreed that as a rule he was polite, considerate, and affable, and that his angry outbursts often were used by him to intimidate his conversation partners and cause them to give up their resistance. Albert Speer said something to that effect: "Some seemingly hysterical reactions which are reported can probably be attributed to such theatrics." If he saw that his counterpart was not induced to capitulate by a staged fit of rage, then he could bring his angry behavior under control in a moment, as Alan Bullock illustrated credibly by a scene between Hitler and General Guderian, which the general described thus:

> His fists raised, his cheeks flushed with rage, his whole body trembling, the man stood there in front of me, beside himself with fury and having lost all self-control.

> His voice cracked, his eyes protruded out of their sockets, and the veins on his temple swelled. When Guderian nonetheless stuck to his opinion, Hitler suddenly smiled very affably and bade Guderian: "Please continue with the conference. Today the General Staff has won a battle."

Up to this point primary personal character traits have been listed, portraying Hitler as a necrophile, a destructive, introverted, extremely narcissistic, sadomasochistic, reclusive and undisciplined person. However, to describe Hitler objectively and unemotionally, it is also necessary to deal with his talents and abilities, to which he owed his spectacular successes and his rise in just two decades, from a marginalized outsider without any professional training to the most powerful man in Europe. Among Hitler's talents, no doubt the most important was his art of impressing other people and convincing them. If one seeks the causes for his enormous gift of influencing people, which set him apart from other successful demagogues of his time, one first discovers his extraordinary skill as a political orator, also combined with dramatic talent. This oratorical ability was his most important instrument on the road to power, and his political acumen consisted in stamping just a very few themes onto the particular conditions of his time and transposing them into a kind of pseudo-religious myth. With his cold, piercing eyes, which exercised an almost magnetic effect on many of his audiences, and the unflinching certainty with which he delivered his theses, he must have been a highly attractive figure to such a socio-politically insecure era as Germany, in the 1920s, and must have appeared to many almost like a Savior with great tactical skills; he knew how to deepen this indefinite feeling among the masses by allusions to the Christian liturgy, for instance when he said:

> I came from the people. In fifteen years I slowly
> worked my way up out of this people through this
> movement. I was not appointed by anyone over this
> people. I grew out of the people, I remained among
> the people, I return back to the people.

These pathetic words were for him not just empty sound; they sprang from his narcissistically stamped conviction of his "political nature as a John the Baptist." At first he believed he was just the proclaimer of a coming Messiah, but starting in 1924 he felt more and more that he himself was this "Chosen One," namely, "der Führer."

Another talent was his ability to portray complicated things in a simplified fashion, and he was also fully aware of this when on one occasion he declared:

> Our problems seemed complicated. The German
> people could not begin to deal with them. Under these
> conditions, they preferred to leave them to the profes-
> sional politicians. I, on the contrary, simplified the
> problems and reduced them to the simplest formula.
> The masses recognized this and followed me.

Of course, that he selectively sought out facts that served his agenda and combined them with things that had nothing to do with the matter at hand, so as to formulate convincing arguments out of this hetero-geneous mixture, remained hidden from the majority of the uncritical masses.

Hitler's unusual memory should also be emphasized, as Percy Ernst Schramm, among others, wrote:

> One quality of Hitler's which repeatedly amazed ev-
> eryone—even those who were not sold on him—was
> his stupendous memory that could retain inessential
> data firmly and store up everything that entered his
> range of vision.

If his generals were repeatedly deeply impressed by his "thorough knowledge" in the military field, this, too, was simply an achievement of his extraordinary memory for numbers and technical details; and the same is true of the evaluation of Hitler's wide reading and general knowledge, to which some biographers pay unreserved admiration. Although it must be gathered from his *Table Talks* that he must have been an avid, indeed an insatiable, reader and have retained an abundance of facts because of his immense memory, still precisely these often cited *Table Talks* unmask him as a very gifted but basically only semi-educated man, without a solid foundation in any field. Through his intelligence, however, he knew how to scatter the bits of information acquired in superficial reading and firmly retained in his excellent memory so skillfully that he was able to simulate knowledge on a wide array of topics. In accord with his character, in his reading he avoided anything that ran contrary to his own ideas, visions, and prejudices, so that actually he didn't read to acquire greater knowledge, but, as Erich Fromm said, to gather new "ammunition for his passion for persuading others—and himself....Hitler was not a self-taught man but a half-taught man, and the half that was missing was the knowledge of what knowledge is." His narcissistic character, always pleased to play the role of infallible and omniscient sage, also found it hard to carry on a conversation with people who were equal or even superior to him, because the illusory edifice of his knowledge might collapse under the pressure. The only exceptions were architects; he liked to converse with them, because apparently architecture was the only genuine interest in Hitler's life. It is not surprising that his taste in architecture, as in other fields of art, was primitive and shallow, as could be expected from his unfeeling, primitive nature.

Despite Hitler's gifts and talents, his meteoric rise to power would still have been inconceivable without the hydraulic power of a grandiose propaganda campaign, which again and again led the masses to believe that both the Führer and every single citizen were under constant threat by dark forces, namely, the Jews, the Bolshevists, and the plutocratic West, a threat that could be warded off only by an iron-willed Führer. The "Führer" thus became an idol that was not merely foisted on the people, but also in part was created by them. Hitler's rise to power is therefore hardly imaginable without the susceptibility of many German (and later also Austrian) citizens to the main tenets of his ideology: hatred of the Jews, restoration of a German great power, and extension of the German living space toward the East. As Stern in his interesting analysis determined—probably correctly—Hitler's personality and the masses' willing receptivity to his warnings about alleged dangers form a solid mutually promoting unity. In speeches that were admittedly diabolically seductive, he conjured up these dangers in greatly simplified form and reduced them to a few enemies of the people. Speer's judgment was similar:

The people around Hitler were also to blame, in the last analysis, that he became more and more convinced of his superhuman qualities. Even a more self-controlled and modest person than Hitler would have run the danger of losing all standards of self-evaluation amid the uninterrupted hymns and constantly resounding applause.

Binion pointed out that "Hitler's eerie personal power over the Germans was based on the fact that he brought his private traumatic anger at the 1918 capitulation into harmony with the national traumatic need." Thomas Aich, however, rightly emphasized that, after all, "mass man" remains an absolute precondition for a mass hypnosis, or respectively a mass delusion. Such a mass man is "a critically weak, ideology-prone, emotionally unstable type of person who has, in the wake of industrialization, freed himself from traditional allegiances and, especially in times of economic crisis, needs the strong psychological narcotic administered to him by Hitler to stabilize his 'self.'"

Since all the concepts of psychoanalysis and depth-psychology can draw only a theoretical picture of Hitler's character and his singularly unique personality, the portrayal by the French ambassador André François-Poncet, who was accredited to Berlin from 1931 to 1938 and got to know Hitler from closest proximity, should be cited; for it is drawn in unusually vivid colors and with exceptional psychological insight. A passage about Hitler from his memoirs published in 1949, cited in de Boor's monograph, gives us a vivid picture of this eerie man, with the eyes of an observer with an extraordinary gift of observation:

A man like Hitler cannot be reduced to a simple formula....I personally knew three faces in him, matching three aspects of his nature. The first was pallid and showed blurry features, and a dull complexion. Without expression, his slightly protruding eyes looked lost in dreams and gave him an absent, distant air; it was an opaque face, disturbing like a medium's or a sleep-walker's. The second was animated, with lively color and passionate expression. The nostrils quivered, the eyes shot lightning bolts; this face was vehement, full of the will to power, rebellion against any coercion, hatred for the opponent, wild energy; it was ready to disregard everything: a face marked with

storm and stress, the face of a madman. The third was
that of an everyday person, who is naive, crude, ordinary, easy to delight, who breaks into loud laughter
and slaps himself on the thigh; a face such as one often meets, without particular expression, one of
thousands and thousands of faces such as are found in
the wide world. Talking with Hitler, one sometimes
experienced these three faces, one after another.

At the beginning of the conversation, he seemed not
to be listening, not to understand. He remained indifferent and as if absent. One had before one a person
who remained sunken for hours in strange meditations
and who after midnight, when his comrades had left
him, again fell into long, solitary reflections, the
"Führer," who reproached his coworkers with indecision, weakness, and vacillation. Then suddenly, as if
a hand had pressed a button, he plunged into violent
speech, spoke in a raised voice, excited, angry, with
rapid logic, like that of a Tyrolian from the hintermost
mountain valleys. He thundered and raged as if he
were speaking to thousands of hearers. Then the orator in him awakened, the great orator of Latin tradition,
the tribune who spoke in the deep tone of conviction,
who instinctively used all the rhetorical figures, masterfully drawing on all registers of eloquence, who
hardly knows an equal in biting irony and diatribe;
and this is for the masses something new and unheard
of, because in Germany political rhetoric is generally
monotonous and boring. When Hitler plunged into a
lecture or a diatribe, one could not think of interrupt-
ing or contradicting him. Sputtering with anger, he
would have smashed down the incautious person who
dared to do that, as he thundered down Schuschnigg
and Hache who tried to show him some resistance.
That lasted for a quarter, a half, or three-quarters of an
hour. Then suddenly the stream of words dried up,
seemed exhausted. One could have believed that his
batteries had run down. He became dull and limp.
That was the moment to raise objections, to contradict

him, to hold a different viewpoint, for then he no longer became outraged, he wavered, desired to think the matter over, and postponed his decisions. And then if you could find a word to move him, a joke to relax him completely, a smile lit up his dark features.

Because of these states of excitement and depression, these crises which befell him—as the people around him said—and ran the scale from the worst destructiveness to the whimpering of a beaten animal, psychiatrists have declared him to be a periodic raving maniac; others see him as a type of paranoiac. Certainly he was not normal. He was a sick creature who can be characterized as insane, a figure such as Dostoevsky called a "possessed person." If I had to stress the main trait of his character, his dominant quality, according to Taine's teachings, then I would think first of his pride and ambition. But it would probably be more correct to use an expression from Nietzsche's language, which he incidentally himself often used: "Will to power." Power, he wanted it for himself but also for Germany, it was one with him....Since childhood he had been chauvinistic and an adherent of the "Great Germany" idea. In his own flesh he endured the suffering and abasements of the nation he regarded as his own fatherland. He swore to avenge himself by avenging it....Since the will to power is by nature oriented to conquest and war, he sought to turn the state into a military state, a police state, a dictatorship....But the will to power is never satisfied. It constantly grows beyond itself, for it finds happiness only in action. Therefore Hitler was not satisfied with creating the Third Reich and breaking the chains of the Treaty of Versailles. He wanted to set up the "Great Reich" in Europe...and had he succeeded, then he would have started on North and South America. Hitler's imagination was wild and romantic. He fed it with elements gleaned from here and there. He was not uneducated but he had the bad education of an autodidact. He had the gift of reducing things to a common denominator and simplifying them and this won him the enthusiastic praise of his admirers.

From the writings of Houston Steward Chamberlain, Nietzsche, Spengler, and many others there rose before his mind the dream image of a Germany that would reestablish the grandeur of the Holy Roman Empire of the German Nation...for a master race based on a healthy peasant foundation, led by a Party that represented a political elite, a kind of knighthood. After this master race had cleansed the world forever of the Jewish poison, which in his view contained all other poisons—the poison of democracy and parliamentarism, the poison of Marxism and Communism, the poison of capitalism and Christianity—he would create a new and positive religion that would equal in scope and depth the one Christianity had produced. These were delusions he dwelled on in his nightly dreams....Sometimes he clothed his dreams in Wagnerian harmonies. He considered himself a hero from Wagner's world; he was Lohengrin, Siegfried, and especially Parsifal, who heals the bleeding wound of the ailing Amfortas and gives the Grail back its marvelous power.

But it would be a mistake to believe that this man who lived in visions, did not also have a sense of reality. He was an absolutely cold realist and a painstaking orator. Although indolent and incapable of devoting himself to a regular job, he knew precisely everything that was going on in the Reich....Thus he cannot escape responsibility. He knew about the worst crimes and excesses; he tolerated or willed them. His will to power was supported by dangerous mental abilities: an extraordinary obstinacy, boundless audacity, a sudden and ruthless power of decision, rapid comprehension, an inner feeling that warned him of dangers and protected him more than once from plots contrived against him....His violence and brutality were accompanied by cunning, hypocrisy, and a penchant for lying. When he looked back over his career, at the marvelous rise that had brought him power such as no emperor had ever possessed, he was convinced that Providence was protecting him and making him invincible. He, the unbeliever, the enemy of Christianity, considered himself the Chosen One of the Almighty, to whom he appealed more and more in his speeches.... He overestimated his own person and his country, and in complete ignorance of foreign countries he underestimated his Russian and Anglo-Saxon opponents. Finally, he considered himself a strategic genius and wanted to equal Friedrich II and to outdo Napoleon. His absolutism, his tyranny became progressively worse. Himmler and the Gestapo set up a reign of terror in the Reich....It is astonishing that the German people followed this insane Führer so long and so submissively. To explain this, it is not enough to allude to fear of the police and the concentration camps.

If one tries to draw a true picture of the man Hitler and his significance for human society based on this brilliant analysis by an eyewitness and on personality traits elaborated theoretically by psychologists, psychoanalysts, depth psychologists, and psycho-historians, then one is immediately confronted with the question posed by Joachim C. Fest at the beginning of his biography: "History records no phenomenon like him. Ought we to call him 'great'?" In fact, John Toland, in his biography held that Hitler surpassed even the greatest movers of world history, such as Alexander the Great and Napoleon, although Bahnsen relativized this somewhat in his introduction to that biography:

> Certainly in our time no other ruler caused the death of so many people. At the same time, however, he was admired and honored....For the few who still are his convinced followers, he is a hero, a fallen Messiah. For all others, however, this man is a "madman," a political and military adventurer, a totally evil murderer, who achieved his successes by criminal means.

Only forensic psychiatry is equipped to prove or disprove this last statement. Wolfgang de Boor, an internationally recognized specialist in penal law, in his extraordinarily thorough and highly instructive study in criminal psychology by the title, *Hitler: Human, Superhuman, Subhuman*, dealt with this question and came to remarkably concrete results which should be summed up here in closing.

HITLER—A PSYCHOPATH AND CRIMINAL?

For his criminological investigation of Hitler's case, de Boor used basically two scientific methods that draw on various typical traits and permit the most objective possible appraisal of a personality's criminal tendencies: namely, the theory of "social infantilism," and the so-called "monoperceptose-concept."

As opposed to somatic and psychic infantilism, de Boor defines social infantilism as the abnormal behavior of an individual within the social field of tension, characterized by various deficits in the area of his social activities. If one follows Neidhardt's definition, which stated that the socialization of an individual is a process "by which the values, norms and techniques of life prevalent in a society are communicated and made binding," then—according to de Boor—in Hitler's childhood hardly any deficits can be discovered that could have exercised a baneful influence on his primary socialization. Despite all his father's negative authoritarian traits, precisely he must have communicated the normative ideas of law and order most impressively to his son. Even the secondary socialization phase, whose most lasting influence comes mainly from school, seems to have succeeded normatively. This assumption is corroborated by Hitler's strong verbal dispute with construction workers at the beginning of his Vienna period, in which he passionately defended "almost the entire catalogue of norms of bourgeois society." During the third phase of socialization, however, in which the final personalization of the individual is supposed to be achieved, and which Erikson calls "the psycho-social moratorium," a normal course of development cannot be demonstrated. His psychosocial moratorium lasted for almost a whole decade and shows no signs indicating a final formation of the personality. However, in that period of time between 1905 and 1914, a few experiences were significant for the further development of Hitler's personality. His mother's death occurred at that time, and it moved him very deeply, as Dr. Bloch, the Jewish doctor who treated her, emphasized credibly in 1943 while in exile in America. Her death thus released just about the only genuine emotional feelings in his life. Another event which left persistent traces was his failure at the Academy of Art in Vienna in 1907, which left a lifelong aversion to all successful and socially integrated people and a hatred of everything that had to do with academies and universities. Since he placed the responsibility for his own failure to achieve his dream goal of becoming a painter or architect not on himself but on the narrow-mindedness and incompetence of the professors, he from then on felt rejected by established bourgeois society, and this led him to go underground in anonymity, first in a homeless shelter, then in a men's home.

Thus the forensic-criminological analysis of Hitler's psycho-social moratorium provides little tangible evidence one way or the other. The only thing certain is that he failed to find his identity because of various identity crises and that these formative years of the Vienna time produced only fear-conditioned defense mechanisms. World War I, his "great positive educational experience," then broke all the more powerfully into Hitler's personality vacuum and thus became a dominant shaping factor in his belated process of maturation, giving Hitler's previously "amorphous" gestalt tangible personal contours. No tendency to cruel actions could be documented. Since there was no "genuine experience of political awakening" after the end of the war, it is difficult to give an exact point in time for the beginning of his political career. Possibly his sudden realization that he had talent as an orator is what pulled him out of his long-lasting crisis of self-worth and caused a real "breakthrough to himself." The final close of his personalization phase was his prison-term in Landsburg Fortress, since from then on he stepped into the political arena. Eitner believed that the "Jordan experience" of his time in prison was the igniting spark for the change of his political consciousness which now took shape.

In the normal average citizen, the lengthy socialization process of an individual results in the building of the all-important structural barrier that prevents the triggering of more severe aggressive actions even under violent emotions. In Hitler, this structural barrier was mostly intact until the end of World War I. Only with the beginning of his political activity did the first signs of increasing deformation of his structural barrier show up, as is evidenced by an interview with General von Seeckt in the Bavarian War Ministry on March 1923. At that time Hitler explained to the dismayed general:

> It will be the task of us National Socialists to put the Marxists, together with the defeatists in the current administration, where they belong—hanging from the lampposts.

But the deterrent mechanisms first failed completely only at the beginning of the seizure of power in 1933. The 1934 slaughter of his SA-officers in the "night of the long knives," the murder of the generals von Bredow and Schleicher, who had gotten in his way, the euthanasia-order for the killing of the mentally ill and other forms of "worthless life" in 1939, the order to murder millions of Jews and other races labeled as worthless subhumans, and finally the inhuman "Nero Command" of 1945 prove that Hitler's leveling of his structural barrier was equivalent to "extinguishing normative substance such as takes place comparably only in the mass murderer."

A further, essential criminological mark of Hitler was his pronounced "social autism," which, according to de Boor, is a typical character trait of schizoid persons who do not display a real schizophrenia but indeed many schizophrenia-like symptoms. As a criminological phenomenon, this "social autism" is paraphrased as follows:

> The inability or difficulty of a person to create social contacts; the tendency to separate oneself off makes it more difficult to solve mental conflicts by conversations with others or by obtaining competent advice. This encapsulation produces aggressive tension. The communication barrier and information blockage make it difficult to adapt to reality.

On the autism of schizoid personalities, Ernst Kretschmer listed other traits that aptly describe Hitler's psyche, namely:

> Harsh and cold egoism, pharisaic self-conceit and immeasurably over-excited self-esteem, striving for the theoretical happiness of mankind according to schematic doctrinaire principles, the wish to improve the world, altruistic sacrifice on a grand scale particularly for general impersonal ideals.

A particularly typical feature of Hitler's "social autism" was his cold affective lack of sympathy—a symptom grounded in his abysmal contempt for mankind. He did not feel the least sympathy for the unimaginable sufferings of the German civilian population in the merciless air raids of the last war years, whereas news of the destruction of opera houses or theater buildings moved him deeply. And he gave not a moment's thought to the wounded soldiers who were sheltered in the subway tunnels and who would have been helplessly exposed to death by drowning by his criminal order to open the floodgates of the Spree. Hitler's weak ego led to extreme distrust that became virtually the "element" he lived in during the last years of his life, as Speer said. That he capsuled himself off in the last phase of his life in the bomb-secure bunker under the Reichs-chancellory is, for de Boor, symbolic of the "close of his life, which had always missed the middle ground between autistic narrowness and unbridled world power—the humane dimension of existence."

From a criminological viewpoint, an important key to explain a criminal's deviant behavior resides in evidence of his inability to toler-ate frustration, to accept failures, disappointments, or insulting humiliations without an aggressive response. Hitler's intolerance of frustration was recognizable at a very early age; and, as a consequence of his biologically grounded high potential for aggression, even in his youth it led to some peculiar ways of reacting. Along with his lack of social conscience, this important criminological trait, so extremely pro-nounced in Hitler's behavior toward human society, explains the horrifying number of the most brutal acts of violence he later authorized.

Another characteristic Hitler shares with many criminals was a series of identity deficits. Such identity deficits arise whenever the formation of a stable identity core is not achieved during the decisive early years of a person's development. Since Hitler could not identify with his feared, despotic father without denying his own ego, he found himself after his mother's death in a kind of emotional vacuum, which also could not be filled in Vienna as a consequence of his own failures. Uncertainty about his biological origin and knowledge of his parents' incestuous relationship may have played quite an essential role among the disturbing factors in the process of his finding of identification. In the view of psychiatrists experienced in criminology, identity defects often push socially infantile people to do spectacular actions in their quest for self-identity. Although, in Hitler, the impulses to do spec-tacular things were at first positive and constructive in nature, after the beginning of World War II they increasingly took on a destructive character. How interconnected the relation between disturbed identity-formation and paranoid phenomena can be, is described by Josef Rudin in his book *Fanaticism; A Psychological Analysis:*

> The rigid behavior of this type of fanatic generally builds up to a complete identification with the idea he advocates. With this we arrive at the second symptom pointing to the schizoid syndrome. Even though the processes of identification, like the processes of

projection, belong to the universally human and therefore necessary mechanisms, depth psychology clearly
recognizes those inadequate identifications which as
defense mechanisms alienate man from his real identity and his innermost self and thus drive him into
neurosis or the unfolding of a latent psychosis....It is
the special peril of permanent identifications and
overidentifications that the real ego shrinks more and
more and is gradually replaced by phantastic, naive,
or paranoid forms of identification.

Hitler thus ranks among the group of criminals whose career, as a result of their identification deficits, is characterized by the stigma of the
"destruction of their world," as Speer described this by the example of
Hitler, who in 1939 was changed progressively from an original
creator to a fanatical destroyer:

He intentionally wanted people to perish with him.
The end of his own life meant, for him, the end of
everything.

Such a complete destruction of the "normative capacity" as was
expressed in Hitler's fanatical destructive drive, unparalleled in history, can hardly be explained, however, by the presence of his "social
infantilism" or by primary criminally pre-formed personality structures;
but here, additionally, as de Boor stated, a "corruption of his normative
capacity" by lack of an overarching corrective or at least admonishing
authority inside and outside Germany must be assumed. Only so did it
become possible for Hitler to satisfy his "infantile needs. He found in
the radical circles of his people...an ideal partner. The two infantilisms
united into one...phenomenon, which is called in psychiatry 'folie à
deux.'...The active partner, the Führer, imprinted his delusionary themes
upon the weaker partner, the ideology-susceptible people, more and
more relentlessly, so that in the course of years an inseparable unity
arose that can be accurately characterized by the word 'mass delusion.'
Mass delusion can, however, arise only when both partners are infantile." Such delusional consciousness processes with deep, far-reaching
social consequences are summed up by de Boor under the concept
"monoperceptosis."

Megalomania, of which Hitler had a good measure, is one of the
typical characteristics of monoperceptosis. For he was deeply convinced "of being a solitary individual towering above the surrounding

world in mental and creative force." His "social autism," with reality-alienated wishful thinking and with the idea that he must owe his extraordinary abilities to a higher power, certainly favored the development of megalomania. This megalomania of his was not a symptom of mental illness, but the result of a long psychological process from childhood on. A partial aspect of his megalomania was a phenomenon that has been termed "construction-megalomania." Thus, as a symbol of his world rulership, the erection of the "great hall" in the Reichs-capital was supposed to be crowned by a huge globe, held in the claws of a Reichs-eagle, decorated with the swastika. And Speer was supposed to prepare an office for him in the new Reichs-chancellory with almost a thousand square meters of area and a planned completion deadline of 1950. William Carr interpreted this as "hypercompensation for an inferiority complex as part of a complicated defense mechanism that helped him overcome the doubts of his mission and the fears about whether he would indeed succeed in keeping the conquests he had already made and would make in the future."

Every attempt to explain Hitler's unexampled aggressiveness has to struggle with the difficulty that, based on the biographical facts, an inborn aggressive character quality is excluded with certainty as a cause of his later excessive aggressiveness. De Boor now called attention to something previously overlooked: the enormous dynamics generated by a monoperceptosis under the dictates of an all-dominant hypervalent idea and mobilized with tremendous forces and psychic energies to realize the respective key theme. Normally, aggressions that are carriers of a "hypervalent idea" with delusionary content are impeded from executing socially disastrous actions uninhibitedly by the threat of penal measures. For Hitler there was, however, from 1934 on, no impeding authority of any kind, and therefore he could with impunity act out aggressions that were constantly being energized by his hypervalent ideas—destruction of the Jews, the struggle against Marxism, expansion of German living space toward the East.

> Since from 1934 on all technical, economic, and military means of a modern industrial state with unrestricted power and authority stood at his disposal, this possibility of realizing his monoperceptory, hypervalent ideas resulted in a historical situation that stands unique in all previous history.

Große Halle
290 Meter

Reichstag
75 Meter

Brandenburger Tor
29 Meter

An example of Hitler's megalomania: the planned "Great Hall" in Berlin, shown behind existing German buildings for comparison

As Trevor-Roper correctly remarked, it is therefore unimaginable that such a baneful conjuncture of three factors should ever occur again. These three factors were:

- a dictatorial and, in de Boor's opinion, most seriously criminal personality;
- the predominance of a mankind-endangering, monoperceptory, hypervalent delusionary idea;
- and the total state potential to realize this hyper-valent idea.

In addition, Hitler's extreme narcissism, by concentrating exclusively on the libido of his own ego, not only caused a feeling of omnipotence, but due to the tendency to "narcissistic vexations," especially pronounced in such persons, it could also lead to criminal acts. In such a case, no psychic trauma, no humiliation, and no vexation can ever be forgotten and forgiven, and Hitler provides enough examples of later revenge on people who had once humiliated or offended him and had to pay for it with their life.

This combination of narcissism and egocentricity led ultimately, with regard to his supposed world-historical significance, to the "extinguishing of the internal value system" with complete disregard of the needs and rights of his fellowmen. As de Boor emphasizes, such a process is actually observed otherwise only in serious mental cases, such as within the framework of a schizophrenic breakdown of the personality. For persons who are not mentally ill, there have until now been no verified ideas on the conditions for the genesis of such an almost complete breakdown of norms, and Hitler is the first such case since the beginning of scientific research on the mental changes in criminal persons.

Among Hitler's dominant "hypervalent ideas," his unparalleled pathological hatred of Jews occupied first place. The eradication of the Jews in Europe was, in the last analysis, the objective of all his military actions. With the start of his conquest for living space in the East in 1942, he came alarmingly close to carrying out his utopian dream of purging Jews and "inferior" Slavs from a huge territory in the East and filling it with members of the "master race" and, by the erection of a mighty Eastern wall, shielding it forever from invading hordes from the Asiatic expanses. Almost all psychological hypotheses, as usually applied in medicine, fail to explain this "virtually Satanical hatred, which mutilated the humane in Hitler to the point of being unrecognizable." Certainly, his hatred of Jews was a truly insane phenomenon, since it coincides perfectly with three of the characteristic criteria required by Jaspers for a schizophrenic delusion. First, the content of his delusionary idea that there exists a Jewish lobby, seeking to destroy the Aryan race and establish world rule, is unreal due to the impossibility of its realization. The second criterion is met by his obdurate conviction of the rightness of this delusionary idea. And finally the third argument is that this delusion could neither be influenced by logical reflections nor corrected by contents of experience. De Boor, in his criminological analyses, therefore came to the conclusion that "all delusionary criteria must be affirmed of Hitler's ideological thought-structure. So it was 'madness,' although 'madness' of a kind exhibited by clinically healthy persons, persons who display no symptoms of schizophrenia. For this reason in 1976 we proposed a special term, monoperceptosis, in order to distinguish the 'madness' of healthy people with its grave social consequences from the 'madness' of the mental ill."

The analysis of the characteristics of the various periods of Hitler's life with regard to the terms "social infantilism" and "monoperceptosis," which enables the expert to make a criminological-social prognosis in trials, in Hitler's case produced a virtually catastrophic criminological prognosis, which de Boor summed up as follows:

> In case of a final victory, cruel trials would have been inflicted on the German people and the people of Europe. One must be grateful to the efforts of the Allies that Germany and Europe were liberated from the dictatorship of a severely criminal personality.

The arguments of a few psychiatrists that Hitler was clinically insane do not hold up to objective criticism. Serious professionals agree that Hitler was a "vindictive, hysterical psychopath and schizoid-autistic fanatic," who must be considered fully accountable for all his deeds. Dr. Bumke, former Professor of Psychiatry at the University of Munich accordingly came to the following forensic judgment about Hitler:

> Schizoid and hysterical, brutally cruel, semi-educated, uncontrolled and treacherous, without kindness, without a sense of responsibility, and absolutely without morals.

Persons of this kind, when they rise to political power, can become an enormous danger to society, as was explained by Dr. Schaltenbrand, Professor of Psychiatry at the University of Würzburg:

> The psychopathic politician represents an especially dangerous intermediary form between the healthy person and the mentally ill person. This type is especially dangerous because the psychopath generally has too many healthy traits to be easily recognized with certainty by everyone as mentally deviant....Typically, the psychopath succeeds in gaining disciples and followers who in their psychic constitution diverge but slightly from the normal. The grotesque and distorted programs accepted by these people produce a kind of mass psychosis.

The rapid spread of this mass psychosis was favored by Hitler's unusual talent for influencing others, so that he succeeded in unleashing a regular group hypnosis. How this reciprocally affected Hitler, so that the "Führer" and the "masses" influenced one another in the manner of a spiral dominated by delusionary thoughts is explained by criminal psychology as follows:

> If the masses develop an almost doglike reverence for a socially infantile creature dominated by delusionary thoughts, then the negative potential of the object of worship must ineluctably be strengthened and finally extinguish the remnant of humanity.

Considering the weird events which unfolded during the few years in which Hitler made himself the absolute ruler of Germany and almost all Europe, no doubt a high, indeed virtually unique, historical rank must be assigned to him, though in a negative sense. He, therefore, most certainly will keep his place as a historical figure for all time in the "pantheon of world history." But, as de Boor so accurately remarked, a similar place of honor is also rightly reserved for him in the "pantheon of great criminals."

Apparently by 1943 the National Socialist potentates, with their "Führer" at the top, were themselves of the same opinion. For Joseph Goebbels wrote in his magazine *Das Reich* on November 14, probably with regard to the monstrous deeds they were already committing and which were to be followed by still more horrible ones:

> As for us, we have burned our bridges behind us. We can no longer turn back, nor do we want to. We will go down in history as the greatest statesmen of all times—or as its greatest criminals.

JOSEPH STALIN

Great Leader
Great Leader of the Soviet People
Great Master of Courageous Revolutionary Decisions
and Drastic Changes
Great Helmsman
Great Strategist of the Revolution
Great Friend of Children
Great Friend of Women
Great Friend of Divers and Long Range Runners
Great Friend of Collective Farmers
Great Friend of Artists
Great Field Commander
Great Genius of All Times and Nations
Father, Leader, Friend, and Teacher...

A selection of Stalin's titles

"Stalin was without a doubt the most hated and most loved, the most highly revered and the most bitterly despised statesman in all history." Within the territories he ruled, there were only enthusiastic followers and irreconcilable enemies. To give a psychological portrait of this monster of a man, objective descriptions and reports by contemporaries from his immediate circle would be necessary. But these types of documents will hardly be possible in the near future, since in his lifetime there were no objective observers in his immediate personal circle, and, moreover, he had everyone who in his opinion "knew too much" about him systematically exterminated—whether they were pre-Revolutionary colleagues in the struggle, fanatically devoted Party functionaries, former friends, or members of his own family. Therefore, an attempt will have to be made to draw on the few existing sources about his youth and his political activity before the October Revolution, which consisted basically of seven arrests and five successful escapes, in order to discover possible causal factors for the development of his criminalistic qualities on his way to becoming one of the cruelest and most treacherous tyrants in history.

It will also be necessary to include in our deliberations the particular historical situation after the October Revolution and the specific structure of the Communist Party organization, with its bureaucratic power apparatus; these two factors were essential preconditions for the living out of Stalin's criminal impulses, which became more and more uncontrollable by any authority. In this context, one must also consider the unique phenomenon of the interdependence that exists between a charismatic "leader," no matter what his character traits might be, and the "masses," in this case, the long-suffering Russian people.

The only direct insight into Stalin's psyche and world of ideas has been communicated to us in the sketches written by his daughter Svetlana, as well as in his own reports, letters, commentaries, or marginal remarks, with which he annotated many of his criminal instructions and orders. From a medical standpoint, finally, we have the memoirs of N. Romano-Petrova, which are based on the personal experiences and observations of Professor Dimitri Pletnev, Stalin's personal physician for many years. Petrova last worked as a nurse in a military hospital reserved for high officers of the NKVD (People's Commissariat of Internal Affairs) and other high-ranking officers of the Red Army. After the hospital fell into German hands in the summer of 1942, Petrova managed to escape to the West, where she later published her memoirs, first in Russian, then in 1989 in an English translation by Michelle Petroff.

BIOGRAPHICAL SURVEY

STALIN'S CHILDHOOD

Joseph Vissarionovich Djugashvili was born on December 21, 1879, in the Georgian town of Gori. In his domestic passport he was identified as a "peasant from the Gori district in the Province of Tiflis," and in fact his parents were of peasant background and were born as serfs. Both were illiterate, as were three-fourths of the local population. After the abolition of serfdom, his father Vissarion Djugashvili had moved to Gori, where as a trained shoemaker he repaired the shoes of the poor. There he met Ekaterina Geladze, who washed, sewed and cooked in other people's homes; and she soon became his wife. The young couple lived in direst poverty. Two of their three sons, Mikhail and Georgiy, died before the age of one year, so that finally the only one left was "Soso," as they called Joseph. But he, too, fell sick at the age of five of a very serious smallpox infection that took him to the edge of the grave and left many disfiguring scars on his face. At the age of ten, Joseph reportedly was run over by an automobile. After ten days in a coma and blood poisoning from badly cleansed wounds, he was left with a stiff left elbow. At least that is how Stalin's own account goes, but it sounds quite implausible because the automobile, constructed by Daimler in 1885, can hardly have appeared on the streets of the small Georgian town just four years later. Whatever the case may be, Stalin's left arm remained stunted all his life and four inches too short.

As described by Jossif Iremashvili (the Georgian Menshevik, who was well acquainted with the Djugashvilis), Stalin's father was a crude, violent man, who was often drunk and struck both his wife and his son. Vissarion Djugashvili had acquired the habit of driving out little Joseph's alleged obstinacy with daily beatings before going to bed, so that the boy soon learned skillfully to avoid his father. As Iremashvili suggests in his memoirs, these beatings, inflicted for no particular reason, must have affected the child's development:

> The unjust severe beatings the boy received made him as hard and heartless as his father was. Since he was convinced that everyone to whom obedience was owed had to resemble his father, he soon developed a deep antipathy to all those above him in rank. From early childhood on, the realization of his desires for revenge became a goal in life to which everything else was subordinated.

Mistreatments by his father, to which Joseph reacted with hatred and vindictiveness were also confirmed by other sources, which pointed out that the boy did not break under them but rather was hardened by

The house in Gori where Stalin spent his childhood

*Stalin's mother Ekaterina G. Djugashvili, a woman of
modest origin and daughter of a serf. Joseph was her fourth
child and was born on December 21, 1879*

his father's "black pedagogy" and made all the more resistant to the
most severe mental and physical burdens he would have to face in
the future.

He was supported in this attitude by his mother's example. She
also frequently became the victim of her husband's outrages, but she
never let herself be intimidated or defeated. For Joseph, with whom
she was bound with loving affection, she was ready to make any sacrifice, which must have been a beneficial counterbalance for the boy.

When the father moved to Tiflis, where he found a better job opportunity in a shoe factory, he soon had the ten-year-old boy join him in Tiflis to learn the shoemaker's trade. Ekaterina, on the contrary, was driven by the ardent desire to help her Soso acquire an academic education; and when Vissarion soon afterward lost his life from knife wounds in a drinking bout, she immediately brought her son back to Gori. With support from an Orthodox priest, whose household she tended, she actually managed to get Joseph into a church-directed school in the firm hope that someday her son would become a priest. For this reason, she did everything possible to raise the financial means for his subsequent study at the Russian Orthodox seminary in Tiflis. Under the greatest personal sacrifices and assisted by state stipends, she managed to have her son attend the seminary until he was nineteen years old. Decisive for obtaining such a scholarship was his outstanding graduation transcript from the church school in Gori, which brought him a written commendation from the authorities.

In 1894 Joseph left Gori to enter the seminary for priests in Tiflis, which the majority of its almost six hundred students regarded less as preparation for a priestly vocation than as a place to obtain a university education; for the Czar had prohibited the establishment of a university in Georgia lest it become a breeding ground for nationalistic machinations. At the same time, under the plan for universal Russification, the Russian language replaced Georgian as the language of instruction. This measure led to frequent conflicts with the government authorities; and the harsh military-like conditions in the seminary, more suitable in many ways for an army camp than as a home for ecclesiastical students, also caused dissatisfaction.

Although Joseph at the age of fourteen was short and physically rather on the weak side, he was soon noticed by both his fellow students and his teachers for a degree of self-confidence remarkable for his age. Probably his mother's role was responsible, for—although herself illiterate—she made it possible for him to enter high school for the fixed purpose of providing him with a better future. With unshakable faith, she counted on the certain success of her only and obviously intelligent son, and this aroused in him the conviction, indeed perhaps even a kind of sense of mission, of someday having to accomplish something significant as his mother's delegate.

The ecclesiastical training in the Gori school and later at the seminary in Tiflis necessarily had an impact on the boy's psychological maturation process. The systematic memorization of religious texts

Joseph Djugashvili in the year 1894 as a pupil in the priestly seminary in Gori

from the Old and New Testaments, to which he gave his undivided attention, helped him acquire a truly phenomenal memory, which would be useful to him later. The years of theological training, from which he obtained the ideal image of a unique Divine Being as the bearer of undivided power and absolute knowledge, surely also contributed to developing in his mind the pattern of "dogmatism" and catechism-like division into "black-and-white categories" so typical for the argumentation and style of his later writings. Adam Ulam calls the later Stalinist traits "declamatory, full of repetitions and liturgical allusions," and this was in part also detectable in his way of speaking with its "typical pattern of repeated questions and answers."

The experiences during his stay in the seminary, however, also had an opposite effect, namely, an ever deeper rejection of religion and its liturgical customs. One thing that contributed to this was the daily routine of long hours of prayer, which seemed senseless to him, but more important was the snooping, denunciatory, and punitive behavior of the monks toward their charges in mostly trivial matters. This living audiovisual instruction of the sanctioned practices in a closed and compact society, whose methods of subjugation to unconditional obedience consisted in uninterrupted supervision, denunciation, and punishment, fed in him a growing resentment for any kind of authority, seeds of which had already been sown in his childhood by his father's abusive treatment. His hatred first concentrated on the monks, but soon also on the official agencies of the strict Czarist regime, and finally also on the craven and simpleminded masses, who submitted meekly and without resistance to the chicaneries of authoritarian domination. Svetlana Alliluyeva later wrote very accurately about her father's seminary training:

> I am convinced that the seminary where he spent more than ten (?) years of his life had great significance for his character-formation and his whole life. His innate characteristics were thereby promoted and strengthened. He had never had religious feeling. The endless prayers and the coercive discipline could only have the opposite effect on a young person who had never for a moment believed in the spiritual, in God....From his seminary training he believed he knew that humans are intolerant and harsh, the herd of them deceived in order to keep them under control, that they intrigued, lied, and, moreover, had many other weaknesses and very few virtues.

Whereas during his school years in Gori he had been a lively, openhearted, and sociable boy, his behavior changed in the first years of his stay at the seminary. He displayed a reserved, introverted temperament and learned progressively better to hide his real thoughts and feelings from the surrounding world behind an impenetrable veil, a quality that later became a determining element of his tactics and enabled him to conceal from his unsuspecting colleagues his cunning and treachery and his absolute coldness of heart and deep hatred.

A hidden variant of resistance and inner rebellion by the boy was the zealous study of books which had been officially disapproved or even prohibited. Among these books smuggled into the seminary were not only Russian classics, but also scientific and political writings with some explosive power, such as Darwin's theory of evolution or Karl Marx's *Das Kapital*. With such a supposedly scientific foundation, the young student, whose head was filled with Romantic ideals, set out to organize a socialistic circle of like-minded colleagues, to which incidentally Iremashvili also belonged. The key ideas of Marxism, particularly the inevitable necessity of class war to remove arrogant, unjust, and corrupt bourgeois society, genuinely fascinated him and seemed to be the only way he could turn into reality his pent-up hatred, his destructive drive, and his marked vindictiveness. By "declaring his enemies to be the enemies of society," as Robert Tucker has stated, he could easily legitimate the motives for his relentless hatred of every form of authority.

While still a seminarian, he had established contact with the first Marxist Social Democratic association in Georgia, which called itself the "Third Group." There he met a member of the study group whom he admired almost to the point of idolization and who for years remained his ideal of a revolutionary warrior, Lado Ketskhoveli. Lado, too, had been a pupil in the seminary for priests at Tiflis. After having been dismissed from the seminary for "causing disturbances," he became politically active in the underground as a "professional revolutionary."

It was, incidentally, not the first time that Joseph clung to an idealized model. During his school years in Gori, he was enthusiastic about the Caucasian hero, Koba, whom he had learned of in the story "Patricide." His heroic battle against the Cossacks and successful defense of the rights of the peasants impressed Stalin so much that he insisted on being called "Koba" himself. This imaginary relationship to the heroic figure with whom he sought to identify quite evidently corresponded to a desire to strengthen his still not definitively formed identity. The words of his colleague Iremashvili can be interpreted in this sense, when he reports:

> Koba had become Joseph's god, the content of his life. He wanted to become a second Koba, just as famous a warrior and hero. Koba's figure was to be reincarnated in him.

In his fifth academic year, Joseph's activity, not least of all under his idol Lado's influence, was felt by the administration to be "creating a disturbance," and so he, too, was dismissed from the seminary "for unknown reasons." What reasons were really decisive for his dismissal can no longer be determined today. Iremashvili wrote later only that Joseph left the seminary with "grim and bitter hatred for the school administration, the bourgeoisie, and everything else in the country that embodied Czarism." In his bitterness, he made the definite decision to burn all bridges behind him and to decide upon a life as a professional revolutionary and political agitator, with all the ensuing consequences. That is how he must have successfully overcome the "identity crisis of his years as a young man," thus avoiding more serious psychological damage in the formation of his self-identity. The words formulated by Erik Erikson concerning Adolph Hitler would apply to Stalin, too: he "remained an unbroken young man" who "decided on a career outside bourgeois happiness, economic security, and inner peace of mind." Robert Tucker points out that Joseph, "from this time on, invested all his energies in the ever-increasing effort to live up to his own ideal self-image in practice and to have this confirmed by others." In this attempt to build up a clear self-identity and design an idealized self-image, he no doubt experienced an inestimable corroboration by the narcissistic identification with his idols Lado and Koba, to whom was soon added the powerful model of Lenin.

THE PROFESSIONAL REVOLUTIONARY

For the dangerous life he faced as a revolutionary agitator in Czarist Russia, which was kept under close scrutiny by Ochrana (the Czarist secret police), Joseph had at his disposal, in the form of Marxism, a philosophical conception that apparently "fully satisfied his need for a substitute for the dogmatic theological system of ideas," which, after all, he had never really accepted. On closer examination the two systems have striking similarities: the exclusive validity of orthodox doctrine, the absolute claim to truth, intolerance toward those who think differently, and the relentless persecution of heretics and apostates. The particular synthesis of the first accepted, but later rejected, religious dogmas partly explains his future striving to systematize every kind of knowledge, to classify and assort things into intellectual categories. Since all his life he always held rigidly to postulates—first Christian, then Marxist ones—he lost all capacity for a critical attitude toward his own ideas, for which reason he declared everything that did not fit into his personal scheme of thought to be heretical or opportunistic.

After Joseph's dismissal from the seminary in 1899, he spent the next decade as a Social Democratic agitator in the Caucasus region, concentrating his "rebellious" activities mainly in the cities of Tiflis, Baku, and Batum. There he led workers' demonstrations and took part in various strikes that sometimes ended in bloodshed, but even then he showed his preferred tendency to act as an organizer and planner of individual campaigns, to draft leaflets and manifestos, and to see to their publication in the underground while avoiding active participation in the actual demonstrations. He also displayed this tendency later in the notorious so-called "expropriations."

The expulsion from the seminary left clear marks on Joseph's character. For he felt not only socially discriminated against, but also was under the impression of having been betrayed by the established society. This led him early on to regard every person with deep distrust and to be convinced that he could rely on no one but himself. This attitude is at the root of several characteristics that were to emerge more clearly later, namely, cold calculation, absolute lack of feeling, contempt for human beings, and the extinction of all moral sensibility in the realization of his set goals. In such a character, there could, of course, be no person for whom he felt honest and lasting affection.

F. Khunyanis, a woman fellow struggler at that time, has left us the description of her impressions on the occasion of her personal meeting with "Koba" at one of the usual political meetings:

> He was short, thin, and gave a somewhat "poor soul" impression, so much so that I was reminded of a petty thief waiting for sentencing. He wore a dark blue peasant smock, a tight-fitting jacket, and a black Turkish cap.... He treated me with distrust. After a long interrogation he handed me a batch of illegal writings....He accompanied me to the door with an unchangingly suspicious, distrustful manner.

Despite this rather wretched-looking profile, he must even then have possessed a certain authority, for her portrayal continues:

> At the agreed time Koba once again was not there. He always arrived too late, not very much, but regularly.... When he arrived, the atmosphere changed...to one of

anticipation. Koba usually came with a book under his stunted left arm and sat down somewhere or other to the side or in a corner. He listened silently until everyone had spoken. He always was the last speaker …and presented his own standpoint with great finality, as if this put an end to the discussion. Thus the impression was given that everything he said carried special weight.

When Stalin was confronted for the first time with the illegal newspaper *Iskra (The Spark),* founded by Vladimir Ilyich Ulyanov (Lenin), he immediately was drawn by its views and theses. In that newspaper in 1902, Lenin published, according to Alan Bullock, "one of the most famous revolutionary manifestos of all times," with the title *What's To Be Done*, demanding a tightly centralized Party with a cadre of genuine professional revolutionaries operating as the "vanguard of the proletariat" with whose help Czarist rule was to be violently removed by the working class.

However, soon afterward, following the founding of the pan-Russian Social Democratic Workers Party overseas, differences of opinion soon led to a split into the moderate Menshevists, who were willing to cooperate with the bourgeois constitutionalists and wanted to replace Czarist autocracy merely by liberal reforms, and the Bolshevists under Lenin's leadership, who uncompromisingly rejected such a plan, demanding a radical approach. Stalin was by nature, of course, a confirmed Bolshevist from the first; Lenin's ideas appealed to him immediately, not only because they were radical, but especially because they stressed the importance of the professional revolutionary as the real driving force of the revolution that needed to be prepared.

With this formal recognition of his "professional status" by Lenin, whom he first met personally only in 1905 in Tammersfors in Finland, his definitive self-identity as the successful professional revolutionary was established once and for all. Moreover, it offered him a satisfying compensation for the often humiliating, arrogant treatment by those Party comrades such as Plekhanov and Trotsky, who, as sons of wealthy bourgeois families, belonged to the intelligentsia and felt superior to him because of their higher education and overseas experiences.

Precisely such men, in Stalin's eyes, knew only from hearsay the terrible living conditions of the Russian people as a result of their capitalist exploitation, whereas he, as the son of former serfs, had grown

up in the worst poverty and had to accumulate his experiences in revolutionary politics with great effort in the hard school of life:

> I became a Marxist because of my social position...but
> above all also through the severe intolerance and the
> Jesuitical discipline that weighed on me so mercilessly
> in the seminary.

Isaac Deutscher therefore says quite accurately that:

> ...his hatred against property-owners and against the
> ruling class must have been much stronger. The class
> hatred which the revolutionaries from the upper class
> felt and preached was a kind of secondary emotion
> which moved in them and which they developed fur-
> ther with theoretically based convictions. In him class
> hatred was not secondary; for him this hatred was
> everything....His socialism was cold, clear, and crude.

Stalin's experiences as a cold-blooded revolutionary and talented
organizer at the very front of the movement were what made him, as a
man with practical experience, so valuable to Lenin. He also gathered
the experiences involuntarily, not least of all during his frequent imprisonment and years in exile. For he was arrested in all no less than
seven times, in five of which he managed to escape. The deprivations
he endured and the humiliations he suffered during the sixteen years he
spent in the underground, in prisons, and in exile, of course, strengthened the character traits he exemplified in his youth, namely, coldness,
calculation, cunning, and distrust. So as early as 1905, "Koba" was
considered an extremely difficult comrade and ambitious intriguer who
could never be trusted and who had already mastered the perfidious art
of pitting competing comrades against one another. Nor did he completely trust any of his collaborators. Contradiction or insults,
derogatory to his narcissistically structured image, caused him to react
with extreme sensitivity, and his excellent memory saw to it that he
never forgot such "insults" and he vented his revenge upon the guilty
parties with full force, even decades later.

In his Caucasus years, Stalin was already very much a loner who
avoided all closer contact and gave the impression that he was incapable of normal interpersonal relations. But in 1906 he married
Ekaterina Svanidze, the daughter of one of his schoolmates. Probably
this marriage did not result just from an internal impulse, but also under a certain pressure, since he first seduced the sixteen-year-old girl,

*Stalin's first wife Ekaterina Svanidze. Her death
in 1907 affected the young revolutionary deeply.*

causing a pregnancy. Yet we learn from Iremashvili that the impoverished household in which he lived with Ekaterina and their son Jacob was the only place where he ever in his life had experienced real love. That is probably true. For when Ekaterina died of typhus on October 22, 1907, half a year after giving birth, Stalin is said to have openly showed his grief and even to have ordered an Orthodox funeral for his wife.

Among Stalin's incarcerations, the one in Batum in April 1902 is worth mentioning. An entry in the police files from that time lists some particular characteristics: "A small congenital deformation: the second and third toes of the left foot were fused together." In 1904 he escaped from a Siberian camp despite the most severe snowstorms and an alleged latent tuberculosis of the lungs. Between 1905 and 1907 his revolutionary field of action was again located in the Caucasus region, where he immediately participated in various "expropriations." These consisted of armed robberies of banks and mail coaches and served to obtain the financial means that Lenin urgently needed to finance his Party. Because of Stalin's alleged part in the spectacular robbery of the state bank in Tiflis, in June 1907, he was condemned by the Menshevists—who were in the majority in Georgia and strictly rejected such violent excesses—and threatened with expulsion from the Party, which is probably why he transferred his activity to Baku as a precaution. There by the fall of 1907 he had established himself as a member of the Bolshevist state committee, and in this capacity he had the task of writing various essays and commentaries for the union's legally published news bulletin.

Once again he was arrested by the police and sentenced to a year and a half in prison and exile. Once again he escaped. On February 8, 1909, during his exile he became seriously ill with typhus and was being transferred to another camp. He was in such bad condition that the guard convoy considered it absolutely necessary to interrupt the transport for at least three weeks, and he was escorted to the town of Voloda. Despite his greatly weakened physical condition, he managed to escape before the planned convalescence stopover was ended. In July 1909, he showed up again incognito in Baku. But he was not to enjoy his freedom for long, for just a few weeks later, during preparations for a general strike of workers in the petroleum industry, he was arrested again and not released until the summer of 1911.

The years of his participation in revolutionary work, the romantic trappings of an unselfish "expropriator," the years in prison, and the years in Siberian exile gradually obtained for "Koba" the reputation of an especially experienced "revolutionary fighter," a man of action, and a "practitioner." Therefore, Lenin brought him into the Central Committee together with his Georgian countryman Ordzhonikidze, who in turn had become especially familiar with the peculiarities of the Russian underground, where the two men were to help coordinate the Party's activities in Russia. Strengthened in his feeling of self-worth in this way, Stalin decided—like Lenin—to underscore the hardness and strong will of his person by assuming a revolutionary pseudonym: from the year 1912 on, Joseph Djugashvili no longer wanted to be called Koba, but rather Stalin, the "man of steel."

Early in 1913 Stalin was sent to Vienna for four weeks by Lenin to study more closely the Austrian Marxist ideas. Immediately, he rejected the view of the Austrian Social Democrats, who saw as the task

Wanted poster for the arrest of the revolutionary Joseph Djugashvili, 1908

of the Party "to preserve the national traits of all folk groups." For him even then the supreme goal was to organize the proletariat for the coming class struggle and to unite the workers of all nationalities into a single, transnational Party. After his return to Russia, Stalin convinced Lenin of this view, so that just a few years later Lenin, relying on Stalin's expertise in this field, appointed him People's Commissar for Nationality Questions.

A few days after his arrival in St. Petersburg, Stalin was arrested again due to a complaint filed by an informant working for the notorious Ochrana, the Czarist secret police, and this time he was banished to one of the most remote penal colonies near Turukhansk, in the high north of Siberia, where the temperatures during the long Arctic winter frequently drop to lower than -40 degrees Celsius, and in the summer the prisoners are tormented by an indescribable plague of stinging flies. Escape from this forsaken region at the edge of the world was absolutely unthinkable, since even with a sled and team, more than six weeks were needed to reach Krasnoyarsk, the nearest railroad station.

The desolate wasteland, the long Siberian winter, and the complete isolation from the rest of the world placed on the exiles inhuman physical and mental demands which not many were equal to. Stalin had the hardness and the endurance to come out alive even of this banishment. But he, too, noticeably dulled in those years, seemed to be interested only in hunting and fishing and hardly participated in the conversations and political discussions of his comrades. Jacob Sverdlov, who, together with his comrade Spandarian, played the central leadership role over the three hundred companions in misfortune, later told about Stalin in a letter to his wife:

> The comrade I lived with there had an impossible personality. We had to avoid seeing each other and speaking with one another.

He had already displayed this difficulty of fitting in socially during his exile in Solvitshegodsk in 1909/1910. This time, there was added a striking political apathy; indeed, in the Turukhansk penal camp, he showed signs of a real reactive depression. In a letter thanking the Alliluyev family, with whom he had found shelter in St. Petersburg prior to his banishment and which later would accept him as a son-in-law, he confirmed the reception of a package and, to illustrate his state of mind, added the request that they send a few postcards:

Joseph Stalin as a revolutionary in 1911

Stalin in exile in Siberia

> Nature in this accursed region is desolate and ugly; in
> summer the river, in winter snow. That is all the land-
> scape we have around us here. So I have an idiotic
> yearning for the sight of the landscapes, even if only
> on paper.

These lines give a clear idea of his depressed mood due to the desola-
tion of the place where he had to stay. What especially depressed him
was the circumstance that he could get newspapers only after considerable delays, so that it could sometimes take months before he got them,
making it impossible to remain informed about the current political
events in Russia.

With the start of the war in 1914, the last signs of the inner concern
for the political events vanished, as well as any desire to escape. One
reason was probably that in wartime the exiles' chances of fleeing were
made more difficult and, moreover, Stalin had no intention of running
into the arms of a recruiting party that could force him into military
service. As it was, in February 1917 he was actually transferred to a
recruiting board in Krasnoyarsk, and he had only his stunted left arm
and the deformation on his left foot to thank for his being classified as
unfit for military service.

This was a lucky break for him, especially since his situation was further improved by his not being sent back to the Arctic wilderness, but he was allowed instead to spend the rest of his exile in Atshinsk, not far from Krasnoyarsk. From the Bolshevist, I. D. Perfilev, who spent some time in this place of exile prior to the October Revolution, we learn that Stalin had a love affair there with a native girl and that a child was born of this relationship. Perfilev was later unable to discover whether Stalin ever concerned himself about the fate of that child or that young woman.

Stalin's passive phase, during the years of his last banishment, was probably also a time of pondering and reflecting on what direction his life should take in the future. After all, he was already forty years of age and, like Hitler at age thirty, hardly had any real prospects for the future. He had no profession, not even that of a shoemaker like his father, had no regular work he could engage in, and had actually never worked before, apart from activities as an agitator and professional revolutionary in the service of politics. Such a sad "internal review" had to convince him it was too late for him ever to think of leaving the path of a professional revolutionary. From this perspective, it is easy to imagine that the news of the anti-war mood reaching as far as Siberia in 1917 and of the storm clouds gathering over St. Petersburg must have given the revolutionary tendencies new courage and faith in a political future.

When in 1917 the Czar was forced to abdicate and a provisional government was set up, Stalin sent a telegram with "brotherly greetings" to Lenin, his shining paragon, and without delay boarded a train for Petrograd, where he arrived on March 12. Hardened by the years spent in the Arctic and equipped with an ice-cold apathy, he believed the hour had come at last to avenge himself on the corrupt class-enemy, bourgeois society, by which he felt betrayed, humiliated, and marginalized. Trusting only himself, he took over the interim leadership of the Bolshevist Party, together with Comrade Kamenev, who had likewise returned from exile, until Lenin arrived from Switzerland. One of his companions from the time of his most recent exile remarked with bewilderment:

> Djugashvili remained just as proud as ever, just as immersed in himself, his own ideas and plans.

Once again people around him noticed his lack of contact, his unusually marked distrust of everyone, but also his ability to hide his own intentions and goals from the eyes of others, with cunning and astonishing patience until the right moment had come to accomplish them just as relentlessly.

THE GREAT REVOLUTION

In the night of February 28th, 1917, the bourgeois-democratic February Revolution, the prelude to the coming October events, was victorious. Contrary to later historical falsifications, neither Lenin, nor the Bolshevists, nor certainly Stalin played any particular role, at least until August 1917. He was indeed on the team forged by Lenin, employed in high political agencies, but he did nothing remarkable in any of them. As the "Representative of Faraway Nations," he remained an inconspicuous functionary who enjoyed absolutely no popularity, and, as Nikolai Sukhanov, one of the Menshevist leaders of that time, wrote, he was "in the political arena no more than a dull gray spot." However, Stalin's *Short Biography*, published later and revised by himself and played up as a kind of catechism for the people, reverses the true historical facts and states:

> In this responsible period Stalin gathered the Party around himself in order to cause the bourgeois-democratic revolution to make the transition to a socialist one....Stalin's articles provided the Bolsheviks with the fundamental guidelines for their work.

The truth is that his weaknesses first emerged during the February Revolution and in the days of the October turmoils. His lack of theoretical knowledge and limited capacity for creative action relegated him to writing articles and withdrawing to the administrative "staff" chambers. Since he did not know how to address a larger audience effectively, he was never drawn to the masses—quite the opposite of Leo Trotsky, who was unequaled in his ability to stir up the masses. Trotsky thereby soon aroused the venomous envy and enmity of Stalin, who was so untalented as an orator.

Thus it is not surprising that Stalin's name appears extremely rarely in the documents of that time. Contrary to the accounts in his *Short Biography*, during the Revolution he appeared neither as an outstanding personality, nor as a leader, nor as a flaming orator, nor as an organizer, but rather as a hardly perceptible functionary of the Party apparatus, who had to carry out the tasks he was assigned. After the victory of the socialist revolution on the evening of October 25, 1917, when elections were held for the Presidium of the Congress of Councils of Workers', Soldiers', and Peasants' Deputies, the ballot included, besides Lenin's name, the names of Trotsky, Kamenev, and Zinoviev among those elected, while Stalin vanished in the events of those days. The future autocrat must have suffered persistently from his shadowy existence. Alan Bullock is probably right: that in this decisive phase, the fact that Stalin could not play the leadership role he had dreamed of must have been for him a deep trauma that shaped his further psychological development.

Not until the end of 1929 did he feel strong enough to take steps to overcome this trauma by commissioning a large-scale falsification of history. By removing files and documents, by arbitrary alterations in the memoir literature, and by the conscious repression of the names of personalities who played vital roles during the October Revolution, the historical events were to be so reversed and manipulated that the achievements and deeds of these persons were now accomplished exclusively by the great Stalin. This made it easy, among other things, to wipe out of the Russian people's memory such a dominant figure as Leo Trotsky in the Communist seizure of power and to replace him by the person of Stalin, who supposedly played a leading role second only to that of Lenin himself.

This crude manipulation of historical events at the same time laid the foundation for establishing the Stalin cult. By raising his shining image onto a high pedestal, visible to all, and requiring that almost divine reverence be paid to it, he was also able to save his narcissistically heightened self-image which he had over all the years been creating with ever more passionate ardor and which he so urgently needed because of his total lack of moral foundation.

Apparently the staged falsification of history was not sufficient by itself to overcome the trauma of having been ignored in the year of the Revolution, which Stalin felt to be a moral failure. To remove this traumatic experience once and for all, he needed an action with which he could outshine even Lenin's achievements. This seemed possible to him, as Alan Bullock remarks, only by adding to Lenin's revolution an even more significant "third revolution." And actually the agricultural collectivization, carried out in the years 1929 to 1933 by the most brutal means, and the coercive industrialization of Russia were—compared with the 1917 October Revolution—an even more drastic transformation of the country.

The legend Stalin later had propagated: with Lenin at the head of the October Revolution (after a painting by E. Kibrik)

The leaders of the October Revolution liked to use metaphors from the French Revolution in their writings. Lenin, for instance, liked to compare his differences with the Menshevists with the conflict between the Jacobins and the Girondists. When in spring 1918 a civil war broke out in the Russian lands still devastated by the World War, a civil war that came within a hair of putting an end to Soviet power, they compared it with the revolt of the Vendée in the years 1793 to 1796, in which the royalist-minded peasants fought against the revolution and for the re-instatement of the monarchy. In the Civil War of 1918 in Russia, whose hardness and irreconcilability showed the deep class hatred and split the populace into two hostile camps, not only did the White Guards and the Red Army fight each other, but a great part of the civilian population was drawn into the conflicts, too.

In these conflicts, Stalin made himself more conspicuous than in previous years. As an extraordinary plenipotentiary representing the Central Committee, he was responsible not only for the procurement of food supplies, but he also had to make military decisions. It is typical of him that he avoided visiting trenches and field hospitals in the war zone, preferring to work at staff headquarters and to send his directives from there. With shocking nonchalance he ordered cruel operations; he ordered people to be shot who had committed no crime other than seeming suspicious and, in his opinion, hurting the cause. Stalin's hardness and brutal intransigence, however, increased his standing in Lenin's eyes and led to his rapid gain in recognition among the higher Party functionaries. By 1918 the Party leadership knew definitely: this is not a man who reliably executes the Central Committee's assignments, but a born specialist in punitive campaigns and "extraordinary measures" and one who has no scruples whatever at passing death sentences without trial, since he firmly believes in the necessity and efficacy of such methods. For the first time, he was able to give full vent to his hatred and vindictiveness and to openly reveal the baneful character traits that later would be the source of unspeakable suffering for individuals and for entire groups of people.

Besides his brutal hardness, his lack of any trace of pity, and his contempt for human life, he now displayed his sadistic inclination to publicly humiliate and debase opponents. What his comrades at this point in time still could not realize was his unusually vindictive character, which later so often led the slightest difference of opinion or offense to draw down Stalin's inescapable vengeance. Almost everyone with whom Stalin came into contact during the Civil War had to pay dearly for it later.

But Stalin was not the only person convinced that hardness and pressure applied at the right moment would yield the desired results. With Lenin's express approval, on December 7, 1918, an Extraordinary Commission, the notorious Cheka, was formed under the leadership of the incorruptible Pole, Felix Dzierzhinsky, and had the assignment of

Felix Dzierzhinsky as prisoner of
"Ochrana," the Czarist secret
police

opposing any counterrevolutionary strivings with the utmost severity. At least two thousand murders and executions, just in the first five years of its existence, are charged to the Cheka's account. The "organizer of victory" in the Civil War was, however, Trotsky, who developed extraordinary skills in the military area and had a considerable share in the creation of the one-party dictatorship after the end of the military conflicts. He and Stalin, together with Kamenev, Zinoviev, and Bukharin, were the men with whose help Lenin hoped in the future to rule the young Soviet state, and these men were also, after Lenin's death, Stalin's most dangerous competitors in the struggle for succession, although at that time almost no one on the highest Party panels saw Stalin as a possible successor to Lenin. For both the Party and the Soviet government were inseparably linked with the names of Lenin and Trotsky, while Stalin operated unnoticed in the background. This must have been even more intolerable to the ambitious aspirant, when Trotsky did not even take him into account and let him feel this clearly by his condescending treatment. In his autobiography Trotsky later wrote about Stalin:

> He had a repelling effect on me by the very qualities which later, in the wave of disaster, constituted his strength: narrow interest, empiricism, psychological crudity, and a peculiar provincial cynicism, which freed

Marxism of many prejudices, but without giving it a fully comprehended world view that could be integrated with psychology.

The somewhat arrogant Trotsky dangerously underestimated Stalin, and he had to pay for it later with his life.

Lenin's approval more than compensated Stalin's inferiority complex for his disdainful treatment by the intellectuals in the top leadership. Lenin ascribed his crudeness and his unpolished behavior to his proletarian origin, which naturally had to differentiate him as a "practical man" from the intellectually oriented functionaries, who stemmed mostly from the bourgeois camp. Although just a short time later, Lenin would change his mind completely, at first Stalin seemed to him a colleague of incontestable value, since in his opinion a dictatorship of the proletariat could not long exist without such hard-hitting Party comrades of Stalin's type. This was shown, for example, by the armed revolt of the sailors at the naval base in Kronstadt on March 2, 1921, which aimed at the violent removal of the intolerable "commissarocracy" and which was put down with great bloodshed by the Red Army, under the command of General Tukhachevsky. In this campaign, according to Alan Bullock, thousands of sailors were simply shot without any trial.

In solving the difficulties to which the Party was exposed in the years 1921/22, Stalin again remained completely in the background, where he proved to be a good pupil of his idol Lenin by his striking flexibility. This flexibility was evident in Communism during the last war years, but even more manifestly with the introduction of the NEP (New Economic Program), which Lenin regarded as an unavoidable concession to the enraged peasants after the brutal mandatory confiscations. Many high functionaries regarded the NEP as a completely incomprehensible reversal of his prior policy. Stalin showed understanding for this measure, and in this period he proved to be an extraordinarily good learner. Later he made many of Lenin's practices, such as the prohibition of the "formation of fractions" within the Party or the introduction of terrorist methods as a legitimate means of maintaining the uncontested power of the Communist one-party system, the principle of his terrorist regime. Since Lenin knew that in every situation he could count on Stalin, the experienced man of action, to take hard, effective measures and since Stalin had proven himself very well as the responsible coordinator of the Party secretariat, Stalin's

*Joseph Stalin in 1919 as
People's Commissar for
Nationalities and member of
the Politburo*

appointment as General Secretary on March 4, 1922, did not surprise anybody. At that time, no member of the Party's top leadership could in the slightest suspect the power-madness of this ice-cold, distrustful, and vindictive man—a power-madness that shattered all normal standards. Even Lenin, from whom Stalin's defects were not hidden, did not feel threatened at all in his top position by Stalin—at least not until his first stroke in May 1922.

The first signs of Lenin's exhaustion and impending serious illness showed up in 1921, and Stalin was apparently the first in Lenin's closer circle to understand the tremendous significance of the unique function of the anonymous power structures of the Party apparatus for the conquest of an Oriental-style autocracy. At the very first symptoms of Lenin's sickness, Stalin began cunningly and with ice-cold calculation to unreel his great game plan of expanding his position within the Party hierarchy as rapidly as possible. Since from the first he saw everything he did as morally justified and he hypocritically propagated it "in the name of building up socialism," later, on his way to the top, he did not shy away from having possible rivals declared "enemies of the people"—even if they had been Lenin's closest collaborators, such as Zinoviev, Kamenev, or Bukharin—or unmasking leading captains of industry and proven diplomats as "harmful pests of the people" and having them exterminated as such. And because he was still underestimated by many high functionaries and very skilled at hiding his intentions through his art of disguise, no one in Lenin's circle, even in his worst nightmare, had any inkling of what a monster was growing up in their midst—a monster like Robespierre, who on February 5, 1794, had declared to the Convention:

> The first law of our policy must be to lead the people with the help of reason and to dominate enemies with the help of terror.

Because of Stalin's brutal procedure in solving the problem of the Caucasus Federation, Lenin, as he was recovering from his stroke, realized that everything was already in the process of slipping from his control—but to little avail. After Lenin's second stroke on December 16, 1922, his original confidence in Stalin had changed to a deep distrust, as can be seen clearly in the so-called "testament" dictated by Lenin between December 23, 1922, and January 4, 1923:

> Since Comrade Stalin has become General Secretary, he combines enormous power in his hands, and I am not certain that he will always know how to use this power with the necessary caution....Stalin is too crude, and this defect...cannot be tolerated in the function of the General Secretary.

Lenin therefore gave his comrades the urgent plan to replace Stalin by another man who is "more tolerant, loyal, and more attentive to the comrades, and less moody." Greatly appalled at Stalin's threat to cauterize the nationalist turmoils in Georgia with a red-hot iron, Lenin at last openly declared the constitution formulated by Stalin to be a delusion, totally unsuited to protect the non-Russians from "invasion by every genuine Russian, the Great-Russian chauvinists, indeed actually scoundrels and men of violence, such as is the typical Russian bureaucrat." Lenin could not have expressed his contempt of his former protégé more strongly. When in March 1923 Lenin suffered a third severe stroke that left him paralyzed on the right side and unable to speak, his previously uncontested supreme authority was removed from the political scene once and for all.

Joseph Stalin together with Lenin (Vladimir Ilyich Ulyanov)

This event was the most serious, indeed the most dangerous, crisis in Stalin's political career, since it involved the succession, and the definitive break between him and Lenin occurred just at that point. Isaac Deutscher, in his biography of Trotsky, wrote:

The realization of Lenin's testament, namely, to remove Stalin from his post, would inescapably have promoted Trotsky to the post of Party leader.

Stalin, too, knew this, and it was probably the distrust of the interim trio of leaders, Zinoviev, Kamenev, and Stalin, for their main rival Trotsky that finally led them, despite many personal differences on the question of Lenin's succession, to proceed in common against Trotsky, whom Lenin in the end favored. Thus Stalin was definitively put in command, because his increasing influence in the Politburo had already so increased his authority within the Party that he needed but little effort to win the majority of delegates at the Party Congress on April 17, 1923, which Lenin no longer could attend. At the very next Party Congress in January 1927, he could demonstrate his power by having both the program and the final decisions set in advance—a practice that became the rule in the future.

Lenin died on the evening of January 21, 1924, from consequences of a fourth stroke, and with his death the only power that posed a danger in Stalin's path to autocracy vanished from the political stage. Trotsky pointed out correctly in his memoirs that only Lenin's illness prevented him from "smashing" Stalin politically. In the same context he stated his conviction that Stalin's arbitrary actions and ruthless leadership style had often exasperated Lenin greatly and, indeed, that this great excitement had a recognizably unfavorable influence on the course of Lenin's illness. The Stalin biographer Dimitri Volkogonov similarly wrote:

> I cannot prove that the "Georgian incident" or the conflict with Stalin hastened the fatal outcome of Lenin's illness, but it is at least very probable.

Together with other high functionaries, Stalin carried Lenin's coffin. As a former pupil in a seminary for priests, it did not seem very difficult for him to hold a moving funeral oration, consisting—as Alan Bullock expressed it—of a liturgical series of solemn assertions and an oath composed in catechetical form. Initiated comrades like Bazhanov, Stalin's secretary for many years, felt Stalin's behavior to be abysmal hypocrisy, since he himself had witnessed Stalin's reaction to Lenin's death:

> I have never seen him happier than on the day after Lenin's death. He ran back and forth in the office with a face beaming with satisfaction.

Now his path was cleared of all obstacles. His belief that fate had selected him for especially great tasks confirmed him in his wishful dream of identifying with the great leader Lenin, the "Vozhd" [leader], whose role he now wanted to take over as his successor.

EXPANSION OF HIS POWER POSITION

Stalin needed about five more years, however—from 1924 to 1929—until he finally could be certain of his victory. By that time he had gotten rid of his rivals, one after another, with brutal though outwardly very cleverly concealed methods of warfare. As a real master of intrigue and disguise, he practiced a very cunning tactic of adroitly playing off his competitors against one another, so that he never faced a unified front of opponents. For such a kind of warfare, he was greatly assisted by character traits he had acquired since youth, as his secretary Bazhanov attests in his memoirs:

> Stalin confided his innermost thoughts to no man. Most rarely did he express his ideas and impressions even to his closest associates. He had the talent of silence to the highest degree....He was clever enough never to say anything before all others had completely elaborated their arguments. After all others had spoken, he spoke out...and then he repeated the views toward which the majority had tended.

Certainly what he intended was to establish himself as a kind of integrating figure and to give the impression of being a representative of the moderate center.

Since Stalin was constantly underestimated by his antagonists, including the highly intelligent Trotsky, they all failed to notice that his thinking always revolved around only one question: "How does one assert power in the Party and how can organizations best be structured from the point of view of power?" as Ruth Fischer astutely noted on the occasion of a meeting in Moscow in January 1924. This becomes especially clear if one studies the *History of the Communist Party of the Soviet Union: Short Course.* This book shows that Stalin does not seem to have at all understood the underlying laws of social development, but rather to have adhered to a kind of fatalistic predestination. Essentially he clung to a crude, vulgar materialism and saw coercion as the means of choice. Basically he scoffed at all who followed a "general morality" or listened to the "demands of reason." Above all, anything that did not fit with his preconceived notions seemed to him suspicious and therefore hostile. His definitions thus were canonized, so to speak. In his dogmatic thinking, one recognizes his primitive, orthodox character and his tendency, probably stemming from the time of his life in the priestly seminary, to formulate his view with catechism-like simplification and strict schematics. Among the many possible variations of socialism, he created his own Stalinist socialism, which, as Volkogonov expresses it, renounced the humanistic foundations of this world view and was transformed into a bureaucratic "victimizing socialism" with a mixture of army camp communism and dogmatism.

This development to Stalinism, of course, did not remain hidden from the "Leninist core" of the Party functionaries, and around the mid-1920s it was even still possible for them to state their reservations publicly. An example of this is Kamenev's speech on December 21, 1925, for Stalin's birthday at the XIVth Party Congress, which has gone down in history and in which he said:

> We are against creating a theory of one-man rule; we are against creating a Führer....I have become convinced that Comrade Stalin cannot fulfill the task of a person who can unite and hold together the Bolshevist staff.

These prophetic and courageous words naturally could never be forgotten by so vindictive a man as Stalin, even if years went by, until someday he could avenge himself for this incredible *"lèse majesté"* by liquidating Kamenev.

Homeless child, sleeping on the street in Moscow, 1926

No doubt, during the 1920s, Stalin gained considerably not only in self-confidence, but also in authority. The Stalin whom Bazhanov described at the beginning of the decade was a completely different man from the man who finally defeated his arch-rival Trotsky in the Central Committee in October 1927. The clever moves, whereby he was finally victorious over the other three factions in the Politburo, have often been referred to as "textbook examples of Machiavellian politics." We can forego the question as to whether he really proceeded according to a fixed plan or whether his success was not rather attributable to a merciless choice of his means applied flexibly and unscrupulously. One thing is certain: by his fiftieth birthday in December 1929, except for Rykov, he had actually succeeded in definitively pushing aside all other comrades with whom he had originally worked in the Politburo—Trotsky, Kamenev, Zinoviev, Bukharin, and Tomsky.

STALIN'S PRIVATE LIFE

With few exceptions, Stalin's "private life " coincided with his work. Whether weekday or Sunday, his schedule always remained the same. Each day between 6:00 and 7:00 a.m., he was visited by his doctor, as Professor Pletnev, his official personal physician reported. The doctor then determined the hours Stalin might work and he also monitored his gymnastic exercises, as well as his facial and body massages. Both procedures took place, incidentally, mornings and evenings. He showered every day. As a rule Stalin rested for two hours before the noon meal. At that time his body was rubbed down with cold water and eau de cologne. One hour before he ate his lunch, it was the doctor's duty to analyze the food for possible unhealthy additives or poison. The food was prepared in a kitchen that was more like an Epicurean institute in which the best cooks competed for excellence. Opulent French, Georgian, and Russian dishes had to be served. Stalin's daughter Svetlana later gave some details about this:

> Fish from special ponds, pheasants and rams from special breeding farms were served at his table, along with Georgian wines of special vintage. Fresh fruits were brought in by plane from the south. He did not know what high transportation costs had to be paid in order to keep him supplied regularly with such things....I don't know whether father knew that this "food supply depot" consisted mainly in having specialized

doctors check everything edible that was delivered to
his kitchen for possible poisonous content by means
of chemical analysis. Every sample of bread, fish, or
fruits was accompanied by a certificate stamped and
signed by the person responsible: "No poison was discovered." Sometimes Dr. Dyakov came into our room
in the Kremlin and took air samples from all the rooms.

Frequently Stalin ordered the table set with silverware that Ivan the
Terrible had often used and had treasured highly as a gift from Queen
Elizabeth I of England. Incidentally, he had a portrait of that Czar
hung in his study, since apparently he felt especially good in his
presence.

Stalin spoke bad Russian with a strong accent. But, according to
Milovan Djilas, he supposedly had command of a rich vocabulary and
seasoned his lively and graphic mode of expression with many Russian proverbs and expressions. Surprisingly, he is also reported to have
had a sense of humor, a "crude, self-confident humor, but not devoid of
all finesse." The only diversions in Stalin's monotonous life were his
get-togethers for parties with his closest associates and with foreign
guests. Milovan Djilas tells that on the occasion of a visit in Moscow
in 1944 he was astonished at the quantities of food Stalin could devour.
"Even for much bigger men, they would have been enormous." He
also was able to empty his vodka glass up to twenty times, without
becoming tongue-tied, and American diplomats also confirm that in
such strenuous rounds of toasts they never saw Stalin drunk. At drinking bouts with Party friends in his dacha (country house) he liked to
use a crude and vulgar manner of speaking. He was then most de-
lighted by slapstick humor, as when a drinking companion put a tomato
on the seat of a neighbor's chair just at the moment he sat down.

Stalin was very worried about his personal safety. That is why he
always carried a pistol in his pants pocket or in his top coat. At night
he laid the gun under his pillow and never parted from it. He was
afraid to be alone, so at night he locked himself in his bedroom and had
armored doors built that could be opened only from inside by a complicated electrical mechanism. All these precautions were taken, even
though his rooms were patrolled around the clock by numerous secret
police of the Cheka. But since he did not trust even these security
forces, he could unexpectedly—day or night—order the entire guard
force exchanged. The enormous sums spent to guard him resulted not
just from personal security in his apartment and office rooms, but also

from the precautionary steps required to police his travel from his dacha to the Kremlin. Hundreds of sentries or secret police lined the streets of his limousine route. Moreover, five cars were always sent out so that not even the secret service knew in which car Stalin was riding. The limousines themselves were hermetically shielded from the outside by gray curtains, so that no ordinary citizen could catch sight of the supreme leader of the workers.

Stalin's appearance was intentionally so touched up in the portraits distributed by the Soviet government that no one, whether in the Soviet Union or in the West, could have the least doubt about the overflowing health of that "man of steel," who watched tirelessly over the people's welfare in sleepless nights. Plainly speaking, with a height of 5 ft. 5 in., he was short like Napoleon. He looked even shorter because, over the course of the years, he had put on weight and always wore wide-cut pants that hung down over his shoes like accordion folds. He had his shoes made with high heels so that he would look taller. His face was pockmarked, wilted and covered with reddish spots. His neck was noticeably wrinkled. His hair was, as usual in Georgia, blue-black. His gray-brown eyes were described by Louis Fischer, on the occasion of a Kremlin interview, as follows:

> The thick eyebrows, the fleshy eyelids, and the moist shimmer of his pupils seemed as if made to shield his eyes from any probing look. In the course of a three-hour interview, Stalin looked me openly in the face only twice.

Very few people had the occasion to get to know this eerie despot very closely. One of them was Professor Dimitri Pletnev, who served as his personal physician since 1927. Pletnev, born the son of a village shoemaker in 1872, had studied medicine with a government scholarship, obtained through the help of the village pastor. His subsequent clinical and scientific activity was so successful that by the time of the October Revolution he was considered probably the most famous heart specialist in the Soviet Union. It was therefore quite natural that in 1927 the quest for a Director of the Polyclinic, established in the Kremlin for the medical care of the highest Party functionaries, should come across the name Pletnev. Since there was nothing political against him, he was quickly nominated head of the clinic, and the comrades Kazakov, Levin, Weisbrod, and Moschenberg were assigned as his colleagues. Pletnev's proletarian origins—he, too, being the son of a simple shoemaker—his dignified demeanor, his open and straightforward nature, and his sense of humor soon led Stalin, who had previously really trusted nobody, to feel increasing affection for this doctor and, to the annoyed surprise of his closest Party comrades, to tie him more and more closely to himself.

Pletnev's notes give the following description of the dictator:

> Stalin was unafraid and brave as a lion, clever as a snake, and weak and cowardly as a rabbit—all at the same time! He had a hard time bearing physical pain, so that sometimes pain in his joints almost drove him mad. He tolerated no resistance, was inclined to boast and loved flattery. He had quite a wide horizon, was astute, resourceful, and flexible, and strongly inclined to adventurism. Nonetheless, his mental abilities by themselves would hardly have sufficed for his successful rise, had they not been accompanied by a devilish cunning and slyness as well as an astonishing knowledge of the human mind with all its weaknesses. He was headstrong, consistent, and had extraordinary willpower and nerves of iron. It was hard to deceive him if you stood in his immediate presence, since you always had the feeling that his eyes were boring through you. He had an excellent memory....With his eyes flashing cunningly and his smirking mouth, whose corners betrayed craftiness, the impression Stalin made warned you to be cautious. Sometimes he seemed deceptively benevolent and friendly, although at that very moment he felt nothing but hatred and hostility toward that very same person....He suffered mainly from two pathological states: megalomania and a persecution complex.

As father of a family, Stalin was a complete failure. He made mental cripples out of his two sons by misuse of power. Yakov, his son by a first marriage, was pushed almost to despair by his father's cool, rejecting behavior, so that one day he even tried to commit suicide by shooting himself, but fortunately he survived. When his father visited him in the hospital immediately after the attempted suicide, he had nothing else to say to his son than to ask him scornfully: "Ha, so you missed, didn't you?" Only with great difficulties did Yakov later

Joseph Stalin with his son Vasily and his daughter Svetlana.

succeed in realizing his lifelong dream of entering a military career. He was sent to an artillery school of the Red Army and at the beginning of the war held the rank of First Lieutenant.

The fate of Vasily, Stalin's son by a second marriage, was also quite pathetic. Since his father had failed to make a hard man of him, after his mother's death, his education was assigned to Major General Vlasik, for many years the head of Stalin's personal guard. But precisely through this decision, as a result of Vlasik's fawning treatment of the boy, for he hoped in this way to win Stalin's special favor, Vasily grew up to be irresolute, moody, and of weak character. In World War II, he showed courage as a fighter pilot, but his arrogant privileges among

Vasily Djugashvili, son from Stalin's second marriage, in the uniform of an air force officer. He died in 1962 as an alcoholic.

the military cadre soon led to quarrels and embarrassing incidents—no wonder, if one reflects that in 1942 he was promoted to Colonel at only twenty years of age. In his military records as a twenty-five-year-old Lieutenant General, one reads:

> He is of a fiery and choleric disposition and has a hard time controlling himself. Incidents of physical assaults on subordinates and personal coarse behavior toward individual officers, as well as fist-fights with the control sentinels of the NKVD have occurred. His state of health is bad, especially with regard to the nervous system. He is extremely irritable....All these inadequacies diminish to a considerable degree his authority as a commander and are not consonant with the rank of a division commander.

To protect the units under his command from this "ill-behaved prince," the only solution that Vasily's superior officers could devise was to transfer him to the military academy. But since he continued to be showered with distinctions and all imaginable privileges, the spoiled, psychically deformed young man slid gradually into alcoholism, so that finally, on orders from his father, he had to be dismissed from his position as commander of Moscow's air defenses. After Stalin's death he was put in jail in Lefortovo, from where he was released again under Khrushchev. He was finally sent to exile as penalty for new incidents committed while inebriated; on March 19, 1962, he died there, a physical and mental wreck, at the age of forty.

Stalin's favorite child was his daughter Svetlana, who strongly resembled him in appearance. She herself, with her moody, domineering, and sly character much like her father's, also felt strongly drawn to him from earliest childhood. Stalin did not succeed in educating her into a real patriot, yet there is some evidence in a few letters that show a loving affection for his daughter. In his letters he liked to call her his "mistress of the house" and signed them as "Your secretary." Nonetheless, such sentimental moments cannot hide the fact that he could reprimand his "mistress of the house" brutally with a flick of the hand when his pathological distrust smelled danger. So he arranged for his daughter's first lover, the journalist and film director A. J. Kapler, to be arrested and sentenced to a work camp for ten years because he "suspiciously had a sister in France and because he was proven to have spoken once with two American correspondents." In the 1960s Svetlana published, in the United States, a critical review of her father's life and deeds, which, despite some doubts as to its objectivity, presents some valuable biographical details.

Boris Bazhanov, Stalin's secretary for many years, describes Stalin as an impassioned politician, who was interested only in power and beyond that allegedly had no vices. He loved neither money—he had plenty to dispose of as he willed anyway—nor pleasure, nor sports, nor women. "Except for his wife, women did not exist for him." Bazhanov's assertion, however, conflicts with Professor Pletnev's views as presented in Romano-Petrova's memoirs—at least as far as Stalin's life after his second wife's death is concerned.

Nadezhda Alliluyeva was the daughter of a railroad man, whom Stalin knew from Tiflis and who had taken him into his home in Petrograd, after his return from exile in 1917. In 1919, during the Civil War, he married the woman, who was twenty-two years younger. Despite her youth, she showed a rather serious temperament. She was a convinced Communist and worked in the People's Commissariat for Nationality Questions. In addition she studied at the Economics University. She bore him two children, Vasily in 1921 and, four years later, Svetlana. Soon Yakov, Stalin's son by a first marriage, moved in with the family in Moscow; he was seven years younger than Nadezhda and she loved the youth as if she were his own mother, although Yakov was not exactly spoiled by paternal affection. Nadezhda admired Stalin, not only as her husband and the father of her two children, but also as the great leader of the Party to which she belonged with idealistic conviction. She soon recognized his difficult character, and she tried —successfully, at first—to keep his moods under control. She sought to avoid any kind of preference or privileged special treatment; therefore she insisted on having their two children educated in a public school, to which they were driven by car by their teachers and driven back to the Kremlin after school. Nadezhda herself was shielded within the Kremlin from everything that took place outside those walls. Only through personal contact with colleagues at the Economic Institute did she now and then hear a few things, and later this would be the cause of her early death.

The Secret Genocide

Probably at the beginning of the first five-year plan (from 1928 to 1933) Stalin first developed a sense of mission, a feeling that fate had chosen him for special political and historical achievements. The mission he felt called to realize was to lift the Soviet Union's economic potential to a level equal to the West's. The only way to attain this objective seemed to him to be the collectivization of agriculture and the rapid modernization of industry. In his present position he felt secure enough to abandon once and for all Lenin's lukewarm compromise, the New Economic Policy, and to undertake this mighty revolutionary transformation of the country by using the most brutal coercive and terrorist measures that had stood him so well during wartime Communism. Such an enterprise seemed not to entail too great a risk for him at that point in time, since with Zinoviev's expulsion from the Party and Trotsky's banishment to Alma-Atu in January 1928, the concept of "opposition" had been stricken from Soviet vocabulary and the road to absolute power lay open before him.

What Stalin intended by this "Third Revolution" was to transform the Soviet Union into a leading industrial state in the shortest time. The head start of the Western industrial states, which had developed in the course of more than a century, was to be overtaken in just a few years, as Stalin proudly proclaimed at the end of 1929, "the year of the great breakthrough":

Firmly in charge as Lenin's successor: Stalin in his office at the end of the 1920s. Inset: Stalin's second wife, Nadezhda S. Alliluyeva, also became a victim of his violence.

> We are now going full steam on the road to industrial-
> ization—to socialism—leaving our ancient Russian
> retardedness behind us....Then let the honorable capi-
> talists who boast of their "civilization," try to catch up
> with us.

In his mad delusion of power, he wanted literally to build the mightiest
industrial nation out of nothing.

To master such a mammoth enterprise, Stalin had to try to inte-
grate peasant-owned agriculture into the scheme of socialist society.
He viewed this branch of the economy, with its mode of labor rooted in
past centuries, in Cohen's words, as "a huge, sluggish, and yet somehow threatening mass of people blocking Russia's road to industrialization, to the modern age, and to socialism—a realm of darkness that
simply had to be overcome before the Soviet Union could emerge as
the Promised Land." To sensitize the Party comrades concerning this
imaginary "class enemy in the countryside" as required, Stalin constructed the image of an exploitatory, capitalistic class of successful
and capable peasants in the form of "Kulaks"—a concept Lenin had
coined at the beginning of the 1920s but never clearly defined at the
time. These Kulaks had to be the first ones liquidated by expelling
them from their homes, confiscating all their property, and deporting
them together with their families to Siberia. In the Ukraine alone, more
than two hundred thousand people were affected by "dekulakization,"
and many of them froze or starved to death on the endless journey.

But Stalin was not satisfied merely with dekulakization. His next
goal was the coerced unification of all farms and small landed properties into collective organizations, the kolchozes. This measure allowed
the peasants to keep their houses, but they had to surrender their agricultural equipment, all their cattle, and their land, which in effect
changed them into rural hired hands on what had formerly been their
own land. At the end of 1929, the "year of the great breakthrough,"
Stalin wrote in *Pravda* literally:

> It involves a radical change in the development of agri-
> culture, the transition from a small and archaic
> individual farm economy to the progressive collective
> agricultural big enterprise.

A few weeks later, on his fiftieth birthday, he demanded, within the
framework of his "October Revolution on the Farm," that his announced
collectivization in the Ukraine, the Caucasus region, and the Central

Volga region should be completed in two years at the latest. While about 30 percent of the poorest rural population joined the kolchozes almost without resistance, the remaining portion, consisting mostly of medium-scale peasants, resisted these coercive measures, at least for a time. But whoever opposed Stalin's decision to change all large-scale farmers designated as Kulaks and, later, all independent peasants into disenfranchised working hands was branded an "enemy of the Soviet power" who had to be neutralized. In this way, without consideration of the actual social conditions, countless peasants were arbitrarily subjected to the project for the "liquidation of the Kulaks." Quite often the decision made by Party functionaries to reclassify a medium-scale peasant to a Kulak, that is, a large-scale farmer, was motivated plainly by ordinary robbery.

To make it quite clear to the medium-scale peasants what they could expect if they continued to oppose collectivization, Stalin announced on December 27, 1929, with cold-blooded decisiveness:

> This means we have moved from the policy of restraining the exploitatory tendencies of the Kulaks to their liquidation as a class.

By Stalin's own data, in this coercive action, probably unique in all history and carried out most brutally by the henchmen of the Party and of the NKVD (in the years 1930 to 1933), about ten million more or less prosperous farmers were liquidated!

Simultaneously with this rape of a coerced collectivization, affecting 120 million rural persons, Stalin began a bitter campaign against the Orthodox Church, which had occupied a central position in the lives of the peasants for centuries and meant for them a harbor of refuge and consolation. To rob the peasants of this spiritual support, thousands of monks and nuns were hauled off to Siberia and a huge number of churches were demolished or put to other uses.

Stalin's policy of the "October Revolution in the Countryside" culminated in the coerced delivery of grain and other agricultural products at prices fixed by the government. The almost unimaginable misery unleashed by this order led to acts of desperation and finally to systematic resistance by the peasants, in which women often took part. Only by sending in the Red Army and NKVD units did Stalin succeed in repressing these peasant revolts and establishing a cemetery-like peace. Many rural workers migrated to the cities to find employment as workers in industrial plants. From 1929 to 1935 almost eighteen million peasants were withdrawn from agriculture in this way. The "domestic passports," so hated in Czarist Russia, were reintroduced and issued only to workers and officials, but were withheld from peasants, so that the peasants were reattached to their place of residence like their serf ancestors and were no longer permitted to leave the land.

This dekulakization and agricultural collectivization marked the beginning of one of the most horrible chapters in Russian history, namely, the "Ukrainian Holocaust." These coercive measures had worse consequences for the peasants in the Ukraine than in the rest of the Soviet Union. But the situation there was drastically worsened, because Stalin considered that the right time had come for him to avenge himself properly for difficulties he had encountered in the Ukraine in the early 1920s as People's Commissar for Nationality Questions. He was determined to crush Ukrainian nationalism forever by any means. Stalin linked his revenge campaign against "nationalist deviation in the Ukraine" with collectivization by accusing the Kulaks of being responsible for the spread of nationalist ideas. By eliminating private ownership of the land, he hoped to undermine the social foundation for nationalist tendencies in the Ukraine.

His procedure was worse than diabolical. He ordered the Ukrainian peasants to give up their grain, which they allegedly were withholding from the government. These arbitrarily ordered, ruthlessly enforced, and excessive demands during this "grain battle" led to an unimaginable famine in the Ukraine and compelled the famished populace, whose grain had almost all been confiscated, to steal grain from the collective farms. Stalin's satanical vindictiveness found a way to increase the suffering of starving children and adults by promulgating an edict written in his own hand, making theft of collective property punishable immediately by the firing squad or, given mitigating circumstances, by a sentence of ten years in a penal colony or prison. All amnesty was prohibited. In Kharkov alone, Bullock reports, fifty-five thousand people were jailed and fifteen thousand executed.

As Dmytro Zlepko, publisher of the documents of the German Foreign Office from the period 1930 to 1934 writes, at that time "the entire Ukraine was transformed into a supradimensional death camp. Maddened with hunger, facing certain death, emaciated people ate the flesh of children who had starved and the abdomens of corpses." Lev Kopelev, a Communist activist at that time, described this unimaginable catastrophe in shocking detail in his book written later while in exile:

Street scene during the "Ukranian Famine Holocaust" 1932/33

Together with others I emptied the cupboards of old
people and blocked my ears in order not to have to
hear the screams of children....I saw women and children turned blue, with bloated bellies and empty,
lifeless eyes, still hardly breathing. And I saw corpses
in tattered sheepskins and pitiful bast shoes, corpses
in peasant huts, in the melting snow of the old city of
Volgoda, and under the bridges of Kharkov.

In this Ukrainian genocide alone, seven million people, among them
three-and-a-half million children, fell victim to this "holocaust of famine," according to historical data that have since been verified.
Robert Conquest states that today the estimate for the dekulakization
program amounts to three million dead; in the Republic of Kazakhstan,
an additional one million victims would have to be mourned. Thus,
the total number of victims who died in this period runs to approximately eleven million, to which would have to be added another
three-and-a-half million prisoners who lost their lives in penal colonies, during the murderous work of excavating the White Sea Canal, or
in the gold mines of Magadan, as well as in other camps in the Arctic
North. Conquest states in conclusion:

Although Stalin's war against the peasants was restricted to only one country, more people died there
than in World War I in all countries combined.

Hardly ever in history did a tyrant build his fortress as unrestricted master over life and death on such mountains of human victims; and not one of them ever looked down so unmoved and pitiless, indeed almost cynically, upon the countless victims who had fallen prey to his intoxication with power and his hate-filled thirst for revenge as did this monster of a human creature. His commentary on all the horrible consequences of his coerced collectivization and the famine he intentionally brought down on the Ukraine was:

> Between the peasantry and our regime there rages a merciless life and death struggle. This year was a test for our struggle and their endurance. A famine had to be brought on so that they would understand who is master in the house. It cost millions of human lives, but the system of collective farms has survived.

However, the press was not allowed to print one word about the famine, and anyone who tried to resist this order was threatened with five years in a labor camp. On top of all this, his crafty, treacherous, and unscrupulous nature was shown by the fact that on March 2, 1930, in an article putting the responsibility on the shoulders of his Party functionaries for their disturbingly "overzealous operations," he described himself as a moderating figure seeking harmony, and he successfully tried to divert any suspicion from his own person as the real initiator of these coercive measures.

Only one person was not impressed by these hypocritical maneuvers and dared to accuse Stalin openly for his incredible crime against the Ukrainian people, namely, his own wife, Nadezhda Alliluyeva. One day in the Economic Institute she learned from Nina Karova, a student and friend of hers, whose mother had died as a victim of the Ukrainian "famine holocaust," that countless victims there were exposed to death by famine caused by the coerced requisitions of food supplies ordered by the government. Greatly excited, she immediately hastened to the Kremlin to question her husband about it. His answer consisted in rejecting the accusations as fabrications and forbidding her to continue attending the university. Nor was she able to get any information from other members of the Politburo, but only a vague suggestion to the effect that the program in the Ukraine was merely a "temporary experimental period of the young Soviet state." In this context Molotov even called her a "cowardly and fainthearted Communist woman." Only

Lenin's widow, Nadezhda Krupskaya, listened calmly to her and recommended that she travel to the Ukraine to appraise the situation with her own eyes.

Although Stalin reacted with rage on learning of this plan and threatened to divorce and banish his wife, Nadezhda held firmly to her plan to travel to the Ukraine without delay. She returned two weeks later, a completely changed person because of the horrors she had witnessed; she immediately wrote an embarrassing report to the Politburo and the Central Committee and threatened her husband that she would give this report to the press for publication unless measures were taken immediately to end these provocative, inhuman acts of violence.

On top of it all, another shock awaited Nadezhda that hit her personally especially hard. When she went to the Economic Institute after her return, she discovered that Nina Karova had been arrested by the GPU, together with other female colleagues. Completely disconcerted at such an arbitrary measure, she immediately telephoned Genrich Yagoda, then Chief of the GPU (the secret police after February 1922), in order to demand the immediate release of these young ladies. Totally aghast, she was told that, unfortunately, he could not fulfill this desire since all the arrested girls had meanwhile "died in prison of an infectious disease."

From those days on, Nadezhda's marriage relationship to Stalin was strained and unnatural, and finally she herself indirectly fell victim to this genocide of her husband's. Deeply disillusioned by the increasing corruption of the Communist Party and its potentates and outraged by her husband's criminal role as the leader of this brutal Party apparatus, she came to an early end. The official report states a "heart stoppage" as the cause of her death, but soon the rumor spread that she had committed suicide by shooting herself. This version was later indirectly supported by a clue from her daughter Svetlana that her mother left a letter revealing her intention to commit suicide. Dimitri Volkogonov, in his biography which appeared four years ago, however, raises the justifiable question whether it really was suicide. His doubts seem to be corroborated by the depiction of the events provided by Professor Pletnev, who allegedly was an eyewitness to what happened.

The notes of Stalin's personal physician reveal that in that critical marriage situation he was asked to use his influence with Nadezhda and "make her see reason." During a meeting then arranged in the doctor's apartment, she reportedly first described her horrible impressions of the catastrophic famine in the Ukraine; then she said outright that her husband was deceiving and betraying the Soviet citizens, complaining to this effect:

> I was deceived by my Party and its leader, whom I wanted to serve with my whole devotion. Now I see clearly that all Lenin's successors vanished into oblivion one after the other. Stalin is a dictator who is driven by the insane dream of a worldwide revolution. Stalin's terrorism rages through the country like a wild animal—I am deeply ashamed.

Pletnev's report goes on to say that a few weeks later, toward midnight on November 22, 1932, he was called to her bedside, where his colleagues from the Kremlin Polyclinic, Dr. Kazakov, Dr. Levin, and Dr. Weisbrod were working on her. She twisted in her pillows, and on looking more closely he perceived that she was mortally wounded. With painful effort she stammered the words:

> This executioner has killed me. He could not bear my truth. He killed the mother of his children; take my children away from near him.

She reportedly also called for her mother and her sister, but they were not present. Only her son Vasily, eleven years old at the time, awakened from sleep by the gunshot, suddenly stood in the room as if petrified at the sight of his mother in her mortal agony. Stalin himself is said to have spent the night sitting in a corner of the room, supposedly crying.

In Romano-Petrova's memoirs the events of that day are described as follows:

> On that day Stalin went to Voroshilov's rooms in the Kremlin to discuss various matters. Suddenly his wife rushed into the room, interrupted the conversation, and accused both men of being responsible for the famine, and she expressly called Stalin's mode of behavior "terrorist." Stalin lost his self-control, threw a few objects to the floor and called his wife a bitch and a whore. Nadya then ran out of the room, followed closely by her enraged husband. Voroshilov hastened after them. As soon as the family's suite of rooms was reached Stalin began hitting his wife with his fists, which Voroshilov tried to prevent. Nadezhda, whose eyes

The Stalin family with Kliment Y. Voroshilov and his wife (1931)

glared with rage, scolded Stalin as a murderer and trai-
tor. Then Stalin hastily reached for his pistol and fired
at her before Voroshilov could do anything. Nadezhda
threw up her arms, struggled for breath, remained
standing for a moment as if petrified, whispering the
words: "You will destroy the Party!" Then, bleeding
abundantly, she fell to the floor.

On the following day, Stalin is said to have openly confessed his
deed to his Politburo, explaining that he could not allow his wife to
interfere with Party leadership and offering his resignation, which his
comrades refused to accept. Of the entire Politburo, only his Georgian
countryman, Ordzhonikidze, dared to accuse Stalin of having killed a
true Communist woman and friend, the daughter of an old revolutionary and the mother of his children. Nevertheless, all agreed that they
must not let the "leader" fall under the least suspicion in this family
tragedy. So Stalin had the announcement aired on the radio and printed
in the morning newspapers that his wife had died unexpectedly from a
"heart stoppage," a completely vague statement certified by the doctors Pletnev, Kazakov and Levin.

In order to erase all traces from possible later investigations, Stalin
did not shrink from violating her grave. Four weeks after his wife's
burial, which incidentally he did not attend, he had the honor guard

Politburo member, Grigori "Sergo" Ordzhonikidze (1886-1937), was driven to suicide by Stalin.

removed from the tomb. In a nightly action he had Nadezhda's corpse removed from the opened coffin and replaced by a female corpse of the same age. The honor guard was ordered back only after all traces of the desecration of the grave had been removed. Then Nadezhda's corpse was cremated. The unfortunate security guards who involuntarily had witnessed the murder in Stalin's apartment were liquidated. Thus, not only the murder victim, but also any witnesses who could later have testified against Stalin, had vanished forever from the face of the earth. Only Vasily supposedly called his father a murderer in Professor Pletnev's presence. Stalin arranged for generous gifts to be given to the doctors who dutifully covered up his grizzly crime, and he reassured Pletnev, after whom the Kremlin Polyclinic was to be named, by offering him the prospect that the clinic would be expanded into the best and most modern facility, not only in the Soviet Union, but in all of Europe.

FURTHER EXPANSION OF POWER

Besides the collectivization of agriculture and rapid industrialization, the third goal of Stalin's "revolution" was the construction of a mighty state, with a single unrestricted autocrat at the top and below him a powerless, weak society trained to fearful obedience. The dominant role in this system of rulership was played by the political secret police—called GPU or NKVD—which was directly under his command. This secret police had already proven its deadly efficiency in repressing the peasants, and now its assignment was centered more intensely on intimidating the technical and organizational leadership cadres in the various enterprises by uninterrupted supervision and stern punishment, if necessary. Stalin's plan was to focus primarily on all specialists with bourgeois background who did not belong to the Party, and only later also to thin out the Party elite.

These programs were initiated with the so-called Shakhty Trial, the first great show trial in Moscow in March 1928, in which twenty-five persons were accused of alleged sabotage and conspiratorial activity. This show trial, where incidentally Andrei Vyshinsky made his first appearance as an especially cynical and sadistically cruel prosecuting attorney, was to serve as precedent for future trials. With the stereotypical themes—"Conspiracy, treason, and sabotage"—and with the cooperation of a servile press, this trial was supposed to create in the whole Soviet Union the climate of fear and terror that Stalin urgently needed for his "intensification of the class struggle," along with the active complicity or at least tacit consent of the intimidated populace. In April 1929 he proclaimed threateningly:

Andrei J. Vyshinsky
(1883-1954), 1935-1939
States' Attorney of the
USSR. He was the
prosecutor in the
Moscow show trials.

Shakhty-people now are sitting in all branches of our industry. Many of them have been fished out, but by far not all. The damaging work of the bourgeois intellectuals is one of the most dangerous forms of resistance to developing socialism.

The Shakhty trial signaled the start of a kind of "cultural revolution," whose first victim was Vladimir Mayakovsky, the main representative of Russian literary futurism. Mayakovsky had just returned from exile in the United States and had already aroused Stalin's displeasure with his writings several times, which indirectly meant a death sentence for the author. Professor Pletnev, personal physician to the all-powerful General Secretary first witnessed the cold-blooded and hypocritical behavior of his prominent patient when he wanted to remove undesirable persons as stealthily as possible: Stalin notified Mayakovsky, through a special order to the author, that due to the pressure he was under, the most purposeful thing for him to do was to save himself from further embarrassing measures by committing suicide, which Mayakovsky finally did. Afterwards Stalin, the master of disguises, expressed his sincere regret at the unexpected loss of this important writer. To remove all suspicion from himself, he ordered his personal physician, who was then treating him for a purulent tonsil infection, to examine Mayakovsky's corpse medically and to certify his suicide as a deed committed in a "temporary state of insanity."

In building up Soviet industry, Stalin seemed to be more flexible and capable of learning than in the collectivization of agriculture. The Shakhty trial was followed by further trials against leading captains of industry and high economic functionaries charged with sabotage or conspiracy against the state and sentenced either to death or to long terms of incarceration in labor camps. But he soon learned that at least for a certain time he could not yet do without technicians from the hated bourgeoisie, although he had scorned them at first; so after only three years he changed the policy announced in 1928. Not to give the impression that he himself had ordered the "hunting down of the technicians" and the accompanying trials, with cynical impudence he blamed his subordinates for supposedly having acted overzealously, just as he had done after the coercive collectivization program. In a speech to captains of industry in June 1931 he said:

It would be stupid and irrational today to regard every specialist and engineer of the old school as a criminal not yet caught and a harmful pest. Among us the "resentment of specialists" has always been considered a harmful and shameful phenomenon and it will continue to be so considered.

A clearer attempt to wash his hands of the bloody trials against innocent men could hardly be possible. Since the end of 1929, there was virtually no opposition. Stalin could arbitrarily manipulate public opinion as needed and convincingly clear himself of any responsibility for terrorist methods. With his clever maneuvers, he could deceive not only the Soviet people, but also foreign countries, which in those years tended to dismiss reports of terrorism in the Soviet Union as anti-Soviet propaganda. Without a doubt, the show trials also contributed to this attitude in other countries, for they were a kind of political stage to carry on effective propaganda; and the confessions of the accused, extorted by mental and physical torture, were published by the media with whatever twist Stalin wished. The most important news articles on the proceedings had to be censored by Stalin before publication and—typical symptoms of his self-infatuation, ridiculous vanity, and arrogance—marginal comments written by himself emphasizing Comrade Stalin's "extraordinary determination and energy" and "wise foresight" had to be inserted into the text.

Stalin had more success with the coercive promotion of industrialization than with the collectivization of agriculture, but here, too, he fell into his old error of false estimates due to technical incompetence; and this, together with his pathological gigantomania, repeatedly caused almost chaotic turmoil. The excessive achievements that he demanded were in the end actually attained; however, this was due to the ruthless removal of all resistance, if necessary by summarily shooting the persons responsible for failure to meet the goals. For this purpose, he sent especially reliable followers with unlimited authorizations out to the various Soviet Republics to check the achievement capacity of important enterprises, on the spot, and to apply the necessary pressure on members of the enterprises by summary executions of the responsible "saboteurs." Molotov and Kaganovich especially distinguished themselves as such inspectors. That Stalin's unrealistic demands, in the mad race to catch up by a rapid industrialization, were ultimately fulfilled, after all, is also partly explainable by the fact that he had a huge army of slave workers at his disposal. These industrial slaves were recruited from camp prisoners condemned to forced labor, who literally were worked to death in the mines, on road and railway construction, or in the megalomanic project of the canal from the Arctic Ocean to the Baltic, built under inhuman labor camp conditions. In this huge network of penal colonies, movingly described in Solzhenitzyn's book *The Gulag Archipelago*, there were always from two to four million men, according to the most recent Russian publications. This archipelago was for Stalin not only the cheapest, but in the early forties also the most important, construction enterprise in the Soviet Union.

When in the winter of 1932/33 the situation of the suffering population had become almost unbearable, skepticism about Stalin's methods began to spread even among the leading Party functionaries, and some brave Party comrades even dared to publicly declare that they did not agree with his approach. During the famine of 1932, it was mainly Martemjan Ryutin, a former member of the Central Secretariat, who now spoke up for a moderation of the Stalinist policies. In a compendious work *To All Members of the Communist Party of the Soviet Union,* he described Stalin literally as "the evil spirit of the Russian revolution, who out of personal greed for power and vindictiveness has brought the revolution to the edge of disaster," and he demanded his deposal as General Secretary. Stalin, in his paranoid fears, saw this proclamation as an open call for his murder, and so he had Ryutin arrested on the spot, together with several like-minded Party comrades, and insisted that the accused men be put before a firing squad. The trial against the so-called "Ryutin platform" was played up as a major large-scale conspiracy threatening the state, in order to create a solid foundation for Stalin's later show trials. The Central Committee, however, converted the death sentences into a ten-year prison sentence—a painful failure for Stalin that he could not forget. Just five years later, his position of power was so consolidated that at last he could quench his thirst for revenge by ordering the execution (without a trial) of Ryutin, both of his sons, and a crowd of followers.

Not just Ryutin, however, but other high functionaries in the Politburo also believed it was time at last to desist from the constant terror and brutal force, now that a breakthrough had been made in Stalin's collectivization of agriculture and industrialization of the country; it was also time to create a better standard of living for the population after all the hard years. Among these "oppositionists" were men like Sergo Ordzhonikidze, who was responsible for all heavy industry, and Sergei Kirov, leader of the Leningrad Party organization, whom Stalin could not eliminate without further ado because of their popularity with the people and their high reputation. So at the XVIIth Party Congress of February 1934, the so-called "Party Congress of Victors," he could not prevent an unofficial bloc of delegates from discussing the possibility of transferring Stalin to a different position of leadership and electing Sergei Kirov as the future General Secretary. Khrushchev characterized the delicate situation at the time as follows:

> The irregular situation that arose in the Party through the personality cult was unsettling to a part of the Party membership, especially the old Leninist cadre. Many delegates to the Party Congress, especially those who knew Lenin's legacy, believed the time had come to transfer Stalin from the function of General Secretary to another post.

In secret balloting, almost one-fourth of the delegates voted against Stalin, while Kirov received only three negative votes out of over one thousand delegates. Stalin was beside himself with rage and offended vanity, so that he felt "personally only hostility and vengefulness for this Party Congress, and of course for Kirov," as Mikoyan noted in his diary extracts, selections of which were published in 1987. As a later examination of the records revealed, Stalin immediately engineered a massive election fraud and assigned a special commission of the Central Committee to destroy 267 of the 270 ballots that had been cast against him, so that at the end of this vote fraud, the appearance was given that he too had received only three negative votes. This election swindle was, however, just the beginning of a revenge campaign he launched against the insubordinate delegates. As Khrushchev reported at the XXth Party Congress in 1956, Stalin's vengeance affected not only the 1,966 Party Congress delegates, of whom no less than 1,108 were arrested for counterrevolutionary crimes, but also the 139 members and candidates of the Central Committee elected by the Party Congress, 98 of whom suffered the same fate and were put before the firing squad.

So, in Robert Tucker's words, the Party Congress of Reconciliation in reality became the "Party Congress of the Final Alienation of Stalin from the Party of the Bolsheviks." This was shown, among other things, by his demand for an improved system of political control within the Party. He began assigning the most important key positions in the Party and in the NKVD to men whom he especially trusted: Genrich Yagoda as head of the NKVD, with Nikolai Yezhov and Lavrenti Beria—later his successor—as his deputies, as well as the reliable comrades Lazar Kaganovich, Georgiy Malenkov, and Nikita Khrushchev. With these men behind him, it was easy for Stalin, by a base, yet masterful, play of intrigue, to link any suspicious action of a rival whom he intended to destroy with an imaginary conspiracy or spy-ring. The salient feature of his tactic consisted in confusing his selected victims by playing them off against one another, thus always protecting himself from having to proceed against a united front. At the same time such an approach gave him the advantage of holding all the threads of the complex web of his intrigues in his own hands.

After the 1934 Party Congress two new secretaries were accepted into the Central Committee, namely Andrei Zhdanov, who was to play an important role after World War II, and Sergei Kirov, the candidate against Stalin at the XVIIth "Party Congress of Victors." It is assumed by historians today that this personnel decision was part of a strictly logical and clever plan Stalin was following that began with Kirov's murder in Leningrad on December 1, 1934, by Leonid Nikolayev, a longtime Party member. From today's perspective it can be accepted beyond all doubt that the murderer had personal rather than political reasons for his act. On the other hand, it is solidly established that there is no way Nikolayev could have gotten to Kirov if the NKVD sentries had not been removed prior to his encroachment, although Nikolayev had already been temporarily arrested twice for trying to approach Kirov with a pistol in his pocket. Moreover, precisely at the time of Kirov's murder, his own bodyguards were prevented from accompanying him on the way to his offices. Finally, we know today that the NKVD was responsible even for the ominous "traffic accident" in which Kirov's bodyguard Borisov was killed on the way to an interrogation to be conducted by Stalin and an investigation committee.

What role Stalin himself played in Kirov's murder has, however, not been clarified perfectly to this day. Khrushchev's report states:

> It must be recalled that the particular circumstance of Kirov's murder are still unexplainable and mysterious to this day....But it is an unusually suspicious circumstance that on the very day one of the Cheka bodyguards removed from his post to protect Kirov was being brought to a hearing, he was killed in a "traffic accident" in which no other passengers suffered even a scratch. After Kirov's murder, high functionaries of the Leningrad state police received only very mild penalties; but in the year 1937 they faced the

firing squad. Presumably they were executed to wipe out the tracks of those who had organized Kirov's murder.

At the same XXIInd Party Congress in 1961, at which Khrushchev made public the findings of a review of this affair by a commission, to the effect that "the NKVD-men were killed to wipe away all tracks," he also said significantly: "The more deeply we study the materials connected with Kirov's death, the more questions arise." If Genrich Yagoda, head of the NKVD at the time, admitted at his own trial in 1938 that "on Abel Yenukidze's instructions he had seen to it that no obstacles would be put in the way of the terrorist act against Kirov," that proves only that the NKVD actually organized Kirov's murder under higher orders. Since we know today by what horrendous means such confessions were obtained, we also know what value such "voluntary confessions" have in the quest for truth. Khrushchev, who himself cooperated for many years as an activist in building up Stalin's terrorist regime, was therefore speaking as an insider in his memoirs, extracts of which were published in 1989:

> I am of the opinion that this murder was organized by
> Yagoda, who could act only on secret assignment from
> Stalin which he had received, so to speak, face to face.

But that was precisely what Yagoda had to keep secret in his 1938 trial and name another scapegoat as his employer, as was usual with Stalin's crimes. The later execution of Yagoda, incidentally, also eliminated the last potential witness in the Kirov affair. But Stalin's "fingerprints" are everywhere.

Once again Stalin had taken care, with diligent precision, to appear to be free of any suspicion. His theatrical appearance at the Leningrad railroad station, where he arrived immediately after the news of Kirov's death, was for this purpose. To show his outrage, he gave Comrade Medved, leader of the Leningrad NKVD, a redounding slap and had him transferred immediately to the Far East. As a further visible sign of his sympathy, he ordered a state burial for his "best friend and brother-at-arms" and personally stood in the guard of honor. By exalting Kirov as a revolutionary hero, he could blame his murder on a counterrevolutionary terrorist group, thus also fabricating a suitable pretext for a harder line in his domestic policy. Kirov's murder enabled Stalin not only to get rid of a dangerous rival, but at the same time to launch a comprehensive conspiracy campaign.

TERRORISM ON THE ROAD TO TYRANNY

Stalin's new revolution, which began in 1934, was now directed, with unparalleled terror, no longer against the peasantry or the captains of industry of bourgeois origin, but rather against his own Party friends. A tyrant ruling with unlimited power, Stalin now raised terror to a "permanent principle of rule," whereby he intended to destroy permanently even the weakest democratic tendencies still stirring within the Party. He saw this as the only effective way he could rise to sole ruler of the Soviet Union and become the mightiest and most fear-instilling tyrant in all history. In this way he could finally replace Lenin's Bolshevist Party by a new Party conceived by himself, which, for Alan Bullock, meant nothing but the development from a one-party state to a one-man state.

One of the most essential bases of Stalin's unscrupulous tyranny was doubtlessly his unusually pronounced instinct of self-preservation, which guided him in his choice of personal staff. As Avtorkhanov rightly stresses, his rise to an uncontested dictatorship was possible only by the creation of a so-called "inner circle," composed of "Comrade Stalin's Secretariat" and the "Special Department." The uniqueness of this invention of Stalin's consisted in this: for every Soviet citizen, as well as for foreigners, his personal dictatorship was masked by the absence of any recognizable external form of appearance. In this inconspicuous "Secretariat," all decisions—from those of the Politburo to the Supreme Soviet—were made in advance. Likewise the "Special Department," which stood under the leadership of Poskrebyshev, his slavishly loyal lackey, was simply an "unparalleled institution in the whole world history of dictatorship and despotisms." Stalin created this institution as his own political police, not subordinate to the official state police. Its organization was so masterful that it provided him constant surveillance of the comrades, including the highest Party elite. No doubt, he was helped in conceiving this clever institution by his long years of experiences with the Czarist secret police, whose masterful conspiratorial techniques he had successfully foiled in his years as a professional revolutionary.

Since Stalin was convinced that the survival of the Soviet regime depended solely on the permanence and unassailableness of his own personal power, he considered it perfectly legitimate to use even the most despicable methods to remove, conveniently and permanently, any obstacle to his attaining and maintaining that power.

Stalin in the year 1939

His pathological greed for power increased with the passion of an Asiatic satrap, and although his cruel actions all unmistakably display a strong sadistic streak, they probably—at least to a considerable extent—were not done primarily to satisfy sadistic desires, but generally to serve strictly logical objectives. So in the framework of the subsequent "wave of purges," he consciously and strategically had millions of people shot in cold blood or deported to the infamous penal camps, until the only Party comrades left were men who had placed themselves at his service as compliant tools. But even such tractable creatures as the NKVD leaders, responsible for the mass liquidations that he had ordered, were unhesitatingly wiped out when the time seemed ripe to remove them permanently from the scene as unwelcome witnesses of his own crimes. Ironically, he always assigned their successor as head of the NKVD to expedite their predecessor to the other life.

With Kirov's murder, the press, as instructed, began incessantly to unmask "conspiracies" and "terrorist groups" and to spread the call for "greater vigilance." To sufficiently underscore the necessity of such greater vigilance, by December 1, 1934, after Stalin's arrival in Leningrad, 102 "White Guardists" were arbitrarily arrested and executed after quick hearings. However, Stalin was mainly interested in the "far-reaching conspiracy" that allegedly had the goal of murdering Kirov and overthrowing the Soviet regime and whose responsible leaders, according to Leonid Nikolayev's "confession," were to be sought in the so-called "Leningrad Center." As in all later show trials, such "confessions" of an accused person were obtained by the mental and

*Alexander N. Poskrebyshev (1891-
1965?), Stalin's first secretary*

physical torture methods of the NKVD, whose refinement could hardly be excelled. These torture methods were checked and optimalized for their effectiveness by scientific tests on political prisoners performed by medical "creatures" of Professor Krasnushkin's type. This criminalistic doctor, working at Rostov University and even honored with the Order of Lenin for his valuable work, had been using imprisoned criminals for his inhuman experiments since the years 1925/1926, but after 1930 he preferred political "guinea pigs" on which to test and develop the most effective methods of interrogation, and he also developed the most suitable implements and tools for optimal torture. The results of these "scientific" experiments were used by the NKVD in its interrogations to obtain the desired confessions, and Krasnushkin, in return, received considerable sums of money from the government as director of his notorious "Kanatshikova Dacha" Institute—later named the "Serbsky Institute." The practical procedure was gruesome and effective. In the preliminary investigations, the persons accused on falsified charges were subjected to a broad spectrum of extremely cruel mental and physical tortures, sometimes lasting for weeks or even months. By refined methods of torture, each was reduced to a crushed wreck of a man and brought to the point where he was ready to make whatever statements the NKVD wanted, even if this meant accusing himself of the most incredible crimes. Then they were forced to memorize the prefabricated confessions, and only when the rehearsals were satisfactory to the henchmen could they be exhibited in the showy spectacle of a public trial, literally as helpless prey to General Prosecutor Vyshinsky or Ulrikh—two cynical and cowardly hyenas in human form.

It is under such preconditions that at the end of December 1934 the trial against the "Leningrad Center" was held under the "honorable" Vasily Ulrikh. It lasted only one day, ending that same night, with death sentences carried out immediately afterward in the cellar vaults of the Liteyni Prison. The names of the members of the "Leningrad Terrorist Center" were brought from Moscow to Leningrad by Yeshov, later General Commissar of the NKVD, on a list written in Stalin's own hand. The list included, as might be expected, former adherents of the Leningrad Party Organization led in his day by Zinoviev and also names from a similar "Moscow Center." So it was not surprising that as early as mid-January 1935 a second trial was begun, directed against sixteen Party members of the so-called "illegal counter-revolutionary Moscow center," among whom Zinoviev and Kamenev were listed. But since no direct link with Kirov's murder could be

*Vasily W. Ulrikh (1889-1951),
presiding judge in the Moscow
show trials*

established, the accused were for the time being sentenced only to several years in prison. As a deterrent for Soviet citizens, in the purge campaigns against friends and sympathizers of Kirov and Zinoviev in Leningrad, almost one hundred thousand persons from the most varied classes and professions were implicated.

When Stalin on November 25, 1936, proclaimed a new constitution, written in large part by the moderate Bukharin, the Soviet people's hope for improved living conditions was given new fuel. But soon this was to prove a regrettably wrong conclusion. For while Stalin spoke of the "only really democratic constitution in the world," in truth he was anchoring down all the preconditions he needed for his terrorist rule. Actually, on this foundation of absolute legalization of his terrorist rule, he immediately struck a new blow against the former opposition, making it clear to everyone that no one was safe from the death penalty any longer, not even the highest functionaries in the Politburo or in the Central Secretariat. With the introduction of hostage-arrests, entire families, even though innocent, could fall prey to destruction. To realize his plan to liquidate all leading opposition forces and eliminate disfavored persons—whether rivals who seemed dangerous or witnesses who could harm him later since he had used them in carrying out his diabolical purposes—he needed the help of the media to convince the

Soviet citizens that a life and death struggle was ahead and that the masks had to be torn from the faces of "spies and murderers," "traitors and saboteurs," as well as of the "terrorist gang seeking to restore capitalism." In his paranoid delusion he saw himself surrounded on all sides by treacherous and murderous enemies. They had to be destroyed before they could implement their murderous intentions and attempted revolts. But even persons who honored him as their great leader, almost like a god, and were ready to carry out his most repugnant directives were not spared.

What treacherous methods could be used in the process were described by Stalin's personal physician, Professor Pletnev, with the example of Vuacheslav Menshinsky, then head of the NKVD and successor to Felix Dzierzhinsky. One year before Menshinsky's death, Dr. Moschenberg of the Kremlin Polyclinic reported in the presence of Dr. Weisbrod, who also worked there, to Professor Pletnev:

> Strange things are going on in Menshinsky's body. Whenever he changed apartment or servants, his condition also changed noticeably: either it improved or it deteriorated radically. Through my blood tests I became convinced that apparently a slow-working poison was being administered to him from time to time. This suspicion also seemed probable to Dr. Weisbrod, so that he decided to report it to Stalin, who however—allegedly laughing—dismissed the whole thing as pure nonsense. Menshinsky died in 1934, after having been given arsenic by his successor, Genrich Yagoda, which he obtained from the toxicologist Dr. Vasiliev, who then himself was executed in 1937.

This passage once again betrays Stalin's "handwriting."

Stalin's attack on the supposed opposition forces in the state coincided in time with the proclamation of the new constitution. In the notorious wave of purges that followed, the three great Moscow show trials that took place between 1936 and 1938 were no doubt the essential component of his well-prepared drama, with which he drove fear and horror into his subjects' bones. In the first of these show trials, a group of Comsomol [Communist Youths] at the Pedagogical Institute in Gorki, was accused of having plotted Stalin's death, allegedly at Trotsky's suggestion. The confessions squeezed out of the accused by great physical pressure, following the same pattern as the Shakhty trial, provided the basis for elaborating falsified accusations. For Stalin, in Khrushchev's words, "The only [adequate] proof, contrary to all norms of jurisprudence, was the confession of the accused himself."

Such self-accusation of crimes never committed was intended to provide proofs for the prosecuting attorney, but at the same time it satisfied Stalin's pathological need to avenge personal offenses or criticisms and to obtain the unconditional subjection of his rivals under his supreme all-dominating power. Alexander Orlov, a famous officer of the NKVD, who later settled in the West, reported that the NKVD was to use the "confession" of an agent who had infiltrated the suspected Comsomol group to track down, as Stalin wished, a "Trotskyist-Zinovievan Center" as part of a broader conspiracy to oust Stalin and his entire leadership staff. Cast as the alleged leaders, Zinoviev and Kamenev had been arrested in December 1934 and were sentenced in spring 1935 to several years in prison for participating in an alleged conspiracy. The old tried and tested methods of the NKVD had no difficulty, by torture, hunger, lack of sleep, and prolonged interrogations, to make it seem probable by the summer of 1936 that their life would be spared if they "confessed." In truth, however, Stalin, who spent that summer in the Crimea, had already certified their death sentences with his signature before the trial began. Thus Vyshinsky's summation, in which, after properly lauding Stalin's wisdom and intelligent foresight, he demanded "that these mad dogs should be executed one and all," was just a tasteless and hypocritical farce. Disregarding the previously given promise, the accused were executed that very night in the cellar of the notorious Lubyanka prison. Even their relatives, if they could be caught, landed in penal camps or were shot. According to Alexander Orlov's information, Genrich Yagoda, only a few days after Zinoviev's and Kamenev's executions, apparently for the purpose of intimidating the populace even more and putting them in a permanent state of fear, got the order to pick out five thousand opposition camp prisoners and have them shot without giving any grounds.

Even high Party functionaries were shocked by this infamously staged, first, great Moscow show trial. They knew that any form of disagreement, even the most timid criticism, or even any oppositional attitude toward Stalin, would be punished mercilessly by death and that this danger threatened even Party functionaries of the highest political strata. Yet the majority of citizens, who obtained their information exclusively from the state-directed media, were convinced that the regime's violent measures actually were aimed only at real cases of impermissible violations, and that the kindly, wise, and just Stalin, as the sure guarantor of law and order, would intervene to protect those affected when he learned of it. The cult of his person and perfect propaganda saw to it that this bloodthirsty tyrant's credibility remained untouched despite the perpetual state of terror. Stalin was determined to maintain his positive image among the masses of the people. His lying nature and his mastery of the art of dissimulation made it easy for him to do so, especially since he unscrupulously kept blaming a series of scapegoats for crimes he himself had personally ordered.

Next it was Genrich Yagoda's turn to be the scapegoat. Under the pretext that he had proven incompetent in smashing the "Trotskyist-Zinoviev Group," he was removed from his post as head of the NKVD and replaced by Nikolai Yezhov, known as the "evil dwarf." With the support of his later successor Lavrenti Beria, Yezhov saw to the rapid ignition of the flames of the wave of terror that would reach terrible dimensions in the years 1937/38 and that went down in history as the "Yezhovtshina Era." First, however, Yezhov devoted all his energies to the conspiratorial work of preparing the second great Moscow show trial. This time, the defendants were seventeen Party functionaries who, though they had never been members of the Politburo, had formerly had a close relationship to Lenin and, in Lenin's cadre in the 1920s together with Trotsky, had shown an oppositional attitude toward Stalin. Grigori Pyatakov was made the central figure of this trial, although after his expulsion from the Party in 1927, he had broken relations with Trotsky and later attained high honors again in the Party as Assistant People's Commissar for Heavy Industry, given up all opposition, and remained a convinced Communist, loyal to the Party; but the serious mistake he made was that his loyalty was to the Party itself and not to Stalin. That mistake alone was sufficient to have him charged with responsibility for a setback in industrialization and to place him, together with the other accused engineers and higher administrative officials, into a group of "saboteurs." Beyond that, several industrial groups were charged with plotting to murder Stalin and other members of the Politburo. The charges were so groundless that Grigori Ordzhonikidze, a friend of Stalin's from Georgian times, personally concerned himself with Pyatakov's fate and protested to Stalin. However, all he could accomplish was that Pyatakov, if he confessed, was assured of his life and that of his wife and ten-year-old child. The public trial began on January 23, 1937, and ended with Vyshinsky's summation:

> This is a fall into a bottomless abyss! This is a pinnacle, the extreme limit of moral and political degeneration!

As in all the other trials, this time too the promise was broken and all the accused were sentenced to death and immediately executed.

Overshadowed by the executions in the Pyatakov trial, in February 1937 other charges were filed in the Plenum of the Central Committee, namely, against Bukharin and Rykov, who were accused of participating in the Pyatakov conspiracy. Bukharin, however, had no intention of submitting to the extortion of a confession and admitting to a crime he had not committed. On the contrary, he testified with remarkable courage that "a conspiracy did in fact exist but its leaders were Stalin and Yezhov, who planned to establish an NKVD-state that would put unlimited power in Stalin's hands." Both Bukharin and Rykov were deposed as Party leaders and condemned to death before the firing squad, although the executions of this verdict followed thirteen months later, after the last Moscow show trial. Before his arrest, Bukharin managed to give his young wife Anna Larina a letter, which, later, after her release from prison, she put at the press's disposal and which said, among other things:

> To the future generations of Party leaders! I feel helpless in the face of a diabolical machinery that has acquired gigantic power...and is using the vanished authority of the Cheka to palliate Stalin's morbid distrust....Every member of the Central Committee, every member of the Party can be wiped out and transformed into a traitor, a terrorist, a deviationist, a spy.

Actually Stalin, by arranging the arrest and trial of Bukharin and Rykov, had succeeded in ultimately depriving the Central Committee of all power. He now was capable at any time to arrest and liquidate any Party comrade who seemed to stand in his way or to be a danger to him—even if he belonged to the highest political strata—and no member of the Central Committee had the power to object. Intoxicated by this feeling of omnipotence and the unlimited possibilities of a tyrant ruling without mercy, on the one hand, and feeling more and more pathologically pursued by constant fear of removal or even being murdered, on the other, his will to destroy everything that seemed a threat intensified immeasurably. After he had, in the first act of his logically constructed purge campaigns, succeeded in smashing the power of the Communist Party and destabilizing it completely by a state of permanent horror, he directed his second act at those "enemies of the Soviet power" who in his paranoid world of ideas seemed even more dangerous, namely, the hired killers from the ranks of the leadership elite of the Red Army, by whom he felt more and more threatened.

As a first step in April 1937, he had his former NKVD-head and willing henchman, Genrich Yagoda, arrested by his own successor, Yezhov, and in the course of that year he had three thousand of Yagoda's officers executed as undesirable witnesses of his earlier crimes. Only then did Stalin order a large-scale purge within the Red Army itself, to which nine generals in the top command fell prey, after having been accused of high treason and conspiracy, among them Marshal Michail Tukhachevsky, who had proven so highly meritorious in the Civil War. After "confessions" had been extorted from them by torture, they were all sentenced to death in a secret trial and executed without delay. Stalin's bloodthirstiness was shown here in an especially repugnant aspect, when to satisfy his sadistic urges he personally ordered the execution of the Marshal's wife, as well as his sister and two brothers. He ordered the deportation of three of Tukhachevsky's sisters and his seventeen-year-old daughter Svetlana to a penal camp for "endangering society." In addition to this first purge of the high command, he assigned the NKVD to make mass arrests and executions of officers and political commissars in all branches of the Red Army.

Nikolai I. Yezhov 1936-1938, head of the NKVD, shot to death in 1940

A second wave of purges followed in the spring of 1938, to which several army commanders and numerous members of the Central Committee and of the Politburo fell victim. The highly decorated Marshal Vasily Blücher, from the high command of the Far Eastern Army, who refused to confess to something of which he was innocent, was tortured until he died of the wounds. The incredible extent of this bloodletting, which Stalin, in his pathological fear of assassination, inflicted on the Red Army with his purge campaign, can be seen from the facts that Robert Conquest gathered together from *Ogonyok* of the years 1987 and 1989: of the 272 marshals, army commanders, fleet admirals, corps and division commanders, 228 fell victim to Stalin's blood-craze. By autumn of 1938 about four thousand army and navy officers had been dismissed from service. By 1941 a total of forty-three thousand battalion and company officers were arrested, suspended from service, deported to penal camps, or shot to death. For this reason the dissident Soviet historian Roy Medvedev described this "overkill," with which Stalin sought to prevent any possibility of a *coup d'état* by artificially induced weakening of the armed forces, in one sentence: "No army has ever lost so many high officers in war as the Red Army has in this period of peace."

But the "Yezhovtshina" was also characterized by severe actions targeted against the leadership cadre of the Party itself, resulting, according to Roy Medvedev, in the removal from office (in the years 1937/38) of 90 percent of the Party members of the regional and central committees of the Union republics. Stalin's instructions typify the psycho-terror he liked to use in such purges. Thus, he required from each district, in advance, the unmasking of a fixed number of traitors to the people, spies, and saboteurs. Moreover, the number of 1500 executions per district required at first was later set even higher. With visibly sadistic joy he commanded the regional Party Secretaries responsible for the implementation of his order to select two successors, in effect letting them know that if they did not fill the required quota of executions they could expect to be shot themselves. Under such pressure, the unimaginable hardness and brutality with which these purges were undertaken is understandable. Of the 102 members of the Central Committee of the Party in the Ukraine, 99 went to their death!

Stalin, however, intended the main blow of the purge campaign to strike in Moscow. Therefore, he personally took into his own hands the organization of the liquidations to be done under his orders by Yezhov. The lists of the persons to be shot, signed by him, contained about forty thousand names, including comrades who had fled from Spain, Germany, or Austria for political reasons and found refuge in Russia. The climax of the Moscow campaign was reached by the third and last great show trial scheduled for March 1938. Among the twenty-one accused were the former members of Lenin's Politburo, Nikolai Bukharin and Aleksei Rykov, who had been arrested and condemned more than a year previously, also Genrich Yagoda, the former head of the NKVD just a year before, and three prominent medical doctors, including Stalin's personal physician, Professor Dimitri Pletnev.

In fabricating this "conspiracy of doctors," several motives were decisive for Stalin, among which the most important probably was the removal of witnesses of many of his crimes. Both D. I. Kazakov of the Kremlin clinic and Professor Pletnev had directly witnessed the violent death of Stalin's second wife, Nadezhda Alliluyeva; and Dr. Kazakov was accused, in addition, of having assisted the accused former NKVD-head, Yagoda, in eliminating high political functionaries (of course, under Stalin's orders) as well as the writer Maxim Gorki, who had become inconvenient for Stalin. That Yagoda was not acting on his own initiative but under Stalin's orders could not, of course, be brought up in the trial. It was impressed on him all too clearly by the NKVD in the prior hearings that he had to be the sole responsible scapegoat. Accordingly, Pletnev, too, declared in his memorized "confession":

> Actually, Yagoda proposed to me quite openly to use my position as the doctor treating Gorki, who had been sick with tuberculosis for years, to hasten his death by counter-indicated treatment.

This statement naturally agreed with the testimony of the third accused physician from the Kremlin clinic, Dr. Levin, who admitted to having caused Gorki's death "not by using poison, but by intentionally administering the wrong treatments."

Professor Pletnev was, moreover, the eyewitness of private, in part compromising, events in Stalin's life and so probably had to be removed just as a precaution. Among strictly guarded secrets, knowledge of which was dangerous, are some episodes from the chapter "Stalin and Women," which show his complete immorality most repugnantly. After the death of his second wife Alliluyeva, Rosa Kaganovich, the daughter of the Politburo member Lazar Kaganovich, was working in his Secretariat. She was suggested to him by Molotov as worthy of a possible new marriage. And according to a statement by Natalia Trushina, who had worked in Stalin's household for a time, quoted in Elizabeth Lermolo's book *Face of a Victim*, she supposedly had been the occasion for jealous arguments in Nadezhda Alliluyeva's lifetime. Pletnev recorded in his notes that Stalin supposedly complained of problems with potency in his efforts at approaching Rosa:

> Michail Kalinin, also a member of the Politburo, then recommended to him that he undergo a rejuvenation operation since this had worked for him.

Stalin therefore instructed Professor Pletnev to locate a surgeon who was especially experienced in this field. Finally they agreed on Professor Rotsanov, head of the Botkin Clinic, who then actually performed a so-called "gland implantation" with Pletnev and Weisbrod as assistants. The result surpassed Stalin's expectations and, overjoyed at this success, he sent Pletnev the original painting "Christ with the Crown of Thorns" by Raphael Santi, taken from the Moscow Museum of Art. The two other doctors each received an automobile and 50,000 rubles. Since Stalin later discovered that Rosa had already had lovers before him, he apparently soon distanced himself from her. The marriage of

Joseph Stalin with two of his later victims: the Central Committee member Abel Safronovich Yenukidze (left, executed in 1937) and the poet Maxim Gorki (poisoned in 1936)

Politburo member Lazar M. Kaganovich with his family. He was known for his cruelty and absolute loyalty to Stalin.

Stalin with Rosa Kaganovich, although affirmed in Romano-Petrova's memoirs, must be a legend, since no mention of it is made by his daughter Svetlana in her writings.

Other intimate clues are found in a letter of Abel Yenukidze, a friend and former companion of Stalin's from the time of the Georgian underground movement and also a friend and godfather of Nadezhda Alliluyeva. Stalin ordered his arrest by Yezhov for alleged contacts with foreigners and "demoralizing activity" in the Comintern's secret service. Yenukidze, taken completely by surprise, was categorically prohibited from any telephone contact with Stalin, his friend of many years, so he wrote him a message from prison, giving free rein to his disappointment and anger, since he rightly appraised the hopelessness of his situation anyway. In this letter to Stalin, he openly declared that he was not an enemy of the people but a convinced anti-Stalinist; in order to adequately express his contempt for his former friend he reminded Stalin of his numerous adulterous affairs with various women. As Pletnev's notes show, Yenukidze mentioned the kidnapping of the fiancée of his friend Ketskhoveli, the seduction of Sverdlov's niece Nastya Elagina, who was only sixteen, and the affair with his friend Sverdlov's wife, whom he ultimately sent into exile. Yenukidze also reminded him of the criminal affair with Kira Andronnikova, who was unwilling to give herself to him; as a result, he had ordered her husband Pilnyak shot and herself separated from her little child and deported into exile. Finally, the especially repugnant affair with Liza Kazanova was mentioned in this letter: this beautiful blond woman worked in Stalin's secretariat and was engaged to an officer of the Red Army. To open his access to Liza, he ordered her fiancé to be sent on a special mission to China; Stalin had arranged for him to be arrested on the train on the way there for "counterrevolutionary activity" and sentenced to twenty-five years at hard duty in a military camp.

Apparently because Liza still did not cooperate, he avenged himself on her by ordering her to be taken to his country home, where she was to be sexually abused by a few men ordered there. Only one of these men, an adjutant of Marshal Budenny's by the name of M. Akhfilianov, refused to take part in this plot and therefore was executed in 1937 as an undesirable witness. Liza was finally arrested by Yagoda, who was to see to it that she was never heard of again. Nonetheless, this sadistic piece of deviltry later became known, since one of the rapists involved—who incidentally had been close to Marshal Voroshilov—boasted in a circle of officers about how cleverly Stalin had staged "this little prank."

According to Professor Pletnev's report, Yenukidze's letter to Stalin supposedly ended with the accusation:

> And now your lascivious desires are directed even at boys, who are supplied to you by Timoshenko [later People's Defense Commissar and Marshal of the Red Army]....Damn you, executioner, sadist, devil!

NKVD-head Yezhov insisted dutifully on passing this highly compromising letter to his lord and master, although Pletnev, once he knew its contents, urgently advised him not to. Stalin burned the letter even before he had read the whole text and ordered Yezhov to immediately bring Yenukidze to the Kremlin. Accompanied by the Kremlin Commander, Peters, he personally went to the prisoner and former friend and shot him with his own hand.

The knowledge of the allegations made in Yenukidze's letter against Stalin meant, of course, that the lives of both Yezhov and Pletnev were to be forfeited. Yezhov was made the scapegoat for the incredible "excesses" during the purges ordered by Stalin, and in December 1938 he was replaced by Lavrenti Beria as head of the NKVD and would be liquidated in the spring of 1939 after the XVIIIth Party Congress.

Thus Stalin repeated his sly tactic that had made it possible for him in 1930 with his article "Exhilarated with Successes" to pin the responsibility for the incredible crimes during the forced collectivization of agriculture on others and by which he had blamed Genrich Yagoda for the excesses he himself had ordered in the mid-thirties.

The affair of Yenukidze's letter was merely a precipitating event for the elimination of his personal physician Pletnev. The real motive for Stalin's decision to rid himself of this inconvenient eyewitness to many of his intrigues and crimes must be sought in the fact that, according to Sterpellone's report, Professor Pletnev, together with Dr. Levin, the senior consultant of the medical clinic at the Kremlin, on the occasion of a medical examination of Stalin at the end of 1937, openly diagnosed a paranoid psychosis. The third Moscow show trial now provided a favorable opportunity to accuse both physicians of being members of a conspiracy of doctors with the goal of doing away with Stalin and other high personages in the government. A "confession" had been extorted from Yagoda that Maxim Gorki had been killed by an overdose of strophanthin, administered with the help of Pletnev and

Lavrenti P. Beria (1899-1953), head of the NKVD, 1938-1945; shot to death in 1953

Dr. Levin, Gorki's family doctor. Both doctors were also accused of being responsible for the death of the former NKVD-head Menshinsky and of Valerian Kuibyshev, chairman of the planning committee (who reportedly had been suffering from heart disease for some time). To make the discovery of a conspiracy of doctors seem more credible, other doctors were accused, such as Dr. V. Choltsman, director of the Central Institute for Tuberculosis, and the well-known surgeon, Dr. K. Koch, along with the internist Dr. Kazakov, who worked at the Kremlin clinic and who had been called to the deathbed of Stalin's second wife Nadezhda and was an eyewitness of the circumstances leading to her death. According to the dissident Soviet historian, Roy Medvedev, Dr. Choltsman died in a gulag, and Dr. Koch was shot to death.

To prepare the public for the arrest and accusation of Stalin's personal physician, a suitable pretext had to be trumped up. This happened as follows: when Pletnev visited Stalin on the next occasion to inquire routinely about his health, Stalin carried on a telephone conversation, in the doctor's presence, with Voroshilov, later a marshal in World War II, in which Stalin told him that Yezhov held incriminating material against Mrs. Molotov which would really have called for her arrest, but that Stalin had till now prevented this.

To understand the effect this conversation had on Pletnev, one must know that Mrs. Molotov was not only People's Commissar for the Food Industry, but at the same time director of a cosmetics institute, established and operated at Professor Pletnev's suggestion. Pletnev had recommended this in response to Stalin's wish for suitable research on more effective treatment of the aging processes in man. For some time, Stalin had increasingly suffered panic and anxiety about aging and therefore set great store on his facial appearance, undergoing regular massages, facial packs, rubdowns and various baths. Several million rubles were allocated to the establishment of such a research institute and by the highest command the work had to proceed with the greatest haste. At the same time, doctors were assigned by Pletnev to produce substances that were supposed to cause rejuvenation of the body's cells and especially a rejuvenation of the skin. For this purpose, Mrs. Molotov was sent incognito to Paris in order to discover various cosmetic secrets. Of course, it was easy to construe this overseas stay as forbidden contact with Western agents or even a spy affair in which Pletnev could have been involved; and the purpose of the telephone conversation was probably to put Stalin's personal physician into a frightful state of uncertainty. Pletnev knew Stalin's methods too well not to realize that as a witness of Yenukidze's incriminating letter he would soon have to be removed. It did not take long before the Moscow daily papers suddenly published articles with the headlines "The Sadistic Professor" or "Professor Rapist," in which Pletnev allegedly had dragged the Soviet citizeness B., a hired prostitute, as it later turned out, to his apartment and there performed sadistic abuses. Although no one in Moscow seriously believed this story, he was ostracized everywhere, and finally his medical degree was revoked. Before his arrest, Pletnev took the precaution of burning everything he considered necessary except for his notes "On the Blood-Thirsty Joseph Stalin I," which he gave to the nurse Romano-Petrova, who had worked with him for many years.

The detailed description of Professor Pletnev's case should show with what infamous means Stalin worked when he wanted to have people liquidated, if they seemed disagreeable or dangerous to him. The former NKVD officer Alexander Orlov knew firsthand that it was for Stalin a "general rule to get rid of all persons who knew too much about his role or who could remember and perhaps tell various details of his life, especially with regard to the enormous crimes of recent years." How far this could go, his daughter Svetlana describes:

> In the year 1937 my father did not hesitate to wipe out even members of his own family—the three Svanidze, Redens, and Enikidze [Yenukidze], my mother's godfather....In the year 1948 the same fate also swept away my aunts. He considered them dangerous because they "knew too much" and in his opinion they "gossiped far too much." Probably he could not forgive them for having been witnesses of all those events that affected our family, in particular, my mother's suicide [which today is considered doubtful] and the letter she left behind.

Stalin was not present in person at the third show trial in Moscow in March 1938. Apparently he was too cowardly to look his victims in the eye, some of whom were former close personal friends now unjustly accused, plus his personal physicians for many years, or to hear from their mouths words that could soil his exaggerated, cult-like, narcissistic self-image. So he preferred to follow the course of the trial through a loudspeaker line to his office. Vyshinsky—who seemed a rather pitiful figure, compared with Bukharin's masterful argumentation—after hearing the "confessions," demanded the death penalty for the whole "band of murderers, spies, and common criminals, lacking all principles and ideals." As always, the trial closed with hate-filled inflammatory tirades of the chief prosecuting attorney, and the accused were found guilty on all charges. Dimitri Pletnev was sentenced to twenty-five years in prison; his fellow defendants, Christian Rabovski and Sergey Bessonov, to twenty- and fifteen-year terms, respectively; all others got the death penalty. The executions were carried out immediately. Pletnev, too, would not outlive Stalin: on September 11, 1941, after a renewed court judgment, he was shot.

After Stalin, with his methods of terrorist purges, had eliminated so many among the Party leadership, the NKVD, and the military that there was a shortage of capable and experienced personnel in almost all institutions, the intensity of the terrorism diminished gradually in the fall of 1938. Out of fear that the people might discover that the originator of all the indescribable acts of violence and mass murders was Stalin himself and in constant fear of an attempt on his life, Stalin now withdrew from the public attention for a rather long time. From Pletnev we learn that these fears had been especially strong after certain criminal decisions and that in such periods "functional disturbances of the heart" could be discerned. Sometimes, until the final success of a particularly crafty plot against powerful comrades—for instance, the arrest of the almighty head of the NKVD, Yagoda, by his successor Yezhov—Stalin was nervous, sleepless and without appetite for days, and he often had been found by Pletnev still sitting at his desk early in the morning. Only after confirmation of the successful coup could he breathe freely again and fall into a deep sleep without first removing his clothes. When in such situations Professor Pletnev had wanted to give him new health instructions, all he had gotten were annoyed replies:

> Don't bother me with such trivia, Professor. We are in
> a critical phase and must drive the devil out by the
> root and kill him in the seed.

At the XVIIIth Party Congress in March 1939, which was characteristically called the "Party Congress of the Survivors" by Bullock, one could see that Stalin's purges had cleared out a good many of the delegates. Of the 139 members and candidates of the Central Committee elected in 1934, 115 never appeared, since 110 of them had been shot, according to data cited by Roy Medvedev. The leadership of the NKVD was now in Lavrenti Beria's hands, after he had carried out his assignment of putting his predecessor Nikolai Yezhov and the entire leadership team before a firing squad. Under Beria, terrorism, which had proven itself so well in the "Yezhovtshina," now was, in Bullock's words, definitively "institutionalized and made into a permanent instrument of government." The total number of persons arrested, deported to camps, or shot to death during the "Yezhovtshina" will probably never be determined exactly. According to an estimate based on the most recent numbers, published by Robert Conquest in 1990, one has the following scenario of Stalin's terrorist rule for the years 1937/38: in January 1937 about five million people were in prisons or penal camps. In the two years between January 1, 1937, and December 31, 1938, the unimaginable numbers were: eight million people arrested, of whom one million were executed and about two million died in other ways. At the end of 1938, about one million were in prison and about seven million in various penal camps of the "Gulag Archipelago."

The responsibility for this unimaginable suffering of millions of innocent people falls on Stalin alone, as *Pravda* in an edition of April 1988, under Gorbachev, openly admitted with regard to the purge years:

> Stalin not only knew of them, he even organized and directed them. Today this is a proven fact.

The horrible thing about it all is that his crimes cannot be explained as the act of an insane person, but that he undertook them with cogent logic and consistent pursuit of his goal, which presupposes considerable intellect. As Volkogonov rightly emphasized, the world-historical tragedy lies in the fact that in Stalin the intellect he had at his disposal was inseparably connected with evil, so that it "functioned like a mechanical, highly efficient calculating machine" and worked mercilessly because it was freed of any ethical ideal. Alan Bullock sums up the significance of Stalin's purges as follows:

> In a psychological sense, the purges diminished Stalin's ever present fear of conspiracy, revolution, and murder. They quenched his thirst for revenge which raged unrestrainedly in this man without a trace of magnanimity or pity. In a political sense...the way to an autocratic form of rule was prepared. This was done by eliminating the last remnants of the original Party of the Bolsheviks, in which there still lived the memory of the 1917 revolution and the Civil War barely twenty

years earlier, of Lenin's style of leadership, of the inner-
party democracy that then prevailed and the ideology
of Marxism-Leninism....Continuity was preserved because the revolutionary tradition was still professed
and Stalin posed as the heir to Lenin's authority....But
behind this façade Stalin created a completely different party than the one in which he had attained power.

STALIN AS A MILITARY COMMANDER

On August 23, 1939, the world was surprised by the nonaggres-
sion pact signed in Moscow between Germany and the Soviet Union.
This pact sealed Poland's fate in a terrible way, since it contained the
agreement that after the country was conquered by the German army a
part of its territory would be ceded back to the Russians. Thus after the
Soviet encroachment into eastern Poland, not only a considerable territory, but also a quarter of a million Polish war prisoners fell into Soviet
hands. Eastern Poland, however, was flooded not only with the Red
Army, but also with swarms of Ukrainians and White Russians, who
were encouraged to murder Polish peasants and property owners and
to move through the country plundering it with the battle cry, "To all
Poles, fine gentlemen and dogs—a dog's death" But the NKVD raged
almost worse, continuing in eastern Poland in its usual fashion with its
purges, which were just ending in the Soviet Union. Arrest, torture,
prison, execution were the orders of the day, and whoever fell into the
clutches of the NKVD was lost. Even after the conquest of the western
Ukraine by the German Wehrmacht in the summer of 1941, meticulous
care was taken that, as the German troops approached, the imprisoned
Polish victims were shot in prison or transported to Siberia. According
to the Polish General Ander's data, almost half of the one-and-a-half
million prisoners died on the way to Siberia. The most sensational
case is the murder of fifteen thousand Polish soldiers and officers, who
were discovered in April 1943 by the Germans in a mass grave in Katyn,
one of three camps that have since become known—murders which
must be charged to the NKVD and which the Soviet government officially admitted in 1989.

In order to obtain control of the territories ceded to him in a secret
codicil to the Hitler-Stalin Pact of September 28, 1939, Stalin began
his effort to gain possession of the Baltic States and Finland immediately after the occupation of Poland. While the Soviet pressures on the

Baltic states succeeded, they failed with regard to Finland, so that on November 30, 1939, the Soviets attacked. Voroshilov assured Stalin that he would be in Helsinki with his tanks within a week, but the resistance of the Finns proved to be so strong that Stalin saw himself forced to mobilize the entire Red Army to bring the war to a decision under Timoshenko's leadership. Even then it still took weeks before this winter war could be ended on March 12, 1940, after battles with heavy losses and without a decisive victory for the Red Army, but more for reasons of foreign policy. For Stalin the high number of about two hundred thousand fallen in battle was of little significance. More important was the great loss of prestige for his much-praised Red Army, whose command structures had, to a great extent, been destroyed by his murderous decimation of the officer corps, of which his own people became aware with bitter disappointment and total incomprehension.

The disappointing performance of the Red Army against Finland showed alarmingly to what a desolate state Stalin had reduced the armed forces. Indeed, his "purges" of the officer cadres had a catastrophic effect during the German invasion army's breakthrough on June 21, 1941. From the outset, the top military leadership saw clearly that this German attack launched with such force would be hard to stop due to a

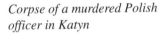
Corpse of a murdered Polish officer in Katyn

shortage of military leaders, and they rightly reproached Stalin severely that the "Yezhovtshina" instigated by him had given the German attack valuable assistance.

Stalin had failed completely because of his prior state terrorism in the years 1937/38 and because of his catastrophic miscalculation of his "ally" Hitler as politician and statesman, to whom the Soviet media ascribed virtually prophetic talents. However, upon the first news of the invasion by German troops into the Soviet Union, he also proved to be one of the most pitiful military commanders of all time. Extolled by the Soviet press as the greatest and most talented military leader in history, on June 21, 1941, he fell into a panic, lost all will to act and behaved as the "very highest deserter," as Avtorkhanov accurately expressed it. After rushing into the defense ministry on June 22 and scolding the entire Red Army as a collection of traitors and cowards, he retreated head over heels to lock himself in his county home, which was built like a fortress. He categorically refused to appear at the extraordinary meeting of the Politburo, the Council of Ministers, and the Supreme Soviet, so that all of them together with the general staff were forced to go to him in Kunzevo. There they had to recognize that their great leader was incapable of deciding on any action, whether of a political or a military kind. Above all, he refused to take over the supreme command of the Red Army in this life-and-death situation, so that General Timoshenko was given that assignment. Stalin did not even dare to speak to the people himself, but assigned even this thankless task

Polish soldiers executed by the NKVD (exhumed skeletons discovered near Kuropaty in the vicinity of Minsk).

to another person, Vyacheslav Molotov. When anyone dared to remind him of his personal responsibility if events should take a catastrophic turn, he scolded all those present with filthy invectives and retreated angrily into his labyrinthine rooms. Not even Beria, as he later reported, was able to tear Stalin out of his fears and to convince him to return from his hiding place and to take over the central command of the army. Completely mindless and pusillanimous, Stalin told him again and again that "all was lost and he was resigned to it."

Astonishment at the behavior of Stalin, their supreme potentate and war lord, was also prevalent in those days in the Russian Embassies abroad. Maisky, the Soviet Ambassador in London, wrote later in his memoirs:

> The second day of the war had dawned, but not a sound came from Moscow; the third, then the fourth day of the war—Moscow was still silent....Neither Molotov nor Stalin gave any sign of life. At that time I did not know that from the moment of the German attack Stalin had locked himself in, was receiving nobody, and did not concern himself in the least with deciding state business.

Anyone else would long since have been shot to death by the NKVD for cowardice before the enemy or as a deserter. At this point the question arises whether Stalin actually was a coward. Boris Bazhanov, his secretary for many years, expressed his opinion on this subject in his book *I Was Stalin's Secretary* published in 1977, as follows:

> It is not easy to give a clear opinion. It is true that in his whole life not a single example can be given of personal courage, neither during the Revolution, nor during the Civil War, since he always commanded from a safe echelon, and all the less so is there any example from peaceful times.

Actually, Stalin had never acted in person as a professional revolutionary even in the notorious "expropriations," including the famous robbery of the state bank in Tiflis, but had always worked only at the planning and organization of such enterprises. That is probably why in Tiflis he remained unnoticed by the Czarist Ochrana.

Today we also know that the same Stalin who sanctioned the death sentences of millions of people, without the slightest trace of pity, had such a boundless fear of death himself that it was forbidden even to speak of death in his presence. He was absolutely obsessed with the idea of postponing the moment of death as long as possible; therefore, he gave generous financial support to Professor Bogomoletz's mysterious and unscientific experiments, believing firmly that the miraculous serum he hoped to discover could enable him to reach a Biblical old age.

The contemptible impression Stalin made at the beginning of the war also caused the generals and marshals to have critical thoughts about the inadequate abilities of their commander-in-chief, although they only dared admit this openly after his death and to refer publicly to him as a "would-be military genius." They were referring to his vain, boastful, and ostentatious behavior during the further course of the war.

When the events increasingly showed a turn for the better, Stalin suddenly began to play the hero before his people. Khrushchev, who was then an eyewitness to his supreme commander's pitiful behavior, later wrote:

> I knew what kind of hero he was. I had seen him when he was crippled with fear of Hitler like a rabbit mesmerized by a giant snake....In the first half of the war, when things seemed bad for us, it did not remain hidden from me that Stalin's signature appeared under not a single document and command.

Actually, according to the testimony of Marshal Vasilevsky, then chief of the general staff, Stalin gradually became able to take over the top leadership of the war only at the beginning of 1943, during the battles near Kursk. Stalin's alleged magnificent achievement as commander in the battle of Stalingrad must therefore be relegated to the realm of legend, as can be seen from an article in the Soviet press, datelined September 1974, which said "probably in the course of the battle at the Kursk arch, he began anew to master the methods and forms of armed warfare."

When Mikoyan wrote on the occasion of Stalin's seventieth birthday in 1949: "Comrade Stalin's leadership assured the peoples of our country of great victories with the least possible losses," this praise of his "leader" contained a double lie. In truth the Red Army's losses of twenty million soldiers killed and just as many wounded represented an almost unimaginable tribute in human lives that had to be kept hidden from the Soviet people in order to maintain the Stalin cult. The second lie was the falsified portrayal of an unsurpassable strategic achievement by Stalin, who in reality had the very least share in the Red Army's victory. Since at the beginning of the war, faced with the catastrophic situation on all fronts, Stalin qualified more and more as a panic-maker. In his fearful despair and helplessness he had already capitulated mentally, so that other men were forced to take over the job of stabilizing the dangerously careening ship of state. These men were Marshal Zhukhov, who took over the supreme command of the army; Beria, who commanded the NKVD troops; and Malenkov, who headed the political headquarters. Stalin himself functioned only formally as the supreme commander.

His daughter Svetlana later tried to explain what must have been going on in her father's mind at the time:

> He had not suspected or foreseen that the Pact of 1939, which he regarded as the fruit of his own great cunning, would be broken by an opponent still craftier than himself. That was the real reason for his deep depression in the beginning phase of the war—the enormous extent of his political misjudgment.

This explanation, however, is not enough to understand Stalin's fear, his panicky sense of doom, and his immoderate reactions toward the leaders of the Army, the NKVD, and the Party when the war broke out, since a psychologically normal person would never have reacted so lamentably. To comprehend his strange behavior, we must reach back to his marked social infantilism and his extreme narcissism that so strangely influenced many of his actions. Such socially immature people cannot bear the least kind of frustration without having their aggressive reactions shoot far over the mark. This was also why no one in his closer circle ever dared joke about him in his presence, for jokes about him amounted practically to the crime of *lèse majesté*. His unusually low tolerance level for frustration was so feared, even in the early twenties, that not even Boris Efimov, *Pravda*'s great cartoonist, ever dared to publish a cartoon of him, although he otherwise spared no prominent Politburo member, not even Lenin and Trotsky. But besides his intolerance of frustration, his "narcissistic notion of infallibility" was another factor that did not permit him to overcome his crassest political misjudgment, since that type of person generally can never admit mistakes.

Inwardly, however, Stalin surely must have been terribly ashamed of his contemptible cowardly behavior and his role as "most supreme deserter," since he was also fully aware of his loss of prestige with the army by his cowardice. In order not to admit his failure, he once again used his proven recipe to shove the blame for his misjudgment on others and at the same time to distract attention from his paranoid rantings in the presence of officers of the Red Army before the war began. So he declared a few high-ranking officers responsible for the overpowering surprise attack on the Red Army by the German invasion forces. These arbitrarily selected innocent scapegoats were then tortured until they finally "confessed" that they belonged to an anti-Stalin conspiracy which caused the army's disaster by sabotage. With similar infamy he tried to repress his own cowardly behavior by overcompensating and declaring any retreat by a military unit to be cowardice before the enemy, even when it was tactically unavoidable; and the same applied to individual soldiers who were compelled by the enemy to surrender. This overreaction led Stalin to respond to news of military failures or necessary retreat operations by giving "instructions for punishment" instead of strategic or operational commands. In such cases, on Stalin's orders, the responsible commanders could count on being "branded on the spot as cowards and traitors" by the NKVD. As retired General Volkogonov reported, many generals committed suicide because they wanted neither to become prisoners of war nor to fall under Stalin's vengeance.

Similar sadistic cruelty marked his command that soldiers or officers who were taken prisoner, then later managed to escape and make their way back to their own lines, should be shot for desertion. He did not allow mercy even for his own son Yakov. First Lieutenant Yakov Djugashvili, in the very first phase of the encirclement of the whole army, became a prisoner-of-war of the Germans and finally was sent to the concentration camp at Sachsenhausen; this was psychologically a hard fate to bear for the unstable Yakov, who in his youth had tried to commit suicide because of his especially difficult relationship with his father. The final blow that destroyed him was given by his father himself; for later when the Germans offered to exchange his son for General Paulus, Stalin turned down the offer on the grounds that, in his eyes, for a soldier to allow himself to be captured was equivalent to cowardice before the enemy. In his hopeless despair, Yakov threw himself with suicidal intent into the high-voltage chain-link fence of the concentration camp. Since he was not immediately dead, the German SS-camp guard, Konrad Haflisch, gave him a *coup de grace*.

Yakov Djugashvili, Stalin's older son, on his capture at the front. He was shot to death in the Sachsenhausen concentration camp in spring of 1943.

This same inhuman command of Stalin's caused hundreds of thousands of Russian prisoners of war, after having endured unimaginable conditions in the German camps and succeeded in escaping alive from that martyrdom, to be branded, one and all, as traitors and deported to Soviet penal camps upon returning to their homeland. Stalin was as unmoved and indifferent to the fate of these men, doubly destroyed by the war, as by the hecatombs of soldiers who fell victim to his often ill-advised and merely obstinate military operations. For, like Hitler, Stalin from his card table had no real idea of the conditions under which the troops had to carry out his senseless orders.

After the Reuters news agency in May 1943 announced the surprising "abolition of the Communist International," Stalin's political pragmatism moved him to redefine the relation of the Soviet government to the country's Orthodox Church, which by his own personal decision had not been permitted to have a top leader since 1925. This step was not intended so much as a reward for the Church's patriotic stand during the great "Fatherland War," as the people believed; rather, it served mainly a foreign-policy purpose. The Tehran Conference, at which Stalin was to meet with Roosevelt and Churchill for the first time, was scheduled for November 28, 1943, and Stalin hoped, by dissolving the Comintern and rehabilitating the Church, to create favorable preconditions to realize his wishes. He was also trying to present as favorable an image of himself as possible to his Allies: he avoided any intimacy, always acted in a courteous tone, and presented well-reflected, realistic arguments, so that even General Brooke, the British chief of staff, whose attitude toward Stalin was extremely critical, was surprised and had to recognize that "Stalin always grasped all the implications of a situation at a quick and infallible glance."

Stalin actually succeeded in obtaining a firm commitment to the establishment of a second front to take some pressure off the Soviets, in addition to massive deliveries of lend-lease war supplies. He participated in detailed discussions on allied collaboration, not only during but also after the war. Important for the future of Europe was, in this context, the decision to establish a "European Advisory Commission" in London at which, on September 12, 1944, a so-called "zone protocol" was signed, setting the boundary between East and West in Germany, which was in force until 1989, and suggesting the Curzon-line as the future Polish eastern border.

Stalin owed these considerable diplomatic successes in Tehran to his skill in drawing advantage from the weaknesses of his two Allies, while at the same time meticulously hiding from them his own weaknesses and his secret plans for the future. So his ruthless, tyrannical character, his distrustful personality full of paranoid delusions, and his pathological greed for power went unrecognized by the conference participants. Churchill, however, distanced himself on several points from various Soviet-American agreements. When, for example, at a meal in the Soviet Embassy, Stalin in a conversation on the postwar order "saw the liquidation of fifty thousand officers who represented the core of German military power as the only means of destroying that country's military strength" and Roosevelt's son even agreed enthusiastically with this proposal, Churchill left the room as a sign of protest. But when Stalin then hastened after him and soothingly convinced him to return, Churchill, too, again became convinced of the kindness and amiability of his Soviet partner, since he later commented on this incident with the following words:

> Stalin has a very charming way when he wants to, and never have I seen him more likable than at that moment.

Apparently Churchill no longer believed that Stalin was serious about that proposal to liquidate so many German officers—a proof that even in the ruling circles of the West the true extent of Stalin's terror, with which he had caused his own army to be almost incapable of battle, was not known at that time. The complete secrecy of Stalin's state terror was possible only by erecting an impenetrable iron curtain around his national boundaries that allowed no news and no document to cross toward the West. Supported by skillful propaganda and ideological embellishment, an imaginary picture thus arose in which Stalin's horror-regime was replaced by the mirage of a well-organized state and a guarantor of peace and social justice that left no room for violence and terror.

Joseph Stalin together with Winston Churchill on the occasion of a visit in Moscow in August 1942

We have a remarkably realistic portrayal of Stalin from those days from the pen of Milovan Djilas, who visited Moscow with a Yugoslavian delegation in March 1944 and was received by Stalin in his country home on that occasion:

> But the host was the plainest of all, in a marshal's uniform and soft boots, without any medals except a golden star—the Order of Hero of the Soviet Union....This was not that majestic Stalin of the photographs or newsreels—with the stiff, deliberate gait and posture. He was not quiet for a moment. He toyed with his pipe, which bore the white dot of the English firm Dunhill, or drew circles with a blue pencil around words indicating the main subjects for discussion, which he then crossed out, and he kept turning his head this way and that while he fidgeted in his seat.

> I was also surprised at something else: He was of very small stature and ungainly build. His torso was short and narrow, while his legs and arms were too long. His left arm and shoulder seemed rather stiff. He had quite a large paunch and his hair was sparse. His face was white, with ruddy cheeks, the coloration characteristic of those who sit long in offices, known as the "Kremlin complexion." His teeth were black and irregular, turned inward. Not even his mustache was thick or firm. Still the head was not a bad one; it had something of the common people about it—with those yellow eyes and a mixture of sternness and mischief.... His reactions were quick and acute and conclusive, which did not mean that he did not hear the speaker out, but it was evident that he was no friend of long explanations.

After reading this apparently objective description, one is not surprised to learn that Stalin again succeeded, in the fateful Yalta Conference from February 4 to 11, 1945, in impressing his Western Allies with his diplomatic skill and his excellent, coolly calculating memory. This conference, at which the future of Europe was decided, was a meeting of the three most powerful politicians in the world: Franklin Delano Roosevelt, accompanied by his personal physician,

Admiral Dr. Ross McIntire, for the United States of America; Sir Winston Churchill, accompanied by his personal physician, Lord Moran, for Great Britain; and Joseph Stalin, accompanied by a whole team of doctors under the leadership of his personal physician, Dr. Vinogradov. The seemingly powerful external impression of the conference must be qualified somewhat, for in reality in Yalta "three men sat, cared for and tended by their personal physicians, and haggled over the division of the booty like three old, exhausted and toothless lions," as Philipp Vandenberg jokingly remarked. In fact, the three were in such poor health that each one reciprocally doubted the others' capacity to negotiate. Churchill later commented that Roosevelt at Yalta had played only a silent role compared with Stalin, which was not an exaggeration if one reads the commentary of the president of the American Medical Association:

Roosevelt had a heart attack eight months ago. He suffered from a swollen liver and was short of breath. He was irritable and became very nervous when he

Meeting of the "Big Three," Stalin, Roosevelt, and Churchill at the Tehran Conference (November 28 to December 1, 1943)

had to concentrate for a longer time. When something was brought up that required reflection, he used to change the subject.

A similar picture is gotten in an entry dated February 4, 1945, in the diary of Churchill's personal physician, Lord Moran:

Formerly when Roosevelt had sometimes not been precisely familiar with the facts under discussion, his mental acuity had made up for this weakness. From all that I have observed here, I must doubt whether he is equal to his task.

But at Yalta, Winston Churchill too was just a shadow of his former self. Even as a young man he had recurrently suffered from bouts of depression—he called his melancholy moods 'Black Dog'—and this mental state had gotten so much worse with the years that his personal physician Moran openly admitted, in the summer of 1944, that he was virtually a candidate for suicide. Moreover, Dr. Moran noticed signs of mental lapses since 1944, and these were also mentioned by the head of the British general staff, Sir Allan Brooke, in his diary on March 28, 1944: "He seems unable to concentrate even for only a few minutes and constantly wanders off the subject." Since Churchill had fallen ill three times during the year 1944 with severe inflammation of the lungs, he was simply not the same man as before.

This more detailed description, in February 1945, of the physical and mental health of Roosevelt and Churchill seemed necessary, because it was not surprising that, under such circumstances, these two negotiators literally stood "in Stalin's shadow," as Lord Moran phrased it. But Stalin too looked unhealthy to the Western team of doctors, noticeably pale and sickly, although he put on his paternal smile at every official appearance. Stalin was a chain smoker and suffered from high blood pressure, which his personal physician, Dr. Vladimir Vinogradov, tried in vain to treat. For like Lenin, Stalin had a low opinion of Russian doctors and tended to distrust them. He had medical examinations several times per year but instead of the medicines prescribed to lower his high blood pressure he preferred iodine drops, which are a standard remedy in Russian folk-medicine, and Siberian steam baths, on whose marvelous effect he set great store.

As to the state of health of the "Big Three," Stalin no doubt had the advantage, and if at Yalta he succeeded with relative ease in obtaining almost all the decisive war aims of the Soviet Union, this was due not only to his diplomatic skill, but also largely to the bad health of his two conference partners. Even the American press sharply criticized Roosevelt's incomprehensible readiness to make concessions and his weak bargaining power. How little the American president realized what had been bartered away is shown by his smug remark to his personal physician, Dr. McIntire: "I achieved everything I came for, and not even at a high price." Churchill expressed himself more cautiously, for, as a "Realpolitiker," he saw clearly that this alliance could hardly outlast the end of the war, which soon turned out to be true with regard to the question of the fate of Poland. Stalin, who came out of that conference as the indisputable victor, had, as the personified embodiment of the Soviet empire, reached the zenith of his personal triumph and of his international reputation. He had climbed up to that place in the book of history which he had been dreaming of during all those years of his sick intoxication with power.

After returning to Moscow, Stalin began in February 1945 to complain of feeling unwell, of headaches, nausea, and a mild dizziness. A few days later, an intense pain in the area of his heart suddenly began, combined with the feeling that his chest was being squeezed by an iron clamp. The famous cardiologist Professor Myasnikov was summoned without delay, but at first the clinical examination showed nothing particular. The clear symptoms of angina pectoris and the spontaneous sharp decrease in blood pressure, however, brought the suspicion that a heart attack was in progress, and this finally was confirmed by a hastily done electrocardiogram. The cardiogram reading, however, showed that it was only a minor infarct event, limited to the region of the apex of the heart. Of course, this illness of Stalin's had to be kept strictly secret by the Kremlin doctors, so that no detail, however insignificant, could reach the outside world, or even the West. The same precautions were taken when a few weeks later a recurrence of the myocardial infarction occurred at the end of April 1945, once again only a minor heart attack.

In this weakened condition on May 9, Stalin received with indescribable satisfaction the records of the ceremony at which the German representatives had signed the unconditional surrender, as demanded in the closing communiqué at Yalta. The Stalin-cult in the Soviet Union reached its zenith when the title of "Generalissimo" was conveyed on him for having brought the "Great Fatherland War" to a successful end by his genial military science. From then on Stalin no longer was considered the legitimate heir only of Lenin, but also of the Czars Ivan the

Terrible and Peter the Great all in one person, as General de Gaulle expressed it. To do justice to this symbolic role, he elaborated the final reconciliation with the Russian Orthodox Church by officially declaring it the state church.

The meeting of the "Big Three" at the Potsdam Conference, which met from July 17 to August 2, 1945, and was to be the last summit conference of the victorious powers, had the goal of regulating the further treatment of a defeated Germany, the reparations claims, and the dismantlings, as well as the establishment of the Allied Control Council in Berlin. Instead of Roosevelt, who had meanwhile passed away, Truman showed up in his elegant, black-striped, double-breasted suit, completely inexperienced in foreign policy and not in the least prepared for this conference. Churchill appeared in his light-colored parade uniform with three rows of campaign medals over the left breast pocket, but with his state of health so deteriorated that in his personal doctor's opinion he "no longer could muster the energy to use his opportunities." Actually in the subsequent negotiations Churchill represented British interests adequately only with the assistance of his successor, Anthony Eden, who arrived on July 29. Stalin, the third of the Allied leaders, wore a white gala jacket with golden shoulder pads and blue-black trousers with wide side stripes. He was the only one to arrive one day late, since, as is now known, he had suffered his third heart attack a few days earlier. Understandably he did not want to discuss this with his two conference partners, although all participants noticed his striking pallor and a certain unsteadiness in walking. In greeting Truman, Stalin offered an explanation, "Please excuse my one-day delay. I was held up by negotiations with the Chinese. I wanted to fly, but the doctors forbade it," pointing significantly at his heart with these words. Despite his recently suffered heart attack Stalin seems to have shown himself extremely fit for action, as we can gather from Lord Moran, Churchill's doctor: "Stalin's toughness and stubbornness have no equal on our side." The postwar order, negotiated in the closing "Potsdam Declaration" August 2, 1945, turned out accordingly.

The fruits of this victory strengthened Stalin in his belief in his infallibility, his mental superiority, and his messianic role in the formation of socialism and thus the future of the Soviet people. But even for the majority of the Soviet citizens, Stalin became a kind of messiah and was stylized to an earthly god, who freed them from Fascist servitude and let them hope in the future finally to be allowed to live more happily and more freely, without violence and deprivations.

STALIN'S POSTWAR ORDER

The hope for a better life for the Soviet people would all too soon prove to be a delusion. Stalin's programmatic speech of February 1946 made it unmistakably clear to the people that, in the foreseeable future, nothing would change, either in the political conditions or in the economic structure of the country. Since after the war's victorious end he still saw himself and the whole Soviet Union threatened by capitalism and imperialism, he declared the continued existence of agricultural collectivization to be as important a component of the Soviet system as the rapid promotion of industrialization of the country. Only by expanding heavy industry, in particular the armaments industry, did he see the possibility of building up the Soviet Union into a dominant great power that not only could equal the capitalist American world power, but ultimately could even be capable of surpassing it.

Such future prospects made it clear to every Soviet citizen that no hope for relaxation of the prior repressive conditions was to be expected and that even harder work would be demanded of them. Furthermore, the catastrophic living conditions of the immediate postwar years 1945/46 were worsening toward another famine. Volkogonov published disturbing documents from this period (which had escaped their destruction ordered by Stalin), revealing a troubling picture of the unimaginable conditions under which many people then lived. In these reports we read:

> In the region of Tshita, carrion animals and tree bark were eaten. An extremely desperate mother of seven children, whose bodies were swollen with famine, killed her youngest, a one-and-a-half-year-old daughter, and used her as food to save the others. Her name is A. Demidenko.

Such reports of famine in wide areas of the Soviet Union which left Stalin unmoved were, on his orders, not allowed to be publicized either by the press or by radio—not even in strongly diluted form— and were for the most part destroyed as ordered. For Stalin in these first postwar years was trying to make the outside world believe that the Soviet Union was in a state of nonviolent domestic peace and social happiness.

Astonishingly, some foreign delegations, whom Stalin even invited to visit his "alleged" penal camps, were naive and simple enough to fall for his deceptive maneuverings, as a British delegation's visit to a women's camp in September 1951 shows graphically. For the occasion of this previously announced visit, 70 percent of the inmates, who were in terrible condition, were removed from the camp as a precaution before the visitors arrived; then the camp itself was cleaned and adapted to suit Western ideas. The remaining female prisoners were instructed emphatically to present themselves as "politically conscious" citizens who were being kept in this communal camp only temporarily. The successful outcome of this deception is proved by an entry of the English delegation of friends in the "Guest Book of the Camp":

> It made a great impression on us with what directness people approached us. Everything is clean. We believe that this valuable experiment will succeed.

Stalin also knew how to conceal from the outside world other severe repressive and coercive measures by which he inflicted unhappiness and suffering on the population by the millions and which once more stemmed from his pathological state of constant fear for his power and his life. For in his mental world, characterized by persecution and murder, he saw even the five-and-a-half million Soviet citizens, who were brought back from Germany and the regions of Europe occupied by the Western powers, as swarms of invisible enemies who could have compromised themselves by collaboration with the Germans. Even the mere contact of these people with Western thinking sufficed for him to suspect them of being "enemies of the people," with nothing else in mind than to undermine the basic pillars of his power structures in the homelands by subversive activity. Thus the long-suffering Russian people were again immersed in a new incomprehensible tragedy. Only one-fifth of the people brought back from the West were permitted to return to their families, while a further fifth was sentenced to death or twenty-five years in penal camps; the rest received sentences of up to ten years' exile in Siberia, where they had to eke out their lives in slave labor and where some died.

A special concern of Stalin's after the war was to avoid having his undeserved "military fame" as Generalissimo, darkened by marshals of the Red Army. For the memory of his failure and cowardly behavior during the first phase of the war remained all too vividly in his mind. A living affront to his bad conscience was a man who had become extraordinarily popular with the people, Marshal Zhukhov, the assistant supreme commander and now supreme commander of the Soviet armed forces in Germany, whom Stalin regarded with particular envy and increasing distrust. In order to remove him from the all-too-frequent gaze of world public opinion and the Soviet people, Stalin had him transferred, without stating any reasons, to a second-rank position in Odessa, where he was far enough from Moscow not to overshadow the Generalissimo's glory and where he remained until Stalin's death. Many high-ranking and top military leaders who seemed to lessen his glory as "genial military commander" were treated similarly.

Stalin was absolutely certain that the ideological authority, endangered by the special circumstances of the first postwar years, had to be imposed with more discipline and hardness for the urgently needed strengthening of the Stalinist principles, so that the Party, which had become anemic through the prewar purges, could again occupy the all-mastering leadership role that was its rightful place. Andrei Zhdanov seemed to him the suitable man for the uncomplaining implementation of such a change of political course. As in the purges in the 1930s, now too in the hated "Zhdanov era," which lasted from 1946 to 1948, Stalin exclusively managed the reins of policy, while Zhdanov, like Yagoda and Yezhov before him, had to take upon his shoulders the blame for the measures ordered by Stalin.

It could not be hidden from Stalin that since the end of the war the cautious desire for change was being expressed in Soviet society, especially among intellectuals. This was particularly noticeable in literature by a "departure from the classical principles." So the witch-hunt that flared up once again in the Soviet Union targeted mainly those dangerous layers of society. Following the same old recipe, appropriate "hearings" quickly "unmasked" disagreeable and insufficiently servile high functionaries of the Politburo or the Central Committee as "degenerate" or "advocates of groups hostile to the Party" and even "persuaded them to make remorseful confessions." In this new Stalinist excess of violence, many family members of the accused also fell prey, and the most ridiculous accusations were enough for a person's condemnation. To eliminate such high functionaries as Kuznetzov and also Voznesensky, whose books were destroyed and who later was executed, it was enough to know that they dared to think "independently" and had not praised Stalin highly enough on various occasions. Stalin still held firmly to his literally formulated principle:

> We will destroy every enemy, even if he is an old Bolshevik. We will destroy his whole clan, his family. Everyone who by his actions and thoughts, yes his thoughts too, undertakes an attack on the unity of the socialist state, we will destroy without mercy.

This wave of persecutions, too, stemmed essentially from his increasingly pathological delusion of being surrounded everywhere by potential enemies. Although no real attempt had ever been made on his life, he lived in constant fear that the majority of Soviet citizens had nothing else on their minds but to depose him or kill him. Despite his total immorality, his unexampled lack of conscience, and his messianic conviction that he stood outside the law and could deal with people however he wished, the memories of his evil deeds were probably beginning to burden him and to foster in him the fear that the more than twenty million fellow-citizens—not counting those who died in the war—who had fallen victim to his mass terror might somehow punish him. One is involuntarily reminded of the furies described by Aeschylus in his *Eumenides*, the avenging goddesses of Antiquity, who confuse the sinner's senses, infusing madness, and pursue him with bloody eyes day and night like hunted prey. Not even the constant strict guarding of Stalin by Chekists, specially trained bodyguards, could give him a feeling of real security. So he had the absurd idea of finding a "double" to replace him on certain occasions and, in his opinion, to provide him the surest protection against a possible assassination attempt.

This story of a "Stalin double," which first seemed like a scurrilous joke, was known long ago to Western secret services, but was first confirmed in Russia in 1991. The January edition of the magazine *Sovyetskaya Molodyozh* (Soviet Youth), whose sharp investigative reporting gathered all the data and facts on this topic, first publicly identified Stalin's former double as a Jewish accountant by the name of Lubizky. Bearing a close resemblance to the dictator, Lubizky was made to resemble Stalin's appearance to a "t" with the help of barbers, cosmeticians, and stylists; and his training made him so familiar with Stalin's personal qualities, movements, and forms of behavior that even members of the government on the review stands on Red Square supposedly had a hard time telling the difference. For unknown reasons probably connected with Stalin's paranoid ideas, Lubizky was arrested in 1952 and deported to a Siberian camp, from which he was freed only after the dictator's death. According to Vandenberg's account, he supposedly had to promise to keep his delicate role as Stalin's double a strict secret, and that is why the full truth first came to light only shortly before his death.

After 1947 Stalin seemed to age visibly. Milovan Djilas, who visited him that year while staying in Moscow also noticed this, though he remarked with reservations:

But in one thing he was still the old Stalin: he was
stubborn, violent and suspicious whenever anyone had
an opinion different from his.

Other visitors also noted that in the last years he looked rundown and
his stride became uncertain. Besides his generally poor health, his
daughter Svetlana complained especially about her father's disturbing
mental attitude. The doctors, who did not go near Stalin without fear,
believed they had found the key to Stalin's mental change and to the
decline of his intellectual capacity in a progressive calcification of the
arteries of the brain.

A clear sign that his thinking mechanism had changed alarmingly
was, among other things, his strange attitude toward science. Formerly
he had always shown a preference for folk medicines and quackery,
but now he felt practically at the mercy of academic medicine, so that
he increasingly showed distrust and menacing rejection for its representatives. In his typical, sadistic way of humiliating or embarrassing
others, he now liked to play the role of antagonizing genuine scientists
and giving charlatans the advantage before all the world.

A grotesque example of this is the great confidence he had in an
agronomist called Trofim D. Lysenko. This dreamer claimed to be the
inventor of a new and revolutionary theory, holding that a person's
acquired characteristics were communicable by heredity—a view in
diametrical contradiction to the classical theory of heredity. Lysenko
was able to win over Stalin, who was completely uneducated in such
matters, by suggesting that his theory was a materialistic, proletarian
agrobiology, in contrast to the Mendelian theory of heredity which was
allegedly permeated with retrogressive bourgeois ideas. Stalin was so
impressed that he had Lysenko sent as a delegate to the Supreme Soviet, awarded him the Stalin Prize, and made him chairman of the
Economic Institute. The previous director of the Institute, Professor
Vavilov, was, despite his fine scientific reputation, expelled from the
academy and sent to prison together with his staff of coworkers for
allegedly having sabotaged the new doctrine of "heredity of acquired
characteristics." In July 1941, Vavilov was sentenced to death for an
alleged "rightist conspiracy and espionage"; he died in January 1943
from the effects of dystrophy [a condition caused by poor nutrition].

A similar slap in the face to science was the promotion by Stalin of
Professor Alexander Bogomolets. This man claimed to have discovered a means of conquering old age and enabling all persons in the

future to live to the ripe old age of one hundred and forty. Bogomolets received approval for enormous sums of money to experiment with his mysterious elixir, which he extracted from the marrow of animal bones. Stalin, who likewise used this Bogomolets serum in order to assure himself of reaching a Biblical old age, regarded Bogomolets as the greatest Russian scholar since Ivan Pavlov, who, since receiving the Nobel prize in 1904, was honored in Russia almost like a divine being. After this "Slavic Faust" died at the age of sixty-five, the Bogomolets legend quickly collapsed. Only in Stalin's mind did it live on!

Khrushchev describes the Stalin of those days with these words:

> Combined with distrust he showed general symptoms of senility, such as memory gaps and an increasing tendency to link the most recent events with experiences from his childhood.

Bulganin added that "gaps in his memory and forgetfulness impeded him more and more frequently, which generally made him angry."

In general, after the jubilee celebrations for Stalin's seventieth birthday in December 1949 his health deteriorated noticeably, and he was troubled increasingly by constant high blood pressure. One evening in the middle of December, just as he was about to be driven to his country home, he was overcome by a severe dizziness followed by a short period of unconsciousness. His personal assistant Poskrebyshev, who helped him up and was supporting him, wanted to call for medical help immediately from the Kremlin clinic, but Stalin rejected this curtly and adamantly. He sat quietly for a few minutes, drank some tea, and noticed that the dizziness was slowly receding and that only a dull pain in his neck remained. The rejection of a medical examination fit perfectly with the increasing mistrust he lately felt toward doctors, which made him feel justified to follow doctor's orders only when they seemed absolutely inevitable and necessary. He underwent medical examinations only in cases of emergency, for example, after his heart attack shortly before leaving for Potsdam. And he also avoided the modernly equipped Central Hospital at the Kremlin, preferring his own hospital near Fili located on the road to Minsk.

His pathological persecution anxiety raged most fiercely in the subsequent period and escalated to the image of a full-fledged persecution complex. No one, not even his closest intimates, was free of suspicion; assassins were waiting to pounce on him everywhere and his fear of death took on indescribable forms. His daughter Svetlana describes her father's condition at that time as follows:

He forgot all human ties; fear began to torment him and in the last years of his life it turned into a real persecution mania. His strong nerves finally failed him. But his mania was not a pathological fantasy: he knew and understood that he was hated, and he also knew why.

Now, like an obsession, his destructive rage turned against nearly everybody. Censorship was enforced with iron rigor and all scientific and technical contacts with the West were prohibited under threat of heavy penalties, on the grounds that the progressive Soviet Union had nothing more to learn from the decadent capitalist West. Professor Bykov of the Academy of Sciences suddenly found himself in the role of a prosecuting attorney against the frightened scientists. Dutifully he registered a mass production of errors, judged and condemned arbitrarily, so that finally even the most famous intellects among Soviet medical doctors were no longer safe from his destructive lightning bolts.

This period from 1948 to 1950 also marks the beginning of Stalin's anti-Semitic campaign, which soon degenerated into a systematic persecution of the Jews. Its goal was the elimination of "Zionist agents of American imperialism," whom he considered dangerous. After the trial of the "Zionist spies," Solomon Losovski—director of the Jewish Anti-Fascist Committee founded during the war and former Assistant Foreign Minister—was executed; Polina, Molotov's Jewish wife, was deported to a central Asian penal camp and freed again only after Stalin's death. Now Stalin smelled Zionist conspirators everywhere. In his eyes this meant any Jew, even if he belonged to the Communist Party, and even Communist functionaries who had a Jewish wife or for whom Jewish ancestors could be established as far as the third generation of their genealogical tree.

In checking out the "ancestral table" at the highest political level, it turned out that of the eleven members of the Politburo, Kaganovich was a Jew, Beria a half-Jew, and the five comrades Molotov, Voroshilov, Andreyev, Malenkov and Khrushchev had Jewish relatives! The irony of fate was that, on laying bare the family tree of Stalin's coworkers in order to unmask conspiratorial elements in their families, he himself turned out to have Jewish relatives. But this did not prevent him from dragging the wives of Molotov and Andreyev, and Kalinin's widow into this artificially created "Jewish Affair," in order to extort from them, under torture, the "candid confession" he desired, that the

"Anti-Fascist Jewish Committee," in truth, pursued the intention of eliminating the Stalinist system under assignment from the American secret service.

The psychic sadism hiding behind the mask of this hypocrite, who understood his roles so masterfully, devised an especially cruel method with which he chose to test the unshakable and unconditional loyalty of his closest coworkers. The method consisted of arresting their wives or closest relatives, banishing them or even having them shot, then slyly observing the reactions of his subordinates. It is almost unimaginable that comrades like Molotov, whose wife landed in a gulag, and Lieutenant General Poskrebyshev, who served him loyally for decades as the head of his personal security force, whose wife Stalin ordered shot after three years under arrest, continued to serve this tyrant with doglike loyalty and did not tell people around them what a catastrophe had happened in their families by order of their "leader."

THE END OF STALIN'S OMNIPOTENCE

Stalin, like all tyrants, was fearful. Indeed, out of fear of being treacherously murdered, he began to distrust even his most loyal protectors, Vlasik and Poskrebyshev, and finally he had them arrested. In his blindness he thereby deprived himself of his most important security shield; for Major General Vlasik, with his Chekists, was responsible for Stalin's personal protection, while Lieutenant General Poskrebyshev was his personal secretary and closest confidant who acted just as brutally as his master and was initiated into nearly all Stalin's secrets and intrigues. By removing these two men, without whose interference previously no one, not even members of the Politburo, could get at him, he himself got rid of the most perfect and reliable security system. For the "Special Department" had also been subject to Lieutenant General Poskrebyshev; its most important function consisted less in guarding members of the Party and the state, and far more in protecting Stalin from any possible conspiracy. As head of this "Special Department" Poskrebyshev, moreover, had commanded an army of spy-agents, so-called Party reporters, through whom Stalin was at all times informed about the deeds and omissions of Party functionaries in the whole country. Therefore, this political police was also a most important guarantee of Stalin's personal safety. Since Stalin was only too well aware of his reliance on the "Special Department," the idea expressed by

Stalin with Voroshilov (left), Molotov (second from left) and Yezhov near the Moscow-Volga Canal, whose construction cost many lives (1937)

Avtorkhanov cannot be dismissed lightly; he felt that Stalin, in removing Vlasik and Poskrebyshev, probably had been the tool of someone else's will (probably Beria's).

Experienced members of the Politburo believed they knew their "leader" well enough to figure out that the removal of his most reliable protectors was the first step in a more comprehensive strategic plan of Stalin's. Khrushchev stated this openly:

> Apparently Stalin intended to get rid of the old Politburo members. He often declared that the members of the Politburo should be replaced by new ones....And presumably he was simultaneously working his way toward later destroying the old members of the Politburo.

This suspicion was strengthened by Stalin's massive interference into the scenario of two political trials abroad, in which Beria's mighty influence on the leading heads of the Communist Parties of Poland and Czechoslovakia was revealed—a circumstance that immediately led Stalin to suspect a conspiracy. Since he was directing the course of these trials anyway, he gave the instruction that, in addition to "repentant admissions" of the accused, statements discrediting Beria and unmasking all the conspirators should also be obtained. From secret agents of the NKVD stationed in Prague and Warsaw, however, Beria, of course, promptly learned all the details about this plot aimed against him; it was clear both to Beria and to his closest ally, Malenkov, that they now could secure their survival only by decisive action in the plenum of the scheduled XIXth Party Congress in October 1952.

In fact they did convince the plenum to reject Stalin's request for the deposal of at least six members of the old Politburo, which amounted to "Stalin's first historical defeat in his Party." Stalin, completely perplexed, now risked everything on one card. Assuming confidently that his followers would never accept his resignation from his function as all-powerful General Secretary of the Central Committee, he proposed to the plenum that they relieve him of this post. Then the impossible happened. The plenum of the Central Committee accepted his offered resignation without discussion. This was his second—incomparably more humiliating—historical defeat.

His daughter Svetlana wrote about this memorable event of October 1952 from her point of view:

> It surely had something to do with his illness that father had twice offered the XIXth Party Congress his resignation.

And indeed at this point in time the arteriosclerosis of the blood vessels in his brain seems to have already reached a considerable degree, which also was manifested in occasional hallucinations and in difficulties with speech. This was probably also the reason why he appeared at the Party Congress only twice, briefly, at its opening and at the closing proclamation. His presence for only ten minutes allowed all the delegates to recognize clearly that his speech had become heavy and awkward. Stalin's daughter, of course, had seen her father's mental decline, and that was why she wanted to link his offer to resign with his sickness. Apparently she did not want to accept the humiliation that his offer was accepted by the plenum, for later she wrote that her father's resignation had "been unanimously rejected as impossible." Dubiously she added: "But did he really want to resign?"

Today we know beyond doubt that at this Party Congress, Stalin at his own request stepped down as General Secretary, and this can be confirmed in the index of the complete edition of Lenin's works. There it is stated under the rubric "Stalin": "From 1922 to 1952 General Secretary of the Central Committee of the Party; after that until his death, Secretary of the Central Committee." From 1952 on, Stalin was thus definitely only one of the Secretaries, while Malenkov took over his former function, which was now no longer called "General Secretary," but "First Secretary" of the Central Committee.

For the first time, Stalin did not take his vacation in the southern part of the Soviet Union, as had been the rule. He seemed to have been worried about his political defeat and the idea of a possible conspiracy hidden behind it. Virtually consumed by distrust, he again directed his suspicion against the doctors, whom he saw as disguised conspirators or murderers hired by foreign governments. One of the first victims was the internationally recognized physiologist Lina Stern, who broke new ground by her research on the significance of the blood/brain barrier. As early as 1949 she was condemned to five years of solitary confinement with bread and water for having cited foreign authors in her publications and for having received letters from foreign colleagues in her field. But the main blow of this persecution campaign was the contrived discovery of an alleged "conspiracy of doctors" in the fall of 1952. It was triggered by a denunciation made by Dr. Lydia Timashuk, employed as a radiologist at the Kremlin clinic, a secret agent of Beria's who "was honored with the Lenin Order for help that she had given to the government in unmasking the harmful doctors." This heroic deed publicized on January 18, 1953, was to be the spur for further denunciations by colleagues at the clinic. However, Timashuk, who was celebrated as "patriot of her homeland," denounced only Professor Vinogradov, a member of the Academy. But it was easy for Stalin, imitating his procedure in the old liquidation of the "harmful doctors" at the Third Moscow Trial, to fabricate a whole group of "doctor-conspirators" based on the "unmasking" of his previous personal physician Vinogradov. Convinced that the discovered "harmful activity" of doctors was part of a general trend, he wrote at the time:

> History already knows examples in which common murderers acted behind the masks of doctors—such as the doctors Levin and Pletnev, who, under assignment from the enemies of the USSR, killed the great Russian writer Maxim Gorki and the outstanding politicians of the Soviet state, Kuibyshev and Menshinsky.

Referring to the "candid admissions of murder" by these doctors who confessed their misdeeds and their relations to their foreign employers, the TASS-chronicle on January 13, 1953, published the recent successes of the watchful state security service, which had succeeded "in detecting a terrorist group of doctors whose goal was to shorten the lives of active politicians of the Soviet Union by wrongful treatment." As can be further read in that article, those involved as "common spies and murderers masking as medical professors" were the Jews, M. S. Vovsi, B. B. Kogan, A. I. Feldman, A. M. Grinstein, G. J. Etinger, and G. I. Mayorov, who allegedly had been recruited by the American secret service and belonged to the "international Jewish bourgeois-nationalist organization called 'JOINT.'" The member of the Academy, W. N. Vinogradov, as well as Professor P. I. Yegorov, neither of whom was a Jew, had proven, according to TASS, to be members of the English secret service. All were employed at the Kremlin clinic, where they functioned as personal physicians to members of the government and the Politburo, as well as to higher officers of the NKVD. Besides having planned the murders of several generals, the accused incidentally also "confessed" to killing the Central Committee secretaries Shadov and Shchebakov, both of whom were, as is known, chronic cardiac patients, and at least Shchebakov certainly died of a heart attack!

This "trial of the doctors" was conducted exclusively under rules dictated by Stalin. Yet once again he tried to divert from himself any suspicion linking him with this campaign behind a hypocritical mask by expressing doubt concerning the wrongful activities of his doctors. His daughter Svetlana's account, based on later information from Valentina Vasilyeva, Stalin's housekeeper for many years, who was especially loyal to him, must be understood in this sense:

> The trial of the doctors was held in the last winter of his life. Valentina told me later that father had been very worried about the turn this affair had taken. She heard the matter being discussed at table during a meal she was serving as always. Father said he did not believe in the "dishonesty" of these doctors, that could not be true....But all those present, as always in such cases, remained quiet as a mouse.

Svetlana herself could not believe this completely, since she knew that Valentina always tried to defend her father. She therefore put the truth of the content of this statement in question with the words:

Stalin's personal doctor, Prof. V. N. Vinogradov (right) in the circle of his colleagues in 1960. Arrested during the "doctors' conspiracy" in 1952/53, he was lucky to survive.

Nevertheless, one must listen to what she reports and cull the grain of truth from her narratives, for she lived in father's house during the last eighteen years, while I lived far from him.

The extent to which the whole affair was Stalin's very own invention was revealed by Khrushchev at the XXth Party Congress in 1956:

Let me also mention the affair of the doctors' conspiracy....Basically, there was absolutely no such affair, if we disregard the statement by Doctor Timashuk who probably was influenced or instructed by someone to send a letter to Stalin—after all, she was a secret collaborator with the state security agency. Shortly after the arrest of the doctors, we members of the Politburo received the files on their admissions of guilt....The case was presented to us in such a way that no one could check the facts on which the investigations were based....When we investigated this "case" after Stalin's death, we discovered that it was invented from beginning to end. This disgraceful case had been

completely fabricated by Stalin, but he had no time
left to bring it to complete termination—to the kind of
ending he wanted.

Today we know that Stalin was pressing for a quick progress of the
trial and had decreed the kind of execution in advance, namely, not to
shoot the condemned men but to hang them. As Khrushchev reported,
Stalin ordered his personal doctor, Professor Vinogradov, laid in chains
and forced by torture and blows to make "spontaneous admission" to
being one of the "harmful doctors." He is said to have literally stated
to Comrade S. D. Ignatiev, then Minister of State Security, in plain
words: "If you cannot get the doctors to confess, then we will make
them a head shorter." Later Lavrenti Beria, while himself under accusation, confessed that all the doctors had been arrested without legal
foundation and under false allegations and had been forced to make
their admissions by "forbidden means." Fortunately these victims, who
faced certain death, were saved just in time by Stalin's own demise.
But by the time these "murderers in doctor's coats," these "execution-
ers of human society," were released from their cells in Lefortovo, two
of their colleagues had meanwhile succumbed to the effects of interrogation under torture.

After Stalin had published his January 13, 1953, article on the "terroristic Kremlin doctors," people expected a "stormy, all-embracing
and merciless" purge to begin. Which "enemies of the people" his
plan of vengeance would target was indicated by his own words:

> Some of our Soviet agencies and their leaders have
> lost their alertness and have been infected with care-
> lessness. The state security agencies did not detect
> the harmful, terroristic organization among the doc-
> tors early enough.

Whom he meant by that was menacingly announced at the end of
the article:

> The Soviet people stigmatizes the criminal band of
> murderers and their foreign masters with rage and in-
> dignation. It will stamp out like obnoxious reptiles
> the contemptible hirelings who have sold themselves
> for dollars and pounds sterling. As for those who in-
> spired these hired killers, they can be convinced that
> revenge will not forget them and will find a way get at
> them and give them an important message.

The "Group of Four," consisting of Beria, Malenkov, Bulganin, and Khrushchev, who held the real power in their hands since the XIXth Party Congress, knew this language of Stalin's only too well and saw clearly that these darts were aimed at them personally. They also knew very well that their days were numbered if they failed to break Stalin's power in time. How this revolution took place is a mystery that still has not been fully solved in detail to this day. One thing is certain: they gave Stalin an ultimatum not only to release the doctors who had been unjustly charged, but also to resign from all his offices. They dared to take such a step only because they had succeeded—probably with the assistance of Beria, who was considered the head of the conspiracy—in first bringing about the arrest of Major General Vlasik and Lieutenant General Poskrebyshev, thus shattering Stalin's insurmountable "inner circle." Possibly the arrest of the Kremlin doctors was even part of this plan, because Stalin thus blocked his own way to the quick medical care he might possibly need. If one believes the recently published statement of a Comintern coworker, Franz Borkenau, then both Professor Vinogradov and Professor Yegorov, head of the medical administration at the Kremlin, had been arrested on Beria's orders with the knowledge and consent of Malenkov, Bulganin, and Khrushchev. Khrushchev's version, claiming that the "Doctor's Conspiracy" had been purely Stalin's invention would, rather, have served to exonerate himself and his friends.

The ideal pivot man in organizing such a conspiracy proved to be S. D. Ignatiev, Minister for State Security. Fully aware of being in exactly the same situation as his predecessors, so that sooner or later he would be liquidated by Stalin, he was quite interested in Stalin's removal and ready to carry out all Stalin's instructions, while also informing the "Group of Four" without delay of any orders aimed against them.

Ilya Ehrenburg, the speaker of the Kremlin team at that time, told his friend, Jean-Paul Sartre, the French author, of the course of events from his own perspective, and this was then quickly broadcast via the French media to the entire Western world. In Ehrenburg's words:

> After the XIXth Party Congress it became clear to everyone that Stalin was suffering from a persecution complex. He was preparing a very bloody purge and intended to physically annihilate the Central Committee of the XIXth Party Congress.

The decisive factor, according to Ehrenburg, was that Stalin believed that a conspiracy of Politburo members was plotting against his life; so he planned to stop it by a devastating preemptive strike. This plan was foiled by the Politburo's decisive actions in a kind of palace revolution, according to statements by Ehrenburg and Ponomarenko, later ambassador to the Netherlands. Ponomarenko reported his version of the events to the West in 1957, as follows: On March 1, 1953, Lasar Kaganovich, in a session of the Presidium, categorically called on Stalin to appoint a special commission immediately to clear up the "Doctors' Affair" and to revoke the order for the deportation of all Jews to remote regions of the Soviet Union. These demands were unanimously approved by the Politburo with the exception of the overly timid Beria. Stalin bewilderedly saw himself facing a plot; he lost his composure and, cursing wildly, threatened to oppose this internal rebellion with the sharpest retaliations. A short time before, such a reaction on Stalin's part could have meant death for many of those concerned, but now the members of the Politburo, knowing that the security police under Ignatiev and the Army under Marshal Zhukhov were on their side, felt strong enough to disregard such a threat. In contrast with earlier times, according to Khrushchev, "when we entered Stalin's room recently, we never knew whether we would come out again alive," Mikoyan now fearlessly told the raging dictator: "If we do not leave this room freely in half an hour, the military will occupy the Kremlin." At that moment Beria, too, felt secure enough to join the rebels; and Stalin lost all composure once and for all. When finally Kaganovich, still angry, tore his membership card of the Presidium of the Central Committee before Stalin's eyes and flung the pieces in his face, Stalin fell unconscious from powerless rage.

This palace revolution, described by Ehrenburg and Ponomarenko, was reflected indirectly in the Soviet press. For while Pravda had, since February 8, been spitting its venom in the daily agitation against the "murderous doctors," "spies," and "enemies of the people," heating up the atmosphere in the whole country to a kind of spy madness, on March 1 the readers were surprised by the fact that now suddenly there was no mention of the doctors' conspiracy and the "Jewish enemies of the people." Once the facts are known, the explanation is obvious: the Presidium of the Central Committee had immediately taken all power. A government statement, first published on March 4, 1953, in Pravda, announced that Stalin was "temporarily" prevented from exercising power by a sudden illness and that this illness was a stroke caused by a blood clot in the brain that had occurred on March 2 in his Moscow apartment. This government declaration, in which neither the place of the event nor the date on which the stroke took place is accurate, closed with the words:

> The Central Committee and the Council of Ministers of the USSR are aware of the fact that Comrade Stalin's severe illness means that for a more or less long time he will not be able to participate in the leadership activity. The Central Committee and the Council of Ministers in leading the Party and the country will seriously take into consideration all circumstances that follow from Comrade Stalin's temporary withdrawal from the work of leading the state and the Party.

STALIN'S DEATH

The exact circumstances of Stalin's death have not been satisfactorily clarified in all details down to this day, so that one still has to orientate oneself by Khrushchev's account, although as a result of repeated additions and changes during the first decade after Stalin's death it must be regarded with some caution.

Averell Harriman, who was the American ambassador in Moscow during the war, was apparently the first person to whom Khrushchev told more specific details about Stalin's death. In his book published in 1959 by the title of *Peace with Russia?* he expressed himself on this topic as follows:

> The so-called "doctors' plot," in which a number of doctors were accused of conspiring to assassinate some leading Communists, was apparently concocted by Stalin to launch another purge, and some foreign observers of Russia have suggested that the men around him, fearful of losing their own lives in another mass terror, murdered the old man himself. I have always questioned this. During one of my long talks with Khrushchev recently, he revealed his version of Stalin's death. Later, at my request he gave me permission to publish it. Stalin, Khrushchev told me, had become far more suspicious, arbitrary and ruthless in his later

years than when I had known him during the war. "He trusted no one and none of us could trust him. He would not let us do the work he was no longer capable of. It was very difficult for us.

"One Saturday night he invited us to his dacha in the country for dinner," he went on. "Stalin was in a good humor. It was a gay evening and we all had a good time. Then we went home. On Sundays Stalin usually telephoned each of us to discuss business, but that Sunday he did not call, which struck us as odd. He did not come back to town on Monday, and on Monday evening the head of his bodyguard called us and said Stalin was ill.

"All of us—Beria, Malenkov, Bulganin and I—hurried out to the country to see him. He was already unconscious. A blood clot had paralyzed an arm, a leg and his tongue. We stayed with him for three days but he remained unconscious. Then for a time he came out of his coma and we went into his room. A nurse was feeding him tea with a spoon. He shook us by the hand and tried to joke with us, smiling feebly and waving with his good arm to a picture over his bed of a baby lamb being fed with a spoon by a little girl. Now, he indicated by gestures, he was just as helpless as the baby lamb.

"Some time later he died," Khrushchev continued. "I wept. After all, we were all his pupils and owed him everything. Like Peter the Great, Stalin fought barbarism with barbarism but he was a great man."

The barbaric terror Stalin had created did not end with his death. I asked whether Stalin had selected a successor before he died. Almost bitterly Khrushchev replied, "He chose no one. He thought he would live forever."

In Khrushchev's narrative it is remarkable that not a word is said about attempts of medical treatment at Stalin's sick bed. Khrushchev probably took this circumstance into consideration in a later revised version. The core of the later story remained essentially unchanged, but now the description of Sunday, March 1, 1953, following the "joyful evening," reads as follows:

> Suddenly the telephone rang. Malenkov was on the line, saying: "Listen, the men from the Cheka have just telephoned from Stalin's dacha. They believe something has happened to him. I think we ought to drive out there. I've already notified Beria and Bulganin. You ought to get started right away." I got dressed quickly and drove to Stalin's place. When we had all assembled, before entering Stalin's room we looked in near the officers who were standing guard. They explained to us why they were disturbed: "Toward eleven o'clock Comrade Stalin always summons someone and orders tea or something to eat. But today he did not do that." The Chekists reported that they had sent Matryona Petrovna in to see after him. Matryona Petrovna was an old house servant who had been taking care of Stalin for years. She was not very intelligent but she was honest and very faithfully devoted to Stalin. After Matryona Petrovna had looked around, she came back and reported to the Chekists that Comrade Stalin lay asleep on the floor in the large room where he usually slept. Apparently Stalin had gotten out of bed and fallen down. The Chekists lifted him off the floor and laid him on a sofa in the little adjoining dining room. After hearing all this, we came to the conclusion that it was inappropriate for us to present ourselves as long as Stalin was in this unpresentable state. We parted and all drove home.

Even in this account, it is immediately noticeable that the "Four" who were summoned to Stalin's dacha on March 1 did not choose to go in to see the patient, who apparently was sick and unable to speak, and they returned home without first sending for any doctors. This happened only later, as Khrushchev again narrated in his memoirs:

> Somewhat later in the night Malenkov telephoned again. "The men from Comrade Stalin's dacha have called again. They say that something definitely is wrong with him. Matryona Petrovna said that he was

sleeping soundly when we sent her into his room once again, but it is an unusual kind of sleep. We really ought to drive out there once more." We agreed that Malenkov should also telephone the other members of the Buro, Voroshilov and Kaganovich, who had not been there at dinner the evening before. We also agreed to send for doctors. The doctors assured us that sicknesses like this one usually do not last long and end fatally.

Now doctors were called in after all, but no one knew them by name and Stalin's recent campaign of revenge against his doctors now turned against himself. Both Professor Vinogradov, his conscientious and highly competent personal physician for many years, and also the head of the medical administration of the Kremlin clinic, though innocent, had been pining away in prison for some time. That is the only way it could happen that Stalin lay without medical care for twenty-four hours or longer on the floor of his room, paralyzed and unable to speak. Another reason, certainly, is the circumstance that no one was allowed to enter Stalin's rooms without expressly being called. Khrushchev confirmed this in 1963 before representatives of the Polish Communist Party and this version of his story naturally also reached the West where it was reprinted both in the French journal *Paris Match* and the German news magazine *Der Spiegel*.

In this version Khrushchev again referred to the telephone call from the Chekists who were guarding Stalin on the eve of March 2, informing the "Four" that Stalin had not shown any sign of life for many hours. Word for word, Khrushchev wrote:

> They did not know what had happened, since the internal communication system between the three rooms, in one of which Stalin lay, is too complicated. Only he himself could open the door with the help of a special electrical mechanism. Since none of the guards knew in which room Stalin was, all the doors had to be broken open, one after the other: they opened the first one, then the second one—and found Stalin. He lay lifeless on the floor, dressed in his Generalissimo uniform.

If this account were completely right, then Khrushchev's earlier version would be incomprehensible. For in that version he reported that on the arrival of the "Four" the Chekists told them they had sent in the housekeeper Petrovna to Stalin to inquire about his health and Petrovna had soon returned with the news that she had found her master asleep on the floor of his room. But how could Petrovna have gotten into this room if it could be opened only from inside by a complicated mechanism?

It should be noted that, on March 2, that is, after more than twenty-four hours, a team of doctors under the leadership of P. E. Lukomsky, a cardiologist and member of the Academy of Medical Sciences, was called in, or rather admitted to the unconscious patient. Svetlana, who like her brother Vasily was not summoned to her father's sickbed until that day, reported:

> Unknown doctors, who were attending the patient for the first time, developed a terrible amount of activity. They applied leeches to the front and back of his neck, they made electrocardiograms, x-rays of his lungs. A nurse kept giving the patient injections and one of the doctors was constantly taking notes on the course of the sickness....All were trying to save a life that no longer could be saved.

Her brother Vasily was, according to Svetlana's account, drunk as always on that day, too, and he continued drinking in the guardroom, "making noise, insulting the doctors, and yelling that they had poisoned, murdered father....He was outraged and firmly convinced that his father had been murdered."

This suspicion can probably be explained by the fact that his father actually had increasingly feared being poisoned by treacherous elements in his closest surroundings and had probably admitted this fear to his son more than once. The possibility of poisoning has been seriously considered in most recent times, probably, in part, because of Vasily's accusations. Avtorkhanov suggests that at least a clever plot had been devised that was to be staged under the code name "Mozart," an allusion to Pushkin's play *Mozart and Salieri*. But such a plan certainly was no longer carried out, since Stalin's stroke could not at all be harmonized with such a version.

Pravda *announces Stalin's death on March 6, 1953*

The interim team of leaders also tried very hard to convince the Soviet people that everything humanly possible was being done to save Stalin's life and that there was no need to fear any harm from the recently so violently attacked "harmful doctors." The March 4 government statement accordingly says that "Comrade Stalin's treatment is being done under constant observation by the Central Committee of the CPSU and the Council of Ministers of the USSR" so that a "wrong treatment" was certainly out of the question.

In the Medical Bulletin of March 5, an attempt was first made to conceal the seriousness of the situation, as the text clearly shows:

> At 11:30 a serious collapse took place for the second time, and it was controlled by the appropriate medical

measures only with difficulty....Later the disturbances of the cardiac blood vessels became slightly milder, although his general state remains very serious.

How serious his condition already was at this point can be learned from Svetlana, who experienced her father's approaching end with her own eyes:

> The last agony was horrible, it choked him before all eyes. In one of these moments he suddenly opened his eyes and let his gaze scan all those who were standing around. It was a terrible look, half insane, half angry. This look passed over everyone in just a fraction of a second, and then—it was incomprehensible and horrifying, I still do not understand it to this day, but I can never forget it—then he suddenly raised his left hand, which still could move, and pointed upward with it and threatened us all. The gesture was incomprehensible but threatening, and it remained unknown to what or to whom it referred.

At any rate, certainly not to the innocent lamb that according to Khrushchev's account hung above the head of the sickbed and at which Stalin is supposed to have pointed! At 9:50 p.m. on March 5, 1953, Stalin's death struggle was over.

When the news of his death spread with lightning speed throughout the land, there was noticeably no real jubilation. The personality cult of this man had reached such a supradimensional level that the comrades, out of deepest conviction, and the rest of the people, at least in respectful fear, looked up to this earthly god. For the people he was apparently at least a "symbol of order, a cruel, relentless order, but despite everything an order." The people's feelings were accordingly varied and contradictory. Many seemed sad and many wept in the streets—which is hard to believe in view of the monstrous crimes he had committed. Svetlana asserted:

> [Vasily was] in a horrible state on the day of the burial and he behaved terribly. Before all those present he cast allegations and reproaches on all sides, accusing the government, the doctors, and all possible persons that came to his mind of not having given father the

proper treatment and now they were giving him a proper burial....He considered himself the "crown prince" and "heir to the throne"!

After the funeral ceremonies, the corpse was brought to the mausoleum where it was supposed to lie embalmed next to Lenin for centuries. No one then expected that soon after the grim exposure of this man's unimaginable crimes his hideous idol would be toppled from its pillar and his mummy removed from the mausoleum as early as the evening of October 31, 1961. Even those dutiful followers who, shortly before had still praised Stalin as their "genial and incomparable leader," soon spoke a different, previously unknown kind of language. A historical example of this is Khrushchev's much-noted speech of June 19, 1964, before a delegation of the Hungarian government:

> Stalin shot at his own people, at the veterans of the Revolution. We condemn him for this arbitrariness.... There are some who betray the current leadership in this country and want to defend all the abuses Stalin committed, but their efforts are futile. No one will be able to exonerate him....In the history of mankind there have been many cruel tyrants, but they all fell under the executioner's axe, just as they had maintained their power by the executioner's axe.

By this last sentence Khrushchev probably wanted to suggest publicly that the former leading Stalinists themselves had a part in Stalin's removal, even if it were only that Beria forbade the bodyguards and house servants in the night before March 2 to call doctors for the unconscious patient for the implausible reason that one "must not disturb the leader's sleep." In this light, the riddle of Stalin's death, given the absolutely correct diagnosis of a stroke, today no longer consists in whether his death was violently induced by poison or other means, but only in what multiple ways his dying was assisted.

The fate of Stalin's son Vasily has already been described. Svetlana escaped to the West during a visit in India in 1961. In the United States, she associated with Lazar Karp, a Jewish immigrant from Russia and the brother of Molotov's wife, who had been banished by Stalin, and he introduced her to the lawyer Dr. Greenbaum, who organized Svetlana's journey to Zurich, where huge sums of money had been transferred for Stalin by his close and trusted private secretary Lieutenant General Poskrebyshev for the last time in 1948. Svetlana ended her life in a psychiatric clinic.

The dead Stalin, exposed in his coffin on Trubnaya Square in Moscow

STALIN, THE PATIENT

*For twenty-seven years I was witness to the spiritual de-
struction of my own father and I observed day after day
how everything human left him and he became more and
more a dark monument of his own self.*

Svetlana Alliluyeva

The medical evaluation of an overview of Stalin's biography en-
counters some difficulties because he strictly forbade any documentation
of the results of his medical examinations. This contrasts with Hitler,
whose blood pressure and laboratory test results, including x-ray and
electrocardiograms, were most precisely recorded and thus were preserved for posterity. The reason for this shortage of medical records is
not only Stalin's pervasive pathological distrust, but also his general
rejection of, indeed almost contempt for, doctors and their medical examinations. He had a complete medical checkup twice per year by
Professor Pletnev, his personal doctor for many years, who was executed in 1941, and subsequently by Professor Vinogradov, his second
personal physician, whom the trial against the "doctor conspirators" in
1953 also had slated for the death penalty. But Stalin regularly put the

medicines prescribed by the doctors into his drawer and would take them only occasionally as he saw fit. Since, like Lenin, he obviously had a very low opinion of Russian doctors, he preferred his own treatments drawn from folk medicine over their prescriptions based on academic medicine. Considering the lack of information this caused and the scanty documentary clues to possible pathological changes, the attempt at a medical analysis of Stalin's mental and physical peculiarities runs into considerable problems. A "psychograph" of this extremely abnormal man is perhaps the easiest aspect to derive from biographical portrayals of his life, while the attempt at an interpretation of physical data can be supported only by the few clues from his doctors and by scattered biographical data.

The difficulties in clearing up somatic peculiarities begins with his left arm which was four centimeters too short and apparently of limited mobility in the shoulder area. Stalin himself officially attributed this "lameness on the left side" to an accident suffered as a child. Professor Pletnev, who repeatedly saw this arm himself, considered the impeded growth and functional curtailment to be the result of an infectious childhood disease he had suffered, possibly poliomyelitis, that is, infantile paralysis. Only after Stalin's death did his daughter Svetlana report that the cause of the shortening and functional limitation of the left arm was said to have been a midwife's mistake. A connection with an earlier syphilitic infection allegedly proven in a clinical examination, according to Vandenberg's indications, seems improbable to me.

At the age of five he survived, with great hardship and distress, a severe smallpox infection that left numerous scars on his face. Subsequent illnesses are first mentioned during his years in exile. Vague reports speak of a tuberculosis of the lungs, which, however, did not prevent him from escaping from the penal camps in an adventurous manner and surviving the incredible hardships of a trek through the endless icy distances of Siberia. In 1909, in a penal camp, he fell sick with a severe case of typhus—typhus of the stomach or spotted fever—and he, therefore, had to be transported via Vologda where he once again was able to escape despite his tremendously weakened general condition.

In the first thorough examination by Professor Pletnev in 1927, gall bladder troubles were diagnosed and this is supposed to have led to repeated complaints due to dietary burdens. Pletnev's notes, however, do not indicate whether the ailment involved gallstones or only functional disorders in the area of the bile ducts. During this examination, a "damaged heart muscle" was also discovered, but the clinical or electrocardiographic data needed for a more precise diagnosis are not provided. For the patient, who was then forty-eight years old, it was probably the beginning of a disease of the coronary art?ries, in which deposits on the inner walls of the blood vessels led to narrowing that impeded the oxygen supply to the heart muscle. In such cases one speaks of a coronary atherosclerotic myocardiopathy. Significant risk factors for this condition are: excessive ingestion of nicotine, high blood pressure, and lack of physical movement.

Precisely these risk factors apply to Stalin in the highest degree. Until the year before his death he was a chain smoker; he also used to consume incredible amounts of food; and he hardly ever interrupted his constantly sedentary way of life by any physical movement. Finally Stalin seems even then to have suffered from high blood pressure, although Professor Pletnev's notes contain no numerical values. Indirect signs of the existence of high blood pressure are the ruddy cheeks in Stalin's otherwise rather pale face, which were observed by various persons from his closer circle, as well as the circumstance that he even then regularly took iodine drops in water, which was a favorite folk medication to lower high blood pressure.

Stalin's blood pressure was first mentioned in writing during the Yalta conference in February 1945. At that time subjective complaints in the form of headaches, ringing of the ears, and spells of dizziness accompanied by mild nausea were first registered. What triggered these symptoms, which are relatively frequent in patients with high blood pressure, must have been the mental strains required for the hard negotiation with his conference partners. How strong this mental stress must have been for Stalin is proven by the serious condition which developed a few days after his return to Moscow. The above-described symptoms were now joined by a persistent intense pain in the heart region and under the sternum which seemed to strangulate the thoracic cage, a typical symptom of an angina pectoris attack. Professor Myasnikov, the cardiologist who was called in, gave a suspected heart attack as the reason for the persistent unvarying heart pain and the severe drop in blood pressure, which can have drastic significance for high blood pressure patients. An immediate electrocardiogram confirmed this suspicion and also showed that it was a minor infarction, limited to the region of the apex of the heart. Just a few weeks later, in

May 1945, a new, again minor infarction occurred once more, and again Stalin survived it without complications. Recurrent infarctions occur significantly more often, as experience shows, in smokers who are not ready to give up the habit, and since Stalin did not follow the doctor's ban on smoking, it is not surprising that a few days before the beginning of the summit meeting in Potsdam in July 1945 he had a third heart attack, which of course, like the previous infarctions, had to be kept strictly secret. No doubt a certain risk was involved in having to undertake the journey to Potsdam nonetheless.

High blood pressure treated for many years with totally inadequate medications and Stalin's chronic smoking habit naturally had their harmful effect on the rest of the circulatory system. Clinically, arteriosclerosis in the area of the blood vessels of the brain acquired increased significance during the last years of his life. Thus Khrushchev described how Stalin in his last years more and more frequently brought up childhood memories and tried to link them with the most recent events, a typical symptom of cerebrovascular disease. Typical of such changes in the brain are disturbances of attention and memory gaps, about which Stalin complained at an advanced age, as well as an uneven, awkward, and difficult speech, such as was noticed by everyone present at the XIXth Party Congress [in 1952].

The term cerebrovascular disease refers to any disease in which one or more vessels in the brain are involved in a pathological process. The most frequent cause involves changes in the blood vessels in the sense of arteriosclerosis, a state frequently found with high blood pressure and leading to a diminished supply of blood and oxygen to various areas of the brain. As a rule the affected artery, or respectively the affected areas of the brain, can be identified by the pattern of neurological failure due to a temporary acute impairment of the blood supply, a so-called transient ischemic attack [TIA]. Such a transitory attack with brief loss of consciousness, following a severe spell of dizziness accompanied by dull pain in the neck area, occurred in December 1949, according to Poskrebyshev's description. Such attacks are clinically very significant because they are often warning signs of an impending infarction of the brain, that is, a stroke.

Such a stroke, then, occurred on March 1, 1953. It was probably triggered by an acute rise in blood pressure in the aftermath of an unusually violent dispute with the members of the Presidium of the Central Committee. He first reacted to their provocative demands by a fit of rage and finally fell unconscious. When the cardiologist, Professor Lukomsky, who was called in with his team finally on March 2, under incompletely clarified circumstances, examined the patient who had been unconscious for a long time, he discovered a hemiplegia of the right side with paralysis of the leg and arm as well as the existence of impaired speech, according to the housekeeper's information, such as is typical for bleeding in the area of the left hemisphere of the brain close to the so-called "inner capsule." The described impairment phenomena develop within minutes, hours, or days, depending on the degree and rate of the bleeding. With massive bleeding, the paralysis on one side and unconsciousness of the patient follow almost immediately and in such a case the condition of the patient deteriorates rapidly.

Stalin's extremely severe breathing difficulty described by Svetlana shortly before her father's death, a breathing difficulty that threatened to choke him and was accompanied by a blue-black discoloration of the neck and face, indicates that an acute failure of the functioning of the left ventricle had occurred, with the formation of massive lung edema caused by an extensive new myocardial infarction, as registered by the electrocardiogram. The treatment measures consisted in removal of blood by means of leeches, as was then still customary in such cases. Besides this, the patient was given strophanthin injections to strengthen the pumping power of the left side of the heart as well as camphor and caffeine to support circulation. To mitigate the extreme degree of breathing difficulty, oxygen was supplied artificially. Since fever and an increase in the number of white blood cells soon developed, penicillin was administered to prevent a pneumonia that often develops quickly with inadequate lung function.

As could be foreseen, all efforts failed. At 9:30 p.m. on March 5, 1953, Stalin's last agony was over. A commission consisting of seven members of the Academy of Sciences was set up to check the correctness of the diagnosis of a "bleeding in the brain, which put vital zones of the brain out of function" made by the cardiologist Professor Myasnikov and the neurologist Professor Konovalov and at the same time to confirm the correct procedure of the doctors in their treatment of Stalin. The findings of this review commission were published on March 7 in the press:

> The results of the pathological-anatomical examina-
> tion confirm perfectly the diagnosis made by the
> professors who treated Stalin. The data of the

Патолого-анатомическое исследование тела И. В. Сталина

При патолого-анатомическом исследовании обнаружен крупный очаг кровоизлияния, расположенный в области подкорковых узлов левого полушария головного мозга. Это кровоизлияние разрушило важные области мозга и вызвало необратимые нарушения дыхания и кровообращения. Кроме кровоизлияния в мозг установлены значительная гипертрофия левого желудочка сердца, многочисленные кровоизлияния в сердечной мышце, в слизистой желудка и кишечника, атеросклеротические изменения сосудов, особенно сильно выраженные в артериях головного мозга. Эти процессы явились следствием гипертонической болезни.

Результаты патолого-анатомического исследования полностью подтверждают диагноз, поставленный профессорами-врачами, лечившими И. В. Сталина.

Данные патолого-анатомического исследования установили необратимый характер болезни И. В. Сталина с момента возникновения кровоизлияния в мозг. Поэтому принятые энергичные меры лечения не могли дать положительного результата и предотвратить роковой исход.

Министр здравоохранения СССР А. Ф. ТРЕТЬЯКОВ
Начальник Лечсанупра Кремля И. И. КУПЕРИН
Президент Академии медицинских наук СССР академик Н. Н. АНИЧКОВ
Действительный член Академии медицинских наук СССР профессор М. А. СКВОРЦОВ
Член-корреспондент Академии медицинских наук СССР профессор А. И. СТРУКОВ.
Член-корреспондент Академии медицинских наук СССР профессор С. Р. МАРДАШЕВ
Главный патолого-анатом Министерства здравоохранения СССР профессор В. И. МИГУНОВ
Профессор А. В. РУСАКОВ
Доцент Б. Н. УСКОВ

Result of the pathological-anatomical examination, Pravda, *March 7, 1953*

pathological-anatomical examination prove that Stalin's disease was irreversible from the moment of the bleeding in the brain. Therefore the energetic treatment measures that were taken could produce no positive result nor prevent the fatal outcome.

The autopsy record, signed by nine doctors and certified by the pathologist, Professor Migounov, ends with this summary:

Hemorrhaging source in the subcortical centers of the left hemisphere of the brain, responsible for the crossed hemiplegia. Arteriosclerosis of all cerebral blood vessels is manifest....In the heart exists a hypertrophy of the left ventricle with bleeding in the myocardial wall.

This autopsy finding confirmed once and for all not only the bleeding in the brain that led to the paralysis of the right side and the failure of the motor center for speech located in the left hemisphere of the brain, but also the fresh myocardial infarction in the hypertrophic wall of the left ventricle, manifestly thickened by withstanding years of high blood pressure. This infarction was responsible for the acute pulmonary edema which occurred last. Finally, the autopsy stressed the advanced calcification of the blood vessels in all arteries of the brain, the consequences of which must have affected Stalin's actions and misjudgments during the last years of his life.

The described findings of the clinical autopsy enable us to exclude with absolute certainty the possibility of a poisoning by a deliberate attempted murder. If later descriptions by Stalin's successors after the XXIInd Party Congress suggest such a version of his death, this probably was done pursuant to a very definite intention. Once Stalin's incredible crimes were discovered, the new potentates could have been trying, for their own rehabilitation, to make the outraged comrades believe that in Stalin's last phase they were already anti-Stalinists and as a "Leninist core" were actively trying to counteract his raging activities. In attempting to build confidence in the new leadership among the Soviet people and within the Party such a hint at conspiratorial plans to poison the dictator could have made some sense.

THE PSYCHOGRAPH OF THE GREAT LEADER

NARCISSISTIC MEGALOMANIA

Thanks to the progress of modern psychology, today we can better understand the psychological contradictions in one and the same individual. Significant is the knowledge elaborated by Sigmund Freud and his school that our mental inner world always develops on two planes, namely, the conscious and the subconscious. Moreover, it is known today that the basic traits of a person's character are preformed by hereditary factors only in part, while its final structure is received only under the influence of education and impressions in early childhood and youth. These original impressions are never extinguished, but are at most repressed into the subconscious, from where they later, to a changing and different extent, influence the emotional world and mode of behavior of the adult individual. It is impossible to understand an individual's character without considering the subconscious factors as well as the conscious ones and without examining the origins of a person's childhood impressions. Therefore, it will be necessary with regard to Stalin, as well as to Napoleon and Hitler, to attempt an overall synthesis of the various stages of development that mark the formation of his character.

If Stalin's childhood biography is exposed to an objective medical scrutiny from this point of view, several phases can be distinguished that were decisive for his later development:

The first formative phase was without a doubt Stalin's early childhood. As can be gathered from the description by his childhood friend Iremashvili, the brutal repressions and punishments by his violent and frequently drunken father left unmistakable, permanent scars. Apparently he suffered not only physical pain from the daily beatings with which his father sought to drive his alleged obstinacy out of him, but also the humiliating experience of an unjustified punitive campaign that had become almost the rule, as well as the feeling of powerlessness with which he had to endure the violent acts of his crude, primitive, and unpredictable "educator." Clear differences exist between the abuse of an adult and of a child, as Alice Miller so impressively shows, insofar as the child cannot live out his hatred against his tormentor. For he is not permitted to hate his father—that is forbidden by the fourth commandment—and basically he does not want to hate him, for he loves him. This paradoxical situation of a "beloved persecutor" can then have an unhealthy effect on a person's further development.

The memory of having been beaten will live on in the child, but not the corresponding emotional content of suffering abuse, which had always been described to him as an educational step necessary for his welfare. The adult will later, as a result of the complete repression of those youthful experiences, tend to face similar events dully and apathetically. The unconsciously stored suffering of their own abuse, or the lack of insight into their own painful childhood experiences, leads these formerly beaten or abused children, by an inner compulsion, to try to repeat their own childhood sufferings later on. They do this typically without pity for the affected victim, because they then identify completely with the aggressor. That is why the most reliable concentration camp guards and henchmen are recruited from such a human reservoir. The formerly enslaved, persecuted child himself becomes a persecutor; even after decades he stands under the tragic compulsion of having to avenge offenses experienced earlier and to project the stored-up hatred onto other persons or entire institutions.

Stalin's friend of his youth, Iremashvili, anticipated this modern knowledge when he wrote:

> The unjust, severe beatings the boy received made him
> as hard and heartless as his father was. Since he was
> convinced that everyone to whom obedience was owed

had to resemble his father, he soon developed a deep antipathy to all those above him in rank. From early childhood on, the realization of his desires for revenge became a goal in life to which everything else was subordinated.

Since his father always stepped into action as the punitive dominator of the family and never showed friendly or even tender sides, the child's mounting hatred was "continual and unambiguous."

About his mother's influence we can only develop hypotheses. No doubt there was no similarly strong bonding with the mother as was the case with Napoleon or even Hitler. We know only that she too had to humbly and obediently submit to the humiliations and injustices, indeed also blows, from the brutal head of the family and that she was forced to witness the child's punishments without doing anything. In the eyes of the child, for whom the mother was eliminated as an ally in self-assertion against the father, she therefore probably seemed to be silently agreeing with the father's rough educational methods—which quite certainly did not promote the mother-child relationship.

On the other hand, it can be assumed that the mother clung with special love to her only remaining son in her otherwise joyless existence, all the more so since with his shortened left arm he must have seemed more in need of protection than any other child. Her great love for her "Soso" found visible expression in her readiness to make any sacrifices to assure him of a life without hardship, by making it possible for him to enter a high school. The boy's self-confidence and capabilities, will power and endurance, noticed very early by his teachers, could, then, indicate that the mother, with her unshakable faith in future important achievements of her son, represented for him the "stronger parental reality," in whom he found his central, delegating parental figure.

With his entry into the church school in Gori and subsequently into the priestly seminary in Tiflis, the second phase that is significant for Stalin's later development begins. First, he had to discover very soon how smooth the transition was from home to school, insofar as the teachers were only too ready to imitate the fathers in disciplining their pupils, and how necessary that was for strengthening their own weak egos. This was made even clearer to him in the priestly seminary, which resembled an army barracks more than a student dormitory. The strict monastic rules with their long hours of senseless prayer, the constant uninterrupted supervision of the pupils by spying, and the denunciations of slavishly obedient monks, who compelled obedience and submission by various degrees of punishment, became another breeding ground for his hatred. Thus during puberty the hatred warded off in early childhood was rekindled, but now, since he obtained a clear image of the enemy, it was changed to the extent that he could "hate freely and permissibly." His stored-up hatred concentrated first on the monks supervising him, but he soon extended it to include other authoritarian power figures, such as the officials and officers of the Czarist government. At the same time he developed a deep aversion for the stupid and cowardly masses which submitted without resistance to all authoritarian coercive measures, whereby he may unconsciously have been thinking of the role of his mother within the family.

In the environment of the priestly seminary, which he found more and more unbearable, he, moreover, received practical graphic instruction on how one can escape the reach of such a crafty and strict system of power, namely, by ruses, lying, and distrustful reserve toward everyone. His daughter Svetlana, therefore, said that even then "from his seminary experience he acquired the belief that human beings were intolerant and crude, and deceived the herd in order to have firm control over them by intrigue and lies." So, even as a seminarian he agreed with the idea of Karl Marx, whose forbidden works he smuggled into his room from a lending library. The key idea of Marxism—to eliminate the corrupt and obsolete bourgeois system of society by a successful class war—seemed best suited to let him live out his mightily dammed-up feelings of hatred for every form of authority and to quench his thirst for vengeance.

When he was expelled from the seminary in 1899 for reasons unknown to us, the third phase of his personality formation began. The commentary of his colleague Iremashvili that young Stalin left the seminary with a "grim and bitter hatred against the school administration, the bourgeoisie, and everything else in the country that embodied Czarism" suggests that he was now determined to build up a clear self-identity. He burned all his bridges behind him and decided upon a life as a professional revolutionary with all the dangers and consequences that this entailed for him, thus concluding and at the same time compensating for the "identity crisis of his youthful years." In this quest for his true identity, he tried to design an idealized image of himself and to live up to it as much as possible in reality. As model for this he used Koba, the Caucasian equivalent of Robin Hood, and he identified closely with him. This imaginary fusionary relation to Koba

was supposed to serve to strengthen his identity, which still was not definitively built. In the framework of modern theories of narcissism, one speaks in such a case of an alter ego relationship, which is meant to express that the respective partner—in this case, Koba, the Caucasian hero—shows no clear psychic demarcation from one's own person, and so is felt to be almost like a twin.

The modern concept of narcissism contributes to the understanding of a personality disorder recognizable by the failure to establish normal relations with the concrete and abstract outside world. A narcissistic personality always recognizes as true reality only what corresponds to its own wishes, thoughts, and feelings. Persons and things that exist outside its egocentric horizon are not considered worthy of its attention, just as anything that other people do is evaluated exclusively in relation to the narcissistic personality. Depending on the extent of the narcissistic mechanisms, which can lead even to the development of a sense of mission, the postulate of personal infallibility and absolute power, subject to no control by any authority whatsoever, can go so far that the least criticism or action that threatens the self-created image of one's personality is punished relentlessly, even to the point of the physical annihilation of its originator.

These perspectives are significant for Stalin's character formation, because in this particular narcissistic person, as a consequence of the action of a double standard, grave deficiencies in judgment and objectivity resulted. Moreover, this led him to create the belief in and idea of his unique greatness and his absolute infallibility, based essentially on his narcissistic megalomania and not founded on his actual achievements as a real human being.

He saw his expulsion from the seminary as an arbitrary act of social discrimination by an arrogant, privileged society. And so now as a self-chosen professional revolutionary, he found the recognition and satisfaction he so urgently needed for his self-discovery in order to build a firmly contoured personal identity, after all the humiliating and degrading experiences he had endured in his parental home and in the seminary. Now he was a full-fledged member of that operative cadre which his great model Lenin exalted so highly as the "avant-garde of the proletariat" and as the real driving force to achieve planned revolution. Such political groups tend to appeal preferably to narcissistic prejudices, because this promotes solidarity and internal cohesion. Group narcissism, in turn, gives contentment and satisfaction to the individual members, particularly to those among them who former

suffered from inferiority complexes and frustrations. By belonging to this significant group, so highly esteemed by Lenin, even the least respected member felt compensated for all disappointments and reprisals suffered in the past. The degree of group narcissism, therefore, always corresponds to the deficit of real satisfaction in the individual's existence. Membership in this group of professional revolutionaries, moreover, also offered Stalin compensation for the perceptible disdain with which he was often treated by Party comrades who belonged to the class of intellectuals.

A fourth phase in his character development was the seventeen years he spent as a professional revolutionary in the underground, in prisons, or in exile. The unpleasant experiences during this period strengthened characteristics that he had already acquired as a youth—coldness of feeling, a calculating attitude, sly craftiness, and especially his distrust of all human beings. As we learn from fellow prisoners, he developed more and more into a loner who avoided all closer contacts with his companions in suffering and became less and less capable of normal interpersonal relationships. He felt best in the companionship of criminal prisoners and other dark existences, which led to additional psychic deformations. Later he was unable to discard the deformations and he remained a rough-hewn, crude and uncouth person characterized by hatred, vindictiveness, and delicate sensitivity to the least offenses or slights—another sign of his extremely narcissistic nature.

A CASE OF NONSEXUAL SADISM?

With great probability the years of deprivation of freedom, in which he was exposed without protection to the arbitrary power of his guards, promoted that malignant aggressive character trait whose foundation was laid in his childhood, namely, his pronounced sadism. As Erich Fromm so convincingly described it in his *Anatomy of Human Destructiveness,* especially significant among the conditions that can produce sadism, are those that communicate a feeling of helplessness in the child or even the adult, for example, fear caused by "dictatorial" punishment. By such a "dictatorial" punishment, Fromm means punitive measures "whose intensity is not strictly limited, and that do not stand in suitable ratio to a specific behavior, but are arbitrarily fed by the punisher's sadism and of a fear-instilling intensity." Such conditions must be assumed in Stalin's case, both in his parents' home and

in the seminary, and especially in the various prisons and penal camps, where he was interned for years.

If one tries to find the reason why Stalin's sadism later took such crass forms, one must consider not just the innate hereditary factors and family background but also the mental climate conducive to the development of social and individual sadism. For we know that the power whereby a ruling group exploits and enslaves another social group usually provokes sadism in the ruling and controlling group. If one considers Stalin's position within the Soviet social system and its baneful spirit, surely one will understand better why his sadistic traits came to the fore in such an unusually crass, stubborn, deep-rooted manner.

Erich Fromm sees Stalin as the prime example of a clinical case of nonsexual sadism. Stalin can boast of being the first person since the beginning of the Russian revolution to have ordered the torture of political prisoners; under his rule the refinement and cruelty of the methods of torture used by the NKVD outdid anything that had ever existed before. Sometimes Stalin allowed himself the exquisite pleasure of personally selecting the kind of torture for a prisoner. But he derived his greatest pleasure from the spiritual sadism of letting a victim dangle in fear and despair between suggestions of his special affection and the subsequent announcement of the death sentence, until he finally eliminated him once and for all. With Satanic satisfaction he assured himself of the loyalty and absolute obedience of the highest government and Party functionaries, by arresting their wives and sometimes also their children and having them deported to labor camps, while their husbands had to continue performing their assignment and did not dare to ask him to release their family members. Indeed, they even had to assure Stalin that the arrests of their family members were justified, although they knew he used to order such measures completely arbitrarily and merely for his private enjoyment. R. A. Medvedev reports that Stalin not only sent the wife of such a high functionary as Molotov to a labor camp, but he also forced the wife of the President of the Soviet Union, Michail Kalinin, arrested and under torture, to sign incriminating statements against her husband, in case the thought ever came to him later to eliminate Kalinin.

This behavior of Stalin's captures the element of his character that constitutes the core of all sadism, namely, the passion "to exercise absolute and unrestricted domination over a living creature"—whether it be a man, a woman, a child, or a whole segment of society. Stalin saw in his power to force someone to endure pain or humiliation, not only the greatest pleasure he could gain but also the confirmation of his absolute mastery. This feeling of absolute power over another being gave him the illusion of being able to solve the problem of human existence—an illusion that someone like him, in whose life all creative force and any spark of joy were missing, desires with particular ardor. In this sense, sadism is, as Fromm once expressed it, "the transformation of impotence into the experience of omnipotence. It is the religion of spiritual cripples." It may be that even the crippling of his left arm, which is supposed to have bothered him mentally all his life, also promoted this rampaging malignant development of his character.

Moreover, in Stalin's sadism, we find yet another symptom typical of his character, cowardice. As Boris Bazhanov, his secretary for many years, stated, in his whole life not one single example of personal courage can be found, neither in the revolution, nor during the civil war, "since he always commanded from the safe rear echelon."

During the Revolution he actually remained, as Nikolai Sukhanov remarked, "no more than a gray speck in the political arena," just as in general he first showed his weak side during that time. Because of his defective education, his lack of creative energies, and his inadequate oratorical skill, he was left with only administrative tasks at "staff headquarters." In this decisive phase he led only a shadowy existence and had no role to play among the leadership cadre, such as his narcissistic self-portrait dreamed of; and this no doubt was a powerful psychic trauma for Stalin—one he would not forget. To avenge himself for this insult and abasement which burned inextinguishably in his soul, he merely had to wait patiently for the right moment to come. Patience was one thing he had of necessity learned in the hard years of his Siberian exile, and waiting for the best opportunity to achieve his goals virtually became Stalin's trademark. Not until the end of 1929 did he think the favorable moment had arrived to avenge himself for past insults and to lay the ground for the future Stalin cult by a drastic revision of history with falsification of sources and destruction of documents.

From then on, too, his inferiority complex toward the leading intellectuals of the Party began to recede more and more, and the seeds of his plan were already germinating secretly to remove his most dangerous rivals who might someday challenge him for his leading position as General Secretary. Above all, by banishing Trotsky, he saw to it that this dominant figure during the Communist seizure of power was relegated to the realm of shadows and that, besides Lenin, the leading role in the buildup of Communist rule was ascribed to himself alone.

He also sought to compensate for the narcissistic offense to his person during, and immediately after, the Revolution, by seeking a way to outdo even his former model, Lenin, by initiating a "Third Revolution" in the form of the coercive agricultural collectivization and the industrialization of the country, during the years 1929 to 1933. This "Third Revolution" outshadowed anything that had ever happened before, not only by the incredible brutality of the methods applied, but also by the enormous revolutionary transformation of Soviet society.

The "Ukrainian Famine Holocaust" of the years 1932/33, ordered and organized by Stalin, whose horrible extent first became known to the world only a few years ago, when the secret files of the German foreign office were opened, shows in a shocking manner the destructive, criminal characteristics of this monster. Millions of Ukrainians fell victim to what was probably the worst genocide in history. It is practically incomprehensible that by threatening drastic punishments Stalin was able to keep this raging series of murders among his own population secret, not only from foreign countries, but also from the Soviet citizens. Apparently, Stalin was also able to convince even those who, day after day, were eyewitnesses of these horrors, including even cannibalism, of the necessity of these draconian measures. Lev Kopelev, who saw these gruesome scenes with his own eyes and who is a man of intelligence, wrote:

> I did not dare weaken and feel pity. We were performing a historically necessary deed. We were fulfilling a revolutionary duty. We were supplying the fatherland with bread.

This justification shows how strongly the Soviet people were caught in Stalin's web of lies, after having fallen prey to his propagandistic tricks and treachery. This explains why Pasternak designated as one of the most important elements in Stalin's policy "the inhuman power of the lie." In fact, deception and treachery had long since become second nature to him; since he exercised his power always only from the background and avoided open confrontation, even during the bloody experiment of his brutal agrarian revolution, he was able to pose as a moderate and compromising figure, who was always trying to act with good intentions and always keeping his eye on the interests of the Party, the welfare of the people, and Lenin's socialist principles. Only on this basis was it possible to stage the horrible spectacle of a "secret genocide," without damaging his image as the great leader of his people.

The planning and implementation of such a diabolical enterprise, however, also required a person, such as Stalin, who had the requisite criminal traits in his character as if focused through a magnifying glass. His abysmal contempt for human beings, his unexampled ruthlessness, the complete lack of any pity, and the cold-blooded cruelty, which were fed by his deep-rooted hatred of everybody, were characteristics that predestined him to use even the most unscrupulous means of power to achieve his objectives. His narcissistic belief in his historical task led to a growing sense of mission that not only became a central instrument of his exercise of power via the "personality cult," but also gave him the feeling of being entitled to act beyond the usual laws. His corrupted, internalized value system made him immune to any kind of guilt or pity, so that he thought he could pursue his longing for absolute supremacy without restriction—a typical manifestation of his nonsexual sadism.

THE PARANOID PERSONALITY STRUCTURE

In contrast with Hitler, Stalin lacked all charismatic talents to secure a loyal following; so, basing himself on historical models such as Ivan the Terrible, he preferred to keep the Soviet citizens, in particular the political power apparatus itself, under constant fear and horror. With his crafty art of mental sadism, he put his closer circle under such pressure that ultimately just about no one felt safe from his unpredictable moods, which could mean physical annihilation. Khrushchev illustrated this in his memoirs with the words:

> When we were called into Stalin's room, we really
> never knew whether we would ever come out alive.

According to Stalin's motto that there is no trust in politics, his own distrust of each and everyone grew and developed into a regular persecution complex.

The first doctor to diagnose Stalin as having paranoia was Professor Bekhterev, a neurologist working in Leningrad, who, after visiting Stalin in the framework of an international congress in Moscow, at the end of December 1927, told his observations to his assistant Dr. Mnukhen and pointed out that Stalin definitely was suffering from paranoia, and that a "dangerous man was at the head of the Soviet Union." The circumstance, that Professor Bekhterev died of a sudden illness in his hotel before leaving Moscow, points to Stalin's typical handwriting, although as always no evidence was found for such an assumption. Bekhterev's accurate diagnosis, which was confirmed by Professor Pletnev and Dr. Levin in 1937, was presented in detail by the Soviet psychiatrist, Dr. E. A. Litshko, in the Russian journal *Literaturnaya Gazeta* of September 1988. Litshko added to his finding by pointing out that waves of a paranoid psychosis, as a rule, are triggered by various pressures and unusual mental situations and typically display a periodic pattern. Examining Stalin's biographical developments, Litshko arrived at the hypothesis that Stalin had a first wave of paranoia after the "dekulakization" program of 1929/30, a second one before the start of the great "purge" of the Party apparatus and army leadership in 1936/37. Probably, as Litshko says, "there was another wave the moment the war began, when he *de facto* gave up his leadership of the government." It is also virtually certain that a wave of paranoia began shortly before his death in connection with the "doctors' conspiracy."

Alan Bullock rightly points out that in Stalin's case—as in Hitler's—it cannot have been a matter of an organic psychiatric disease in the framework of a genuine schizophrenia, but rather of a paranoid personality structure, and that he accordingly must be held accountable for absolutely all his actions. In the view of current psychiatry, what is involved in a paranoid personality is a "systematically elaborated and unshakable delusionary system" that first manifests itself in middle age. Since this delusionary system is strictly separated from all other cognitive functions, the personality retains complete vital functions and can deal appropriately with all necessary demands of life. The famous psychiatrist Kraft-Ebing pointed out that in a paranoid psychosis, along with a delirious aspect, a "lucid" stage can also be observed, in which the affected person displays inconspicuous, normal behavior and arouses no suspicion among his associates.

The most prominent feature of a paranoid psychosis is a persecution complex, expressed in pathological distrust and finally leading to an *idée fixe* of being surrounded everywhere by enemies and traitors. In Stalin, the paranoid delusions went so far that ultimately he liquidated almost all his former fellow strugglers, including those in top positions, under the pretext of conspiratorial activities and terrorist plots. His notorious "waves of purges" did not spare former friends and even members of his own family. In many cases, to have known "too much" about Stalin's past was enough to target a person for victimization. His mounting fear of an attempt on his life sprouted grotesque blossoms: his dacha was remodeled into a veritable fortress, where he slept behind an armored door that could be opened only from inside by a complicated mechanism and surrounded by a vast number of Chekist guards, whom in his distrust he ordered changed suddenly at the most impossible hours. He always carried a pistol, which lay under his pillow at night. His short route to the Kremlin was lined by hundreds of secret police, and he always used a different one of five swift limousines, whose windows were shielded from outside view by gray curtains, so that his own guards could not know which of the cars he had boarded. His food had to be prepared in special kitchens under strictest surveillance and had to be analyzed before serving by an especially trained toxicologist for possible harmful substances or poisons. Finally even a double for Stalin was installed to exclude possible dangers with certainty by his appearance on certain occasions.

Although he probably was never plagued by moral qualms about all his crimes, this extreme persecution mania probably did stand in some connection with the fear that an avenger's arm could someday punish him for his millions of murders.

Certainly another factor was that Stalin again and again recalled the centuries-old tradition of political conspiracies in Russia's history, and for that reason, as a precaution, on the least suspicion of a plot against him, he had the supposed "conspirators" eliminated. In order to shield off his fixed delusionary system, he had to have the rightness of his paranoid suspicions confirmed by the "candid" confessions of the condemned persons, who were generally completely innocent. At the same time through the staged show trials in which anyone could be implicated, he experienced the sadistic satisfaction of having shown once again that he was the master of life and death over his fellow citizens. The power-madness fits perfectly into the profile of an extremely paranoid personality.

In addition to his power-madness and his persecution complex, Stalin also had megalomania, a third characteristic trait of a paranoid personality. Like Hitler, Stalin too lived under the delusion of "being an individual who towered alone above his surrounding world in intellectual power." At the zenith of the Stalin cult, the Party made Stalin a "superman with godlike supernatural qualities, a man who allegedly knows everything, sees everything, thinks for everyone, can do everything and is infallible in his whole behavior." This glorification is not simply the product of fanatical, believing worshippers; Stalin himself wrote about Stalin in such tones in his *Short Biography*. In this self-description he calls himself the great theoretician, the leading power

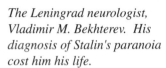

The Leningrad neurologist,
Vladimir M. Bekhterev. His
diagnosis of Stalin's paranoia
cost him his life.

of the Party and the state, the genius who developed the advanced Soviet military science, the field commander with genial insight and the master of military operations. This self-description illustrated better than any scientific treatise what is understood in medicine as "delusionary intellectual megalomania." In the last years of Stalin's life, his megalomania rose to such a crescendo that in 1949 he instructed Soviet historians systematically to attribute to the Soviet state, with which he totally identified himself, primacy in all important technical and other scientific achievements of this century, including the "discovery of the radio." In his megalomania and his infantile feelings of omnipotence he had by that time completely lost sight of the fact that by such instructions he was exposing himself to ridicule before the world.

Stalin's megalomania was not based primarily on metaphysical contents but purely and simply on his delusion of power. Convinced that he had been selected for a historically unique role because of his extraordinary abilities, he saw himself forced to fulfill this task of becoming the absolute ruler of the whole Soviet Union, so that the transformation of the Bolshevism, constructed by Lenin, into a Stalinism based on his own megalomanic ideas, became inevitable. This plan was in complete accord with his megalomanic and power-crazed autistic thinking and his extremely narcissistic personality structure. In a world completely detached from reality, such persons habitually concentrate their entire care and attention upon their own person and have long since lost the ability to really see other persons. To provide a suitable ideological foundation for this role of "Vozhd," that is, "Leader," the *Short Biography* of the "Leader" written by himself was published and declared mandatory reading, not only for all Party members, but also in all universities of the land. By the establishment of that kind of perfect personality cult on an oriental pattern, the possibility of any free exchange of opinions—which had still been exalted under Lenin—was repressed forever and the unity of the Party demanded by Stalin was equivalent to uncontradicting obedience to his directives and total submission to the arbitrary rule of its "Leader." This coupling of megalomania and greed for power in a paranoid personality, so dangerous to the state and the citizens of the country, underwent an additional disastrous culmination through Stalin's extreme nonsexual sadism, which made his total power over people an exhilarating experience and led him to inflict unspeakable suffering on millions of human beings.

It sounds like a contradiction that this highly stylized "superman" showed himself to be completely helpless at the most critical phase of the Soviet Union's existence, the German invasion in June 1941, when he capitulated mentally in his fear and despair. Seized by panic, he crawled into the labyrinthine protective rooms of his dacha during the first days of the war, but not without first having accused the officers of the Red Army, one and all, of treason and cowardice. This latter behavior is a typical form of defense mechanism of a paranoid personality, namely, to ascribe to others, by projection, the errors and defects it did not want to tolerate in itself. Stalin was in this way trying to justify his cowardly behavior and his betrayal of the people in his own eyes, and in those of his immediate circle, by accusing the army leaders of this shameful behavior. It seems important to point out that cowardice is an essential element in the broad spectrum of sadism.

Stalin, incidentally, was not merely cowardly—no one was permitted to speak of death in his presence—but also obsequious, a trait which again typically fits into the sadism syndrome and is most distinctly manifested in his uncritical devotion and accommodation to Lenin during and after the Revolution. Because of the close relationship between sadism and masochism, one should perhaps really speak rather of a sadomasochistic character, even when in a particular person one or other of the two aspects is dominant. Erich Fromm also calls the sadomasochist an "authoritarian character" when the psychological side of his character structure is related to his political attitude. As a rule, people who are politically impressive as "authoritarian characters" display the sadomasochistic elements of their character, on the one hand by their wish to dominate their subordinates, and on the other by their obsequious behavior toward their superiors.

Like every paranoid personality, Stalin reacted very sensitively to his shameful cowardly behavior and his general incapacity to act during the first period of World War II, since these defects impaired his self-respect and tarnished the narcissistic self-image he had created. To prove to his people that the victory was due to himself alone and to his "genial performance as a military commander," he decided upon an overreaction. Immediately after the war he removed from positions of leadership those persons who really had earned the military victory and the stabilization of the ship of state, which had been endangered by the storm of war—above all, Marshal Zhukhov and Malenkov—and he transferred them to regions far from Moscow. He also demonstrated his hardness and contempt for cowardice before the enemy—again a typical projection mechanism—by the order to deport to Siberian penal camps hundreds of thousands of prisoners of war brought back from German camps, since in battle they had preferred captivity to death.

These unjust overreactions were the expression of his intense intolerance of frustration, a trait which criminological analyses frequently find to be the key to understanding the deviant behavior of criminals. What this means is the incapacity to endure disappointments, failures, insults, or humiliations without excessive reactions. People with intolerance of frustrations are therefore always inclined to aggressive actions. This is one of the typical traits of socially immature people, among whom Stalin must be ranked. His "lack of social contacts" was thus one more thing that contributed to his aggressiveness.

In 1949 a new wave of Stalin's paranoia triggered the second great "wave of purges," in which his obsessive urge for destruction was aimed at just about everybody. In his persecution mania he began to see "Zionist agents" everywhere, and with the systematic persecution of the Jews, which now began, he demanded even of his highest functionaries a "table of ancestors" down to the third degree of their family tree. Family members of the highest Politburo cadre fell victim to his terrorist rage, and it became clear to his closest coworkers that Stalin, in his fear of dangerous rivals, was now about to get rid even of his old Politburo members. The only thing that prevented this, and also prevented the liquidation of the "doctor conspirators," already under arrest in the fall of 1952, was that Stalin died first, just in time.

Dimitri Volkogonov wrote:

> At the dying man's bedside, the people's tragedy ended, even though this fact was to be recognized only later. A tragedy that was inseparably linked with this man's life. It seemed then as if his death were the people's tragedy, but then the people came to understand that the crimes of his life were the real tragedy.

Since his death, Stalin's empire has disintegrated; freedom and democracy now have a chance, even in Russian society—what remains is the memory of millions of innocent victims of Stalinism and horror at a man whose life was filled with contempt for, and destruction of, human lives.

EPILOGUE

The supreme commander should, however, be intrinsically just and yet also humane. This task is therefore the most difficult of all; indeed, its perfect solution is impossible: out of such crooked wood as man is made of, no carpenter can make something perfectly straight. Only the approximation to this idea is imposed on us by nature.

Immanual Kant
Ideas for a Universal History in a Cosmopolitan Sense, 1784

Written six years before the outbreak of the French Revolution, these prophetic and yet thoroughly skeptical words of the great philosopher are, nonetheless, also vibrant with hope and confidence that, despite all man's weaknesses, it will be possible in the future to find personalities to govern who will not misuse their freedom. But the course of world history in these last two hundred years seems to have proven Kant wrong; indeed, the anticipated "approximation" to the ideal he postulated has threatened to change into its opposite: the specter of nationalism and new totalitarian ideologies have led to a previously unknown political radicalization of broad circles of the population; a propaganda machine operating with all means and tricks had built up the myth of self-appointed redeemer figures, who brought only misery and death to their countries. The names Napoleon, Hitler, and Stalin stand symbolically for this development—they mark its pinnacles of infamy, those perverse moments in history when empty slogans were everything and a human life was considered worthless.

It would be false to compare the crimes and cruelties of these three men one with another, for each of them is inseparably bound with his society and his time; a comprehensive judgment of their political activity must, therefore, also consider economic and social aspects—a task which, of course, goes far beyond the framework of this medical study. But I believe it can be said that these biographies have shown one thing penetratingly: the terroristic reign of a dictator is never an inexplicable "accident" of history; rather, individual and social preconditions develop a mutually stimulating dynamic that is indeed susceptible to analysis. As for Hitler and Stalin, their decisions display a new, terrible quality of dictatorial action: killing as a cold bureaucratic act that sends countless innocent victims to their death merely for some external trait, such as their nationality or their social position. Dominated by a cynical technocratic calculation, these despots established, in advance, "production quotas" governing the number of people to be killed and, by an unprecedented "division of labor," they turned murder into a routine activity for otherwise "harmless" people.

In view of the unimaginable crimes committed by these dictators—excluding Napoleon for the moment—two fundamental questions can be raised:

- Did Hitler and Stalin have an "innate ethical defect" in the sense of the familiar "moral insanity hypothesis," or was their deeply amoral behavior made possible—as Kant already feared—by the fact that their criminal actions were not hindered and controlled by any higher authority?

- And how was it possible in all ages for tyrants to have at their disposal any number of willing, slavishly devoted, and unscrupulously cruel henchmen to carry out their inhuman objectives?

Wolfgang de Boor, in his critical analysis, cited in this context, referred to Lipót Szondi's highly interesting monograph, *Cain: Figures of Evil,* in which the author, with his "psychology of destiny," tried to give an answer to these burning questions, which certainly are decisive for all political practice. Szondi holds the thesis that the "killing mentality" of a person is based on an innate character disposition in the sense of a "Cain nature," which he labels the "e" radical. Szondi estimates that about 6 percent of people in an average population display such a Cain characteristic and that an additional 14 percent are covert, disguised bearers of this trait—these he labels "Abelized everyday Cainites." Based on comprehensive psychological studies of this question, Szondi suspects that the mass murders of all times, and especially those of National Socialism and Stalinism, first became possible at all only through the relative frequency of occurrence of this "e" radical. To identify this mental trait, Szondi developed his own specific test procedure.

According to Szondi, if bearers of the Cain characteristic are not in a position to release their pent-up "killing attitude" by corresponding perverse actions or ecstatic expressions, then, under special circumstances, during revolutionary and/or military events, thus spurred on by political or ideological motives, they are quite capable of killing thousands of people. In this way, insignificant, harmless "everyday Cainites" become bloodthirsty mass murderers and war criminals. Szondi summed up the results of his many years of research as follows:

> That a megalomaniac emperor or king, politician or leader, anywhere in the world and in all epochs of world history, can and could mobilize millions of people for shameful enterprises, which he propagates as a "holy war or struggle," and incite them to perform criminal deeds, is and was possible only because the so-called "people" consists partly of hidden Cainites. These ultra-chauvinists and ultra-racists are just waiting for a chance to live out their Cainite urges safely and freely, disguised as "patriots." Indeed, the masses, as such, are already an excellent camouflage, under which one can slip in as a Cainite, for the masses abolish personal responsibility.

Whatever one may think of Szondi's terminology and theses, his model could offer an explanation for how an excessively narcissistic, sadomasochistically disposed psychopath with paranoid delusions can succeed in finding a following: the moment he becomes the unrestricted ruler over life and death and assures his subordinates and countrymen of absolute immunity to punishment, even for the most inhuman crimes, the affected society suddenly sprouts forth those torturer-henchmen and slaughterers of mankind, such as could be found by the thousands in the Nazi concentration camps, in the Stalinist penal colonies, and the torture chambers of the NKVD.

The Viennese psychiatrist, Erwin Stransky, from the world-famous Wagner-Jauregg School, whom I knew personally as a young clinical assistant many years ago, with his typically fiery rhetoric, made the admittedly unrealistic demand that actually every leading statesman with a sense of responsibility should undergo a psychiatric examination once per year. Now, the present book is by no means intended to lend support to such conclusions, but does certainly support a healthy distrust of and a critical and rational attitude toward all the enticing slogans that promise freedom and greatness, but in reality mean only oppression, discipline and death.

BIBLIOGRAPHY

NAPOLEON BONAPARTE

ABBATUCCI, S.: L'hépatite suppurée de Napoléon Ier, à Sainte-Hélène. In: Presse medicale 63, 1934

ALBERT-SAMUEL, COLETTE: Napoléon à Sainte-Hélène. Bibliographie 1955-1971. In: Revue de l'Institut Napoléon, Nr. 120, 1971

ANDREWS, EDWARD: The diseases, death and autopsy of Napoleon. In: Journal Amer. Med. Assoc. 1895

ANTOMMARCHI, FRANCESCO: Les derniers moments de Napoléon. Paris 1898 (Erstausgabe 1825)

ARETZ, PAUL: Napoleons Gefangenschaft und Tod. Dresden 1924

ARNOTT, ARCHIBALD: An account of the late illness, disease and post-mortem examination of Napoleon Bonaparte. London 1822

AUBRY, OCTAVE: Sankt Helena. Der Tod des Kaisers. Zürich 1950

AUBRY, OCTAVE: Napoleon privat. Erlenbach-Zürich, Leipzig 1940

AYER, WARDNER D.: Napoleon Buonaparte and schistosomiasis. In: Journal Amer. Med. Assoc. 1966

BANKL, HANS: Viele Wege führen in die Ewigkeit. Vienna Munich Bern 1990

BAUDOUIN, M.: Remarques cliniques sur da dernière maladie de Napoléon. In: Gaz. med., Paris 1901

BELLINI, ANGELO: Igiene della pelle. Milano 1900

BERTAUT, JULES: Napoléon ignoré. Paris 1951

BERTRAND, HENRI-GRATIEN: Cahiers de Saint Hélène de chiffres. Par Fleuriot de Langle, Paris 1950

BETT W. R.: An Hypothalamic Interpretation of History. In: Bulletin of the History of Medicine, Vol. 27, 1953

BOUHLER, PHILIPP: Napoleon. Kometenbahn eines Genies. Munich 1942

BRETON, GUY: Napoleon and his ladies. London 1965

BRICE, RAOUL: The Riddle of Napoleon. London 1937

BROCK, RUSSEL: Napoleon's death. In: The Lancet, 3. February 1962

CABANES, AUGUSTIN: Napoleon et la gale. In: Journal des maladies curanées et syphilitiques. 1892

CAULAINCOURT, ARMAND AUGUSTIN LOUIS MARQUIS DE: Ünter vier Augen mit Napoleon. Denkwürdigkeiten des Generals Caulaincourt. Trans. by Friedrich Matthaesius. Bielefeld, Leipzig 1937

CHANDLER, DAVID GEOFFREY: Napoleon. Munich 1974

CHAPLIN, ARNOLD: The illness and death of Napoleon Bonaparte. London 1913

CHEVALIER, A. G.: Die kaiserlichen Leibärzte. In: Ciba-Zeitschrift Nr. 75, 1 p. 2578, 1940

CHEVALIER, A. G.: Napoleon and his physicians. Ciba-Symposia, 1941

CHEVALIER, A. G.: Krankheiten und Tod Napoleons. In: Ciba-Zeitschrift Nr. 75, p. 2590, 1940

CRONIN, VINCENT: Napoleon. London 1971

DIBLE, J. H.: Napoleon's Surgeon. London 1970

DUMAS, ALEXANDRE: Napoleon Bonaparte. Berlin, [no date]

EBSTEIN, ERICH: Napoleon. Leipzig 1926

FLEURIOT DE LANGLE, PAUL: Napoléon et son geôlier. Paris 1952

FORSHUFVUD, STEN: Who killed Napoleon? London 1961

FORSHUFVUD, STEN: Arsenic content of Napoleon's hair probably taken immediately after his death. In: Nature, 14. Oct. 1961 (London)

FRÉMEAUX, PAUL: Napoleons letzte Tage auf St. Helena. Berlin 1912

GANIERE, PAUL: Corvisart: Médecin de Napoléon. Paris 1951

GANIERE, PAUL: La mort de l'Empereur: L'Apothéose. Paris 1962

GEYL, PIETER: Napoleon: For and against. Utrecht 1846, London 1964

GODLEWSKI, GUY: Napoleons letzte Krankheit. In: Ciba-Zeitschrift Vol. 5, 1 p. 94 (Aux confins de la vie et de la mort. Paris 1957)

GROEN, J.-J.: La derniere maladie et la cause de mort de Napoléon. In: Etude psychologique, historique et medicale. Leiden 1962

HENRY, WALTER: Surgeon Henry's trifles. London 1970

HERRE, FRANZ: Napoleon Bonaparte. Wegbereiter des Jahrhunderts. Munich 1988

HILLEMAND, PAUL: Pathologie de Napoléon. Paris 1970

KALIMA, TANO: De quelle maladie est mort Napoléon? In: Acta chirurg. scand. 72, 1, 1932

KARLEN, A.: Nicht Wellington besiegte Napoleon bei Waterloo. Vienna 1985

KEITH, ARTHUR: The history and nature of certain specimens alleged to have been obtained at the post mortem on Napoleon the Great. In: Brit. Med. Journal, 1913

KEMBLE, JAMES: Napoleon immortal. The medical history and private life of Napoleon Bonaparte. London 1959

KEMBLE, JAMES: St. Helena during Napoleon's exile. London 1969

KIRCHEISEN, FRIEDRICH MAX: Selbstmörder Napoleon? In: Münchner Med. Wochenschrift, 1 p. 503, 1933

KNOTT, J.: The fatal illness and death of Napoleon the Great. In: Journal of Irish Med. Assoc., 1913

KORNGOLD, RALPH: The last days of Napoleon. London 1960

LAURENT, P. M: Histoire de Napoleon I. Paris 1870 (contains many illustrations by Horace Vernet)

LUDWIG, EMIL: Napoleon. Berlin 1931

MANFRED, ALBERT ZACHAROVI´C: Napoleon Bonaparte. Berlin Ost 1978

MARTINEAU, GILBERT: Napoléon à Sainte-Hélène 1815-1821. Paris 1981

MASSON, FRÉDÉRIC: Napoléon dans sa jeunesse, 1769-1793. Paris 1922

MAUROIS, ANDRÉ: Napoleon. Reinbek bei Hamburg 1966

MÉNEVAL, CLAUDE FRANÇOIS DE: Napoleon und Marie-Louise. Geschichtliche Erinnerungen. 2 vols. Berlin 1906

METS DE, A.: Comment mourut Napoléon. In: Revue de la Corse ancienne et moderne. Antwerpen 1931

MONTHOLON, CHARLES-TRISTAN DE: Geschichte der Gefangenschaft Napoleons auf St. Helena. Leipzig 1846

MONTHOLON, CHARLES-TRISTAN DE: History of the captivity of Napoleon. London 1847

NAPOLÉON, BONAPARTE: Lettres de Napoléon à Joséphine. Paris 1891

NAPOLEON, BONAPARTE: Mein Leben und Werk. Aus dem Gesamtwerk ausgewählt und herausgegeben von Paul und Gertrude Aretz. Berlin 1936

NEUREITER, F.: Ein Bericht über die Sektion der Leiche Napoleons I. In: Wiener Med. Wochenschrift 44, 1901, 1921

O'MEARA, BARRY E.: Napoleon in exile. London 1882

PEVERIL V. D. PICK, W.: Das Leben des Kaisers der Franzosen Napoleon Bonaparte. 8 Bände, Danzig 1827

REUBEN, F.: The Emperor's Itch. The Legend Concerning Napoleon's Affliction. New York 1940

RICHARDSON, FRANK: Napoleon's Death—An Inquest. London 1974

SAVANT, JEAN: Napoleon wie er wirklich war. Bern 1955

SAVANT, JEAN: Les amours de Napoléon. Paris 1956

SCHIFF, LEON: Diseases of the Liver. Philadelphia 1975

SOKOLOFF, BORIS: Napoleon: A Doctor's biography. New York 1937

TISCHNER, R.: Napoleon und die Homöopathie. Leipzig 1933

TULARD, JEAN: Napoleon oder Der Mythos des Retters. Eine Biographie. Tübingen 1978

WAIRY, LOUIS CONSTANT: Mémoires sur la vie privée de Napoléon, sa famille et sa cour, Paris 1830

WALLACE, D.: How did Napoleon die? In: Med. Journal Aust., 1964

WENCKER-WILDBERG, FRIEDRICH und KIRCHEISEN, FRIEDRICH MAX: Napoleon: Die Memoiren seines Lebens. 14 vols. Vienna, Hamburg, Zürich, 1930/31

WHIPPLE, WAYNE: The Story-Life of Napoleon, New York 1904

WOLFF, G.: Die letzte Krankheit Napoleons. In: Med. Wochenschrift, 1963

ADOLF HITLER

AICH, THOMAS: Massenmensch und Massenwahn. Zur Psychologie des Kollektivismus. Munich 1947

BAHNSEN, UWE: Foreword by John Toland: Adolf Hitler. Bergisch-Gladbach 1977

BAHNSEN, UWE: Die Katakombe. Das Ende in der Reichskanzlei. Bergisch-Gladbach 1981

BELOW, NICOLAUS VON: Als Hitlers Adjutant. Mainz 1980

BINION, RUDOLPH: Hitler's concept of Lebensraum. In: History of Childhood Quarterly, 1973

BLOCH, EDUARD: My patient, Hitler. In: Colliers Magazine, 1941

BRAUNMÜHL, ANTON VON: War Hitler krank? In: Stimmen der Zeit Bd. 145 H/8 Munich 1954

BROMBERG, NORBERT: Hitler's character and its development. In: American Imago, 1971

BULLOCK, ALAN: Hitler und Stalin. Parallele Leben. Berlin 1991

BULLOCK, ALAN: Hitler. Eine Studie über Tyrannei. Düsseldorf 1957

CARR, WILLIAM: Adolf Hitler. Stuttgart 1980

DALMA, G.: Un pazzo al timone del mondo. Referto psichiatrico su Hitler. In: Cosmopolita, 1944

DE BOOR, WOLFGANG: Hitler: Mensch, Übermensch, Untermensch. Frankfurt am Main 1985

DIETRICH, OTTO: Zwölf Jahre mit Hitler. Munich 1955

DOMARUS, MAX: Hitler. Reden und Proklamationen. 1932—1945, 2 Vols. Munich 1965

EITNER, HANS-JÜRGEN: Der Führer. Munich/Vienna 1981

ERIKSON, ERIK H.: Identity, Youth and Crisis. New York 1968

FEST, JOACHIM C.: Hitler. Eine Biographie. Frankfurt am Main/Berlin 1989

FRANÇOIS-PONCET, ANDRÉ: Als Botschafter in Berlin 1931—1938. Berlin/Mainz 1962

FRANK, HANS: Im Angesicht des Galgens. Deutung Hitlers und seiner Zeit aufgrund eigener Erlebnisse und Erkenntnisse, Hrsg. v. Oswald Schloffer, Munich 1953

FROMM, ERICH: The Anatomy of Human Destructiveness. New York 1973

GIBBELS, ELLEN: Hitlers Nervenleiden—Differentialdiagnose des Parkinson-Syndroms. In: Fortschritte der Neurologie u. Psychiatrie, 1989

GIBBELS, ELLEN: Hitlers Parkinson-Syndrom. In: Der Nervenarzt, 1988

GISEVIUS, HANS BERND: Adolf Hitler. Versuch einer Deutung. Munich 1963

GOEBBELS, JOSEPH: Tagebücher. 5 Vols., 1993

GRAU, RUDOLF: Gehört er ins Pantheon der Weltgeschichte? Wiesbaden 1947

GRIMM, G.: Kranke Männer am Steuerruder der Staaten. In: Saeculum, 1969

GUDERIAN, HEINZ: Erinnerungen eines Soldaten. Heidelberg 1951

HAFFNER, SEBASTIAN: Anmerkungen zu Hitler. Munich 1978

HANFSTAENGL, ERNST: Zwischen Weißem und Braunem Haus. Memoiren eines politischen Außenseiters. Munich 1970

HESTON, L. L. AND A. R.: The Medical Casebook of Adolf Hitler. London 1979

HITLER, ADOLF: Hitlers Zweites Buch. Ein Dokument aus dem Jahre 1928. Stuttgart 1961

HITLER, ADOLF: Mein Kampf. Munich 1938

IRVING, DAVID: Die geheimen Tagebücher des Dr. Morell. Munich 1983

IRVING, DAVID: Hitler und seine Feldherren. Berlin 1975

IRVING, DAVID: Wie krank war Hitler wirklich? Munich 1980

JETZINGER, FRANZ: Hitlers Jugend. Phantasien, Lügen—und die Wahrheit. Vienna 1956

KARDEL, HENNECKE: Adolf Hitler—Begründer Israels. Marva/Genf 1974

KEMPKA, ERICH: Die letzten Tage mit Adolf Hitler. Preußisch-Oldendorf 1975

KERSTEN, FELIX: Totenkopf und Treue. Heinrich Himmler ohne Uniform. Hamburg [no date]

KOGON, EUGEN: Der SS-Staat. Das System der deutschen Konzentrationslager. Frankfurt am Main 1965

KRAUSNICK, HELMUT: Anatomie des SS-Staates. Freiburg im Breisgau 1965

KRETSCHMER, ERNST: Geniale Menschen. Berlin 1942

KUBIZEK, AUGUST: Adolf Hitler. Mein Jugendfreund. Graz/Göttingen 1953

LANGER, WALTER CHARLES: Das Adolf-Hitler-Psychogramm. Vienna/Munich/Zürich 1973

LINGE, HEINZ: Bis zum Untergang. Munich 1983

MASER, WERNER: Adolf Hitler. Das Ende der Führerlegende. Düsseldorf/Vienna 1980

MASER, WERNER: Adolf Hitler. Legende, Mythos, Wirklichkeit. Munich/Esslingen 1973

MILLER, ALICE: Am Anfang war Erziehung. Frankfurt am Main 1980

OLDEN, RUDOLF: Hitler the Pawn. London 1936

PICKER, HENRY: Hitlers Tischgespräche im Führerhauptquartier 1941-1942. Hrsg. von Percy Ernst Schramm, Stuttgart 1965.

RAUSCHNING, HERMANN: Gespräche mit Hitler. Zürich/Vienna/New York 1940

RECKTENWALD, JOHANN: Woran hat Adolf Hitler gelitten? Munich/Basel 1963
ROEHRS, HANS-DIETRICH: Hitler—die Zerstörung einer Persönlichkeit. Grundlegende Feststellungen zum Krankheitsbild. Neckargemünd 1965
ROEHRS, HANS-DIETRICH: Hitlers Krankheit. Tatsachen und Legenden. Medizinische und psychische Grundlage seines Zusammenbruchs. Neckargemünd 1966
Rudin, Josef: Fanaticism; a Psychological Analysis, translated by Elisabeth Reinecke and Paul C. Bailey, C.S.C., Notre Dame, Ind., 1969
SCHALTENBRAND, GEORG: War Hitlergeisteskrank? Festschrift, Göttingen 1961
SCHENCK, ERNST GÜNTHER: Patient Hitler. Düsseldorf 1989
SCHUSCHNIGG, KURT VON: Ein Requiem in Rot-Weiß-Rot. Zürich 1946
SMITH, BRADLEY F.: Adolf Hitler: His Family, Childhood and Youth. Stanford 1967
SPEER, ALBERT: Erinnerungen. Berlin, Vienna 1969
STEINERT, MARLIES: Hitler. Munich 1994
STERN, JOSEPH PETER: Hitler. Der Führer und das Volk. Munich/Vienna 1978
STIERLIN, HELM: Adolf Hitler. Familienperspektiven. Frankfurt am Main 1975
STOLK, P. J.: Adolf Hitler. His life and his illness. In: Psychiatr. Neurol. Neurochir., 1968
STRASSER, OTTO: Mein Kampf. Frankfurt am Main 1969
SZONDI, LIPÓT: Kain. Gestalten des Bösen. Bern 1969
TOLAND, JOHN: Adolf Hitler. Bergisch-Gladbach 1977
TREVOR-ROPER, HUGH R.: Einleitung zu Hitlers politischem Testament. Hamburg 1981
TREVOR-ROPER, HUGH R.: Hitlers letzte Tage. Frankfurt am Main 1963
TREVOR-ROPER, HUGH R.: Lügen um Hitlers Leiche. In: Der Monat, 1956
WALTERS, J.: Hitler's encephalitis: a footnote to history. In: Journal Operat. Psychiat., 1975
WEISSBECKER, MANFRED AND KURT PÄTZOLD: Adolf Hitler. Leipzig 1995 (nach Fertigstellung des Manuskripts erschienen)
ZIEGLER, HANS SEVERUS: Hitler aus dem Erleben dargestellt. Göttingen 1964
ZOLLER, ALBERT: Hitler privat. Erlebnisbericht seiner Geheimsekretärin. Düsseldorf 1949

JOSEPH STALIN

ACCOCE, PIERRE AND RENTCHNICK, PIERRE: Kranke machen Weltgeschichte. Düsseldorf 1978
ALLILUJEWA, SWETLANA: Zwanzig Briefe an einen Freund. Vienna 1967
ALLILUJEWA, SWETLANA: Das erste Jahr. Vienna-Munich-Zürich 1969
ANTONOW-OWSSEJENKO, ANTON: Stalin. Porträt einer Tyrannei. Berlin 1986
AWTORCHANOW, ABDURACHMAN: Das Rätsel um Stalins Tod. Frankfurt-Berlin-Vienna 1984
BASCHANOW, BORIS: Ich war Stalins Sekretär. Frankfurt 1989
BLEULER, EUGEN: Lehrbuch der Psychiatric. Heidelberg 1969
BOOR, WOLFGANG DE: Terrorismus. Der "Wahn" der Gesunden. Berlin 1978
BORTOLI, GEORGES: Als Stalin starb. Kult und Wirklichkeit. Stuttgart 1974
BULLOCK, ALAN: Hitler and Stalin. London 1991
BULLOCK, ALAN: Hitler und Stalin. Berlin 1991
CHRUSCHTSCHOW, NIKITA S.: Chruschtschow erinnert sich. Edited by Strobe Talbott. Hamburg 1971
CONQUEST, ROBERT: Die Ernte des Todes. Munich 1988

CONQUEST, ROBERT: Der große Terror. Sowjetunion 1934-1938. Munich 1992

DEUTSCHER, ISAAC: Stalin. Eine politische Biographie. Stuttgart 1962

DJILAS, MILOVAN: Gespräche mit Stalin. Frankfurt 1962

DOLLARD, J. et al.: Frustration und Aggression. Weinheim 1972

ERIKSON, ERIK H.: Kindheit und Gesellschaft. Stuttgart 1971

ERIKSON, ERIK H.: Identität und Lebenszyklus. Frankfurt 1966

FISCHER, RUTH: Stalin und der deutsche Kommunismus. Frankfurt/M. 1948

FROMM, ERICH: The Anatomy of Human Destructiveness. New York 1973

HINGLEY, R.: Joseph Stalin. Man and Legend (cited from Sterpellone)

IREMASCHWILI, JOSSIF: Stalin und die Tragödie Georgiens. Berlin 1932

KOLENDIC, A.: Machtkampf im Kreml. Bergisch-Gladbach 1983

KOPELEW, LEW: Und schuf mir einen Götzen. Lehrjahre eines Kommunisten. Hamburg 1981

LERMOLO, ELIZABETH: Face of a victim. New York 1955

LEWYTZKYI, BORIS: Die rote Inquisition. Frankfurt/M. 1967

MEDWEDEW, ROY A.: Die Wahrheit ist unsere Stärke. Frankfurt 1973

MEDWEDEW, ROY A.: All Stalin's Men. Garden City, New York 1984

MILLER, ALICE: Am Anfang war Erziehung. Frankfurt 1983

ORLOW, ALEXANDER: Kreml-Geheimnisse. Würzburg 1956

PALOCZI-HORVATH, GEORGE: Stalin. Gütersloh 1966

PAYNE, ROBERT: Stalin. Aufstieg und Fall. Stuttgart 1967

PIRKER, THEO: Die Moskauer Schauprozesse 1936-1938. Munich 1963

PORTISCH, HUGO: Hört die Signale. Wege und Irrwege des Sowjet-Kommunismus. Vienna 1991

ROMANO-PETROVA, N.: Stalin's Doctor—Stalin's Nurse. Princeton 1984

RUBEL, MAXIMILIEN: Josef W. Stalin in Selbstzeugnissen und Bilddokumenten. Reinbek bei Hamburg 1975

SMITH, EDWARD ELLIS: Der junge Stalin. Munich-Zürich 1969

SOLSCHENIZYN, ALEXANDER: Archipel GULAG. Reinbek bei Hamburg 1988

STERPELLONE, L.: Pazienti illustrissimi. Rom 1985

SZONDI, LIPÓT: Kain. Gestalten des Bösen. Bern 1969

TOLSTOJ, NIKOLAJ: Die Verratenen von Jalta. Munich-Vienna 1977

TROTZKI, LEO: Stalin. Eine Biographie. Hamburg 1971

TUCKER, ROBERT: Stalin in Power. The Revolution from Above 1928-1941. New York 1990

ULAM, ADAM B.: Stalin, Koloß der Macht. Esslingen 1977

VANDENBERG, PHILIPP: Die heimlichen Herrscher. Munich 1991

WAKSBERG, ARKADI: Gnadenlos. Andrej Wyschinski - Mörder im Dienste Stalins. Bergisch-Gladbach 1991

WOLKOGONOW, DIMITRI: Stalin: Triumph und Tragödie. Düsseldorf 1989

ZLEPKO, DMYTRO: Der ukrainische Hunger-Holocaust. Sonnenbühl 1988

ACKNOWLEDGMENTS

Österr. Nationalbibliothek bzw. Bildarchiv der Östereichischen Nationalbibliothek: Napoleon, p. 10, 14, 16, 20, 21, 27-30, 45, 57, 58, 61, 65, 71, 77, 79, 86, 87, 103, 113, 129, 142, 145, 146; Hitler, p. 155, 161, 169, 173, 179, 183, 188, 191, 201, 203 (top), 203 (bottom), 205, 213 (top), 233, 234, 269 (bottom); Stalin, p. 314, 323, 335, 347, 376, 379, 420, 428

Österreichisches Institut für Zeitgeschichte Wien, Bildarchiv: Hitler, p. 148

Bayerische Staatsbibliothek Miinchen, Fotoarchiv Hoffmann: Hitler, p. 200, 210, 211 (bottom), 223 (top and bottom), 242, 249, 250, 257 (bottom), 259 (bottom), 262, 265, 270, 303

Ullstein Bilderdienst, Berlin: Hitler, p. 157, 211 (top), 215, 229, 257 (top), 261; Stalin, p. 311, 324, 373, 385, 386, 395

Contrast/Archiv Interfoto/TRANSGLOBE: Hitler, p. 219, 231

Bundesarchiv Koblenz: Hitler, p. 176, 185, 195, 269 (top), 276 (top and bottom)

Bundesarchiv Preußischer Kulturbesitz, Berlin: Hitler, p. 251, 259 (top); Stalin: p. 308, 333, 365

Votavafoto Wien: Hitler, p. 217; Stalin: p. 355

Deutsche Presse-Agentur: Stalin, p. 312, 321, 329, 344, 391

Presseagentur Novwosti Wien: Stalin, p. 356, 423

Russian Central State Archive for Documentary Films and Photography: Stalin, p. 347 (inset), 357, 366, 368, 377, 407, 411, 441

David King Collection: Stalin, p. 325, 343

Political Archive of the Foreign Office, Bonn: Stalin, p. 351

Ernst Weizmann Collection: Hitler, p. 209, 213 (bottom)

Ciba-Zeitschrift, Nr. 5, 1940: Napoleon, p. 55, 67, 68, 75, 81, 85

Archiv für Kunst und Geschichte, Berlin: Hitler, p. 253

Süddeutscher Verlag Bilderdienst, Munich: Stalin, p. 393

Friedrich M. Kircheisen and F. Wencker-Wildberg: *Napoleon. Die Memoiren seines Lebens*. Vienna 1930/31. Napoleon, p. 35, 43, 69, 73, 93

The illustration on p. 73 is taken from Richard Toellner, *Illustrierte Geschichte der Medizin*, Salzburg: Verlagsbuchhandlung Andreas & Andreas; reprinted with the kind permission of the publisher.

The map drawing on p. 78 came from Octave Aubry: *Sainte Hélène, Vol. 1: La capitivité de Napoléon*, copyright by Flammarion, Paris, 1935.

The drawing on p. 154 is taken from Werner Maser: *Hitler. Legende, Mythos, Wirklichkeit*. copyright by Bechtle in the F. A. Herbig Verlagsbuchhandlung GmbH, Munich.

The illustration on p. 194 is taken from the book *Illustrierte Geschichte des Dritten Reiches*, ed. by Kurt Zentner (Vienna, 1965; copyright by Südwest Verlag Dr. Neumann & Co. KG, Munich); reprinted with kind permission of the publisher.

The photographs in the chapter on Hitler, p. 181, 224, 225, 235, 237, 238, 263, are reprinted from the book, *Das Dritte Reich*, Wien 1965.

The letter on p. 246 is taken from the Museum catalog "Konzentrationslager Dachau 1933-1945," IMT Document NO 296 (Munich 1978); reprinted with kind permission of the KZ-Memorial Site, Dachau, Germany.

The marriage certificate of Adolf and Eva Hitler, p. 271, is reprinted with kind permission of the Eisenhower Library, Abilene, Kansas.

The portrait of Dzierzynski, p. 331, and the photograph of the homeless child on the street in Moscow, p. 338, are taken from *Geist und Gesicht des Bolschevismus* by René Fülöp Miller (Zurich-Vienna 1926).

The photograph of the shell-crater where the corpses of Adolf and Eva Hitler were found, p. 273, is reprinted from *Wie sie wirklich starben* by Bankl; published by Wilhelm Maudrich, Vienna 1989.

ABOUT THE TRANSLATOR

DAVID J. PARENT, who translated *Dictators* from the German language, is Professor of German at Illinois State University, specializing in nineteenth and twentieth century prose fiction and drama. Dr. Parent has translated many books and articles on philosophy, political theory, and literature.

ABOUT THE TECHNICAL EDITORS

MARILYN FUCHS, PH.D., who reviewed the psychological terminology in the text, is a psychologist in private practice in Washington, D.C. Dr. Fuchs performed her undergraduate work at George Washington University and at Mount Holyoke; she obtained a masters degree from Harvard and a doctorate from the American University.

VICTORIA J. BROCKHOUSE, D.O., who reviewed the medical terminology in the text, is a physician in private practice in Bloomington, Illinois, special-izing in family practice. Dr. Brockhouse completed her undergraduate work in the biological sciences at Illinois State University; she graduated from the Chicago College of Osteopathic Medicine and completed a fam-ily practice residency in Decatur, Illinois.

INDEX OF NAMES